MW00608214

01 Mar 07   3258 3426

Dhyanyoga Centers, Inc.
P.O. Box 3194
Antioch, CA 94531
925.757.9361
www.dyc.org

© 2004 Dhyanyoga Centers, Inc.
All rights reserved. Published 2004
Designed by Insight Design
Printed in China by Palace Press International

10 9 8 7 6 5 4 3 2 1

Library of Congress Cataloging-in-Publication Data is available.

ISBN 1-883879-50-7
ISBN 1-883879-51-5 (paperback)

Photo of Swami Vivekananda used with permission of Vedanta Society of Southern
California. Illustration on page 50 from Ramayana: A Tale of Gods and Demons by
B.G. Sharma © 2002 Mandala Publishing, used with permission.

THIS HOUSE IS ON FIRE

LOOT ALL YOU CAN

The Life of Shri Dhyanyogi

AS TOLD BY SHRI ANANDI MA AND DISCIPLES

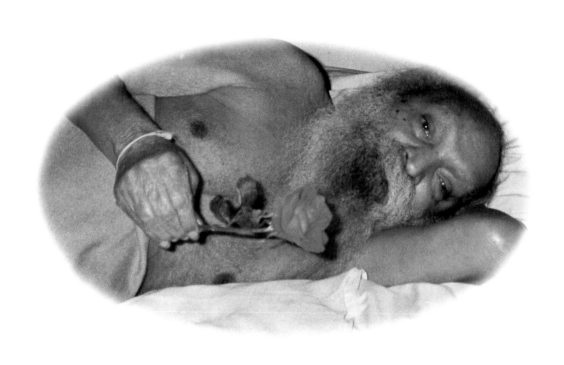

*In tune with Dhyanyogi-ji's heart,
we dedicate this book to all who seek
the True One, within and without.*

Hum To Ram Te Ram
By Dhyanyogi-ji

I am a wandering sadhu.
My peace and joy come from beyond this world.

Affected not by happiness and sorrow
Nor profit and loss
I live not in the past nor in the future.
I do not weep in the face of criticism
Nor laugh when being praised.
I am a wandering sadhu.

Sometimes I live among kings
Enjoying all the comfort and luxury of their palaces.
I eat the most delicious foods
And my senses enjoy the best of everything.
I am a wandering sadhu.

Sometimes I go to the jungle and live under the trees
Eating only fruits and flowers.
I control my senses
And practice severe austerity.
I am a wandering sadhu.

Sometimes I dress up in silk robes
Sometimes I wear only a loincloth
Sometimes I live with the wealthiest of men
Sometimes I seek the company of yogis.
I am a wandering sadhu.

Sometimes I give charity and serve the poor
Sometimes I just meditate on my Lord.
But no matter where I am or what I am doing
The voice inside this body
Inspires me to do only good deeds.
I am a wandering sadhu.

Note: This was a song that Dhyanyogi-ji wrote about his life. He typically sang this when disciples asked him to chant.

CONTENTS

MESSAGES

MESSAGE FROM SHRI ANANDI MA

Although I do not remember whose face I first saw after my birth, I am sure it was my mother's, and then my father's. Since then, as the years have gone by, I have seen many faces. On the journey of life, we encounter so many people. Some are just passersby. We say, "Hi, hello, good morning," never to see them again. Some we see every day until they move, pass on, or we go away. Some faces we see only once, yet they have a permanent place in our hearts. Certain people may say a thing or two that we never forget. Still others may perform certain actions that become the foundations of our lives and roots of our inspiration.

Of all the faces that I have seen so far, there is one that stays always in front of my physical eye as well as the third eye, appearing constantly to me with each and every heartbeat. I feel his presence in all parts of nature, in the wind, the waves of the sea, the day and night, the summer and winter, the fall and spring. I hear his voice in my ears saying, "I am always with you." My Guru, my Master, my All in All, Shri Dhyanyogi-ji. He left such a mark upon my being—his eyes of love, care and grace, his protection and guidance, his tenderness and gentleness like a bed of rose petals. Oh, what more can I write! His face, his words, his actions, all have left their imprint—not only on this life, but on life after life after life.

There is an old verse that asks, "What's the use of gaining the whole world but losing your own soul?" Many may think that they must give up one to have the other. But Dhyanyogi-ji gave me everything. He brought me to my soul and gave me the whole world as well. Only he has given me the love, strength, courage, hope, sight and vision—all of this—to help you, to help humankind. I adore his grace for choosing me and making me a part of him so that now I in turn can help you become the part of God that you truly are. He often inspired me with the words of Swami Vivekananda: "Arise, awake, and stop not till the goal is reached!" This biography offers a handful of petals from the huge lotus of Dhyanyogi-ji's life. Smell it, touch it to your eyes, preserve its contents in your heart and mind, and you too shall find *Satyam Shivam Sundaram*—Truth, Absolution, and Beauty.

In Service to God, Guru and Humankind,
Anandi Ma

Message from Dileepji

Have you ever wondered how many steps you have walked from the time you took your very first step? Have you ever thought about the directions in which you have gone? What were your goals? How many were positive? How many of these steps do you now feel you should not have taken because they hurt you or someone else?

Nowadays we rarely take steps. We hardly ever walk. We drive or fly. But once, there was a child in India who, six years after he took his first step, began a life of walking. He had no worldly goal, only the ultimate goal of life—to meet the One who is the cause, the effect, and all that lies in between these two states, to discover the answer to the question "Who am I?" to attain realization and see All in One and One in All. That child was Kashinath, who later became Dhyanyogi Madhusudandas-ji, one of the greatest yogis of India. He walked miles and miles across India, from east to west, from the Himalayan peaks to the southernmost tip of the country. He walked barefoot on ice and snow, on sand and thorns, in sun and rain. He never worried about the next day, where he would sleep or what he would eat. He thought only about God, just, "God, where can I find you?"

For 30 years, he met teacher after teacher. He learned, practiced, and experienced. Then, finally, the *sadguru*—the true teacher—appeared in front of him, smiling and bestowing grace and energy. At last his wandering was over. By his sadguru's grace, the unknown became known. He saw the face of God, and began to merge with the Divine.

Once he had attained his goal, he continued to walk, this time for his fellow humans. Never pausing, even in times of pain and suffering when his legs could walk no more, his heart cried, "Who can I help? Let all be happy." Such is the legacy of this great being. Blessed are those who saw him or will hear of him and even see him in ages to come.

As he took his countless steps to help humankind, I was very fortunate in that he allowed me to take a few steps by his side.

Dhyanyogi-ji liked to take walks every day and I don't know of anyone who could keep up with him, even when he was in his late 90s and early 100s. Once, in 1964, while we were walking by the ocean in Mumbai, an elderly gentleman of about 65 walked towards us from the opposite direction. He passed us, but very soon turned around, came running back, and stood in front of Dhyanyogi-ji. He held his hand and asked, "Are you really God?"

In 1977, Dhyanyogi-ji and I were again walking. This time, we were in Buffalo, New York. Two children about 10 or 12 years old walked towards us with their bikes. As in the earlier incident, they went by us, but soon turned around and came riding back on their bikes, stopping in front of us. One of them stood holding onto Dhyanyogi-ji's robe and asked, "Are you really God?"

Although *Maya*—the veil of illusion—hid the true Dhyanyogi-ji from me, after these incidents, I could see his real identity. On many such occasions, his unity with the infinite was revealed, crystal clear, to me. Yes, for me, and for a few others, he was truly God!

Dhyanyogi-ji was anxious to demonstrate the spiritual phenomenon in scientific ways whenever possible, but he taught that in matters of spirituality, both the heart and mind are important. He reminded us of Vivekananda's words: "Spirituality begins where intelligence ends." We should try to understand spirituality in a scientific way as much as possible, but there is not an answer for each and every question. Many things need to be accepted without a logical explanation. In 1965, I was taking some photographs. I had purchased a camera and flash for the first time. I was to photograph an important event—a fire ceremony at Bandhwad ashram. Right away, the flash would not function, and I was very disappointed. I told Dhyanyogi-ji that I would not be able to take the photos since the flash didn't work. He said, "Don't worry, just go and put the flash in front of the statue of Hanuman, and then start using it." My rational mind thought this was stupid, but I had faith in his words. I did as he told me, and a minute after I placed it on the floor in front of the altar, the flash began to go off on its own, and it worked fine for the next 15 years!

Dhyanyogi-ji always said that the path to realization is a spiritual one, and that we should distinguish between spirituality and religion. An individual may be of a particular religion, but at the level of spirituality, the soul is reaching God, and that God is universal. We are all one.

For me, Dhyanyogi-ji proved to be not just a spiritual teacher, but also a father, mother, friend and guide. He fulfilled everything that I have ever wanted. He taught me, giving me expertise in all that I wanted to learn. He was unique—the kindest, gentlest, most loving, caring, giving, tolerant and sacrificing of all persons that I have ever met. His eyes were the eighth wonder of the world, so vast and infinite, so empty, like the void—the goal of life itself.

His qualities as a simple and pure saint were clear to see in the way he lived, by the humble appearance of his ashram and its location in a rural part of the country where villagers lived at a subsistence level. He taught simply, by example. He showed respect to all—to the elderly and children alike. Although most of his older disciples were younger than he, he addressed them with great respect, as if they were his elders. No child ever expressed any fear of him; children felt comfortable playing with him, even pulling his beard. He often said, "A true yogi fears no one and no one is afraid of him." And he never complained. One devotee, who owned a tiny betel leaf and nut stall, said that Dhyanyogi-ji would often come and rest in the back of his stall on the bare floor.

His sense of humor was out of this world. People could see the twinkle and mischief in his eyes when he was about to crack a joke, although he could manage to do it with the most serious face. Once, a lady who invited him for lunch insisted on knowing how the dessert was. She had made a sweet popular in the state of Gujarat because she knew Dhyanyogi-ji liked it, but since she was originally from another state in India, she was not quite sure exactly how to make it. As usual, Dhyanyogi-ji, extremely conscious not to hurt anyone, simply said, "It's good." Over and over, the lady asked how he liked the sweet. Dhyanyogi-ji kept repeating, "It's good," but the lady continued to press him for an answer. Finally Dhyanyogi-ji said, "If you want to know the truth, whosoever eats this will not die, but surely will fall sick!"

Another time, when Dhyanyogi-ji was traveling, he took with him the barber from Bandhwad, the village where his ashram was located. This fellow had not seen much of the world outside his tiny village. They were visiting a disciple and when they were served lunch, the barber noticed that the spoons were made of sterling silver. Very excited, he told Dhyanyogi-ji, "Did you know these spoons are fine sterling silver?" Dhyanyogi-ji chuckled and said, "Why don't you swallow a spoon and when you go home you will be rich!"

He never got angry. He was in absolute control of the negative emotions that frequently plague the rest of us. His saintliness was demonstrated repeatedly, but one incident stands out the most for me. A group of disciples were traveling with him. In the evenings, Dhyanyogi-ji had only a cup of milk as dinner, but on one particular evening, it was impossible to find milk for him. We searched all over the village but no one had any milk to spare. We finally found an old woman in her 90s who said, "You cannot allow your Guru to go to bed hungry. Here please take this milk for him. I also have nothing but milk at night, but today I will offer it to your Guru." We were relieved and happy that Dhyanyogi-ji would get his cup of milk.

After we returned and he had finished his evening practices, we offered him the milk. Immediately he asked, "Where did you find the milk?" We all were a little hesitant to answer. Finally someone said that an old woman had given it to him. He became a little upset and said, "How can you feed me and expect an old woman to go hungry? Go and return the milk to her. I cannot let anyone suffer on my account." Such was his simplicity and nobility.

On another occasion, Dhyanyogi-ji and I were at a railway station. Before the train arrived, as we were waiting, a beggar approached us. I was still in the eighth grade at the time and did not have any money. Dhyanyogi-ji put his hand in his pocket and pulled out all the money he had—two or three hundred rupees—and gave it to the beggar. I was stunned. I later asked him, "Guruji, you did not keep any money for the rest of our trip. What if we run into a situation where we need some?" He said, "The Lord will always provide." Such was his faith and charity.

Years later, after we had come to America, we were in Desert Hot Springs, California. A group of disciples was on our evening walk with Dhyanyogi-ji when all of a sudden, for no apparent reason, he just fell down. He sprained his shoulder and got a bruise on his nose, but he said nothing by way of explanation to us. About two weeks later, a letter came from Bihar, India, where Dhyanyogi-ji was building a hospital for the community. It said that at the construction site, an 8-year-old boy had fallen from the third story but had escaped without a scratch. At this point Dhyanyogi-ji stated that he had seen and felt the boy falling in India, and that he took it upon himself to protect the child. Such was his compassion.

Once, when he was sitting in a car, someone slammed the door and his thumb got smashed between the car frame and the door. Can you imagine the pain? But very gently and calmly he said, "Would you please open the door? My thumb is caught."

When the door opened, I saw that his nail was pulled out and hanging. He was bleeding, and the bone was visible. Yet the person who had slammed the door seemed to be in more pain than Dhyanyogi-ji. Forgetting his own suffering, he comforted the disciple. "Such things happen. Don't worry, it is not your fault." Such was his tolerance.

In 1976, Dhyanyogi-ji came to America. Mother Earth was especially happy. The steps she had felt on her in India, she now felt on another part of her being. America was truly blessed. The blessings of great saints like Swami Ramtirth, Swami Vivekananda, and Yogananda were pulling other great teachers and yogis from across the ocean.

The four years I spent here in America with Dhyanyogi-ji were the best years of my life. The opportunity to be so close to him, serve him and learn was a priceless gift. Every day was a new experience, a new teaching. The joy, the happiness, the state of my mind was like a free bird, but with a great shadow of protection. Life was so carefree—no worry of any sort, no pressure, just being in the present. It was like a void, yet filled with everything. No matter what happened around us—some good things, some not so good—he was always the same. No change. Although he had planned to come for six months, he ended up staying for four years, because the requests of the people here and their enthusiasm melted his heart.

The experiences of love that his disciples have reported are as infinite as the ocean and the sky. I don't know where to begin and how to end, but maybe, as you hold and read this book, you will have a dip in that ocean, a glimpse of that sky. All I can tell you is that many who knew him, even those who just met him, often shed tears of love. We love him. His love for humankind was so apparent that even those who were against him loved him. Just a year before his *mahasamadhi*, although he was bedridden, he said, "My attitude to help humankind attain its welfare has never changed. It is as strong today as it was when I was traveling."

My pen and paper are too dry and short to do justice to the uniqueness of Dhyanyogi-ji, but this biography will surely be a spark of the universe that could lead you to light and freedom, granted by the love and grace of this infinite being.

It is with great pleasure, joy and the deepest feelings of accomplishment that we publish this biography of one of the "last guard" yogis. Many difficulties have had to be overcome to bring his story out. A biography was written in Gujarati by a disciple of Dhyanyogi-ji's and published in March 1972. It was translated into English by the late Mr. C. Patel. Since it was primarily written for the disciples in India, the writing was in the context of the Indian culture, so the style and flavor were very devotional. Rewriting the book so that it would be accessible to a wider range of readers presented a challenge. Also, Dhyanyogi-ji revealed very little about his own self or his past. He always said, "I am serving the dessert with love, just eat and be satisfied. Don't waste time in inquiring who grew the grain in which field, who ground it and sold it to the store, etc. All that is useless. Just eat!"

Since its translation, several writers who are disciples of Dhyanyogi-ji worked and corrected the language and grammar. To Dr. Marsha Newman (Moti), Margaret Herrell, and Dr. Jyoti Prevatt we owe our special thanks. Besides that, a host of disciples, particularly Eric and Sally Biggar, have worked hard in several ways over the past few years to present this biography as an inspiration for fellow seekers, now and for future generations. The book that you are now holding like a flower emanates its beautiful fragrance through the love and work of Dr. Ellen Balis and Meredith Goad.

Keep an open heart when you read it. Please understand but don't try to analyze; the mind will only block your efforts. We are certain that just by holding this book in your hands, and further, by reading it, in some way or another, known or unknown to you, no matter what path or teacher you follow, his energy will come into your life, and his grace and love will always be with you, boosting you to your Highest Self.

FOREWORD

"If only even a drop from the unlimited depths of the waters of the great ocean falls into our throats—dry for so many births—the thirst of all these births will be quenched. And so, this story is shared in the hope that the quest for spiritual union will be ignited in others. As that quest is realized, service to humanity and to this beautiful Earth who supports us will be actualized."

—Pranav Parekh, *Pathway to the Self*

FOREWORD

We offer this book at the feet of Shri Dhyanyogi-ji and Shri Anandi Ma. We have tried, in these pages, to give you a sense of this extraordinary man who embodied the essence of love and sacrifice, who embraced hope even when confronted with seemingly insurmountable obstacles, who spanned the worlds of ancient yogis and post-modern America, and devoted himself for more than a century of life to the welfare of humankind.

We cannot promise total accuracy in what is presented here. Dhyanyogi-ji rarely discussed his life, and when he did, his memories were sometimes inconsistent—perhaps because he felt it was not a story's details that were important but the underlying lesson he was trying to convey. Furthermore, some of his disciples' experiences with him may challenge the beliefs you hold about what is possible. We did what we could to stitch together the pieces that we heard from those who spent time with him, but it was never Dhyanyogi-ji's way to teach his students to stick to the facts or stay in their left brains. More than once, he showed us that the truth often lies in that vast, mysterious territory beyond the workings of the mind, and that facts can be manipulated by a yogi!

In *Raja Yoga*, one of Dhyanyogi-ji's favorite books, Swami Vivekananda tells how Indra, the king of Heaven, took the form of a pig and was happily living a pig's life, to the horror of the other gods. No matter what they said, the gods couldn't persuade Indra to abandon his pig life and return to Heaven. When he finally remembered who he was, Indra laughed to think that he could have gotten so lost. Vivekananda writes that we have all forgotten our true, glorious identities, and that when someone tries to point this out to us, we begin to "squeal and bite." The yogis tell us that we are living in a dream world, where, to escape the miseries of our condition, we become slaves to our desires, while in fact, our real nature is limitless and free. This was Dhyanyogi-ji's mission: to awaken us to our true identities, to free us from illusion.

Dhyanyogi-ji may always remain, to some extent, an enigma. He certainly can't be contained within the boundaries of his life, or grasped within the pages of a single book. But we are sure that he has blessed this project, and that his energy is in your hands at this very moment.

Ellen Balis and Meredith Goad

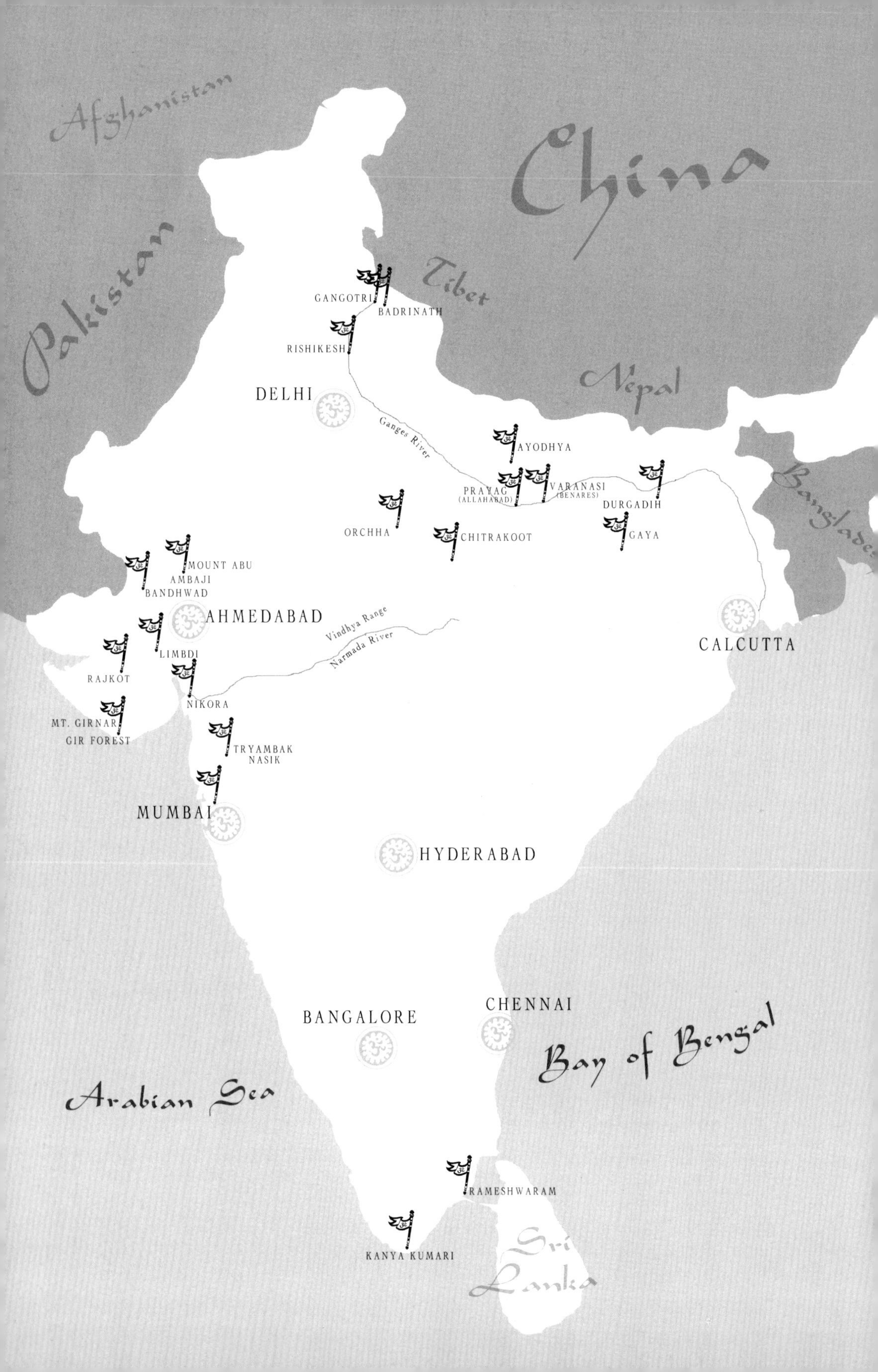

Afghanistan
China
Pakistan
Tibet
Nepal
Bangladesh
GANGOTRI
BADRINATH
RISHIKESH
DELHI
Ganges River
AYODHYA
PRAYAG
(ALLAHABAD)
VARANASI
(BENARES)
DURGADIH
ORCHHA
CHITRAKOOT
GAYA
MOUNT ABU
AMBAJI
BANDHWAD
AHMEDABAD
Vindhya Range
Narmada River
CALCUTTA
LIMBDI
RAJKOT
NIKORA
MT. GIRNAR
GIR FOREST
TRYAMBAK
NASIK
MUMBAI
HYDERABAD
CHENNAI
BANGALORE
Bay of Bengal
Arabian Sea
RAMESHWARAM
KANYA KUMARI
Sri
Lanka

PART 1

"Do or die."

CHAPTER ONE

THE GOLDEN DAY

On the slopes of Mount Abu in northern India was a cave, carved deep into the mountain and overhung with rock. A lone figure, sitting cross-legged on a worn piece of cloth, formed a silhouette against the mouth of what was known as the Elephant Cave. Warmed only by a white loincloth and his rugged full beard, the man was as immovable as the rocks around him as he recited a litany of sacred verses in the brisk mountain air. He was a yogi, and he had spent his entire life looking for answers to two questions that had tormented him since childhood: "Who am I?" and "What is death?" This quest had taken him from the bitter cold of the Himalayan peaks to the warm breezes of Sri Lanka. Now it was 1920, and the wandering was over. More than 30 long years of fasting, meditation and prayer had purified his body. Living in the wild, exposed to the harshness of the elements, had weathered his face and limbs. Yet his austerity had given him something more; his dark eyes shone with compassion and his heart was filled with love for all humanity. Powerful waves of spiritual energy seemed to emanate from his body.

His name was Madhusudandas, later to be known as Dhyanyogi-ji, and he was a man determined to reach enlightenment or perish in the attempt. He had worked hard to master many difficult yogic disciplines and was steeped in the knowledge of ancient Indian scriptures. He had survived starvation, illness, bandits, sudden encounters with tigers, as well as the frustrations and inevitable disappointments of the spiritual path. So far all his efforts had not given him the state of God-realization he longed for so desperately, but that did not stop him. "Do or die" was the guiding principle of his life. And so, on this day as on so many others, he sat alone on the rocks, repeating the verses of the sacred *Ramayana* and pouring his heart out to God.

But on this day, something different happened, something that would change his life forever. Dhyanyogi-ji saw a stranger approaching, a huge coil of matted hair spiraled high atop his head. This was the great swami Yogiraj Parmeshwardas, head of an ancient lineage of yogis. He set his water-gourd on the ground, sat down in front of Dhyanyogi-ji, and smiled.

"You seem to be a good *mahatma*," he said sweetly. "But don't you know that you have to clean a cloth before you can dye it?"

Dhyanyogi-ji asked the yogi what he meant. Parmeshwardasji replied that without complete purification, it is impossible to reach God.

Dhyanyogi-ji sensed that this was the teacher he had been waiting for all his life. He bowed down and said, "You are my Guru. I have struggled to reach God for such a long time, and have had no success. Please have mercy on me." Moved by Dhyanyogi-ji's humility, Parmeshwardasji answered, "Come see me tomorrow."

The next day, after bathing, Dhyanyogi-ji sat in front of Parmeshwardasji. Parmeshwardasji told Dhyanyogi-ji to close his eyes, and then held his hand over his new student's head.

"I felt like my body was on fire," Dhyanyogi-ji later wrote, "and I saw a wonderful and inexplicable light. After five minutes my Guru told me to open my eyes, but I didn't want to, and I remained in that ecstatic condition for 25 minutes. I lost body consciousness and experienced divine bliss. Finally he opened my eyes and smiled warmly. "I have initiated you. What was your experience?" he asked.

"I could not describe the bliss I had felt, and I prostrated at his feet. He lovingly caressed my head and gave me some instructions I was to follow for the rest of my life."

Parmeshwardasji gave Dhyanyogi-ji the *Bhuta Shuddhi mantra*, a verse especially potent when passed from teacher to student, which purifies the mind and the body to receive divine grace. For the next several months, Dhyanyogi-ji meditated and performed spiritual practices intensely under the direct guidance of his guru. His body underwent a dramatic cleansing, and he experienced a number of unusual phenomena, some of which frightened him. Several times, while meditating, he heard loud sounds like gunshots, that seemed to come from inside his head. Other times he felt his body fill up with spiritual energy and begin to assume positions on its own. His teacher assured him that during purification, these experiences were not uncommon.

One of the caves at Mt. Abu where Dhyanyogi-ji did austerities. (This photo was taken in 1988. When Dhyanyogi-ji was here, the cave had no walls or door.)

After five months, while suffused with joy, Dhyanyogi-ji began to run a high temperature that continued for several days. The heat generated by his practice was so strong that he went without proper clothing and sprinkled water over his bed before lying down. Then, one night a month later, while chanting the sacred name of Ram, he spontaneously went into the deepest state of meditation, known as *samadhi*. He felt as if his body were filled with divine light, and in this state, he experienced the answers to the questions that had haunted him all his life.

Suddenly, I felt like I was suffocating and I could not seem to exhale. I was very scared and I wondered if I were dying. Would I ever come back down to the normal plane of consciousness?

But then this stage passed, and I felt as if my skull were bursting with bliss. Ecstasy was sprinkling like a fountain out of the hair follicles of my head. I was submerged in the sea of bliss. I have no words to describe this condition. Not only had I never before experienced such supernatural bliss and magnificent light, I had never even heard of it! I wanted to stay in that state forever.

The experience of samadhi can only be grasped by the soul. That was a golden day in my life. My joy and bliss were like the joy felt when a drowning man reaches the shore, when a life-term prisoner is set free, or when a warrior emerges victorious after a grim battle. My body felt light and the weakness caused by fasting disappeared like magic. I was very alert and energetic. The vague uneasiness of mind that I'd had since childhood, the search for my true identity, and my constant fear of death vanished into oblivion. Life seemed full of joy, and realizing that I had reached my goal, I understood the importance of this life.

Dhyanyogi-ji's meeting with his teacher on Mount Abu was the pivotal moment of his life. During their time together, Shri Parmeshwardas prepared him to become the next leader of their spiritual lineage. From that day forward, Dhyanyogi-ji dedicated himself to the betterment of humankind and the welfare of all beings, pouring out his spiritual energy unconditionally so that others might not have to suffer as he had in their search for enlightenment.

Six months after meeting his guru, Dhyanyogi-ji resumed his solitary life in the forest. Then, after many years alone in the wilderness, he moved to a tiny village and devoted himself to its people for three decades. In the late 1950s, he broke with tradition and started teaching meditation and giving initiation to anyone who asked. Over the years, thousands of people flocked to him. Offering himself in this way required his body to go through major transformations—as extreme as those as he went through during the months leading up to his enlightenment—until he became like a human battery, sending out energy to everyone who came into contact with him.

Despite the hardships he endured on his 30-year quest, the twists and turns of the years that followed, and the risks he took throughout his life, Dhyanyogi-ji never strayed even an inch off his path. He was solely committed to attaining self-realization and then bringing others to that level of awareness. In later years he wrote, "Remember, I have devoted each of my breaths and the whole of my life for all of you." Over and over, he urged people to take whatever he had to give. "This house is on fire. Loot all you can!"

This is the story of his extraordinary life.

CHAPTER TWO

ROOTS OF DEVOTION

Those who met Dhyanyogi Madhusudandasji when he came to America in the 1970s knew they had encountered a remarkable being. He performed what appeared to be acts of magic, controlling the rain and changing his (and others') body temperatures at will. He could make people smile for no reason or suddenly burst into tears. He was nearly 100 years old, yet no one could keep up with him on a walk. He was comfortable in any environment, no matter how out of place he might have seemed. Although American students intuitively understood that he was special, no one really had any idea who he was.

Dhyanyogi-ji[1] came from a long tradition of *sadhus*, people who forsake home, family and wealth to become penniless, wandering holy men. Consumed with devotion to God and the goal of enlightenment, they seek to live outside the reaches of the temptations and attachments. Dhyanyogi-ji's story is part of the legacy of ancient yogis who traveled barefoot in the forests of India, across the snowy Himalayas, and through the steamy jungles. When these spiritual masters emerged into

---

[1] The suffix "ji" is added to indicate respect.

civilization—and some never did—their gazes were so powerful that they rarely looked ordinary people in the eye, their energy so palpable that they avoided physical contact. Dhyanyogi-ji's generation of sadhus and those before him formed a silent network of yogis living lives dedicated to loving God and serving humanity, working to bring about world peace and an end to suffering.

India is a land of extremes. Her icy rivers crash through craggy mountain ranges or slowly meander through villages baking in the sun. Barren plains and lush, green rice paddies stretch as far as the eye can see. The calls of wild birds and monkeys reverberate through jungles teeming with life, and dry riverbeds wind for miles and miles in total silence. From the towering Himalayas in the north, the subcontinent sweeps down to her tropical coasts, bordered by palm trees swaying by the sea.

In the cities and towns, women dress in endless layers of brilliantly-patterned cloth with luscious colors and textures. Smells of spices and incense waft by. The eyes are greeted by all manner of temples. Some are as small as dollhouses, decorated only with twinkling lights, housing primitive-looking statues with intense eyes. Others are large and intricately carved, displaying whole families of deities, each with its own story to tell and its own priest to attend to it. Everywhere there are flowers—garlands of flowers, carts stacked with flowers, flowers floating down rivers on tiny leaf boats—and exotic fruits and vegetables stacked in pyramids beside towers of colored powders sold for offerings in the nearby, always a nearby, temple. The ears are assaulted by a cacophony of motorcycle, car and truck horns, bicycle bells, vendors calling, children shouting.

Right in the middle of all this lively activity and excitement are the aspects of life we dread most. Illness and poverty have touched many people. Families cook and eat meals in the street. Children approach strangers with their hands outstretched. Men sleep by the side of the road, with not even a blanket to cover them. Yet somehow, in the midst of these extremes, there exists a unique stillness and peace, a subtle energy not experienced in any other part of the globe.

India presents duality in its most blatant form, but she also offers centuries of wisdom from yogis whose life work was focused exclusively on understanding the meaning and purpose of this duality. Their compassion for suffering motivated some of them to pass on what they discovered on their spiritual quests, so that we, too, could resolve our deepest and most troubling doubts. They hold out the promise that peace of mind is possible for everyone in all conditions.

While America is blessed with material riches, India is bountiful in its subtle energies. Dhyanyogi-ji told his American students that what his country had to offer was spiritual power derived from centuries of practices done by the yogis. He explained that in India the earth actually retained this etheric energy, like a deposit of priceless, holy ore. He said to look beyond the pollution, the unsanitary conditions, because on a deeper level the land was very pure.

There is a state in northeastern India called Bihar that is particularly known for its sanctity. In ancient times, it was the birthplace of many saints including Lord Buddha and Emperor Ashok, who, in the 3rd century B.C., was renowned for repudiating violence and uniting India under his peaceful rule. It was also the home of Mahavir, who helped to establish the Jain religion in the 7th century B.C. It is believed that the earth of Bihar was so honored to receive the energy endowed by these men that it continued to produce great beings. An Indian saying inspired by the soil of Bihar translates, "Mother Earth is full of gems." Dhyanyogi-ji was born here.

Although he preferred not to speak about his past, because he believed that it is only the present moment that counts, some facts are known about Dhyanyogi-ji's ancestry. He was born into a family named Mishra, who lived in the little village of Durgadih situated between two famous places of pilgrimage—Benares, where dying souls are guaranteed liberation, and Gaya, where Buddha attained enlightenment while meditating under the Bodhi tree. The Mishras were a devout Brahmin family, with a long spiritual tradition. For them, devotion, honesty and purity were as important as breath.

The level of spiritual attainment in Dhyanyogi-ji's family is exemplified by his great uncle, Maunibava, a saint born around 1850 in a little cottage in Durgadih. For 12 years, as part of his spiritual discipline, Maunibava observed a strict vow of silence in order to build his own internal energy and to help him quiet his mind. *Maun* means silence, so from that time on he was known as Maunibava. As a result of this practice, he acquired what is known as "the power of speech." Whatever Maunibava spoke would come true.

Maunibava's cave

Maunibava lived very simply and rarely asked for anything from anybody. His trust in God was so complete that he never worried about how his modest needs would be met. Yet once a year, during the festival known as *Ramalila* or *Navaratri*, he hosted an elaborate feast.

Navaratri takes place during the nine days that correspond to the battle between Ram and Ravana depicted in the *Ramayana*. Ravana was a demon with 10 heads. Five represent the *sattvic* (pure) aspects of humanity, and the other five signify the *tamasic* (impure) tendencies. Ram's triumph over Ravana symbolizes the victory of the higher forces of spirituality over the lower influences of desire. Each year during Navaratri, many people experience the powerful current of uplifting energy that flowed during this war, making it an ideal time for doing intensive spiritual practices—what is known in Sanskrit as *anusthan*. Maunibava always performed an anusthan during this period. The Vedic scriptures dictate that at the end of an anusthan, a yogi should prepare a feast and invite Brahmins and sadhus to attend. Despite his austere life, Maunibava managed to fulfill this tradition, feeding the many saints and devotees who came to celebrate on the final day of Navaratri.

Maunibava's *ashram* stood a mile away from Durgadih, at a place called Morauna. There were wild animals in the forest surrounding his cottage. Ancient wisdom teaches that these creatures recognize and show respect for ascetics who turn their backs on worldly desires. Those who knew Maunibava believed that the animals around him sensed his loving nature, and accepted his hospitality, going to and from his hermitage whenever they wished, without ever exhibiting aggressive behavior.

In the middle of the forest was a lake where many varieties of aquatic birds came to feed each winter, and to live in the peaceful silence there. One day, British hunters came to the lake for sport. Maunibava considered these birds his guests and could not bear to let them be killed, so he called the hunting party to his cottage and tried to persuade them not to shoot the birds. Unmoved by Maunibava's pleas, the hunters raised their guns to fire, but to their surprise, the guns did not discharge. The hunters fired their weapons once more, but again, no shot left their barrels. Puzzled, they examined the firearms and tried again, with the same result. Now they were frustrated. They exchanged their guns but still could not fire. The hunters realized that this yogi must have some kind of power stronger than their guns. Humbled, they fell at his feet, begging his pardon and vowing never to hunt again.

To us this may seem like an impossible fairy tale. But this was the India into which Dhyanyogi-ji was born. It was normal for people to seek blessings from local holy men to cure illnesses or solve other difficulties in their lives. Mantras were used routinely to heal fevers, headaches, diseases and wounds resulting from the bites of dogs, snakes and scorpions. When he was older, Dhyanyogi-ji recalled, "I saw with my own eyes that when natural calamities like a drought or an epidemic occurred, people of the area got together and chanted for a few days, and the calamity was overcome. In the case of drought, rains came. In the case of an epidemic, it disappeared."[2] Until modern times, Indians accepted without question that yogis could defeat kings, and that their *siddhis*, special spiritual powers, could overcome armies. Once, a king in the state of Gujarat commanded that all the residents of a certain area be relocated so that he could expand his city. There was a yogi who would be forced to leave his ashram if he followed the king's orders. He sent word to the king asking that he be allowed to remain, but his request was denied. The yogi had several small copper vessels that he used in his spiritual practices. When he learned of the king's decision, he inverted the vessels and said, "So be it." At that moment, the entire city collapsed into ruin. Events like this one were not considered unusual.

During the early years of Dhyanyogi-ji's life, ordinary people, struggling to survive, lived side by side with sadhus who had renounced everything in their search for self-realization. These spiritual seekers ranged from students fueled by a passionate love for the divine, to saints who had attained an exalted state, their mere existence a blessing. Maunibava was considered such a being.

Maunibava's ashram became a refuge for members of the Mishra family who grew weary of life's limited pleasures. One of Dhyanyogi-ji's aunts, Janakidasi, and her brother, Manrakhan Pandey, went to live there. The hermitage was also a special source of shelter for Maunibava's

[2]Dhyanyogi Madhusudandas, *Brahmanada* (Santa Cruz, CA: Dhyanyoga Centers, 1979) xv.

great-nephew, who as a little boy was deeply called to the spiritual life.

Although the other members of Dhyanyogi-ji's family were also very religious, most lived their days in the context of village life. Dhyanyogi-ji's grandfather, Shivlochan, was by nature quiet and patient, and was known for never becoming angry. He was a Sanskrit scholar and served as royal priest of the state of Tekari. Of his three sons, only Dhyanyogi-ji's father, Ramdahin, survived into adulthood.

Ramdahin, who was also a priest in Tekari, was much like Shivlochan in his gentle and serious temperament. He studied Sanskrit in Varanasi, and became an expert in Vedic astrology. His devotion to God was so deep that he, like Maunibava, acquired the power of speech—whatever he said was sure to come true.

Ramdahin expressed his devotion through constant chanting. Wherever he went, he sang *Sita Ram*, a mantra that honors two divine forms—Ram, an incarnation of Vishnu and hero of the *Ramayana*, and his wife Sita, a form of the divine mother. Whenever they heard the chanting of *Sita Ram*, people knew that *Baba* (father) of Durgadih, was approaching, so he became known as *Sitarambaba*.

A traditional story illustrates the spiritual benefits of devotional chanting. A sage named Narada, who was the son of Brahma, was on his way to heaven to visit Lord Vishnu when he passed through a forest, and saw a sadhu who had been meditating in the same position for so long that ants had built their anthill all around him. When this man learned of Narada's destination, he requested that Narada ask the Lord how many more lifetimes he had to endure before he was liberated from the cycle of birth and death.

As he walked on, Narada met another holy man. This one was in an ecstatic state, dancing and singing the names of God. When he heard that Narada was going to see Lord Vishnu, he also asked Narada to find out when he would be liberated.

When Narada met the Lord, he asked about the two saints, and Vishnu said, "Tell the first sadhu that he has three more lifetimes, and the second, that he has as many lives as there are leaves on the tree under which he is dancing."

On his return trip, Narada went to the ascetic sitting perfectly still in his meditative pose, and told him that he had only three more lifetimes. Hearing the news, the sadhu exploded in anger. "After all the practices I have done, I still have to come back three times? That is so unfair!"

Narada shrugged his shoulders. This is what Lord Vishnu had said.

Next, Narada came to the other yogi and reported to him, "You have as many lives to live as there are leaves on this tamarind tree. Then you will achieve self-realization."

This sadhu jumped with joy. "How fortunate I am!" he exclaimed. "I have all these lives ahead of me in which I can chant God's name and praise the divine, and then, after such bliss, I attain enlightenment!" At that very moment, he was liberated.

Like this second saint, Ramdahin's continuous chanting reflected his intense spiritual devotion. He built a temple to Durga, another form of the divine mother, which still stands today. He inspired awe in those around him, and the residents of Durgadih showed him enormous respect. It was understood that any sadhu or saint was always welcome in his home and would receive a filling meal.

Ramdahin's faith remained firm despite many crushing losses. Two of his brothers died, followed by two of his sons, Brijbihari and Vishvanath, both at the age of five. He lost four more people in his family, before being tested once again with the death of his sixth

Durga temple established by Ramdahin

child Ramrup, who died suddenly after graduating with honors from a university. Having suffered these tragedies, it was not surprising when Ramdahin became very attached to his youngest son, his most deeply spiritual child, who would grow up to be known as Dhyanyogi-ji.

Dhyanyogi-ji's mother, Sampattidevi, was a quiet and virtuous woman who, like her husband, was known for her reverent nature. Each of her eight children was said to surpass the others in appearance, intelligence, asceticism and devotion. Four months before Dhyanyogi-ji's birth, Sampattidevi had a dream in which she had a vision of Lord Krishna, who told her that her eighth child was a special soul.

"A very great being is going to be born to you," he said. "Don't misunderstand him. Don't mistake him for an ordinary person. Take great care of him."

Overjoyed with this forecast and with absolute faith, Sampattidevi eagerly awaited the birth of her son.

CHAPTER THREE

TWO QUESTIONS

*L*ike many of the world's great saints, Dhyanyogi-ji was born into a simple life. Durgadih was a humble village consisting mainly of rice fields surrounded by trees. Flat, moist and lush green, its stillness was broken only by the constant flutter of singing birds.

The Mishra home was a one-room hut with a clay tile roof. Inside, there was an area used as a kitchen, but there were no partitions and no furniture. The cooking was done on the floor, and bedding was unrolled each night for sleeping.

Yet Dhyanyogi-ji's arrival on Earth was anything but ordinary. Sampattidevi had great hopes for the new life developing in her womb, but nothing could have prepared her for the child who arrived during the winter of 1878. She named the infant Kashinath, which is a name for Shiva meaning "Lord of Kashi."[5]

Dhyanyogi-ji's birthplace in Durgadih

[5]Kashi is another name for Varanasi and Benares.

Lord Krishna had told Sampattidevi in her dream that her new son was an enlightened being in his previous life, yet he had self-lessly chosen to take another body and return to this world to help others reach this same state.

In the years to come, it would be said that merely being in Dhyanyogi-ji's presence would free people from their suffering. In his

Interior of Dhyanyogi-ji's birthplace

first months, there may have been few signs that something was differ-ent about the boy, but as young Kashinath grew, it became more and more apparent that he was an unusual child. Reading, writing and arith-metic were a waste of time, he complained, when he could be learning about God instead. Though he loved his family, he had no interest in household responsibilities and found that kind of life suffocating.

The saying "boys will be boys" did not apply to Kashinath. While other children fell into much mischief or were occasionally ill-tempered, he remained calm and in control even in the most difficult circum-stances. When another child beat him or abused him in some way, he forgave them and showed no signs of anger or resistance.

Most of the other boys of Durgadih naturally spent much of their time and energy playing. Kashinath did not enjoy playing like his friends, and when he did, he was prone to injury. Once his eldest brother, Shivkumar, convinced Kashinath to play "horse." Kashinath climbed onto Shivkumar's back, but before he was settled, Shivkumar suddenly bolted ahead. Kashinath lost his balance, fell off, landed on a stone slab and began to bleed. Shivkumar worried that his parents would blame him, but Kashinath claimed full responsibility for the accident so his brother wouldn't get into trouble.

Another time Shivkumar and some friends dragged Kashinath out of the house to wrestle. Even though he knew nothing about wrestling, Kashinath jokingly issued a challenge: "Come on, whoever wants to wrestle me. I am the strongest of all!" Shivkumar took him at his word and threw his brother down in one swift motion, pinning him to the ground. Kashinath's arm got caught in a hole and dislocated at the elbow with a pop. Kashinath's older brother, Ramsagar, had to carry him on his shoulders to the hospital, where the arm was reset. Although he received immediate treatment, it took a long time for the injury to heal, and the pain was so unbearable that Kashinath fainted. Dandiswami, a saint from a local Shiva temple, gave him a treatment of milk foam and black salt, which helped, but for the rest of his life Kashinath carried a scar on his right elbow.

While most growing boys are known for their voracious appetites, Kashinath was indifferent to food and showed unusual self-restraint for someone his age. Even *sanyasis* (renunciates) who have shaken off all worldly possessions like dust from the body have to work hard to gain control over their appetites by doing many austerities and experiments. For example, to help themselves view food as medicine rather than as a source of pleasure, some sanyasis eat only pepper for a period of time. But Kashinath's detachment came naturally to him during his boyhood. He ate what he was served in silence, and showed neither pleasure nor disappointment with the taste of his food.

When his family wanted to pierce his ears in the customary fashion, he protested, "Why should this golden body be pierced?" Kashinath also worried that if he accepted earrings, he might start wearing other ornaments on his wrists or neck. He wanted to avoid developing any attachment to worldly things.

There was one quality he did share with his young friends: He loved to run. He excelled at it, in fact, and his endurance was exceptional. For that reason, the one sport that Kashinath liked was a game called *kabaddi*. In kabaddi, there are two teams that stand opposite each other. One person runs over to the other side and tries to tag someone and get back to his team without getting caught. Kashinath's talent as a runner meant that he was excellent at this game, and his extraordinary speed would stay with him for the rest of his life.

As much as he loved running, by far Kashinath's favorite thing to do was to sit with Shivkumar and worship God. Watching Shivkumar's daily spiritual practices awakened and strengthened Kashinath's innate devotion, and Shivkumar was so impressed that he often invited his little brother to join him in performing ceremonies.

One day, when he was just 5 years old, Kashinath's family realized they hadn't seen him since early morning. Shivkumar was surprised, but thought, "He is still a child, and he may have gone off to play." But when lunchtime came and the boy was still nowhere to be found, the family grew anxious and began to search in earnest. When they discovered Kashinath, he was deeply absorbed in meditation, trying to merge with God. His father Ramdahin felt that finding the child sitting with eyes closed, tender hands joined in a mudra, was the beginning of the fulfillment of Sampattidevi's dream.

In fact, Kashinath's spiritual education had already begun. He was strongly attracted to the spiritual energy at Maunibava's ashram and was soaking up whatever he could during his visits there. He was also receiving instruction from Dandiswami, a *siddha* (enlightened person) who was the head of the temple of Lord Shiva known as Kastar Mahadev, located about two miles from Durgadih. Dandiswami was fond of Kashinath's older brother and once a month, the saint would come from Kastar to give his blessings to the Mishra family. During these visits he became especially close to Kashinath, and he took the young boy under his wing.

Born in Gujarat, Dandiswami was dedicated to serving the sadhus and the destitute, and through his service, he became well known. People came from far and wide to see him, including a great contemporary Indian saint named Shankaracharya (named after Shankara, the eighth-century Indian philosopher who founded Advaita Vedanta[4]) who, accompanied by hundreds of sadhus, horses and elephants, paid him several visits.

Once Shankaracharya sent word to Dandiswami that he would like to spend four months doing practices at Kastar Mahadev. However, because he would be bringing with him an exceedingly large number of aides and animals, Shankaracharya assured Dandiswami that he would understand if he could not bear the expense of their stay. Dandiswami replied that not only could they come for four months, they were welcome to remain as long as they pleased. The expenses, he said, would be covered by God. At the end of the four-month's stay, Shankaracharya, in an unusual gesture of honor and respect, came to bid farewell personally to Dandiswami.

Under the guidance of his mentors, Kashinath began to recite the *Ramstavraj*, a set of mantras praising Lord Ram. He listened spellbound

---

[4]Advaita (non-dualistic) Vedanta teaches that the Atman, the individual soul, and Brahman, the cosmic soul, are one and the same. Shankara (ca 788-820) established four monasteries located in Puri, Shringeri, Dwarka, and Joshimath, the east, south, west and north corners of India. The leader of each of these is known as "Shankaracharya." The Shankaracharya who visited Dandiswami was the Shankaracharya of Puri.

when Maunibava and Dandiswami told him about Ram's adventures in the *Ramayana* or about the lives of saints. He particularly liked to hear Dandiswami tell the story of Jadbharat, a realized being who had his own ashram. One day, near this ashram, a doe gave birth to a fawn. The doe died, so Jadbharat began taking care of the fawn. Over time, he became so attached to it that when Jadbharat died, although he was already realized, he came back to Earth again to look after the deer. Kashinath loved this story of an enlightened being who took another birth simply because of his desire to care for others.

When Kashinath read tales of children who had reached self-realization, he wondered, if they were blessed by the vision of God in their childhood, why can't I be, too? The stories that most inspired him were about Dhruva and Prahlad, two children who immersed themselves in thoughts of God and received divine visitations. Dhruva was known for his steadfast perseverance in seeking God. He was the son of a king who had two wives. The younger wife favored her own son and wanted him to ascend to the throne, so she convinced the king to banish Dhruva and his mother, Queen Sunita, into the forest. There they stayed until Dhruva reached the age of 7 and began asking questions about his father. Sunita wept and confessed to him that his father was the king. The boy decided to go see him.

The king was overjoyed to see his son, but once again, his young wife turned Dhruva out of the palace, and he returned to his mother in the forest.

"Is there anyone more powerful than the king?" Dhruva asked her.

"Yes," she replied. "Narayana, who lives in the mountains." Narayana is a name of Lord Vishnu.

Without telling his mother what he was planning, Dhruva left home in the middle of the night and headed for the mountains, making his way through a jungle filled with tigers and bears. The child had never been alone in the forest before, but he walked on without fear. He was barefoot, yet even when thorns pierced his tender feet, he would not stop. He searched without resting for Narayana, with no luck. Still, the child continued on because he heard the Lord in his heart, calling "Come to me!"

Finally, deep in the darkness of the forest, he met the sage Narada. "Where can I find Narayana?" Dhruva asked.

Narada answered, "Stay here. You have reached the edge of the northern sky. Concentrate all your thoughts on Narayana and have patience."

Dhruva sat down and began to meditate. Day after day, he remained there, yearning for the *darshan* (literally "viewing," having an audience before a diety or guru) of the Lord. Although the ants built their towering homes all around him, he never wavered in his determination. Finally, Lord Vishnu in the form of Narayana came down from heaven and revealed himself. Because Dhruva had shown such inestimable patience, Vishnu turned the boy into the most important star in the heavens, the North Star.

The story of Prahlad, another inspiration to Kashinath, is also a tale of unwavering faith, and love and devotion for God. Prahlad was the son of Hiranyakashyap, a demon king who had been granted certain boons from Lord Shiva, due to the king's intense austerities. Hiranyakashyap could be killed neither by man nor beast. He could not be killed by day or at night, inside of a building or outside of a building. This fierce king demanded that all demons and men worship only him, and no one in the world dared to defy him. But his son, Prahlad, was a spiritual child who constantly thought of the Lord. This infuriated his father, who was determined to squelch his son's desire for the Divine.

As Prahlad continued to talk of nothing but the Lord, the king became extremely angry—as demons are wont to do. He told his guards to throw his son to the bottom of the ocean, and then pile rocks on top of him. He hoped that the threat of death might force his son to relent and worship him instead of God. But Prahlad was so absorbed in thoughts of the Lord that he didn't even realize what was happening to him. Instead of sinking and being pinned to the bottom of the ocean, he effortlessly rose back up to the surface.

Again and again, the guards went to any lengths to kill him. They even threw the boy into a pot of boiling oil, but his skin remained cool to the touch. No matter what they tried, he was unhurt every time, because he was protected by the love of God.

Defeated, the guards returned Prahlad to the king. When Hiranyakashyap learned what had happened, he was filled with rage. At dusk, he confronted his son as he approached the entrance to the palace.

"Where is this God of yours?" he thundered.

"Everywhere," Prahlad said.

The king pointed to one of the columns supporting the threshold of the palace. "Even in this pillar?" he asked.

"Yes," his son replied.

"Then let the Lord appear to me in a form of his choosing," the king said.

With that, the pillar cracked open and Narsimha, a being that was half man, half lion, sprang out and tore him limb to limb. All that the king had asked for had come to pass: He was killed by a creature that was neither man nor beast; he died neither at day nor in the night, but at dusk; and his death occurred not inside or outside a building, but on its threshold.

Kashinath loved hearing these stories, and like Dhruva and Prahlad, he never forgot God. Once, while he and his friends were bathing at a nearby pond, splashing and giggling as children do, Kashinath quietly slipped away and began praying, offering the water to God in his cupped hands. When his friends realized what he was doing, they started teasing him, splashing him with water. But by now Kashinath had learned the lesson of detachment so well that he just ignored them and remained fully engrossed in his prayers.

It was during this time that Kashinath developed his lifelong devotion to Lord Hanuman, an incarnation of Shiva in the form of a monkey. One of the principle characters of the *Ramayana*, Hanuman attained immortality through his impressive feats of courage, supernatural strength and devotion. He is depicted with the head of a monkey and a muscular human body, carrying a large club. Hanuman is the epitome of devoted service and loyalty, and is considered an example of the perfect disciple. Kashinath was so enchanted with him that whenever he happened upon a statue or picture of Hanuman, he would gaze at it without blinking and it was hard for him to tear his eyes away. Reciting *Hanumankavach*, a set of mantras asking Hanuman for protection, always brought him peace of mind. When he visited Maunibava's ashram, he worshiped Hanuman over all other deities.

As he grew spiritually, Kashinath also developed a strong desire to repeat the *Gayatri* mantra, one of the most sacred Sanskrit mantras. Translated, the mantra says, "We are meditating upon the Almighty, who is in the form of supreme luster. May He inspire our intelligence."

Every Brahmin son is expected to recite the Gayatri mantra daily to ask for wisdom. But before he can begin this practice, he must undergo an initiation known as the sacred thread ceremony. During this ceremony, the child is given the mantra by his father, priest, or guru. This marks the beginning of the child's formal spiritual training. The ceremony is called *Upa nayanam*, which means "to be closer to God." The Indian scriptures state that the first humans were Brahmins created by Brahma. Since this is their origin, Brahmins believe that the Gayatri mantra will grant them liberation and return them to God.

Kashinath had not yet been through the sacred thread ceremony, but he didn't want to wait for his family to arrange it before he began reciting the mantra. Boldly, he approached his elders and said, "I can no longer live without being able to chant the Gayatri mantra. With or without the ceremony, I will begin." And so, ignoring tradition, he began reciting the mantra without having received the initiation. The very first time he practiced it, he became so immersed in the sacred words that he lost all outward consciousness, and remained motionless in the same posture for hours.

One day Kashinath and his brother decided to collect some fruit from a *jambu* or rose-apple tree. His brother climbed the spreading tree and shook it, sending heaps of fruit tumbling to the ground. As if drawn by a magnet, children came running from every direction and started picking up the fruit.

Since his brother had done all the work, Kashinath thought that only he had the right to gather the fruit, so he chased the children away. He was so busy chasing them that he didn't pick up any fruit for himself. His brother scolded him from his perch in the tree. "Dear brother, why are you wasting your time driving away the boys? Your job is to collect fruit, not to chase away children." Listening to his brother, he stopped worrying about the others and gathered more fruit than he could carry.

This experience stayed with Kashinath for the rest of his life, and became a metaphor for his understanding of the relationship between the guru and the disciple and the obstacles along the path of meditation.

"The fruit is the goal. The one who shakes the tree branch and gives fruits is the *sadguru* (enlightened teacher). The gatherer of the fruit is *jiva*, the individual soul, and the children who had come to steal the fruit are the tendencies of the mind. If efforts are made to attain spiritual growth, without being distracted by the tendencies of the mind, then, by the grace of the sadguru, the goal will definitely be reached."

At the heart of Kashinath's desire to draw closer to God were two simple questions: "Who am I?" and "What is death?" By the time he was just 7 years old, Kashinath was constantly haunted by these eternal puzzles, difficult even for the wisest sage to understand. Whenever the question "Who am I?" arose in his mind, he became restless and grief overpowered him. Peace only came to him when he sat near Maunibava and Dandiswami or chanted the names of God.

His fear of death was so profound that he would faint if he heard that someone had died. Once, while crossing the river on his way home from school, Kashinath saw a corpse floating downstream. He was so terrified that he refused to go back to school for several days.

Whenever a relative or a family member died, he became obsessed by the question "Will I also die like this?" He knew that, as sure as the sun would set in the west, one day he, too, would die and nothing could prevent it. This prompted him again to ask himself the question "Who am I who will leave this body behind?" He knew he was different from his body, yet at the same time he argued, "If I am different, then who is performing the acts of walking, eating, laughing and speaking?" No adults around him other than Maunibava and Dandiswami took his questions seriously. When he asked his friends, "Who are we?" they laughed and said, "You must be mad to ask such questions. We are the children of our parents. We are Brahmins. Who else can we be?" But Kashinath was not satisfied with these answers.

Whenever he was especially troubled by these questions, he ran for solace to the peace of Maunibava's ashram. On one occasion when he was feeling conflicted, a spontaneous idea popped into his head. "Why shouldn't I leave home to be free from all this?" At that moment, it was as if a series of closed doors opened one by one. He began to visualize, like images in a movie, past members of the Mishra family who had freed themselves from the bondage of worldly life. Maunibava, Janakidasi, and his maternal uncle had all released their possessions as if scattering leaves to the wind. They had realized the transient nature of earthly happiness and advanced far on the path to renunciation.

After this vision, Kashinath knew he had no choice. To find himself and his future with God, he would have to leave his past behind.

CHAPTER FOUR

THE RELUCTANT SCHOLAR

The ultimate aim of human life is enlightenment. When souls become intently focused on this goal, life at home becomes too restrictive. Though they feel love and gratitude to the parents who gave them life, blood bonds are not strong enough to hold back their yearning. They become driven to sacrifice the warmth of family life so that they may follow a path that in time will help hundreds, if not thousands, of others.

In western cultures, breaking away from the family is associated with hurt, anger and rebellion, all of which are rooted in the ego. But in yogic tradition, leaving home is a positive affirmation that the goal of life is to attain God. The yogis believe that while human relationships can be beneficial and beautiful, they all ultimately must end. Our relationship with God, however, is permanent. This relationship, in fact, is the true basis of all other loving relationships we have. People always have expectations of each other, and we see our interactions with one another as a give and take, but a relationship with God is unconditional.

Spiritual seekers who strike out on their own may leave their families heartbroken. Yet their painful decision to shun the life of a householder is, in a way, also a great gift to their families. The yogis say that if even one person in a family attains God-realization, that single moment of enlightenment can not only liberate the parents, but have a positive effect that reverberates through seven generations.

In Durgadih, Kashinath had made the decision to follow in the footsteps of the saints and leave home. He was relishing the prospect of setting out on his spiritual journey in earnest. But his father had other plans.

The Mishras were learned Brahmins, and Ramdahin was determined for his son to continue the family tradition and become a scholar. This was not simply a matter of ambition, but a matter of honor. It would be a disgrace for a child in this family to remain illiterate. Kashinath had the wisdom to recognize that accumulating academic knowledge was not the key to conquering the cycle of birth and death, but he did not want to dishonor his father. When Ramdahin insisted that he go to school, Kashinath reluctantly but dutifully agreed.

The prospect of studying books instead of contemplating the nature of God quite simply broke Kashinath's heart. At school, he felt like a fish out of water. Although he easily won over his classmates, impressed his teachers with his sharp intellect, and quickly rose to the top of his class, his mind was elsewhere.

His best friends were two boys named Paramahansray and Shamaji Tiwari. The three were inseparable and they all excelled in their courses. But while the others were eager and attentive when the teacher was giving a lesson, Kashinath was preoccupied with thoughts of meditating in the quietest corner of his house.

Kashinath did so well in school that one of his older brothers, Ramrup, told him, "Finish your studies in school quickly. Then I will teach you English. I want you to become a successful lawyer." Kashinath firmly declined. For him, that kind of study was superfluous. He believed that by knowing God, he would be connected to the source from which all knowledge flows.

After Kashinath and his two friends graduated from their school in Durgadih, they began to study two-and-a-half miles away in the village of Suryapura. They traveled on foot across the bright green rice fields, sometimes stopping to eat ripe mangoes together, and had to cross a river to reach the school. During the monsoon, the river was sometimes too full to cross in the afternoon, and they were forced to stay at the school until the water level subsided.

The boys created a good impression in Suryapura. They gained the complete trust of one particular teacher who encouraged any spiritual tendencies in his students. Once, when the river was flooded and Kashinath and Paramahansray were trapped at school, this teacher asked them if they would perform the devotional ritual called *puja* for the Jain saint Mahavir, and the boys eagerly agreed. Both had spiritual experiences at the end of the puja—Kashinath had a vision of a white cow, and his friend heard the sound of temple bells, both classic experiences that indicate spiritual growth.

During his time in Surypura, Kashinath had an experience that was so disturbing to him that it had enormous impact in shaping the man he would become. One day, on his way to school, Kashinath got into an argument with another schoolboy, and the other boy began using foul language. Kashinath was upset to hear these words, and without thinking, he lost his temper and smashed his writing slate violently against the other boy's forehead. The blow was so forceful, it drew blood.

Stunned by the intensity of his anger, he deeply regretted that he had actually brought pain to another being. Despite his tender age, he came to understand the extreme importance of developing self-control.

All during his school years, Kashinath continued to balk at traditional forms of learning. He saw no need to memorize long lists of Indian kings and their dynasties. The only lessons he valued were the ones that would give him knowledge of God. The conflict between his parents' wishes and his own desire for self-realization created a growing emotional turmoil. He became more and more impatient, feeling that precious years of his life were being wasted.

One day, Kashinath, now 10 years old, finally gathered his courage and spoke to his family. "I do not wish to learn, nor do I wish to go to school," he told his parents.

Kashinath's family, shocked and disappointed, attempted to persuade him that he was making a mistake. They tried tempting him, tricking him, and punishing him, but he stood firm. Finally, they relented.

Free of school, Kashinath experienced a tremendous lightness, as if shackles had been removed from his legs. ॐ

CHAPTER FIVE

LEAVING HOME

Kashinath hoped that leaving school would give him peace, but the bondage of school now gave way to the bondage of home. Day and night he grew more obsessed with finding the answer to his question "Who am I?" He began to distance himself from his family. At home, he spoke to no one and didn't seem to enjoy it when someone spoke to him. Gradually he lessened his association with friends his own age, and spent more time sitting alone in a corner of the house meditating. He passed his days in a sorrowful mood. He lost interest in eating and unless he was called to a meal, he went hungry. His family naturally started to worry. They could not understand his indifference to them and his detachment from the world.

Kashinath realized that his profound questions about life and death would never be answered if he remained at home. I am the son of the great father—God, he thought. How can I remain confined in this little house in Durgadih? If I stay here, I will be only of this house, but if I leave, the whole world will be my family.

To Westerners, the idea of a little boy running away from home is a kind of quaint reminder of all our childhoods, along with memories of catching fireflies on a hot summer night or hitting a home run in Little League. It's almost a rite of passage in the United States for children to grow exasperated with their parents' rules and regulations and try to strike out on their own, carrying only a few meager possessions in a small bag. Ordinarily, the story ends with the child growing hungry or homesick and returning to the family roost within just a few hours, crawling into bed, the lure of independence only a faint memory.

But in India, leaving home can be a noble path. Indian history is filled with stories of sacred journeys taken by saints such as Dhruva, Prahlad, Buddha, Shankaracharya, Jnaneshwar and Chaitanya. More recently, saints like Yogananda, Anandamayi Ma, Ramana Maharshi and many others turned away from worldly life.

Though Kashinath was following in hallowed footsteps, his decision to leave home was painful. He wondered whether his departure might actually cause the death of his parents, who would have sacrificed their lives for him. On the other hand, if he stayed in the house, his work of self-realization would remain unfulfilled. It was like deciding whether it was better to lose his right eye or his left. The greatest difficulty was that he would be completely on his own if he left the house. He couldn't enlist the help of Maunibava or Dandiswami because they would be obligated to alert his parents. If anyone suspected his plans, the doors of his cage would be locked. His family seemed disappointed when Kashinath missed a meal, or even arrived late for dinner. How would they react if he told them he was leaving forever? It would be a thunderbolt to their hearts.

As difficult as it was to renounce his ties to his family, he knew it would be even more challenging to live the life of strict discipline that he had chosen. Renunciates often do not know where their next meal is coming from. Their bed may be under a bush or in an open field. And going alone into the jungles and forests, hills and mountains with nothing but faith in God is a choice fraught with danger. At the time Kashinath was beginning his spiritual journey across India, tigers were still common in the forests. Cobras, kraits and other deadly snakes were everywhere. A careless step could result in death. But the burning desire to know the truth still drove many away from the shelter of society and into the embrace of Mother Nature, where the essential questions can be asked in solitude. And so it was in the case of Kashinath. He resolved to leave the next morning.

The evening after he finally made his fateful decision to leave home, he visibly relaxed. For the first time in weeks, he ate dinner with his family. They were pleased to see him smiling and talking with everyone after such a long period of withdrawal. In retrospect, their mood was not unlike the happiness the people in Ayodhya felt the night before Lord Ram's scheduled coronation. Early in the *Ramayana*, the King of Ayodhya decided to retire and chose his son Ram to succeed him. The citizens of Ayodhya were overjoyed. Since his childhood, Ram had been the darling of the city. He was seen to be the embodiment of gentleness, compassion, wisdom and courage. All night long, they celebrated in their anticipation that their dear Lord Ram was to be crowned king the next day. But that night, there was a terrible betrayal, and the next morning, instead of becoming their king, Lord Ram discarded his royal clothes, exiled from Ayodhya, and took up the life of a hermit. The people of Ayodhya were stunned, completely unprepared for this heartbreaking turn of events. Similarly, no one in the Mishra family had any inkling of the loss that awaited them the next day.

Kashinath slept soundly that night, feeling he was, at long last, about to fulfill his soul's purpose. At 3:00 the next morning, long before the sun would spread its rays and an hour before Venus would rise, the figure of a small boy stirred in the Mishra home.

From a distance, Kashinath bowed to his sleeping parents. He carefully opened the door without making a sound and said goodbye to his relationship with his family. His small bundle held only two changes of clothing, a book of Sanskrit grammar, a thin blanket, a metal cup for water, and his horoscope. He knew his father, an extremely skilled astrologer, would be able to find him if he left his horoscope behind.

He had told only one person of his plan—his friend Indrajit, who also had decided to renounce the world and join Kashinath on his spiritual quest. At the last minute, however, Indrajit was unable to join him. He told Kashinath to go ahead and he would join him later, but afterwards, Indrajit became so entangled in worldly life that he was unable to leave it behind.

So Kashinath hurried alone from his house in total darkness. There was only one hour before his family awoke, as they did without fail each morning at 4:00 a.m. His safety lay in getting as far away as possible before then. As soon has he stepped outside, without looking back towards his house, he ran as fast as he could. His love of running and his endurance were a blessing that morning.

Kashinath was now free, but without food or money. In the coming weeks he would thoroughly test Lord Krishna's promise in the *Bhagavad Gita*, "But if a man will worship me, and meditate upon me with an undistracted mind, devoting every moment to me, I shall supply all his needs and protect all his possessions from loss."[5]

The Mishras were shocked and grief-stricken when they found Kashinath's empty bed. The entire village loved the boy as their own, so everyone began looking for him. Some tried to follow in his tracks, but he had made a clean escape. With empty hands and heavy hearts, they returned to Durgadih. Kashinath had vanished, and a dead silence swept over the house and village. The family now realized why Kashinath's sorrow had disappeared the night before, and why he had been full of unexpected smiles.

---

[5]Christopher Isherwood, *The Song of God: Bhagavad-Gita* (New York: New American Library, 1972) 83.

CHAPTER SIX

A TASTE OF FREEDOM

When Kashinath left home, his destination was Kashi, a three-day walk from Durgadih. For more than 2,000 years, this holy city on the west bank of the Ganges, also known as Varanasi and Benares, has been a spiritual center of pilgrimage for devout Hindus, and a great seat of Hindu culture and learning, especially Sanskrit scholarship. Shiva is worshiped here as Vishvanath, or "Lord of the Universe," and the Vishvanath Temple is one of the most powerful temples in India. It constitutes one of the 12 *Jyotir-lingani*,[6] considered the purest manifestations of Shiva. Devoted Hindus long to take their final breaths within the city limits of Varanasi because the scriptures state that if they die there, Lord Shiva will liberate them by whispering Lord Rama's name into their ear. This simple whisper is all it takes. Shiva sets them free as a reward for remembering God at the moment of death. Buddhists consider this area sacred as well because Buddha gave his first teachings at Deer Park in Sarnath, just six miles away.

From an early age, Kashinath had longed to visit Varanasi and have the darshan of the mahatmas who dwelt there. So entrancing was

---

[6]A lingam is a phallic shaped form that represents Lord Shiva. Jyotir-lingani are not man-made, but instead appear spontaneously.

the idea of visiting Varanasi that Kashinath occasionally broke into a run during his three-day journey. He ignored the protests of his empty stomach and pushed himself until his legs were shaking and blisters formed on his feet.

When he finally arrived in the ancient city, he wasn't disappointed. The atmosphere of Varanasi is enough to make a person swoon. Everything in the city is so infused with the energy of Lord Shiva that the entire place throbs with *shakti* (spiritual energy). When the great 19th-century saint Shri Ramakrishna visited Varanasi, he reported that he saw that beneath its superficial appearance, the entire city was made of gold. There are more than 1,000 temples squeezed into the city, and hidden paths lead to a myriad of tiny ashrams where highly evolved yogis practice meditation in privacy, just steps away from the hordes of pilgrims and grieving families who bring their loved ones there to die.

At dawn, the river is covered in a mist. Then, as the day breaks, the sunlight reveals the intensity of the colors of the city and the masses of people coming to take a dip in the river. For two miles along the bank of the Ganges, there is a continuous row of "bathing ghats," wide steps that descend from ashrams and temples down to the river. Here pilgrims bathe in the river to purify themselves. Most of the ghats gleam with gold and orange paint. Some correspond to important places of pilgrimage in India. It is believed that, for instance, a visit to the Kedarnath Ghat brings the same benefit and blessings as going all the way to the Shiva temple in Kedarnath, high in the Himalayan Mountains. The great saint Tulsidasji, the poet who wrote the *Ramayana*, lived and bathed at what is now called the Tulsidasji Ghat.

Manikarnika, known as "the burning ghat," is where the cremations take place. Unlike the other brightly painted ghats, Manikarnika is gray and austere, with wood piled on its steps. Clouds of smoke perpetually obscure it in haze. All day long, processions of people, carrying bodies on their shoulders, proceed to Manikarnika for the final rites. But death in Varanasi is not a tragedy, it is a triumph. The deceased person has attained the ultimate blessing by leaving the body here.

Kashinath eagerly began visiting and serving the yogis, sadhus and saints who had gathered in the city. For two months, he absorbed their teachings and followed the instructions they gave him for spiritual practices. But all this time, he kept a very low profile, remaining hidden to avoid being recognized by anyone who might know him from Durgadih.

After a while, he grew careless, assuming perhaps that his family had stopped searching for him. He became freer in his movements, walking in the streets without fear of being seen. One day he was spotted by a sadhu from Durgadih who knew him well and was aware of his disappearance. The renunciate left without letting Kashinath see him, and returned to Durgadih to tell the boy's family the good news. "Go," the sadhu said. "Your Kashinath is wandering in Kashi."

Ramrup and another brother set out immediately for Varanasi. They soon found Kashinath openly wandering the narrow lanes of the old city. Ramrup gathered up his wayward sibling and they returned directly to Durgadih. They marched him into the village like a prisoner. From then on, the family kept a vigilant eye on him so that there was no further chance of escape.

Soon after returning to his village, Kashinath wrote a letter to his fifth brother, Vidyapati Mishra, requesting to be given the sacred thread ceremony. Defiantly, he wrote that if no one would give it to him, he would put the thread on himself, without the ceremony. The family agreed, and Kashinath received the sacred thread on the day that his brother Shivkumar was married.

At one point in the thread ceremony, the initiate's head is shorn and he dresses in the attire of the sadhu. Lines are painted on his forehead with sandalwood paste. He wears only a loincloth and carries a walking stick and a begging bowl. He enacts the behavior of the renunciate by reciting, "*Om bhavati, bhiksham dehi,*" which means, "Om, I am a monk." It is a request to be given alms. By playing this role, the child experiences first hand the humility of the sadhu. At a deeper level, the ritual signifies that the child is entering a period of renunciation as he begins to study spiritual practices. In effect, he is begging for wisdom and knowledge that he will receive from the sacred scriptures, the holy *Vedas.*[7]

"At that time, I really felt that by repeating the phrase 'bhiksham dehi' and becoming a renunciate I would finally be able to discover the true purpose and meaning of life," he said. "I realized that I was destined for the spiritual life, and this gave me great joy! I wondered if everyone who went through the sacred thread ceremony had this same experience. Was I the only one?"

Now that he'd received this initiation, he had society's sanction, and

[7]Hindus classify four stages (ashramas) of life: student (brahmacharya); householder (grhastha); householder devoted to spiritual pursuits (vanaprastha); and ascetic who renounces worldly ties (sanyas). The thread ceremony initiates the child into the first stage.

32

no one could stop him from performing austerities to intensify his worship. The very next day, Kashinath stood in water up to his neck for an extended period of time, while doing yogic breathing techniques called *pranayama*. He considered the sacred thread the only precious ornament he required. Later in life, when his disciples offered him wristwatches and other fine jewelry, he accepted the gifts out of his love for them, so they would not feel hurt or disappointed. However, none of those watches ever reached his wrist; he gave them all away. He'd smile, show his thread and say, "This is my ornament."

After the sacred thread ceremony, his family began pressuring him to return to school, and he finally agreed. As before, he excelled, getting an upper rank in sixth grade and a first rank in the seventh. But Kashinath remembered the pure, limitless joy he had experienced while in Varanasi in the company of saints. Now, worldly life seemed worthless and full of misery, and he became more and more restless every day. The thought "Where shall I find peace?" consumed him.

Even though he had run away and was clearly very unhappy, the affection and respect for him in the village actually increased, and he received numerous offers of marriage. His brother's wife tried to persuade him to take a wife. He was 12 years old and in those days, Indian marriages were routinely arranged by the family while the children were still very young. But Kashinath knew that if he married, he would be firmly bound to worldly life forever. Tormented by this thought, he became completely detached from everyone, not speaking unless spoken to. He lost all interest in eating or sleeping, and was profoundly sad.

As much as he didn't want to lose Kashinath to the life of a renunciate, Ramdahin felt compassion for his son. He knew the boy longed for a simple, spiritual life, and it hurt him to see relatives press him to marry. One day, when he could bear it no longer, he resigned himself to the inevitable and called the family together and said, "From now on no one should speak to Kashinath about marriage. My son is going to become a mahatma. He will never get married. It is useless to pursue this any more. Nobody should talk with him about it again."

After this merciful intervention, no one uttered another word about marriage. Kashinath was relieved, and felt greatly indebted to his father for saving him from the obligations and responsibilities of married life.

One-and-a-half years after his sacred thread ceremony, Kashinath's beloved mother died. Sampattidevi had gone on a pilgrimage to the Temple of the Sun at Devmani, in the district of Gaya. When she returned, she fell seriously ill. Her oldest son had some medical training and struggled to cure her, but day-by-day her condition grew more serious. Although death was approaching rapidly, she was completely without fear. One day when all of her relatives were sitting anxiously at her bedside, Sampattidevi said, "Lord Ram's chariot has come to take me up. Please let me go now."

The Vedic scriptures state that a chariot of the Lord comes to take the soul when we die, and many dying people have described having this vision. Hearing Sampattidevi describe her experience upset her relatives. She tried to soothe those gathered around her. "None of you should cry. The chariot of Ram has come to pick me up," she said.

Someone asked, "Where is the chariot? We don't see anything."

Sampattidevi spoke confidently, as though the chariot were right in front of her. "But I see it. Here it is." Five days later, Kashinath was at her side as she took her last breath, and spoke the name of Ram.

Sampattidevi's death severed an important family tie for Kashinath. Everyone could see his complete detachment from Durgadih and ordinary existence. His family sensed they were about to lose him again, and did everything they could to persuade him to stay, even promising to build a small hut where he could worship God. But there could be no more bargaining or compromises. For Kashinath, attaining God-realization was now a "do or die" proposition.

CHAPTER SEVEN

THE WANDERING SADHU

*I*n the early 1890s, six months after Sampattidevi passed away, Kashinath again left home while the family slept. He was 13 years old, and this would be his final flight from Durgadih. Before he left, he destroyed his horoscope so that his family could not search it for clues to his whereabouts, or use it to find a girl who could be his match in an arranged marriage.

The next 30 years would be difficult, lonely ones as he wandered through holy cities and other far-flung sacred places, hunger and fatigue his only companions. But these trials were to be expected, for they are part of the centuries-old Indian tradition of searching for enlightenment. Renunciates believe that enduring hardships and moving from place to place during their *sadhana* (spiritual practice) helps them to develop the detachment they need to shut out illusion and temptation and become true seekers of God. In this way they escape from the traps of physical pleasures that can keep them tied to the world.

Tota Puri, a highly realized practitioner of Advaita, never stayed in one place for more than three days, believing that a wandering monk must live like a running stream if he is to avoid attachment to worldly life. He broke this rule only once, when he stayed in Dakshineshwar for 11 months to teach Ramakrishna.

Wandering sadhus generally visit places connected to their *ishta-devatas*,[8] or sites that all pilgrims consider holy, such as Varanasi, Allahabad, Rishikesh and other spiritual centers drenched in thousands of years' worth of shakti.

Consistent with the nature of this vagabond lifestyle, there is no record of this period in Kashinath's sadhana. No one documented the places he went, the people he met, or the things he did. And, as an adult, Kashinath felt that such details were unimportant; he wanted his students to concentrate on their own paths so they could move forward. When pressed by his very closest disciples to discuss this period in his life, he would gently rebuke them, saying, "I am serving you this sweet with love, just eat and be satisfied. Don't waste time in inquiring who grew the grain, in which field, who ground it, and sold it to the store, etc. All that is useless. Just eat."

Despite this attitude, a few details have been passed down over the years. During Kashinath's first decade away from home, he wandered around, mostly in northern India, studying under various teachers. He spent some time in Ayodhya, paused for a very brief period in Varanasi, and lived among lions and crocodiles in the Gir Forest in Gujarat. Then he spent another 10 years in the Himalayas, finally sequestering himself in a cave on Mount Abu. There he performed intense spiritual practices for another decade.

Over the years, he learned Sanskrit and Pali, a language related to Sanskrit that is used in many Buddhist texts. He absorbed himself in the *Ram Raksha Stotram*, a powerful mantra to Lord Ram, and in yogic practices that he later referred to as the *Vajra Panjar*[9] techniques. He studied hatha yoga with a blind yogi named Hari Hara Baba, who lived on a boat deck on the Ganges, and he learned about traditional Indian medicine called *Ayurveda*. He studied music formally for one year, mastering the classical Indian instrument called the harmonium, and becoming skilled at *bhajan* singing, praising God with song.

---

[8]From all the different forms of God, devotees can choose a specific form that they feel most drawn to for purposes of worship. This becomes their ishta (principal) devata (deity).

[9]Vajra Panjar literally means "Shield of the Thunderbolt." It consists of a large number of esoteric spiritual practices perfected by Dhyanyogi-ji.

Kashinath struggled tremendously at times during these three decades of his life. "I did not put on shoes for 20 years," he once said. "I walked on the snow of the Himalayas with bare feet, and also on the scorching earth of India's central province in summer, when the temperatures were 110 to 120 degrees Fahrenheit and the tar was melting. I developed calluses half an inch thick from walking in all types of weather. They were so hard that they broke the strongest of thorns. My feet would not be harmed. It was simply a matter of training."

He once said that the first five years were the hardest. It is clear from other remarks he made that hunger was a constant obstacle. Often he would be so absorbed in his spiritual practices that he did not want to waste time begging for food. At these times, he only ate when people freely offered him food or temple authorities gave him a meal. But even then he was very careful about what he put in his body, sometimes even rejecting food if it was offered by someone he felt had an impure motive.

Upon his arrival in Varanasi at age 13, Kashinath had not eaten for three days. As he sat on the bank of the Ganges, deep in thought, his empty stomach tormented him. Soon a man came by and slipped into the holy river to wash. After finishing his bath, the gentleman sat some distance away and began eating mouth-watering sweets from a bag. Kashinath had no need to open his own bundle because it contained only his Sanskrit text.

Suddenly the gentleman rose and approached Kashinath. "Would you like some food?" he asked.

An ordinary boy would have impulsively accepted, but Kashinath hesitated. Growing up, he had been firmly instructed in the Brahmin rules governing the purity of food. Hindus believe that food contains significant amounts of *prana*, life force. The way food is prepared, who cooks it, and the thoughts and emotions of the cook, all affect the energy of the food, and therefore the mental and spiritual energy of the person who eats it. A Brahmin will eat only food prepared by another Brahmin. These ancient rules may seem strange or excessive to Westerners, but Kashinath would not deviate from them even slightly, no matter how famished he might be.

"What is your caste and what is your occupation?" the 13-year-old bluntly asked the man.

"I am a Brahmin from the district of Gaya, and I work at the police department at Faizabad," the gentleman serenely replied. Kashinath was reassured by the man's conduct and spiritual nature, so he accepted the food.

"We considered fried food to be pure," he later recalled, "so I had some *malpooras.*" Malpooras are shallow-fried sweets that bear a resemblance to eggless crepes.

Kashinath was extremely cautious as he moved around Varanasi because this was where his family had discovered him the last time he ran away from home. He knew this time that he could not be overconfident and careless. He remained for a short while, but a nagging sense of insecurity soon overcame him and he decided to leave for Ayodhya, the birthplace of Lord Ram and the site of many events of the *Ramayana.* Before going to Ayodhya, however, he walked to Orchha, a village 300 miles away in north central India on the Betwa River.

Many years ago, a king in Orchha had a dream in which Lord Ram appeared to him and said, "Near Ayodhya, in the river Sarayu, there is an image of me. Find it and install it in a temple."

The king commanded his servants to search for the *murti* (statue) and bring it to him. They found the statue and carefully placed it on a palanquin to be carried back to the king. But when the servants reached Orchha, the palanquin bearing the murti suddenly stopped, and they were unable to move it again. Assuming this to be God's will, the king built a temple at that site and installed the statue inside. This murti of Lord Ram is considered a miracle sent by God, and is now a popular pilgrimage destination.

By the time Kashinath arrived in Orchha, pangs of hunger were once again gnawing at him. He had not eaten for two days. He took a bath in the river, then sat on a bench built around a pipal tree, where there were many monkeys, and chanted a mantra. As soon as he finished, a gentleman he had never seen before came up to him and asked, "Would you like some food?"

"I am very hungry, but I don't see anything here to eat," Kashinath said.

"Don't worry about that," the stranger replied. "Food will be made available."

The stranger soon returned with a leaf plate upon which was some vegetables, yogurt, and a pound of fried wheat bread, called *puris.* He simply placed it in front of Kashinath and walked away.

Just as Kashinath was about to place the first morsel of food in his mouth, he heard the jangle of temple bells announcing the evening *arati*. Arati is a sacred ceremony, typically performed at temples twice a day, at dawn and dusk, in which worshippers sing and wave a lamp with many flickering flames, offering the light to God.

Kashinath now had quite a dilemma. If he ate before going to the temple, he would miss the arati. But if he waited until after arati, the red-faced monkeys that scampered around the temple surely would eat the plate of food while he was gone. If he left this food to the monkeys, he was not sure when he would eat again.

But Kashinath had left home for God, not for food. "By the Lord's inspiration this food was offered to me," he thought. "If it came to me truly by His grace, then the monkeys will leave it alone. If they take it, it's fine. I have come here for darshan at the temple, and I should not miss that."

So he left his leaf plate under the pipal tree and went into the temple for arati. When he returned a half-hour later, he found the food untouched. Rather than eating the meal, the monkeys had formed a circle around it to keep away other creatures until Kashinath reappeared. Once again, the promise of protection by Lord Krishna in the *Bhagavad Gita*, as well as his devotion to Lord Hanuman, had been fulfilled.

Kashinath walked on to the legendary city of Ayodhya, his head full of stories about the miracles that have occurred there, but he quickly became disenchanted. Just a few days after his arrival, he saw two people quarreling near the temple known as Hanumangadhi. The fight was so aggressive it frightened him. "I was very upset to see people quarreling even in the city of God," he recalled later.

So the next day Kashinath set out for Prayag, the city that is known today as Allahabad. Prayag is a spiritually significant site because it sits at the confluence of three rivers—the Ganges, the Jamuna, and the subtle, invisible Saraswati, which runs underground. The convergence of three rivers increases the spiritual energy in the area, and bathing in the waters is considered very beneficial.

Within the human body there are six *chakras*, centers of subtle energy. The *ajna chakra*, or third eye center, is also called Prayag because it is the junction of the three major energy channels called *nadis*—*ida, pingala* and *sushumna*—located in the spinal column. The Jamuna, the Ganges and the Saraswati rivers are external representations of these nadis.

Lord Ram called Prayag "the king of holy places," and said, "The ripples of the Ganges and Jamuna are his royal whisks, the very sight of which destroys all sorrow and distress."[10]

Once every 12 years, when specific configurations of the planets and constellations appear in the heavens, millions of people gather here to take a "holy dip" in the Ganges to cleanse themselves of past karma. This month-long celebration, known as the *Maha Kumbha Mela*, is the largest gathering of people on the planet.

After a few days in Prayag, Kashinath found himself with nothing to eat but a few pieces of rock salt. "I swallowed this salt with sweet Ganges water," he said. "I did this for one day, but on the second day I became desperate with intense hunger." Once again, God sent a stranger to satisfy his physical needs. A man approached him and gave him a pound of chickpeas.

Next, Kashinath began walking toward Chitrakoot, following the same path through the forest that Lord Ram walked with his wife Sita and his brother Laxman during their 14-year exile. The sage Valmiki recommended that Lord Ram go to Chitrakoot for a retreat, describing it as a heaven on earth. "Charming is the hill and lovely the forest, the haunt of elephants, lions, deer and bird." He said that the river at Chitrakoot, the Mandakini, a tributary of the Ganges, was "quick to drown all sins," and that the land was saturated with the blessings of the many great sages who had practiced austerities and "muttered sacred formulas" there.[11] It is a place so infused with Lord Ram's presence and the love of his devotees that people frequently experience visions of him there.

Kashinath had heard poetry describing the magic of Chitrakoot since his early childhood days at Maunibava's ashram:

There was a crowd of saints on the bank of Chitrakoot.
Tulsidas rubs sandalwood paste and Lord Ram applies a tilak.[12]

The verse refers to a story about the saint Tulsidas, who once asked Lord Ram, "How can I see Lord Ram?" Lord Hanuman told him

---

[10]Tulsidas, *Shri Ramacharitamanasa* (New Delhi: Motilal Banarsidass Publishers, 1994) 316.
[11]Tulsidas, 333.
[12]A tilak is a religious mark, usually applied to the forehead.

that if he recited the Ram mantra in Chitrakoot, Lord Ram would pass by and give him darshan.

Tulsidas began reciting the mantra, and after a long time two princes came by. It was Lord Ram and Laxman, but Tulsidas did not recognize them. After they passed by, Lord Hanuman appeared and asked Tulsidas, "Did you see Lord Ram?"

Saddened, Tulsidas had to say, "No." But he did not give up. For the next 14 years he stayed in Chitrakoot, reciting the Ram mantra. One day, as Tulsidas was preparing sandalwood paste during his puja, Lord Ram once again passed by. This time he stopped, took some sandalwood paste and applied a tilak to the forehead of Tulsidas, but still Tulsidas did not understand what was happening. So Lord Hanuman took the form of a parrot and started singing the verse, "Tulsidas rubs sandalwood paste and Lord Ram applies a tilak." It was only then that Tulsidas recognized that he was in the presence of Lord Ram.

It took Kashinath six days to cover the 45 miles of dense forest to Chitrakoot. He had no money, so he walked steadily, stopping only at night to rest.

He lived for a year in the Chitrakoot ashram of Guru Premdas, a 50-year-old, fully realized scriptural scholar with whom he continued his studies in hatha yoga and raja yoga. Then he moved into some caves in a place called Janaki Kund, near the sacred river Mandakini.[15]

It was in one of these spiritual hideaways that Kashinath met a master named Mauni Maharaj. This teacher told Kashinath that it would fulfill his heart to do a 40-day anusthan of the *Ram Raksha Stotram*.

The *Stotram* is a set of mantras that poetically and ecstatically express devotion for Lord Ram. Chanting these verses gives the *sadhak* (disciple) physical protection and accelerates spiritual evolution. Years later, Kashinath said that repeating the *Stotram* can help a person attain anything and everything they desire, from worldly things to liberation from the cycle of birth and death.

An anusthan is an intense spiritual commitment that requires many hours of practice a day over an extended period of time. When doing an anusthan, it is ideal to keep silence and break all contact with the outside world, so the sadhak makes advance arrangements for food and any necessary supplies.

---

[15]Janaki is another name for Sita, because she was the daughter of King Janak. Janaki Kund is the site of a rocky pool where Sita bathed.

Kashinath knew he would need milk, firewood and food for the 40-day anusthan and the feast that traditionally follows, but he had no idea where he could get the 500 rupees it would cost. In India, it is customary for people to take care of sadhus, but Kashinath always moved around, so he didn't know anyone who could help him.

After three days of worrying, while Kashinath was performing his puja, a man came to him and handed him an envelope. The man simply said that it was a letter and walked away. After his puja, Kashinath opened the envelope and found five 100 rupee notes. There was no letter inside.

Kashinath was concerned because he didn't know where the money came from. By accepting it, he might inadvertently be a part of some negative action that would compromise the purity of his anusthan. For example, if a sadhu takes money that was obtained by stealing from others, he would incur some of the negative karma.

That night, however, Kashinath had a dream in which the guru who had taught him the stotram told him not to worry, that the money had been given to him by a devotee of God, and it was meant to be used to finish his anusthan.

But soon there was another problem. It is best during an anusthan not to leave the area where practices are being performed, but Kashinath had to have some milk every day for sustenance. The mantras would take eight hours a day to complete, and the nearest source of milk was four miles away. It would take too long for him to get it himself. For several days he wondered how he would take care of his food needs. Then, out of the blue, another sadhu came and offered to serve him.

Kashinath told the young man about his predicament, adding that he didn't even have a pan to hold the milk. His bowl was his hands, his bed the earth.

"I have a pan, and I'll get the milk every day," the sadhu said. "Anything else I'll do, too. Just write down your schedule, and I'll do whatever you need."

So the sadhu walked eight miles round trip each day to bring him milk, the only food Kashinath allowed himself during the 40-day anusthan. Another sadhu appeared and offered his services as well, so Kashinath had two people to look after him and all the money he needed.

During an anusthan, it's common to experience the body becoming very hot. In fact, Kashinath's anusthan was so intense and required such physical discipline, it was more correctly termed an austerity, or in Sanskrit, *tapas*, which literally means "heat." The fire of his tapas eventually would burn away his karmic impurities and *samskaras*—mental attitudes and values acquired over many lifetimes.

On the tenth day, Kashinath began running a high fever but he continued with his practices, bathing twice each day in the cool Mandakini River. When he sat on his *asan* (meditation mat) each morning, his temperature was normal, but by the time he completed his mantras, the fever returned. It went on this way for three weeks. Saints living nearby warned him that he might have malaria. They advised him to seek medical attention. But Kashinath always told himself, "Lord Ram is my doctor, he'll take care of me."

On the 40th day, the anusthan came to an end, and Kashinath was flooded with ecstasy. This was the first spiritual height he had reached since leaving Durgadih. At last, he felt like he was making a little progress.

Next, Kashinath performed a fire ceremony and cooked a meal large enough to feed a hundred Brahmins. Much to his surprise, word of the feast had spread and 400 people showed up. Mauni Maharaj appeared and said, "Don't worry. Cover the pans with a cloth and keep serving, but don't peek."

Kashinath's guests ate and ate, but the food never ran out. When the cloth came off the pan at the end of the meal, there was still enough food left for 15 people. Years later, Kashinath shared with his own disciples the lesson he had learned from this experience. "Whatever we do, if we do it in the name of God, it will be successful."

Soon after this, Kashinath met a saint in the ancient Saraswati order of monks, and decided to take an important step in his spiritual life. Impressed by the saint's purity, Kashinath asked him for *sanyas*.

Sanyas is a formal ceremony in which individuals take a vow to renounce their former lives and give up all but the most basic necessities. Placing their full faith in God, they begin a life dedicated only to spiritual realization. Kashinath wanted to take the formal sanyas initiation because he thought that it might prevent his family from trying to bring him home again. It also gave him a way to sever symbolically all ties with his past. As part of the ritual, the saint gave him a new name—Madhusudandas Maharaj—servant of Lord Vishnu.[14]

Free of all worldly attachments, he could now completely focus on *moksha*, spiritual liberation. The saint told Kashinath, now dressed in white, that he would become a great teacher and must dedicate his life to serving others.

Every day while Kashinath lived in Chitrakoot, he walked two-and-a-half miles in the company of four other sadhus to receive a handful of chickpeas and barley to eat. On the way, they chanted "Sita Ram" together. They collected the chickpeas and barley for a month, then had it ground into flour and made loaves of bread, which they ate with some chutney.

There were also plenty of days when Kashinath's physical needs went unsatisfied, and he had to find creative ways to silence his rumbling stomach. Many years later, his disciples asked him what he had done during his wanderings when he had no food.

"When that happened," he replied, "I sometimes ate pieces of rock salt, or I prepared a 'vegetable' dish from pebbles. First, I would boil water. Then I dropped the pebbles, which had been washed clean, into the hot water. After a while I put whatever spices I had on hand into the pot. That's all. The 'vegetable' was ready."

"But how did you eat this vegetable?" his disciples asked.

"How do we eat the beans of the saragva tree?" he said, referring to a plant that is eaten like an artichoke. "In the same way, the spices are licked off and the pebbles discarded."

Apparently, Kashinath became very familiar with this "meal." As the years went by, he began speaking about it as if he were a connoisseur.

"Pebbles," he said, "have a particular flavor when gathered from the banks of a river."

Along with pebble soup, Kashinath subsisted on spinach and herbs. Sometimes he filled his stomach with *muth*, the roots of a grass that grows in marshy places.

Most of us have difficulty imagining the suffering that comes with prolonged, intense hunger and physical pain. We might not last a day or two, much less 20 or 30 years. For Kashinath, physical concerns were secondary. He had such drive and eagerness to find God that no obstacle

---

[14]Madhusudana is one of the names of Vishnu, and das means "servant." Maharaja is a formal title that literally means "Great King," and is also used to address sadhus and saints.

distracted him or shook his faith for long. Instead, these challenges only seemed to push him deeper in his search.

During this time, Kashinath focused on the 3,000-year-old scripture known as the *Durga Saptasati* or *Chandi Path*.[15] In these verses, the Divine Mother teaches devotees how to develop true vision and purify the ego so that they can break free from worldly bonds and the anxieties they bring.

Chandi Path tells the story of a king and a merchant who, despite many spiritual virtues, are still plagued with desires. They go to the feet of a great *rishi* (sage) for guidance, and the rishi regales them with tales of the Divine Mother and how she defeats the Ego in a 100-year-long war. In that war, representative of our struggles with inner demons, she battles the negative forces called Fickleness, Haughtiness, Deception, Memories, Wandering To and Fro, and Hypocrisy. She fights Self-Conceit and Self-Deprecation and kills the Lord of Thought. She destroys Too Much and Too Little. She is named "She Who Tears Apart Thoughts." In her warrior form, she becomes ferocious, but in her heart, she is pure love.

The rishi guarantees both men that by surrendering to the Mother, they will definitely attain peace and be released from the desires that torment them.

Shankaracharya, a great devotee of Shiva, wrote a poem in the 8th century about the Divine Mother that has been an addendum to the *Chandi Path* for the last 1,300 years because it so vividly expresses the heart of the seeker crying out for Divine Mother's grace. His inspiration for the poem came during a journey through the Himalayas, where an unusual encounter made him realize he had been neglecting to honor the Goddess in his spiritual practices. During the journey he became very ill with dysentery, growing dehydrated and so weak that he was unable to move, even to fetch a cup of water from a pot just inches beyond his reach. Desperate with thirst, he reached out to an old woman who happened to be walking by and asked her if she would give him a drink.

"Well, you are young and strong," the old woman replied. "Why don't you get it yourself?"

Shankaracharya looked up at her, too exhausted to move.

"Ah, so you don't have any shakti!" she said.

---

[15] *Durga Saptasati* or *Chandi Path* are both names for the 700-verse scripture in praise of the Goddess.

Shakti is both the word for divine energy and one of the names of the Mother. Laughing at her own play on words, the old woman transformed herself into the Divine Mother. Shankaracharya, healed and humbled, composed a poem that speaks with the voice of a child who can hide nothing from his mother and feels only love and longing for her, as this excerpt expresses:

> *Mother, I don't know mantras nor yantras nor can I sing your praise. I don't know how to welcome you, nor how to meditate on your presence. Neither do I know how to sing your glories, nor how to show your mystical signs, nor even how to lament. But I shall keep on calling you, you who take away the difficulties of all.*
>
> *Oh Energy of Infinite Goodness, Mother of the Universe, I don't know the systems of worship. Neither have I sufficient wealth with which to serve you. My nature is lazy, and I don't know the correct performance of worship. Please pardon whatever deficiencies exist in my service to your lotus feet, Oh Mother, because a child can be bad, but a Mother can never be bad.*[16]

Like a child tugging on his parent's sleeve, Shankaracharya's words persistently remind the Mother of her promise to deliver him to his final destination.

In the first years of the 20th century, Kashinath traveled through the rugged Vindhya Mountain Range. He visited Nepal's holy spots and all the major Himalayan shrines in India. He stayed for long in places that had been found to have especially high spiritual energy, spending his time doing intensive sadhana. During those periods, his typical day consisted of four or five hours of yogic practices, including hatha yoga, mantra repetition, advanced techniques of pranayama, and, of course, meditation. Another four or five hours were devoted to studying the Vedas.

For three years, Kashinath lived in Rishikesh, a beautiful spiritual settlement nestled in the foothills of the Himalayas, on the banks of the Ganges River where it enters the Deccan plain. Thousands of pilgrims flocked to this small town each year, sharing the narrow streets with sweet-faced cows and chattering monkeys that clambered around its temples. The paths to the Ganges were lined with stalls selling murtis,

---

[16]Swami Satyananda Saraswati, trans., *Chandi Path* (Napa, CA: Devi Mandir Publications, 1997) 397-8.

Ganges River at Rishikesh

crystal and wooden *mala* (rosary) beads, brightly-colored powders, *ghee* (clarified butter) lamps, incense and flowers—all the necessities for performing puja on the river at dawn and dusk. Ashrams lined the forested cliffs overlooking the water, its two banks connected by a swaying footbridge, marking the spot where Laxman is said to have crossed the river. Here, for two hours each day, Kashinath studied raja and hatha yoga under the tutelage of Guru Yogiraj, a teacher he met in Rishikesh, at his Shanti Shadan Ashram.

On a narrow road rising sharply up from Rishikesh is a tiny village called Devprayag, perched on a wedge of mountainside carved out where the Bhagirathi and Alakananda rivers merge. Devprayag offers breathtaking views. A temple sits at the confluence of the rivers, with stairs that lead down to the chilly, tumbling waters. Kashinath spent two years here, living in a cave by the side of the steep road.

In this remote corner of India near the border of Tibet, Kashinath studied hatha yoga and esoteric yogic techniques with Jivandas, an ascetic so advanced that Kashinath once witnessed him stop a snowfall. Under Jivandas's guidance, Kashinath performed a year-long anusthan during which, for five hours a day, he recited a mantra beseeching Lord Ram for his grace. From Jivandas, he learned a powerful pranayama called *Shaktichalan Kriya* (the "energy heating" movement), used to activate the *kundalini*, the primordial spiritual energy that lies dormant at the base of the spine, to move it upwards to pierce the chakras. Jivandas also taught Kashinath how to consciously astral travel, and how to protect his physical form during these journeys out of the body.

Life in the mountains was beautiful, but it could also be dangerous, especially during winter. In the warm and dry months, walking was rigorous. During the rainy or winter months, the roads and footpaths were impassable. The yogis who lived up in the mountains remained there throughout all the seasons, and as Kashinath climbed higher, he learned from them how to survive the brutal winters. Some sadhus went into meditation for the entire six months. Others had knowledge of herbs and special remedies with which they could control their vital functions. They knew of a particular kind of leaf they could eat and not grow hungry for months. They raised their temperature using the deep and rapid breathing technique called *bhastrika* (literally "bellows"), and prepared musk according to the principles of Ayurveda so that it produced tremendous body heat.

After these years in northernmost India, Kashinath migrated south to Mount Girnar, a major pilgrimage center for both Jains and Hindus, in western Gujarat state. He did practices there, and later, in eastern Gujarat, at a place called Aarasuri Ambaji, near Mount Abu.

The temple at Aarasuri Ambaji was built on the site where the Divine Mother had appeared to a king in her form as the Goddess Amba. The object of worship in the temple is a *yantra*[17] that is never shown to the public. Kashinath found it to be a very powerful place. Much later in his life, he would return to this area and stay for more than 50 years.

---

[17]Yantras are geometric figures that represent the subtle body of God, in both its form and formless aspects.

Confluence of Alakananda and Bhagirathi rivers at Devprayag

CHAPTER EIGHT

Repaying a Debt

There is a legend that thousands of years ago, in the age of the Vedas, the demons and gods joined together in a rare moment of collaboration to churn the divine ocean and extract a sacred nectar for immortality. Harmony between these rival factions couldn't last, and inevitably a struggle over the nectar ensued. During the battle, drops of the nectar fell and one of those drops fell upon the city of Allahabad. As a result, every 12 years, at the time of the Maha Kumbha Mela, the water of the Ganges at Allahabad is said to literally transform into this sacred nectar. Pilgrims who bathe in the river during the days of this celebration undergo a powerful purification, and receive tremendous grace just by being in the company of the thousands of saints and holy people who come from near and far for this spectacular occasion.

During the Maha Kumbha Mela, an enormous and surprisingly organized tent city springs up on the flood plain and riverbanks adjacent to the confluence of the rivers. It is India at its most intense, packed with stalls selling flowers, colorful powders and highly perfumed incense, streets filled with orange-clothed sanyasis and sadhus wearing the costumes of various deities. Rousing aratis ring from temple walls, and gurus hold court in makeshift tents. The river is lined with men wearing only their *dhotis*, long pieces of cloth wrapped around the waist and legs, and ladies in their best saris, all getting soaking wet as they dunk themselves in the Ganges to rid themselves of *karma* (fruits of past actions). Despite the millions of people clamoring at the water's edge and spilling out on the streets and alleys—at the Maha Kumbha Mela in 2001, more than 50 million people came—there are plenty of peaceful, calm places away from the crowds that arrive continuously, day and night.

In 1905, at age 27, Kashinath was known as Madhusudandas,[18] the name he received when he took sanyas. In his on-going quest to be in the presence of people who had attained inner peace, he traveled to Allahabad for the Maha Kumbha Mela. As he wandered through the city streets, he was unaffected by the noise, the dust, and the confusion, completely happy to be among so many true saints and sincere devotees.

In this ocean of humanity, Madhusudandas ran into Mahabirdas, a disciple of his great uncle Maunibava from Durgadih. Madhusudandas's appearance was radically changed from the boy, Kashinath, who had left home at 13. Sadhus don't shave during anusthans, so he had a full, dark beard and wore only a loincloth. Mahabirdas would never have recognized him, but at this point, Madhusudandas had no reason to hide away, so when he saw Mahabirdas, he introduced himself. After a few words of greeting, the sadhu began to tell Madhusudandas about his family.

"After you left home, your elder brother Ramrup died. Everyone in your family has been miserable since your departure. Your father Ramdahin does not want to hear about anything except 'his Kashinath.' His grief-stricken condition is like King Dasharath's state when his son Lord Ram was exiled to the Dandaka Forest for 14 years." According to the *Ramayana*, no matter what reassurances he received from Lord Ram or his other family members, King Dasharath never recovered from his grief and he died from the pain caused by separation from his son.

Mahabirdas's words touched Madhusudandas's heart. Here he was enjoying a pilgrimage in Allahabad, while in Durgadih his father was desperately unhappy. Inwardly he resolved to fulfill his father's wish and return home.

---

[18]Madhusudandas is pronounced Mah-doo-SOO-dan-das.

Madhusudandas knew that Mahabirdas had planted a seed in his mind that was disturbing his inner peace, but he also was aware that this seed would never have taken root if he did not still feel a lingering attachment to his father, despite the fact that he had taken the vows of a sanyasi.

According to the Vedas, only a soul in a human body can realize God. Therefore we are all profoundly indebted to our parents, who provided us with this unique opportunity. Madhusudandas felt this debt keenly. Furthermore, by beginning his son's spiritual education, Ramdahin had been, in essence, his first guru, and Madhusudandas was deeply grateful that his father had understood his heart's desire and released him from the burden of marriage. However, the sense of obligation that he felt towards his father was a distraction from his absolute focus on God and it subtly blocked his spiritual progress. He was aware that true detachment from the physical world came from within, not from external acts like taking sanyas. He could give up everything—family, friends, material possessions—to pursue his search for God, but if any corner of his mind was still preoccupied with thoughts of home, he would not attain his goal. He had to let go of his attachment to the past completely.

So, to honor his spiritual debt to his father and thereby break his karmic bond to him, and to free himself from any further family obligations, Madhusudandas decided to make a pilgrimage to Gangotri, the source of the Ganges, high in the Himalayas. There he would collect water from the river and offer the merits of the pilgrimage to his father.

In many spiritual traditions, pilgrimage to a holy place is viewed as a way to move closer to God, to become purified, receive blessings, and gain spiritual wisdom. A pilgrimage is prayer in action, and it inevitably entails considerable sacrifices. When people survive these tests of commitment, their faith deepens. Most make this effort for their own benefit, but sometimes a pilgrimage is performed on behalf of someone else, and the sacrifices made and the blessings received are offered for the sake of others. In the yogic tradition, all of humankind and even the land itself are beneficiaries of these selfless acts. The more spiritually advanced the pilgrim, the more powerful the offering. For Madhusudandas, at his level of attainment, giving his father the merits gained by his pilgrimage was an inconceivably precious gift.

We cannot be certain why Madhusudandas chose to go to Gangotri, but perhaps it was because for a yogi, going to the source of the Ganges was like going to the source of creation, to the point where this world connects with the realm of the gods. According to the Vedas, the Ganges descended to earth from the heavens because of the intense austerities performed by a prince named Bhagiratha on behalf of his ancestors. However, once the prince's prayers were answered, he had a new problem—how to protect the world from the earth-splitting force of this celestial river. He prayed to Lord Shiva, the only one strong enough to help him, and Lord Shiva broke the fall of the river in the locks of his hair. This is why the Ganges is considered an aspect of Lord Shiva, and bathing in her waters is said to wash away sins. Just a drop of her water can cure diseases, and, at the time of passage from life to death, it helps the soul in its journey. Water collected from the source is at its purest and most sacred. Perhaps Madhusudandas was inspired to trek high in the Himalayas to Gangotri because he wanted to collect the water that came down from heaven as a result of the austerities performed by another son, long ago, on behalf of his fathers.

Today it is possible to make the trip to Gangotri by bus, but in the early part of the last century there were no roads beyond Rishikesh. Years of wandering, hatha yoga and austerities had left Madhusudandas in excellent physical condition, but the walk to Gangotri was a difficult and

dangerous journey into the Himalayan wilderness. Once Madhusudandas reached Rishikesh it probably took him two more months to hike the final 100 miles to Gangotri.

The uncertain nature of mountain travel tests the endurance and resolve of even the most devoted pilgrim. Progress was slow, since to penetrate the mountains the trail constantly had to switch back and forth, ascending and descending repeatedly. Weather in the mountains is notoriously unpredictable. Rain showers, hailstorms and blizzards are all possible, even in the same day, turning the rough dirt trail into a muddy, slippery, and extremely treacher-

Ganges River in the Himalayas

ous track. In these conditions, the traveler is at great personal risk; one slip on a narrow mountain trail could be fatal. Temperatures fluctuate dramatically, even with the mere passing of a cloud. It can be broiling hot in the high-altitude sun, and then, around the next bend in the trail, in the deep mountain shadows, it can be freezing cold. For a barefoot sadhu with only a blanket for protection, these conditions were tremendously challenging. There was always the possibility of a landslide or an avalanche. At times Madhusudandas was forced to cross deep mountain gorges on precarious rope bridges that swayed violently in the wind, testing his courage and faith in God. Food was scarce. Only a few hardy villagers lived in the mountains and there were no tea stalls catering to the pilgrims as there are today. The only people he met on his journey into the Himalayas, other than rugged

Valley of the Shiva temple at Kedarnath, with 23,000 foot high Mahapanth peak as its backdrop

mountain folk and migrating shepherds with their huge flocks of sheep and goats, were other sadhus and pilgrims.

The physical conditions could have led to moments of deep despair, paralyzing fear and pure exhaustion. But Madhusudandas used the yogic techniques he'd mastered during his years of sadhana as the need arose—pranayama and hatha yoga to increase his physical endurance and control his body temperature, *japa*, mantra repetition, to calm his mind and overcome fear, and a meditative practice of focused vision called *tratak* for concentration and protection.

Once while traveling, Madhusudandas met a tiger face to face at a turn on a narrow mountain trail. He stood absolutely still and gazed into the eyes of the great cat, silently repeating the mantra "*So Ham Hansah*" which translates "I am That, That you are. God is in you and in me," affirming their mutual identity as One in God. The tiger left the trail, passed around Madhusudandas, climbed back on the path, and quickly vanished.

Despite these frightening aspects of the journey, Madhusudandas never lost sight of the purpose of his mission—to collect the precious water from the Ganges to give to his father, and thereby free himself from family attachments. His intention gave him strength. And the mountains themselves offered gifts that undoubtedly lifted Madhusudandas's spirits. A breathtaking glimpse of snow-clad Himalayan peaks, glistening in the sunshine or glowing in the moonlight, perhaps made the hardships a little bit easier to handle. The sound of the rushing river soothed his tired heart. Misty rainbows, ethereal reminders of God's promises, appeared after torrential showers, making up for the difficult trail conditions. Waterfalls cascading from tremendous heights offered a cooling shower and a thirst-quenching drink. All of these natural blessings were a bit of divine encouragement as he made his way into the

Gaumukh, the glacier that is the source of the Ganges

thin air that embraces the upper reaches of the Ganges. Climbing higher and higher into the mountains, Madhusudandas sensed he was entering the abode of the gods.

During these months, the river was his constant companion, for its watercourse is the easiest pathway into the mountains. The Ganges is the holiest river in a country of sacred rivers, and from Gangotri to Rishikesh it plunges through the mountains, sweeping along with elemental force.

Gangotri is a tiny village nestled in a thick pine and deodar (Indian cedar) forest, straddling both sides of the spectacular rocky gorge cut by the Bhagirathi River, the most revered branch of the Ganges. The actual source of the river is the ice cave at the leading edge of the Gangotri glacier, a stark, primordial place known as Gaumukh, 10 miles farther up the valley at the base of the Bhagirathi peaks. By the time the river reaches Gangotri, it falls with tremendous force through the gorge. The Gangotri Temple, dedicated to the goddess *Ganga* (Ganges) and containing her silver image, is located in the center of the village.

When snow and icy winds force most people down out of the mountains, some very few sadhus and hermits remain behind, performing their practices and keeping their solitary vigils in isolated mountain caves. Once Madhusudandas made it to Gangotri, he collected the holy water that he had come for and immediately headed back down to Rishikesh. He did not linger, even for a short while, after such a punishing journey, for he could not risk being caught in the mountains by an early winter storm.

Descending as rapidly as possible, he quickly moved from cool air back into the hot, dusty, dry conditions of the flat Gangetic plain of northern India and walked the 500 miles to Durgadih. Upon his arrival, he went to Maunibava's forest ashram rather than his father's house because now that he was a sanyasi, he no longer belonged to his family.

Madhusudandas was concerned that his family would once again force him to stay in Durgadih. The ability to make a clean break with the ones we love is rare, but Madhusudandas knew from the scriptures that even the great sage Vishvamitra, guru to Lord Ram, had been distracted when Lord Indra tested him by sending an *apsara*, a beautiful, celestial dancer, to seduce him. Madhusudandas was determined to resist being lured back into family life.

His aunt Janakidasi greeted him at the ashram and sent the good news of his return to his family. An elder brother came running to persuade Madhusudandas to come home, but saw instantly that this sadhu was not the same Kashinath who had left Durgadih 15 years ago. Madhusudandas refused his brother's request to return to the Mishra household and the two men argued, neither one giving an inch. Finally Maunibava and Janakidasi intervened and begged Madhusudandas to go home. Not wanting to offend anyone, and out of respect for his elders, he agreed to go.

When Madhusudandas reached his childhood home, Ramdahin was sitting on the verandah of his household shrine, worshipping Mother Durga. Madhusudandas bowed to his father. Ramdahin was speechless. He could not believe that "his Kashinath" had finally returned. Seeing his beloved son revitalized the old man, working like a tonic on his tired body. His eyes brightened, and he began to feel better immediately.

While Madhusudandas spent time with his family, he decided that he wanted to offer to his dear father not only the spiritual fruits of his recent pilgrimage, but all of the practices he had done during his years away from home. According to the Indian scriptures, by offering the merits of all his spiritual practices, he would help his father to reach God. He thought hard about how to bring up this plan since, knowing his father, Madhusudandas suspected that Ramdahin's reaction would not be favorable. Ramdahin would think it was wrong for a child to sacrifice so much for his parent. One day he hesitantly raised the subject.

"Father, I have brought Ganges water that I collected in Gangotri," he said. "I would like to honor my debts to you by offering you all the merit of my practices, and I will use this sacred water for my *sankalpa*."[19]

Ramdahin flatly refused to accept the benefit of his son's anusthan. He greatly appreciated the love behind the offer, but was concerned that to accept this proposal would, in fact, dilute the positive results of Madhusudandas's sadhana. Also, as a learned Brahmin, he understood certain prohibitions set by scriptural texts. Spiritual merit cannot be exchanged like material things, or, as he put it, "good is not something that can be bought at the marketplace." Beyond these reasons, Ramdahin was emotionally overwhelmed by the enormity of what his son was proposing.

"Son, what happiness have I given you that I could be considered worthy to receive your priceless offer?" Ramdahin said in a choked voice. "You have not given me a chance to fulfill my duties towards you."

But Madhusudandas's resolve had been forged by years of continuous wandering and spiritual practices. He pressed on, using his own form of persuasion.

"You do not know how much I am obliged to you," Madhusudandas explained to his father. "You instilled devotion in me, you taught me the Vedic scriptures, and how to perform ritual worship. You excused me from life as a householder. Is this not a great obligation? Doesn't a son

---

[19]Sankalpa is a ritual vow.

have a right to honor his debts to his father?"

As Madhusudandas gently argued with his father, his older brother Avadhbihari joined in the discussion, forcefully taking up his brother's case. Finally, with tears in his eyes, Ramdahin agreed to accept his son's gift.

Using some of the precious water from Gangotri, Madhusudandas anointed his father and symbolically offered libations to his ancestors, to formally confer the benefits of his practices to his father. Madhusudandas felt inspired to offer the remaining water back to Lord Shiva on his father's behalf by pouring it on the embodiment of the energy of Shiva, the jyotir-lingam in the Shiva temple in Rameshwaram in the southern reaches of India. In Tulsidasji's *Ramayana*, Lord Ram promises that anyone who offers water from the Ganges to Lord Shiva at Rameshwaram will attain liberation and be absorbed into his divine essence. Madhusudandas told his father to touch the container of Ganges water so that he could complete this anusthan in his father's name, thereby ensuring that Ramdahin was freed from the cycle of birth and death.

Before leaving for Rameshwaram, a scholar advised Madhusudandas that it was not necessary for him to pour water on the lingam of Lord Shiva since river water is always falling on Lord Shiva somewhere. Madhusudandas dismissed this suggestion.

"I made a vow to pour Ganges water on Lord Shiva at Rameshwaram," he responded to the speechless scholar. "If I do not fulfill that vow, I will incur the sin of promising falsely. It is written in the scriptures that there is no sin worse than telling a lie."

Madhusudandas believed that the Indian scriptures were written by the rishis, who, through their spiritual energy and by the grace of God, received the words of the scriptures while in meditation, not through their intellects. The Lord's promise to liberate anyone who completes this anusthan was scripturally based, so Madhusudandas had absolute faith in it and he followed all of the instructions for the pilgrimage with precision. Unlike many of his peers, Madhusudandas was not interested in interpretations or technicalities. His reasoning was simple and from the heart, his promises literal, not symbolic.

It was now time to leave Durgadih. Madhusudandas did not want to stay too long and risk forming new attachments. This time he did not need to creep out of the house in the middle of the night. His father and family members were pleased with the undertaking he was about to make, and more importantly, they now understood his spiritual state and would not insist that he live the life of a householder.

Madhusudandas began another long, arduous journey. Rameshwaram was more than a thousand miles away. He walked until he was exhausted, then he boarded a train and rode until the conductor told him to get down, since he had no money to purchase a ticket, at which point he started walking again.[20] It probably took him several months to reach his destination.

Rameshwaram is an island at the tip of a narrow peninsula jutting out into the Gulf of Mannar towards Sri Lanka. It is an important Hindu pilgrimage site because it is featured in the *Ramayana*, and it is one of the four divine *dhams* (abodes) situated at the four compass points of India. The other three are Badrinath to the north, Dwarka in the west and Puri to the east. One pilgrimage for devout Hindus is the circumambulation of Mother India to visit these four holy corners of the country.

The Shiva temple here, Ramanathaswamy, is well preserved and one of the largest in India. It has magnificent stone corridors flanked by massive, intricately carved columns. In the *Ramayana*, before Lord Ram crossed over to Lanka to kill Ravana and retrieve Sita, he formed a lingam and installed it here. It is called *Rameshwara* which means, "Lord of Ram." It is considered one of the 12 Jyotir-lingani in India because although it didn't emerge spontaneously, it was not man-made.

In the moment when Kashinath poured the water from Gangotri over the jyotir-lingam in Ramdahin's name, he was finally released from his karmic debt to his parents.

For a short while during the last leg of his pilgrimage, Madhusudandas had corresponded with Dr. Paramahans Mishra, whom he knew from Durgadih. About six months after Madhusudandas left for Rameshwaram, one of his elder brothers died at age 52 and Dr. Paramahans relayed to him this painful news. Madhusudandas wrote back and said that he could no longer continue any correspondence, that this would be his last letter.

This attitude may seem harsh, but the ritual of sanyas is like a funeral, a letting go of ordinary life, to free the sanyasi from all attachments other than longing for the divine. For Madhusudandas, this pilgrimage was the culmination of his decision to take sanyas. But he

---

[20]In those days, it was common for sadhus to ride on trains until asked to disembark.

never forgot his father, his first spiritual teacher. Half a century later, he dedicated his book, *Light on Meditation* to Shri Ramdahinji Mishra.

Throughout the remainder of his long life, Ramdahin prayed to see his son again, but this was not to be. A few days before he died at the age of 100, Ramdahin spoke to his grandson, Kailash Mishra, and predicted, "Kashinath has left the house, but he will surely come back, and when he returns he will not come empty-handed. He will come either as a great scholar or a great mahatma, a God-realized being. He is destined to be the messenger of God."

CHAPTER NINE

A VISION OF SWAMI VIVEKANANDA

After he completed his anusthan, Madhusudandas traveled to visit shrines in south India, continuing his search for a teacher. By 1907, his frustration had grown. He had spent more than 15 years wandering around India, and despite the spiritual experiences he'd had, he was still plagued by the question "Who am I?" that he'd had since childhood. He had hoped that by leaving home, he could find someone to help him. Though he had met many capable yogis and learned scholars, few had themselves attained true inner peace. Frequently he detected a feeling of pride and superiority in these men. Many of them arrogantly held their own chosen paths in high esteem, dismissing others as inferior. Madhusudandas believed that all paths were equally valid. He was convinced that through honest efforts and the guidance of a teacher, seekers could reach the final goal of liberation no matter which method they chose. He was certain that if someone had an intense longing for God, a guru would appear to provide the necessary guidance. Yet at times, he felt like he had wasted years swinging between hope and despair.

His sadhana was intense. "I was performing austerities and ritual ceremonies, often having only milk as food, other times eating only peanuts with molasses, or observing a total fast. I was happy when I was successful and disappointed when my labor did not bear fruit. But day by day, my restlessness increased."

Throughout it all, Madhusudandas felt an unseen hand guiding his efforts. At crucial moments in his practices, he received clear instruction through an inner voice or the sudden appearance of a teacher.

It was during this time in south India that Madhusudandas finally reached a turning point. He had met a hatha yogi who, though competent to teach the physical poses, was himself not at peace. Madhusudandas was deeply disappointed when he detected the yogi's inner turmoil because it represented yet another dead end in his search for a true teacher. Shortly after this encounter, while sleeping in a meditative posture in a temple, Madhusudandas suddenly had an electrifying vision of Swami Vivekananda,[21] the foremost disciple of the 19th-century Bengali saint Ramakrishna.

Madhusudandas had seen Vivekananda's photograph, so when the saint appeared to him, he instantly recognized him. He remembered that Vivekananda was a great mahatma, and that Ramakrishna had made God-realization possible for him. Madhusudandas started weeping at the sight of Vivekananda and poured out the agony of his heart.

"Swamiji, what should I do?" he implored. "I cannot concentrate my mind, and I am very unhappy."

Years later, telling this story, Madhusudandas described what happened next:

"Swami Vivekananda laughed heartily and softly pressed his hand against my forehead. 'Do not worry,' he said. 'Everything will be all right.'

"Then he disappeared. In a flash, I felt that my body and mind had become very light, and I felt as if a great burden had been removed.

"A few days after this episode, I came across *Raja Yoga*, a book written by Swami Vivekananda, and I read it umpteen times. I received

---

[21]Vivekananda is both a saint and a national hero in India. At a time when Western religious views were touted as vastly superior to Indian spirituality, he traveled to the United States and England to introduce the concepts of yoga and Vedanta to the west. In a few short years—he died in 1902 at the age of 39—he made Ramakrishna and the highest teachings of India well known and respected throughout much of the Western world. His one-pointed concentration on fulfilling this mission was dramatized when once, while giving a lecture, some troubled member in the audience actually fired a gun at him (and missed) while Swami Vivekananda continued his lecture without missing a beat.

divine inspiration from this book and became unbelievably fond of it. I had previously studied Patanjali's *Yoga Sutras*, but I was unable to understand it properly. After reading Swami Vivekananda's comments, everything became crystal clear to me. It was then that my real sadhana began."[22] Madhusudandas cherished this experience, and *Raja Yoga* became his bible. For the next 12 years, he continued to search, wander and practice. Whenever he didn't attain the peace he was looking for, he simply moved on, willing to go as far as necessary in his search. He still focused on the question "Who am I?" but now, with Swamiji's grace, his faith was steadier and he had a more thorough grasp of the subtle principles underlying yoga. He no longer struggled with disillusionment or impatience.

As Madhusudandas encountered more people and more suffering, he noticed that only those who chanted God's name seemed to be at real peace. He was reminded of something that Guru Nanak, the founder of the Sikh religion, once said: "This world is full of miseries. Only the one who has taken refuge in God is happy." These were the people who impressed Madhusudandas as having true spiritual attainment.

"I experienced immense peace and pleasure only when by the grace of God I came across true saints," he said.

From his experiences, Madhusudandas reached the conclusion that spiritual practices performed externally were limited in what they offered. They might ignite a fire in the seeker to merge with the Divine, but the most important work in yoga takes place in the heart. Few of the yogis and sages he had met were at peace. Despite all of their knowledge and years of practices, they were caught up in the details of yogic science, in evaluating their progress, and proclaiming their achievements. What they were missing was knowledge of their ultimate goal. Merging with the infinite means dissolving completely into the divine, and there is nothing left except that unity. Any other state, no matter how profoundly spiritual, is insignificant compared to this. It is like the story told by Ramakrishna about a salt doll who went to measure the depth of the ocean. The doll wanted to learn how deep it was so it could then go and tell others. But it was an impossible task because as soon as the doll entered the water, it was completely dissolved in the ocean. In the same way, when we dissolve our separate selves in the ocean of infinite love, in God-realization, all thoughts of religious achievement,

---

[22]Dhyanyogi Madhusudandas, *Message to Disciples* (Mumbai, India: Shri Dhyanyogi Mandal, 1968) 9.

scholarship, or debate become forever moot. It was this complete union with the divine that Madhusudandas sought, and nothing less would give him peace.

CHAPTER TEN

AUSTERITIES AT MOUNT ABU

For 20 years, Madhusudandas had roamed from place to place like a restless tiger, collecting the spiritual energies that permeate the subcontinent's holiest mountains, rivers, and plains. After leaving Rameshwaram and spending several months in south India, Madhusudandas was drawn to return north, heading back towards the vicinity of the Ambaji temple in Rajasthan, near the border of the western state of Gujarat. He may not have been aware of it at the time, but he was en route to Mount Abu, a lovely hill town near Ambaji that was to become his spiritual base, in a region of India that would figure prominently in the rest of his life.

Sometime around 1910, Madhusudandas arrived in Ahmedabad, the largest city in Gujarat. Gujarat was very different from Bihar, the state in which he had been born. While Bihar was impoverished and undeveloped, Gujarat was progressive and had flourished economically for centuries because of trade on its western shores. Ahmedabad was the center of a booming textile industry, and the kings and merchants spent lavishly on building beautiful, ornate Hindu and Jain temples. It was also the home of Kashinath's contemporary, Mohandas Gandhi and other figures significant in India's struggle for freedom.

In Ahmedabad, Madhusudandas stayed at the Jagannatha Temple, a Krishna temple with a large courtyard filled with a herd of well-loved cows. The head priest, Shri Nrusinhadasji, grew very fond of the new arrival and urged him to stay on. But Madhusudandas, as ever, resisted those kinds of attachments. He remained in Ahmedabad for six months and then moved on to Mount Abu.

The hill retreat of Mount Abu must have provided a refreshing contrast from flat, hot and dusty Ahmedabad. It was cool and wooded, with clear air, streams and a serene lake. But beyond its physical beauty and charms, it was an important spiritual location. It was particularly sacred to the Jains, and it had been home to Lord Ram's guru, the celebrated Vedic sage Vasishtha. The Abu Hills were known to be an ancient and powerful place to do austerities, and many great saints had been attracted to its high spiritual energy.

"I had many beautiful experiences in that area," Madhusudandas would later recall when he talked about the years he spent at Mount Abu. "It's a very holy place, even to this day."

One legend has it that Mount Abu was actually once a mountain in the Himalayan range. The story goes that Indra stole one of Brahma's cows and hid her in the Himalayas. Brahma was about to find her, so Indra, scared of getting caught, moved the entire mountain upon which the cow was living and relocated it to Abu.

Another account states that during Vasishtha's lifetime, he lived in his ashram with the wish-fulfilling cow Nandini. One day, Nandini was grazing by a lake when she fell into the water and was desperately struggling to stay afloat. Vasishtha instantly flew to the Himalayas for help from the divine beings residing there. They sent Arbuda, the cosmic cobra, to rescue Nandini. Arbuda brought with him a Himalayan peak. He dropped it into the lake, creating Mount Abu, and Nandini clambered upon it to safety. This new land was called Arbudachala, the name under which Mount Abu is mentioned in the *Mahabharata*, and it is speculated that the name Abu is derived from Arbudachala.

The town of Mount Abu sprawls across a rugged 4,000-foot-high plateau that rises over a mile above the hot plains and deserts of southwestern

Rajasthan and northern Gujarat. It has always been a place where yogis performed austerities, but in modern times it also became Rajasthan's only hill station—a place where the British colonials and the royal families of Gujarat and Rajasthan could escape the broiling Indian summer. Today it is a resort with a distinctly European influence. It's one of the only places in rural India where you can get a cappuccino. There are comfortable guesthouses and luxury hotels catering to tourists and honeymooners, but tucked up in the hills are the tiny caves still used by ascetics who shun

Nakki Lake at Mount Abu

such comforts, leading the same existence as their ancient predecessors. The atmosphere at Mount Abu is saturated with this odd mixture of modern pleasure-seeking and ancient renunciation.

The hills surrounding the town are dotted with temples from the distant past. The Dilwara Jain temples are perhaps the finest examples of Jain architecture in all of India. These five temples are made of pure marble, intricately carved in breathtaking detail and delicacy. There are also Hindu temples dedicated to Durga, Shiva, Ram and Hanuman scat-

Elephant Cave, where Dhyanyogi-ji attained shaktipat and realization. At that time, there were no walls or door, just an open cave with overhanging rock.

tered across the 14-mile long plateau, accessible only by lengthy stone paths. Some of these temples have spectacular panoramic vistas over the plains.

When Madhusudandas lived there, Mount Abu was a pleasant but much wilder place. The folded hills were covered with lush, jungle-like vegetation during the monsoon. Tigers, bears, monkeys, elephants and other wildlife abounded in the area. The caves where sadhus practiced their austerities were also home to snakes, mice and black ants, which peacefully coexisted with the meditating yogis.

Madhusudandas did his practices in five caves. Today these caves have been modernized and some even have doors with padlocks, but back then, they were just natural openings in the rocks, with rough and cramped interiors. One cave was so small that Madhusudandas could not lie down with his legs stretched out. In another, he could not stand up without bending over. The sun did not peek into a third until 9:00 in the morning, late in the day for a yogi. Only *Hathigufa,* "Elephant Cave," the cave where Madhusudandas lived for six years, was reasonably comfortable. Hathigufa, so named because the huge boulder that formed it was shaped like an elephant, was six feet high and 50 feet long, and there was a spring inside. A mango tree grew near the three-

Interior of Elephant Cave, as it looks today. When Dhyanyogi-ji lived there, this was an open cave. Only the ceiling looks as it did then. The finished floor and walls are much more recent.

foot-high entrance, and several steps from it was a sweeping view of the blue waters of Nakki Lake, in the center of Mount Abu.

When a sadhu performs austerities in a cave, no one else is permitted to enter. The spiritual energy that accumulates must be strictly preserved. So Madhusudandas stayed alone in his cave, day after day, doing his practices, leaving only to visit the nearby Ram temple once a week. At one point, he completed a long and arduous anusthan without leaving Hathigufa at all.

Temple of Lord Ram at Mount Abu. Elephant Cave belonged to this temple.

Such devotion could not help but attract the attention of the head priest of the temple, a man named Damodarji Maharaj.

The Ragunath Temple sits on the shore of Nakki Lake. Paths from the lakeside temple snake their way up into the rugged hills, past the caves where Madhusudandas was meditating and doing his spiritual practices. Damodarji Maharaj must have seen hundreds of sadhus and mountain yogis over the years, but something about Madhusudandas particularly impressed him. They soon developed a special relationship, with Damodarji Maharaj often going out of his way to help Madhusudandas. The temple took care of all the renunciates who lived in the caves, but it was customary for these sadhus to perform *seva*, service, for the temple, in exchange. Damodarji, however, permitted Madhusudandas to take his meals at the temple without accepting any service in return. Madhusudandas was reluctant to accept this arrangement, but Damodarji insisted that Madhusudandas dedicate his time to his practices, rather than doing work for the temple. For Madhusudandas, the priest was an instrument of God, providing for his basic needs so that he could remain absorbed in worship. Madhusudandas later wrote an account of this period.

During my disciple stage, when I went to Abu for the first time, Paramhans-Shri Damodardasji Maharaj, the Mahant *(head of ashram or temple) of the Ram temple, lived there. At that time, I was with a good friend, a sadhu named Shatrughnadas. We were very fond of each other. We had been staying in the temple for a few days, when I began to feel that I wanted to find a remote place to do practices in seclusion. Without informing Damodarji Maharaj, I went to a small cave near an open plateau called Ramjharukha. Since those days, it has been fixed up, so if you went there today, it might seem quite comfortable, but back then, it was extremely small and without a door. I had enough gol-papadi (sweets) to last me for four days, and I stretched them out for five days. The sixth day I had nothing but water. By the seventh day, I was restless with hunger. I hoped that Damodarji Maharaj would call me to come for a meal without my asking. Since I had come to the cave without his knowledge, I was embarrassed to go to him now. Because of my intense hunger, I could no longer concentrate on my spiritual practices.*

But by the grace of God, it so happened that on that very day, a rich man from Ahmedabad had prepared a feast for all the sadhus and saints in Shri Raghunathji's temple. At mealtime, Damodarji Maharaj asked my friend Shatrughnadas, "Where is the mahatma who was with you?"

Shatrughnadas replied, "Maharajji, he is doing practices in Ramjharukha."

"If he is doing practices there," Damodarji Maharaj asked, "then what is the arrangement for his meals?"

"Maharajji, I have no idea about that, but it is certain that he will not leave the cave," answered Shatrughnadas.

Then Damodarji Maharaj ordered Shatrughnadas, "Call that Mahatma right now!"

Shatrughnadas ran to my cave and said to me, "Maharajji is calling for you."

I was very happy to hear these words, and realized that God was showing mercy on me. When I arrived at the temple and saw Damodarji Maharaj, he scolded me.

"What sort of mahatma are you, going off to do bhajana without food? Seven days ago you left quietly without informing anyone. What arrangements were made for food while you were in the cave?"

I answered, "Maharajji, for the first five days, I ate some sweet sukhadi, but for the past two days, I have been starving."

Listening to me, Damodarji Maharaj laughed heartily and told me, "What a fool you are to start your spiritual practices without arranging for food! Is it possible to do practices without taking care of the body? If you want to do practices, come to the temple for meals and then you can enjoy your practices."

"But, Maharajji," I argued, "those who stay in the temple should offer some service in one way or another. But I can't do this because I am spending all my time doing my practices. How can I come for food when I am not doing any seva?"

Damodarji Maharaj again laughed heartily and said, "What sort of a business policy is this? Is it necessary to perform any other service if one is doing bhajana? Doing practices to reach God is the highest service there is."

I answered, "Maharajji, I understand what you mean, but will the others who are offering their seva understand?"

"Are you concerned with me or them? I am telling you that as long as you are doing bhajana in the cave, you are to come to the temple once or twice, whenever you find time, and have your meals. I will instruct the others to feed you, and no one will ask you to perform any seva."

From that point on, I stayed in the cave for two months, and whenever I had time, I went to the temple for meals.[25]

Early one winter morning, some months later, Madhusudandas was caught in a sudden, torrential hailstorm. Drenched, he decided to go to the Raghunath Temple to ask for help. The sadhu's thin blanket, his only defense against the ice-cold nights on Mount Abu, had been soaked by the storm.

Damodarji Maharaj listened quietly to Madhusudandas's story, occasionally nodding his head and saying, "Yes, yes." Still, he did not offer

---

[25]Madhusudandas, *Message to Disciples* 72-4.

to give him another blanket, preferring that the shy young man ask him directly for what he wanted. But Madhusudandas had surrendered himself completely to the will of God, so he was determined to accept whatever situation was put into his path and could not bring himself to ask for a new blanket.

That night, as the temperature plummeted and a deep, bone-chilling cold tightened its grip on Mount Abu, Madhusudandas lay down on half of the damp blanket and wrapped himself with the other half. He curled his legs up to his chest like a child.

"I passed the entire freezing night wrapped in a wet blanket," Madhusudandas later recalled, "but my body did not suffer as a result. In fact, my body heat dried the blanket."

A week later, Damodarji Maharaj unexpectedly sent him a new blanket.

In his first years at Mount Abu, Madhusudandas did a lot of austerities and anusthans, gaining mastery of various techniques. Based on the teachings he later gave, this may have been when he perfected several obscure and esoteric yogic practices, including the *Plavnik Bhastrika*, and the *Shaktichalan Kriya*, two techniques of pranayama that forcefully activate the kundalini, and the *Durgama Kriya* for astral travel. He studied the science of yantras and performed anusthans of the *Ram Raksha Stotram* using *bija* (seed) mantras, the potent sounds that form the bases of all other mantras.

Now that he was relatively settled in one place, he developed companionships with some other yogis. For a time, he and his friend Brahmachari Shatrughnadas both lived in the temple complex in nearby Achalgarh, where there was a powerful, ancient Shiva temple that housed a rock believed to embody the toe of Lord Shiva.

Madhusudandas and Shatrughnadas often did their spiritual practices together. They each had fears that they helped one another to overcome. Shatrughnadas was not one to shrink from hardships in his pursuit of God. He liked to sleep outside, for example, no matter what the season or how bad the weather. His boldness in facing austerities head-on helped Madhusudandas cope with his fear of the dark, a problem he'd had since childhood, and his reluctance to spend the night in potentially dangerous places.

Mount Abu was a wild forest in the early 1900s. Tigers and

elephants roamed free. It never bothered Shatrughnadas to see tiger footprints clearly visible near the cave every morning, even though he had been sleeping out in the open. He was not afraid of tigers, nor of death itself.

Although Madhusudandas also loved to sleep out in the open, the thought of tigers kept him in his cave. If he was traveling and had to sleep outside, he always kept a campfire burning through the night. Shatrughnadas tried to help Madhusudandas confront his anxiety. "If it is your destiny to die," he said, "the tiger will come attack you inside the cave. After becoming a sadhu, why is there any fear of death? What better death is there than one that comes while performing spiritual practices for God?"

Hearing these words, Madhusudandas realized it was not appropriate to have such a strong attachment to his body when he was striving for God-realization. But when the night came, fear took over and once again, he slept inside the cave.

One night an incident occurred that permanently eliminated this fear. Shatrughnadas and Madhusudandas were sleeping in Ramjarukha, an open plateau above Hathigufa. As was his custom, Madhusudandas lit a fire, but then he fell asleep and the fire went out. Later that night, a tiger passed by the sleeping sadhus and made his

Ramjharukha, the plateau above Elephant cave

way to a bungalow belonging to a lawyer, located about a mile away. He went into the yard of this dwelling and caught a dog for his supper. The tiger then dragged the dog back to Ramjharukha, killing and eating it within 50 feet of where Shatrughnadas and Madhusudandas lay sleeping.

In the morning, Shatrughnadas awoke to find the bones and blood of the dog. He immediately called Madhusudandas and showed it to him.

"See how the Lord has protected us?" he said. "When the tiger passed by, he was definitely hungry because he ate this dog. But he left us alone. This proves that God protects us. Never lose faith in God."

Madhusudandas never forgot this incident. It convinced him that the thread of life and death lies in God's hands alone. "After that, my faith became 100 percent," he said. "My fear was gone completely."

Madhusudandas also helped Shatrughnadas conquer his lingering doubts, particularly his fear of going without. One morning, the two friends set off for Guru Shikhar, a two-and-a-half mile hike along a forest path to the end of the plateau. As the sun neared its apex in the sky, Shatrughnadas's stomach began to rumble with hunger. They had not eaten for days, and they were utterly alone in the wilderness with no food in sight.

"I fear we will go hungry today," Shatrughnadas said.

As they were walking along, there was a crow cawing. Madhusudandas listened to it and said, "The crow says someone is bringing us food."

"Who in this forest is going to feed us?"

As they continued, they came across an old woman collecting firewood. When she saw them, she invited them home, saying she wanted to give them something to eat. When they reached her hut, she gave them some wheat flour and *jaggery* (brown sugar) so they could make bread. She was poor, and these meager rations represented just about everything that she had, but she was so delighted to have the darshan of these two sadhus that she handed over the food without any hesitation.

They took the food the old woman had given them and went to the bank of the river, and there they prepared the flour to make *bati*, a kind of stuffed bread. They washed off a stone and kneaded the dough upon it. Next they collected cow dung for fuel and made a fire. They rolled out the dough, put the jaggery inside, then sealed it up and baked it over the crackling fire, thanking God for his protection and grace.

"I have never forgotten the taste of that bati made from the flour given by that old woman," Madhusudandas said years later. "I could feel the energy of the Divine Mother working through her, and all my other human benefactors."

Madhusudandas had another companion named Janardhandas. Later in his life, Janardhandas became known as Tapasi Maharaj and served as the chief of the Valmiki ashram in the nearby village of Koteshwar. By that time, Madhusudandas had disciples who lived in Koteshwar and Tapasi Maharaj would tell them stories about Madhusudandas's severe sadhana during the days they lived together in Mount Abu. Tapasi Maharaj estimated that for five or six years, Madhusudandas lived without normal food, subsisting on leaves, wild vegetables and roots. He told them how Madhusudandas would select certain kinds of leaves and boil them thoroughly in an earthen pot filled with water. After they were properly boiled, Madhusudandas filtered the liquid through a piece of cloth and subsisted on this leaf water for days and days.

This self-denial had a very important purpose. For spiritual growth to be lasting, there must be a transformation of the physical body and the brain. As a person evolves and the kundalini becomes more active, the body must also evolve to be able to hold and make use of this increased energy. Just as a house must be wired properly for electricity, so must the body be "wired" appropriately to handle the flow of shakti moving through the nervous system without overloading its "circuits."

Traditionally, this has been accomplished by performing anusthans and undergoing severe austerities. The austerities bring about an indifference to physical discomfort. The internal heat generated by anusthans burns out the impurities in the body and cleanses the mind, preparing the aspirant for divine revelation.

Madhusudandas meticulously followed this ancient path for transformation, preparing himself in the strictest and most exacting way for the ultimate meeting with a sadguru, the spiritual teacher who would take him to meet God. During his time at Mount Abu, Madhusudandas perfected and deepened his sadhana, completely surrendering to the will of God. His years of painful searching were nearly over. He was now ready to receive the grace of his true teacher.

सबै भवन्तु सुखिनः ॥१६४१॥

CHAPTER ELEVEN

THE TRUE TEACHER

No, it is not easy in all the three worlds
To find a teacher, like the alchemist's stone,
To turn a student's raw ore into gold.
How much more precious then,
Is one who turns the other not just to gold,
But to his very likeness.

—Shankaracharya[24]

Throughout Madhusudandas's 30 years of sadhana, even at the most discouraging and agonizing moments, he had held in his heart the words of Swami Vivekananda, "Arise, awake, and stop not until the goal is reached." He had overcome every obstacle that appeared along his way, and had absolute faith that his life was in God's hands. He possessed all the essentials, save one—a sadguru.

A sadguru is a spiritual teacher who can liberate people from the cycle of birth and death. We have many teachers in our lives, starting with our parents, then friends, schoolteachers and those who teach us

[24]*Aditi: The Living Arts of India* (Washington, D.C.: Smithsonian Institution Press, 1985) 158.

our vocation. But a sadguru, a human being who has reached the ulti-mate spiritual state and is capable of taking others there, is extremely rare. Meeting a sadguru is crucial because that person can transfer his or her energy—shakti—to the disciple. Once that happens, the energy forever will protect and guide the student, even in the physical absence of the teacher.

The sadguru shows us our true identity, which inevitably leads us to merge with the source from which we have come. This transformation of consciousness is called God-realization. Yogis compare the relationship between the self and God to the sun and its rays. We think of the sun as something that is far away, but we feel the warmth of its rays on our skin. The energy of the sun and its rays is the same, but it exists in different forms. The sadguru gives us the direct experience that God is the sun and we are the rays. In reality, we are one.

The extraordinary power and compassion of the sadguru, who has incarnated for the sole purpose of serving as a bridge between the dis-ciples and God, inspired the 15th-century Indian poet Kabir to write, "The Lord and the Guru are standing together. To whom shall I bow first? I would bow to the Guru, because I can see the Lord only through the grace and energy of the Guru. Even if the Lord were in front of me, without my teacher, my Guru, I may have failed to recognize the Lord." Even God Himself, in the form of Lord Ram, took a guru to set the example for others of the significance of the guru.

Swami Vivekananda demonstrated the powers of the sadguru in his dramatic accounts of how his guru, Shri Ramakrishna, gave him the direct experience of God. Vivekananda, plagued with doubts about be-ing a disciple, went to visit Shri Ramakrishna. It was only their second meeting. As Vivekananda was entertaining one of his skeptical thoughts, Ramakrishna "placed his right foot on my body. Immediately, I had a wonderful experience. My eyes were wide open, and I saw that every-thing in the room, including the walls themselves, was whirling rapidly around and receding, and at the same time, it seemed to me that my consciousness of self, together with the entire universe, was about to vanish into a vast, all-devouring void...Then, touching my chest with his hand...to my amazement, this extraordinary vision of mine vanished as suddenly as it had come. I returned to my normal state and saw things inside and outside the room standing stationary, as before."[25]

---

[25]Christopher Isherwood, *Ramakrishna and His Disciples* (Hollywood, CA: Vedanta Press, 1980) 197.

Since childhood, Madhusudandas had longed to achieve this stage, described in one of his favorite verses from the *Ramayana*:

Shankara sahaja svarupa sambhara
Lagi samadhi akhanda apara.

Shiva contemplated on his essential self
and entered the state of samadhi.

He had studied with many yogis, of whom several were enlightened masters, but he had not met the one who would bring him to the door-step of the Lord. He longed to meet his sadguru.

There is a common saying that "when the student is ready, the teacher appears." One chilly, wintry day, Madhusudandas was sitting in his cave reciting the *Ramayana* when the sage Yogiraj Parmeshwardas appeared. Madhusudandas's extraordinary energy had pulled the saint from the Himalayas to the little cave on Mount Abu.

Parmeshwardasji was a large, heavy-set man with a beard and hair knotted on top of his head. He wore only a loin cloth despite the bitter cold. He had 200 disciples, most of whom lived in Rishikesh, and he roamed around northern India, spending time in the Himalayas and in the Mount Abu region. Madhusudandas sensed that he had never met a teacher as advanced as Parmeshwardasji, yet he had the distinct feeling that he had known him before. He was impressed by the wisdom of Parmeshwardasji's instructions regarding the importance of purification. Like Madhusudandas, Parmeshwardasji exhibited a focused mind and an indifference to discomfort. His voice was sweet, and his simple and straightforward manner appealed deeply to Madhusudandas.

As Parmeshwardasji watched Madhusudandas perform his japa, he must have been struck by Madhusudandas's humility, a trait that was es-pecially meaningful considering how much Madhusudandas had already achieved. But more significant than any of his external observations was his internal recognition of Madhusudandas as his primary disciple. On the spot, Parmeshwardasji offered Madhusudandas *shaktipat* initiation.

Shaktipat[26] is a transfer of divine energy from guru to disciple that activates the student's own dormant spiritual energy, the kundalini, so that he or she can progress more quickly on the spiritual path. Awakening

---

[26]Shaktipat literally means "touch of energy."

the student's kundalini through shaktipat is like lighting a candle with another one that is already lit and glowing. This special initiation bonds the guru and disciple together forever.

There are other ways to awaken kundalini, including meditation, intense devotion, perfection of hatha yoga postures or pranayama. But these methods can take years, or even lifetimes. With shaktipat, the awakening is quick and permanent, and the subtle spiritual connection enables the teacher to continuously guide the student's progress.

Only realized beings who have complete control over their own prana can transfer it to others and awaken kundalini. There are many realized gurus who can give students a mantra and teach them to meditate, but only a sadguru can transmit spiritual energy directly. This can be done in four ways: by touch, gaze, sound or thought.

Shaktipat begins an internal process of cleansing and purification that opens up the subtle central passageway in the spine called the sushumna. The kundalini, lying dormant at the base of the spine, stirs and begins its journey upward through the sushumna, piercing the chakras along the way until it reaches the *sahasrara* chakra at the crown of the head. When this happens, the student attains samadhi. In this state of transcendental consciousness, the jiva unites with Shiva—the individual soul merges with God—and the person gains the ultimate knowledge of his or her true identity, and is liberated.

Once the kundalini is awakened and the journey to enlightenment has begun, students may start to have a variety of unusual experiences. They may see flashes of light or colors, hear internal sounds of bells ringing or birds singing, or experience *kriyas*, the spontaneous movements of the body caused by the activity of the prana.

The process may take years and may not even be completed in a single lifetime. How quickly students progress depends upon their own karma and how well they have prepared themselves for this demanding journey. All the samskaras of their previous lifetimes need to be "burned off" through spiritual practices and the cleansing action of the kundalini. The ego and intellect must be tamed.

No one can experience samadhi without the complete purification of both the physical body and the nadis, the channels within the subtle body that carry the prana. If there are any impurities in either the physical or subtle bodies, these act as blocks to the flow of the prana and prevent the piercing of the chakras. Most significantly, even after the kundalini has moved through the lower chakras, blocks can prevent the *agna* chakra at the third eye from opening, making it impossible for the kundalini to travel upwards to pierce the sahasrara. Only when the sahasrara opens is the student directly united with the infinite ocean of divine energy.

Madhusudandas was like a ripe fruit waiting to be plucked from the tree. Parmeshwardasji asked him to repeat a mantra for subtle cleansing, and as a result of Madhusudandas's sadhana, he was instantly purified. He was so well prepared that at his sadguru's first touch he immediately entered samadhi. He lost bodily consciousness and found himself submerged in a sea of bliss and ecstasy, surrounded by "a wonderful and inexplicable light."

After this initial experience of samadhi, which was a taste of the enlightened state, the kundalini immediately began to transform Madhusudandas's physical body. To remain in a stable and permanent state of samadhi, the body must be pure and strong so that it can channel the force of divine energy without being harmed.

For the next six months, the kundalini soared from the *muladhara*, the root chakra, to the sahasrara, at the top of the head. A fire of purification burned within him. After meditating, there was extreme heat in his body that could only be cooled by drinking warm milk with ghee. At first, he noticed changes in his breathing and found that in less than a minute after sitting down for meditation, he would fall into a deep state of "supreme bliss." After about a month and a half, he began to feel a peculiar sensation, as if an ant or an insect were crawling up from the base of the spine.

"After some time, I had visions of a small baby, or a cow, or a beautiful deity," he recalled. "Sometimes I completely forgot myself, and became overjoyed while observing a lotus or colorful scenes."[27]

Three months went by, and Madhusudandas began hearing loud, internal sounds that resembled gunshots. "I was not scared of the small ones, but the big bangs made me nervous." His heart raced, and at times he feared he would die of heart failure. Parmeshwardasji lovingly reassured him that there was no reason to be afraid. He explained that these sounds were produced by the prana cleansing the chakras as it moves through the sushumna.

---

[27]The quotes on these pages concering Dhyanyogi-ji's experience of enlightenment are from *Message to Disciples*, pages 14-16.

After about five months of being purified by this yogic fire, Madhusudandas started to run a temperature of 104 to 105 degrees. This shakti fever lasted for three to four days during which he had some difficulty walking and carrying loads of firewood from the nearby forest. But he did not feel weak. To the contrary, he felt joyful and alert.

Finally, at 9:00 p.m. on the auspicious full moon day in March called Holi, Madhusudandas reached his final, blessed goal while chanting the name of Ram. His 30-year struggle was over.

Within five minutes of beginning to chant, he lost consciousness. A cyclonic thunderblast reverberated through his body, which was suddenly filled with divine light. The kundalini began ascending gradually from the muladhara chakra. The experience brought him "a peculiar pleasure," but Madhusudandas also felt as if he were suffocating. The lower part of his body became numb.

"I was scared to death and wondered whether I would ever come down to the normal plane of consciousness," he said. "When the kundalini traveled above the eyebrows, I felt as if my skull were bursting with bliss and as if bliss were sprinkling like a fountain through the hair follicles of my head." Madhusudandas compared his bliss to the joy a desperately ill man feels when he is suddenly healed. He wanted to stay in this state forever. Later, he realized he had been swimming in the sea of bliss for two-and-a-half hours.

"I realized that my fears were baseless. The uneasiness of mind that I had since childhood, the search for 'Who am I?' and the constant fear of death vanished into oblivion," he said. "Life seemed full of joy, and realizing that I had reached my goal, I understood the importance of this life."

Humbled with gratitude, Madhusudandas gently knelt first before his ishta-devata, Lord Ram, and then before his guru. He mentally prostrated before Lord Hanuman and all the saints and teachers from whom he had received guidance during his sadhana. He bowed low to Swami Vivekananda, who had been such a great inspiration to him.

Madhusudandas's experience made both him and his guru deeply happy. He had come home to divine knowledge and love, the place all human souls are meant to be.

The spiritual lineage of Kundalini Maha Yoga that Kashinath joined through shaktipat initiation can be traced back to Lord Ram's guru, the great sage Vasishtha. Vasishtha gave shaktipat to Lord Ram. In turn, Lord Ram gave shaktipat to his wife Sita, who was the Divine Mother, an incarnation of Lakshmi. Sita gave shaktipat to her loyal disciple Lord Hanuman, an aspect of Shiva who incarnated to serve Lord Ram. Lord Hanuman gave shaktipat to the great saint Ramanaujacharia. The lineage, therefore, uniquely combined the aspects of Vishnu, Shiva and the Divine Mother. During shaktipat, this tremendous energy poured from Parmeshwardasji into Madhusudandas.

In his later years, Madhusudandas revealed that he had attained self-realization in a past life. Once a soul reaches that state, it can either choose to merge with the divine consciousness or decide to take another birth—not for the sake of its own evolution, but out of a desire to serve God or out of compassion for other beings. If the soul elects to come back in a new body, it will not immediately remember everything from previous lives. The person must put forth effort to regain that information, and to resist the temptations that appear in the present. This is the law of karma, and submitting to that law is the price that must be paid when taking another birth. The danger of reentering the material world is that the soul is exposed again to the all-encompassing influence of *maya*, the worldly aspects of life including material objects, careers, relationships, the physical body. Maya makes us value things that are impermanent, and distracts us from the one truth that is God. Maya creates longing and desire, likes and dislikes, attractions and repulsions, and induces us to care more about the aspects of life that come and go than we do about the welfare of our own souls—the only thing that lasts beyond the boundaries of time.

Although Madhusudandas had chosen to reincarnate to help uplift humanity, once he took rebirth as a boy living in a Indian village, the veil of maya engulfed him. But unlike most of us, even as a small child he ached to get beyond the illusions of worldly life, and he worked hard to achieve detachment from maya. As a result of his sadhana, the questions that had plagued him were spontaneously resolved when he received shaktipat initiation, and his memories from his previous enlightened state, temporarily obscured by maya, returned to consciousness. He remembered why he had come.

"After receiving shaktipat by the grace of Lord Shri Ram and my Gurudeva, I felt the intense desire in my mind to give benefit to as many people as possible. Remembering the sufferings I had undergone to remove the uneasiness in my life, I felt pity for all beings of the world. Seeing their plight, I felt the constant urge in me to try all possible means to relieve them of their miseries."

With his inner vision, Parmeshwardasji saw that his new disciple was destined to bring the hidden teachings of Kundalini Maha Yoga out into the world, so he set about preparing him to take over the lineage, to become the conduit for this ancient, transformational energy. This work had several dimensions. First of all, in order to give shaktipat to others, Madhusudandas would need to build up his strength so he could give away his energy without negatively affecting his own spiritual state. The yogis say, "A two-quart vessel cannot hold 16 quarts of milk and nectar," referring to how our bodies are limited and most of us are unable to contain the vast power and sweetness of the universal energy that surrounds us. That is why the few who are blessed enough to reach a state of samadhi often have only a brief and passing experience of it.

Secondly, the pull of maya is very strong. Unless all seeds of worldly desires are removed, even extremely evolved saints are susceptible to their allure. In order to resist maya, Kashinath would need to be beyond any attachments to worldly things and yet humble enough to surrender completely to the will of God.

Parmeshwardasji instructed his new disciple to follow a specific regimen of meditation for 42 days. During those six weeks, Madhusudandas had visions of divine figures and teachers. He felt Shri Ramakrishna and Swami Vivekananda sitting with him. In *Message to Disciples*, he wrote that on the final day, "I felt that my body was floating in light, like a boat on water. I saw my astral body in front of me. I felt aloof from both my physical and astral bodies. Of course, at first I wondered whether I had died, but as I had the experience of samadhi previously, my doubt disappeared." Madhusudandas felt himself reenter his gross body with the absolute understanding that he was different from it. "Since then I have no more attachment for this body."

To further develop Madhusudandas's capacities, Parmeshwardasji gave Madhusudandas even more advanced instructions in various yogic techniques, from plavnik and other advanced pranayama to astral travel and tratak. After practicing plavnik pranayama, Madhusudandas's energy was so active that he said he could eat enough food for 10 men and still be hungry. Although Madhusudandas spoke very little about his relationship with his guru, he did recall that Parmeshwardasji lovingly teased him about his ravenous appetite.

In later years, Madhusudandas explained that the purpose of these techniques is to "attract energy from the universe and channel it in our bodies so that we are connected to the infinite source of God's energy. If you take a bottle, put a little sea water in it, then seal it and throw it in the ocean, the water of the ocean will never get inside the bottle. There will always be a difference in the two bodies of water. The water inside and outside are identical, but the glass separates them and the seal prevents them from uniting. If the seal is broken and the water from the ocean enters the bottle, then the two waters become one. Energy is always flowing through your body, but if you are not aware of it, you can lose a lot. If you learn how to absorb the energy, control it, and contain it within your body, then over a period of time, you can obtain so much energy that no one can harm you."

In addition to this training in yogic practices, Parmeshwardasji tested Madhusudandas's faith, humility and detachment. Some of the tests at first seemed odd. Parmeshwardasji asked Madhusudandas to perform unpleasant tasks or to do things that appeared illogical. Madhusudandas later recounted stories of some of these tests to his own disciples to teach them about surrendering the ego.

"When I was staying with my Guru at Abu," Madhusudandas said, "he awoke me in the middle of a winter night and said, 'Go and bring me water from Nakki Lake.'

"'There is water in the small earthen pot,' I replied. 'I brought it here last evening.'

"'But I want to drink fresh water,' he said. 'Go right now and bring it to me.'

"Then I realized that he didn't want to drink, he wanted to test me. Immediately I rolled off my bed, stood up, and grabbed the pot. I went out of the cave into the freezing cold, walked to Nakki Lake, fetched the water and placed it in front of my guru."

Another time, on a calm, sunny day, Parmeshwardasji sat outside the cave reading a book. When Madhusudandas came out of the cave, Parmeshwardasji called him over, showed him the book, and asked him, "Can you read what is in this book?"

"Yes, it is very clear what is written here," Madhusudandas replied.

"For some reason I cannot read clearly," Parmeshwardasji said. "Why don't you go inside and get a candle so I can read better?"

Madhusudandas disappeared into the cave, lit a candle and brought it to his teacher. Parmeshwardasji sent his student back into the cave on another errand, and promptly blew out the candle. When Madhusudandas returned his teacher said, "There seems to be a strong wind. The candle has blown out. Please light it again."

This happened not once or twice, but 10 times! Finally, Parmeshwardasji called Madhusudandas and said, "It is a nice sunny day. The bright light makes the text very clear. The letters are easy to read. When I asked you if you could read, you said you could. But I said I couldn't. Didn't you doubt for a moment what I was saying? I asked you to light and re-light the candle many times. Didn't you wonder what was going on, even for a moment?"

"Yes, I did wonder what was going on," Madhusudandas answered. "But I know you are a much greater being than I am, and have a deeper understanding. I firmly believe what you are doing is for my benefit, so I just accept whatever you are doing."

"Your face clearly showed that you had some doubts in your mind," Parmeshwardasji said, probing further.

"Definitely I had doubts, but they were momentary," Madhusudandas replied. "I did not let the mind run away, because I stopped it immediately with the thought that my Guru knows what is best for me and whatever he is doing is for the welfare of my soul. This is not something to be analyzed. I just did whatever you asked me to do. I just let my heart flow, and I didn't let my mind enter the picture."

Parmeshwardasji must have been delighted that Madhusudandas's reactions were flawless, his obedience unflinching, proving that he understood clearly the meaning of surrender, which is the essence of the guru-disciple relationship. In most cases, even yogis who have practiced with great devotion will reveal that their egos are still in charge when they are put to the test. Some will question the logic of their teacher's requests because they still regard their own intellectual grasp of the situation as the highest wisdom. Others will obey their teachers because they believe they are supposed to, in a spirit of submission rather than surrender. Madhusudandas freely conceded his momentary doubts—the natural response of an intelligent, thinking person—but his discriminating mind was in command of his egoic mind, and he chose his response accordingly. This is the action of a disciplined yogi, who observes the ego but is not controlled by it. This is the action of a yogi who is free of attachments, beyond the reaches of maya. Parmeshwardasji must have sensed that his work with his student was complete.

As far as we know, Parmeshwardasji left Mount Abu and Madhusudandas never again spent time in his physical presence. Madhusudandas stressed repeatedly that the subtle relationship with the guru is all that is needed for the disciple to attain the goal. As important and beloved as Parmeshwardasji was to him, Madhusudandas never confused sentimentality with spiritual truth.

Even though Madhusudandas had attained enlightenment and passed his teacher's tests, his work was not over. Enlightenment is not a static condition. True saints do not stop developing spiritually, even after having the "ultimate experience," as if there were nothing else to attain. That would be like getting off a train only part of the way to your destination. Once a spiritual seeker reaches samadhi, that is just the first stop, for there are many levels of samadhi and each takes us deeper and deeper into the consciousness of God. Many people have heard how the Inuit people of northern Alaska and Canada use many different names for snow. Each name corresponds to a physical variation that is subtle yet describes a completely different state of that snow. Similarly, yogis use more than one term to describe different states of samadhi,[28] each progressive state moving us out of gross physical reality into a state in which we are liberated from our bondage to the physical world.

---

[28] In *Raja Yoga*, Swami Vivekananda explains that there are two categories of samadhi. In *samprajnata* samadhi, we still maintain a sense of duality; in *asamprajnata* samadhi, we are beyond duality. Samprajnata samadhi includes progressive states of awareness. First, in *savitarka* samadhi, "samadhi with question," the mind meditates upon aspects of nature, thereby gaining control over them. Next, the mind meditates upon these elements outside of their context in time and space. This is called *nirvitarka* samadhi, "samadhi without question." Higher than this state is *savichara* samadhi, "samadhi with discrimination," in which the object of meditation is the subtle elements out of which creation is made. When we eliminate time and space and think of the subtle elements without any context, it is called *nirvichara* samadhi, "samadhi without discrimination." In the next level of samadhi, both the gross and subtle elements are given up and the object of meditation is the interior organ of thinking. When we think of this organ as being beyond the qualities of activity and dullness, we attain *sananda* samadhi, "blissful samadhi." When the mind itself is the object of meditation and only the pure state of the ego remains, but is still differentiated from all other objects, it is *asmita* samadhi. In this state, we have not yet completely transcended the mind and still think of ourselves as having a subtle body. In the state of asamprajnata samadhi, however, we go beyond nature. We meditate on the mind itself and extinguish all thoughts and all forms. If we can truly accomplish this, we are free.

Swami Brahmananda, a close disciple of Ramakrishna, claimed that spiritual life actually begins with *nirvikalpa samadhi*, the high state of absorption in God that Madhusudandas attained after receiving shaktipat. Only through continual and constant practice can one reach even higher states. Furthermore, as the soul advances, although the energy becomes more stable and the soul moves farther away from the influence of maya, the threat of maya is always there. Even realized beings must maintain their purity and their impeccable lifestyle. Otherwise, there is always the chance that even a saint will devolve. The great saints have always known this and so they never give up, always pressing onward with their spiritual work.

Tota Puri, one of Shri Ramakrishna's gurus, used to meditate for hours every day, and never failed to polish his brass waterpot and fire tongs. One day Ramakrishna asked him, "Why do you meditate? You have already reached the highest state." Tota Puri pointed to his glistening waterpot and replied, "It will lose its shine if it isn't polished daily. It is the same with the mind, it gets dirty if it isn't kept clean by daily meditation."

When Madhusudandas was asked why he continued to do his spiritual practices once he attained samadhi and completed his training with his guru, he explained in his characteristically humble and humorous way, "I have formed a habit of devotion, now I cannot break it." This lighthearted response belied his very serious and firm dedication to a simple, ascetic lifestyle. Madhusudandas held absolute respect for the power of maya.

He told his students once, "If you are a clerk and are promoted to CEO, don't act like a clerk anymore. Once you have attained a higher state, you must behave in the way that befits that level. Then your lifestyle will constantly remind you of God, and you will continue to progress and not be tempted to slide back down from the heights you have achieved."

He taught the same principle by telling a story about Lord Krishna and the sage Narada. Narada and Krishna were talking one day and Narada asked him, "What is this maya of yours?" Lord Krishna answered by suggesting that they go for a walk. As they strolled along, he said he was thirsty, and asked Narada to get him a glass of water.

Narada saw they were approaching a village, so he went to the village well to get water for Lord Krishna to drink. When he arrived, he met a beautiful young woman who said, "You must be hungry," and invited him back to her hut for dinner. Narada went with her to her family's home and enjoyed a delicious meal, during which time her father offered the young woman to be Narada's wife. She was so lovely and pure that Narada was quite smitten, and agreed to marry her. They married and had two children and were very happy until one day, the monsoons came and the whole area became severely flooded. The water level kept rising until the whole family had to clamber up on the roof of the house to escape drowning. As the storm continued, and the family members held on to the bobbing house for dear life, the father lost his grip and fell into the water. Narada's family was very upset, but realizing that the father was an elderly man, they consoled themselves that his time to leave his body must have arrived. But soon, Narada's mother-in-law also slipped off the roof and drowned. In an effort to lighten their grief, the others reminded themselves that she too was old.

Shortly after this, one of the children slid off the roof and was lost in the water, and Narada's wife began to wail. Narada was comforting her by promising that they could still have another child, when their second child met the same fate. Narada and his wife clung to each other, but in her weakened state, his wife lost her grip and she too slipped off the roof. Narada was beside himself with grief when he felt himself begin to slide down into the water.

At that very moment, he found himself standing next to Lord Krishna, on the spot where they had been standing before Narada walked to the village. The Lord looked at Narada and asked, "Did you bring me the glass of water?"

Madhusudandas never underestimated the enormous influence of maya. He adhered to the strict rules of the yogis, and never did anything that would suggest his own desires were more important than his service to God. He taught that living this way is "like watering the roots of a plant rather than its leaves."

As his practices deepened, Madhusudandas began to manifest siddhis. Like his great-uncle Maunibava, the saint from Durgadih, he gained the power of speech—whatever he said came true. Eventually, many people witnessed his ability to see into the minds of others, but the first time Madhusudandas himself mentioned becoming aware that he could do this was when he was doing an anusthan in worship of Lord Ganesh in a cave in Mount Abu. As the anusthan neared its end, Madhusudandas knew he would need money to pay for the traditional feast for Brahmins and sadhus. The owner of the nearby Siddhapur Mill named Sheth Babulal Chunilal Shah came to the cave, and placed some money in front of Madhusudandas as a gift. But Madhusudandas, of course, would not accept donations during an anusthan, especially from someone unknown to him. So he gave the money back, even though he needed it for the feast. Shah was disappointed and asked permission to return the next day at 4:00 p.m. By the time he returned, he had learned about Madhusudandas's dilemma and he pressed the yogi to accept his gift. Noting the man's insistence, Madhusudandas searched his benefactor's mind.

"I saw in meditation that he was a man with a pure heart," Madhusudandas said. "His offer was in accordance with the subtle pre-arrangement of God. So I agreed to accept his gift."

We have little information about Madhusudandas's remaining years in Mount Abu. We can only assume that he spent his remaining time there continuing his sadhana until he knew he was in complete control of the energy moving through him. Just as Lord Shiva had to absorb the impact of the Ganges River when it was brought down from Heaven so that it would not destroy Earth, the guru must learn to contain and absorb the force of the kundalini so it helps rather than overwhelms the disciple.

After 10 years, Madhusudandas felt that the time had come for him to leave the rarefied atmosphere of Mount Abu and devote himself to serving humankind by taking others to higher spiritual states. He was now a master of Kundalini Maha Yoga. In Sanskrit, the word for meditation is *dhyan*, and since meditation is the central practice of Kundalini Maha Yoga, he began to refer to himself as Dhyanyogi, to identify himself with his path of dhyan yoga. From this point on, he would be known to the world as Dhyanyogi Madhusudandas Maharaj. He walked down from Mount Abu onto the plains of Gujarat to fulfill his destiny, eventually teaching the highest yogic wisdom to thousands of spiritual seekers in India and the United States.

PART 2

"A saint's heart is softer than butter.
Butter requires heat to melt,
but the heart of a saint melts just
seeing the pain of others."

CHAPTER TWELVE

PURIFYING THE VILLAGE OF ZALOR

Dhyanyogi-ji's American students hungered for him to tell them stories of his early life. They loved to hear about his days living in jungles, confronting cobras and tigers. These stories were a bridge between the seemingly mythical world out of which he emerged and our modern, Western reality. Like children who love to hear about their ancestors, they listened intently when Dhyanyogi-ji, tears in his eyes, spoke about his teacher. They were stunned to learn that once he found this incredible spiritual guide after so many painful years of searching, Dhyanyogi-ji parted from Parmeshwardasji after only several months. But Dhyanyogi-ji's attachments to people never competed with his focus on enlightenment and his surrender to the divine will. Once he had received shaktipat initiation, he was permanently established in God consciousness and in his subtle link with Parmeshwardasji and the lineage. This was the only connection he needed. Now his single focus was his mission to relieve suffering and help others in their spiritual quests.

Dhyanyogi-ji's companion from Mount Abu, Bramachari Shatrugh-nadas, had taken over the leadership of the Sutharana Temple, a Ram temple in the walled town of Radhanpur, 35 miles from the Pakistan border, near the vast barren salt flat called the Little Rann of Kutch. Shatrughnadas invited Dhyanyogi-ji to come be a priest at his temple, so this was where Dhyanyogi-ji began the next phase of his life. He walked the 150 dusty miles to Radhanpur and spent the next eight months working there.

In his free time, Dhyanyogi-ji offered spiritual lectures to the public. Now in his mid-40s, Dhyanyogi-ji's looks betrayed his years of exposure to the wilds of India. His skin and feet were toughened from his austerities, his body lean from his fasting. But his most striking feature was his eyes, which poured out love to all who met his gaze. Just being in his presence influenced the emotional states of those who came to him for darshan. His compassion was palpable, his humor contagious, his wisdom inspiring, and his purity and simplicity calming.

As Dhyanyogi-ji drew an increasingly large following, Shatrughnadas's own reputation seemed to pale. Shatrughnadas said nothing, but Dhyanyogi-ji could see that he was outshining his companion, and knew that the situation was causing his friend to suffer. Dhyanyogi-ji decided it would be best for him to leave Radhanpur.

Dhyanyogi-ji's intuition directed him to go to Zalor, a nine-mile walk from Radhanpur, to do intensive sadhana there. Once an inhabited area, Zalor was now in ruins. It was mostly overgrown jungle and had a reputation of being a very dangerous place. Even in broad daylight, people were nervous when they stepped foot there, and at night, those who lived nearby reported hearing haunting cries coming from the vicinity of Zalor. Some heard voices chanting, "Kill, kill, kill." A sadhu named Gordhan Maharaj of Sirvada cautioned Dhyanyogi-ji that Zalor had become the residence of ghosts, evil spirits and dangerous animals, including wolves and hyenas. Hyenas have immensely powerful jaws with which they kill their prey, and legend said the saliva of the hyenas in Zalor was itself so deadly that just the touch of these animals' tongues would begin to melt flesh and bone. Gordhan Maharaj warned that if Dhyanyogi-ji went there, he would not return alive.

In the early 1800s, a local resident dreamt that there was a well in Zalor in which there were statues of the Divine Mother and a set of Her footprints. Following the guidance in his dream, the man went to the well, found the statues, and took them to a nearby village called

Artifacts found in Zalor

Devgam, where they were installed in a temple. Years later, archeologists excavated the area and identified the buried ruins as belonging to a 2,000-year-old Hindu city known as Godha, destroyed 700 years before by the Mogul conqueror Ala-ud-din Khilji. The invaders had brutally killed 60,000 people including 1,000 priests.

When Dhyanyogi-ji arrived in 1921, no one was yet aware of what exactly was wrong with Zalor, only that it was a place that inspired terror. But Dhyanyogi-ji was no longer a boy beset with fears. In retrospect, his insistence on doing anusthans at the very spot where the bloodshed had occurred would seem to indicate that he was determined to heal the subtle, negative energy that poisoned Zalor. His attitude was reflected in his statement, "If I do not come back alive, so what? I don't want to begin family life anyway." So Dhyanyogi-ji moved into a small hut on a hill and lived there for the next 18 months.[29]

Zalor was surrounded by desert. The local water supply came from Brahmasar Lake, which filled up during the monsoon season but quickly dried up as soon as the rains ended. This created a hardship for the people. Shortly after he arrived, Dhyanyogi-ji became aware of the situation and did an anusthan to help with the water shortage. After seven days of intensive practices, he took a shovel and began digging a hole in the dry lakebed. When the hole was about three feet deep, a strong current of water began to flow as if he had tapped into an underground spring. The lake filled, and no matter how much water the villagers drew out, the water level never dropped. The villagers celebrated their good fortune and spread the news about this miracle.

Legend has it that in a few rare cases in history, great saints have manifested the Ganges River in locations far from the river's actual course. According to each of these accounts, the Ganges sprang out from the big toe of the saint's right foot. The locals believed that Dhyanyogi-ji's powers had manifested the same phenomenon by digging a small hole. Crowds began to flock there to have darshan of the "Ganges in

---

[29]Later, he discovered several small murtis near his hut. Local residents planned to build a shrine for them at the spot where Dhyanyogi-ji lived.

Zalor" and of Dhyanyogi-ji, the saint who had brought the goddess Ganga—the Ganges incarnate—to this parched and forsaken land. He had begun to transform the energy at Zalor, not simply by bringing water to the area, but by harnessing the energy of the Ganges, the purifier of all spiritual negativity.

Several days after the miracle at Brahmasar, something else happened that demonstrated how far beyond fear Dhyanyogi-ji had come. At one point, he had begun an anusthan to Lord Ram during which he was observing a strict vow of silence. When he needed to communicate, he wrote his message on a small slate that he carried with him. One morning, on his way down the footpath to the shore of the lake for his daily bath in Brahmasar Lake, he encountered a cobra slithering towards him like a raindrop flowing down a window pane. The deadly snake moved a little, stopped for a while and peered at Dhyanyogi-ji, then continued gliding closer.

Dhyanyogi-ji wondered if the cobra would bite him, but then he thought, I am doing an anusthan to Lord Ram. How could he bite? His next thought was, what's wrong if he does bite me? What could be more auspicious than to die while doing an anusthan?

While Dhyanyogi-ji noticed his thoughts, the cobra advanced steadily towards him. He had to make his decision quickly. Shouting for help was out of the question because of his vow of silence. And he was certain that no one could avoid death if it was the will of God.

If I am destined to die at this very moment, he said to himself, death is sure to follow me wherever I run. It is far better to stand in front of death, repeating the name of Lord Ram with eyes closed, than to succumb to death as a coward or without faith in God. It is best to leave this world greeting death with a smile when it comes, not to run away from it with fear in my heart.

Standing squarely in the middle of the trail, directly in the path of the approaching cobra, he closed his eyes. After some time passed, Dhyanyogi-ji opened his eyes. To his surprise he caught only a glimpse of the retreating cobra, which was rushing away into the cover of nearby bushes.

Some time later, a similar episode occurred when a pack of snarling dogs encircled Dhyanyogi-ji. As before, he silently repeated Lord Ram's name until the pack moved along.

The *Ram Raksha Stotram* states that one who takes refuge in the name of Ram cannot be harmed, that "the roaring thunder of the sound Ram" repels the messengers of death. For Dhyanyogi-ji, these incidents were proof that he was under Lord Ram's protection.

Dhyanyogi-ji went on to complete his anusthan, and to plan the feast to be offered at its conclusion. Zalor was in such a state of ruin that providing an elaborate feast was impossible. Since the most important part of the meal was the dessert, Dhyanyogi-ji arranged for a variety of sweets to be brought from Radhanpur. After the first group of guests had eaten their fill, it became clear that there would not be enough for everyone. It would take nearly half a day to make the round-trip journey to Radhanpur for more sweets, and it was unacceptable to keep the guests waiting.

Dhyanyogi-ji began to repeat Lord Ram's name and, after a few seconds, he told the person serving, "It is not necessary to go to Radhanpur. Cover the container of sweets with a cloth."

When this had been done, he said, "Now, go ahead and serve but don't look into the box." To everyone's surprise, the servers continued to dish out sweets until everyone had eaten and was satisfied. Even then, 20 pounds of dessert remained. To the villagers, this was further evidence that Dhyanyogi-ji could perform miracles, and the residents of Zalor grew in their faith that he was a great mahatma.

Soon people who had learned of his powers began to invoke his name in times of need. In the nearby village of Subapura, there lived a blacksmith who had a cow that bled from her teats instead of giving milk. He tried all the traditional remedies, but nothing cured her. He had heard about Dhyanyogi-ji and vowed, "If my cow begins to give milk, I will supply Dhyanyogi-ji with her milk free of charge for as long as he lives in Zalor."

After the blacksmith made his vow, the flow of blood stopped and the cow began to produce milk. The blacksmith was jubilant. With profound gratitude, he not only kept his promise, he became a lifelong devotee of Dhyanyogi-ji. Over time, his neighbors noticed that his life improved, and he grew more and more content.

These events are difficult to comprehend intellectually, but it would be a mistake to dismiss them out of hand. In fact, Dhyanyogi-ji himself did not consider them to be miracles. He believed they were the simple result of one-pointed devotion, and he taught that with firm and constant faith, incidents like these were easily obtainable by anyone.

Shri Ramakrishna used to tell a story about a man who wanted to cross the ocean from Sri Lanka to India. He sought the help of Vibhishana, king of Sri Lanka, who wrote Lord Ram's name on a leaf, tied it in a corner of the man's dhoti and said, "With this you will cross safely. You will be able to walk on the water. But be sure not to look at it, for the moment you do, you will drown."

To the man's amazement, he discovered that he could indeed walk on water, and he headed for India. Understandably, he grew more and more curious about how he was performing this feat. Finally, about halfway across, he couldn't resist any longer and he peeked at his clothes. He tore the leaf from his dhoti and exclaimed, "What is this? It is only a leaf with the name of Ram written on it!" Instantly, he sank beneath the waves.

Dhyanyogi-ji's faith had no limits, so what might seem impossible to most was perfectly plausible to him. That's what had seen him through his 30 years of searching. Now that he was beginning to have more contact with people, he served as a living example of the power of that faith, and the unlikely solutions it could provide.

CHAPTER THIRTEEN

BANDHWAD ASHRAM

Afew miles down the rough road from Zalor was another small village named Bandhwad. In the early 1920s, the villagers there had a problem. Bandhwad was home to a very modest ashram with an ancient statue of Lord Hanuman. Over the years, a succession of three priests had lived there and cared for the murti. It was expected that the chief priest of the temple who performed the daily worship would be unmarried and celibate, so when the third priest, Madhavdas, decided to marry and raise a family, the village leaders had to find a replacement.

The conditions in Bandhwad were primitive. The isolated hamlet, situated 11 miles north of Radhanpur, had no electricity, running water or paved roads. Moreover, although some of the residents were farmers and shepherds, the area was better known as a sanctuary for bandits. Most of the men in the village supported their families by stealing. They typically made forays to distant communities and then retreated to Bandhwad to hide from the authorities. It wasn't a place that would

Typical home in Bandhwad village

readily attract the type of candidate suitable for tending an ashram.

By this time, word of Dhyanyogi-ji's feats had spread like wildfire. The elders of Bandhwad were extremely impressed by the legends they heard about the great mahatma of Zalor who had transformed that lonely, tortured place by bringing the Ganges Herself to fill the barren Brahmasar Lake. If they could persuade Dhyanyogi-ji to come to live at the Bandhwad ashram, think what he could do for their village and its reputation. Aside from his practical help, his presence there would be a source of enormous pride for the villagers.

The Bandhwad ashram dated back to the early 1800s, when a farmer from Arjansar, another small village in the area, had a dream in which Lord Hanuman said, "I am lying in your land. Plow the land softly. Please get me out!"

The next morning, this farmer gathered together some of his neighbors and they set out to find Hanumanji. With a little digging, they unearthed 1,200-year-old statues of Hanuman and Bhairav, a name for Lord Shiva. Their plan was to bring the statues back to Arjansar and install them in their village temple. They had no difficulty moving the murti of Bhairav but Hanumanji, apparently, had a different idea. Though the statue was only three feet tall and weighed no more than 200 pounds, no matter how much the people tried, no matter how many tugged and pulled, Hanumanji would not budge an inch.

A few nights later, Hanumanji appeared again, this time in the dream of a prominent citizen in Bandhwad named Raja Dosa. "Come to Arjansar," he told Mr. Dosa, "Bring nine people and a cart yoked to two small bullocks and take me to Bandhwad."

Mr. Dosa followed the instructions from his dream. This time, to everyone's astonishment, they lifted the murti with ease and loaded it onto the bullock cart. Once Hanumanji was on board, instead of guiding the bullocks, the villagers followed behind the cart. Without any hesitation, the bullocks led the way back to a field in Bandhwad. When the cart stopped, the villagers unloaded the murti and curiously, once they set it down, no one was able to move it again. Hanumanji had chosen his home.

The people from the village constructed a modest temple around Hanumanji, and founded a simple ashram. Soon after the murti was installed, the Hindu Premier of Radhanpur was passing by Bandhwad when the horses drawing his carriage stopped abruptly and refused to go any further. The Premier was a religious man, so he interpreted their behavior as a sign that there was a temple in the vicinity and made inquiries. When he learned of the tiny temple, he went there to take darshan of Hanumanji. Only after this did his horses move on. The Premier was so moved by the power of the murti that he persuaded the Navab of Radhanpur, the ruler of the local Muslim community, to give some land west of the temple to the ashram.

Shri Ramdas, the second priest to preside over the ashram, built a wall around the compound, and acquired some land. But after 100 years, the ashram was still a very humble operation when the delegation of prominent men from Bandhwad went to Zalor to convince Dhyanyogi-ji that he should become its head priest.

The village elders knew that it was a long shot. They suspected that Dhyanyogi-ji might not wish to be tied down because he was a wandering sadhu. They tried to imagine their conversation with him, thinking of all the ways they could frame their invitation to make it most appealing.

When they came upon Dhyanyogi-ji, however, their meeting was not at all what they expected. They had imagined bowing with appropriate reverence to this venerable holy man, and humbly making their request. Instead, they found Dhyanyogi-ji sitting, absorbed in a deep state of samadhi. There was no way they could have prepared themselves for this sight. Tingling with excitement as they wondered what to do next, they grew even more eager to persuade Dhyanyogi-ji to come to Bandhwad.

The men in the delegation huddled together and came up with a clever scheme. The crucial part of the ceremony for appointing the head of a monastery was to place a shawl over the body of the appointee. What if they threw the shawl over Dhyanyogi-ji's body while he was still in meditation? Then he could not refuse them!

When Dhyanyogi-ji woke up, the deed was done. True to the reputation of their village, the men had, in a sense, stolen Dhyanyogi-ji!

Taking charge of a village ashram was an unexpected turn of events for Dhyanyogi-ji. Since his childhood, he had never wanted to settle down, let alone assume the kind of responsibilities that would be required of a temple priest. Such a role would restrict him and create the kind of bondage he had always resisted.

Characteristically, no matter how surprised or distressed Dhyanyogi-ji may have been, he went along with the script he was handed because he believed that everything that happens is the will of God. But he was insistent that he not lose his freedom. He said that he would come only on the condition that they arranged for someone else to live at the ashram, so that the murti would not be left unattended when Dhyanyogi-ji's intuition guided him to leave the ashram to do his spiritual work.

The delegation was more than happy to agree to his condition, so the bargain was struck, Dhyanyogi-ji moved to Bandhwad, and the ashram became his chief place of residence for the next 60 years.

It only took a few days for Dhyanyogi-ji to realize the unsavory character of most of the villagers. Just as he did in Zalor, he undertook the daunting task of improving the undesirable elements in Bandhwad.

Ayurveda teaches that the effect of the medicine called love is very slow, but its benefits last forever. According to the villagers, it was through Dhyanyogi-ji's loving guidance that this tiny outpost and its simple people underwent a metamorphosis. He worked to raise their consciousness, and gradually, they began to turn away from their criminal lifestyles. As the resident saint of Bandhwad, Dhyanyogi-ji was God incarnate to the villagers.

They compare their story to the tale of Valiya, a famous thief, who robbed and murdered people without the slightest remorse. For Valiya, this was simply his profession, how he supported his family. One day Valiya captured a saint and demanded he turn over his possessions. The saint was the sage Narada, and he told the thief, "I have nothing. Why are you doing this?"

Valiya answered, "I do this to take care of my family."

"In that case," Narada advised, "perhaps you should go and ask your parents and children if they're willing to partake in the karma you are creating by your actions. You can tie me to this tree so I can't get away."

Narada's words piqued Valiya's curiosity, so he tied Narada to the tree and went to put the question to his family members. "I am doing all of this for you," Narada said to them. "Are you willing to share in the karma?"

"It's your duty to provide for us," they said. "How you do it is your business. The karma is your own."

Valiya had always assumed that since he stole in order to take care of them, they shared responsibility for his deeds. He suddenly saw his situation with new clarity and determined to change his ways. He ran back to Narada, untied him, and fell at his feet, asking for guidance. "What should I do so that I can erase this terrible karma?"

Narada had the intuition to give him the mantra *Rama* because he knew that would bring Valiya to the state of God-realization. However, because Valiya had killed people all his life, his character had become so negative that he was literally incapable of reciting something so pure. So he told Valiya to reverse the mantra and repeat, instead, the word *Mara*, which means "death." When Valiya recited this mantra continuously— mara, mara, mara—he would, in fact, be chanting Rama, Rama, Rama.

Valiya did his japa with such intensity that he lost all outward awareness. His concentration was so deep that he didn't move even as termites built a hill over his body. Through his sadhana, he became one of the greatest saints that ever lived, and was later known as Valmiki Muni.[30]

A similar story is told about Angulimal of Shravasti, another well-known outlaw, who used to chop off the fingers of the people he killed and make garlands out of them. Influenced by the teachings of Lord Buddha, he gave up his ways and chose instead the path of renunciation, in the end becoming a great saint.

Some of the people of Bandhwad believed that like Valiya and Angulimal, they had been transformed. Simply by being in Dhyanyogi-ji's company, their lives had turned around.

The villagers noticed another phenomenon that took place when Dhyanyogi-ji lived among them. Although the Hanuman murti had con-siderable energy—it had stopped the Premier's horses in their tracks— with Dhyanyogi-ji's arrival, the energy of the place grew exponentially. Sadhus began to appear at the ashram on a nearly daily basis. Given the reclusive nature of some of these sadhus' lives, it surprised the villag-

---

[30]Valmiki means a "termite mound."

ers that so many of them heard about Bandhwad. It seemed that Dhyanyogi-ji operated like a magnet, drawing them in. Even in the 1980s and 90s, when he no longer stayed at the ashram, saints would turn up to give their blessings whenever his students came to do anusthans.

Approach to Bandhwad ashram

Although these holy men somehow knew to trek across the desert to this little ashram tucked away in the middle of nowhere, most people would never find their way there. Even now, in the early 21st century, Bandhwad is a small and unassuming place. It has a population of only a few thousand, many of whom are shepherds and farmers. The turn-off from the road to Radhanpur is a one-lane road well traveled by bullock carts, herds of camels, sheep, goats and cows,

people carrying firewood on their heads, and a few bicycles. Motorized traffic is still so rare that it generates a great deal of interest. Fields lie on either side of the road, and children study and play outside a small complex of concrete school buildings, part of Dhyanyogi-ji's legacy to Bandhwad. With only the slightest invitation, many of them will run together to form a loud, uninhibited chorus, and sing devotional songs for visitors.

Past the schoolyard, the lane passes a seasonal watering hole and ends at the archway that is the entrance to the ashram. People visiting there today walk through the cool archway, step out of their shoes, and emerge into the sanctuary of the ashram. While still open to the sky and the heat of the day, the atmosphere is tranquil, strikingly different from outside.

The first thing visitors notice at the center of the ashram, 15

paces ahead, is a temple painted decoratively in pastel pinks and greens, the home of Hanumanji. All of the other structures in the ashram are held in orbit around Him.

Women collecting drinking water from the village well

Immediately to the right of the entrance is a steep stone staircase leading up to what was Dhyanyogi-ji's bedroom. The bed was on the north wall, with a window situated in such a way that he could have the darshan of Hanumanji even when he was lying down. To the left, there was a room that belonged to Dhyanyogi-ji's spiritual heir, Shri Anandi Ma, who came to the ashram in 1972. This room is gone now, demolished by the February 2001 earthquake that devastated this region of Gujarat. Below

the ruins of that room is Dhyanyogi-ji's sitting room, where he received visitors and held *satsang*[31] with members of the village each afternoon. On hot evenings he liked to sit on a bench outside his sitting room and talk with the disciples and villagers who gathered on the verandah in the welcoming shade of a spreading neem tree. Next to this room is a small shrine displaying a marble casting of the feet of the ashram's first mahant, Shri Janakidas.

Entrance to temple and ashram and view of Dhyanyogi ji's bedroom upstairs

The Hanuman temple is an example of big things coming in small packages. Five feet square and about eight feet high, only two people can fit inside, but the power of the murti defies description. Visitors have said that when they sat before the murti, their hearts exploded with feelings of inner peace, joy and love. Tears streamed down their faces and many have found it difficult to physically pull themselves

---

[31]Satsang literally means to stay close to the truth. Here, it is used to refer to a gathering in the presence of the guru.

away. "I remember walking into this little primitive-looking temple," commented one visitor, "and being caught completely off guard by the energy. I thought I would faint. I wanted to stay in that tiny space forever."

Hanumanji stands directly on the floor. He is about three feet high, slightly over one foot wide, and covered with gold foil. He holds his club overhead, his long tail forming the shape of the Sanskrit syllable "Aum." His penetrating gaze connects with something deep inside. If a puja has been recently performed, He may be adorned with flower garlands or a silver crown, and his face may be painted a characteristic orange with *sindoor*; vermilion powder mixed with oil.

Hanuman Temple at Bandhwad (with entrance to cave on the right)

Beside Him, there is a small murti of Ganesh, and hanging above Ganesh is a silk painting of Hanumanji performing one of his many heroic acts, flying across the length of India carrying a mountain peak above his shoulder. The *Ramayana* tells us that to save the life of Ram's brother Laxman, Hanumanji flew to the Himalayas where an herb grew that could revive Laxman. Hanumanji—being just a humble monkey—was unable to identify the plant he sought, so he simply lifted the entire mountain and carried it south to Sri Lanka, thereby saving Laxman's life.

Dhyanyogi-ji's bed in Bandhwad

Installed in their own niches on the outer sides of the three walls of the Hanumanji mandir are murtis of Indra, God of the Heavens, Varuna, God of the Waters, and Kubera, God of Wealth. On the gleaming white temple spire are lions, the "vehicle" or mount associated with the Divine Mother Durga, facing in all four directions.

To the right of the Hanuman temple is the brightly painted yellow and turquoise wooden door that is the entrance to the man-made cave where Dhyanyogi-ji performed his daily practices and anusthans. A dozen steps descend to the main room of the cave, seven feet below ground, which has space enough for 30 people packed tightly together. On the eastern and northern walls are small, screened windows to let in air and light. For years, old photographs of Dhyanyogi-ji and the villagers hung on the walls, one of which was an extraordinary picture of Anandi Ma at age 14, with a ray of light streaming from her heart.

Just down a short, narrow passage is another smaller cave directly underneath the Hanuman murti with room enough for two people to sit and perform practices. Visitors find it difficult to resist falling into meditation when they sit down on the smooth, tiled floor of the cave. One remarked that when it was time to leave there, she felt as if her body were leaden and bolted to the floor. That was how difficult it was to uproot herself. This tiny space is saturated with Dhyanyogi-ji's energy and love because this is where he spent months at a time doing anusthan.

Just as Dhyanyogi-ji never allowed any discomforts to interfere with his sadhana on Mount Abu, his power of concentration was tested repeatedly during his frequent encounters with the insects and animals that shared his cave in Bandhwad. Once he felt something heavy on his leg and assumed it was a frog. He was about to push it away with his hand when he thought, maybe I should

Cave where Dhyanyogi-ji did practices. The picture on the altar was taken around 1967.

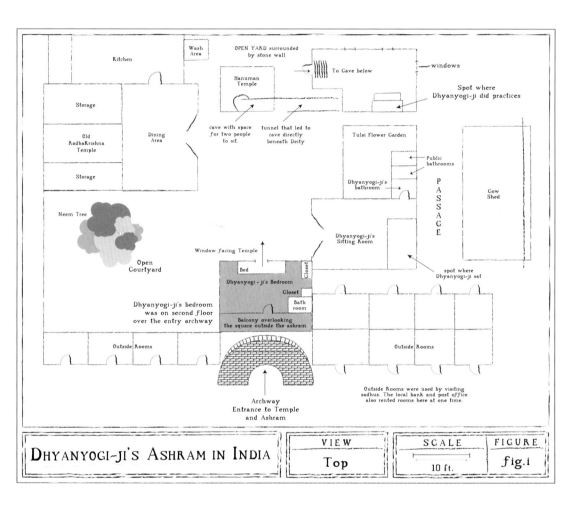

Kitchen

Wash Area

OPEN YARD surrounded by stone wall

To Cave below

windows

Storage

Hanuman Temple

Spot where Dhyanyogi-ji did practices

Old RadhaKrishna Temple

Dining Area

cave with space for two people to sit.

tunnel that led to cave directly beneath Deity

Tulsi Flower Garden

Storage

Public bathrooms

Dhyanyogi-ji's bathroom

PASSAGE

Cow Shed

Neem Tree

Window facing Temple

Dhyanyogi-ji's Sitting Room

Open Courtyard

Bed

Closet

Dhyanyogi-ji's Bedroom

Closet

spot where Dhyanyogi-ji sat

Dhyanyogi-ji's bedroom was on second floor over the entry archway

Bath room

Balcony overlooking the square outside the ashram

Outside Rooms

Outside Rooms

Archway Entrance to Temple and Ashram

Outside Rooms were used by visiting sadhus. The local bank and post office also rented rooms here at one time.

DHYANYOGI-JI'S ASHRAM IN INDIA	VIEW	SCALE	FIGURE
	Top	10 ft.	fig.i

see what it is; it may not be a frog. He opened his eyes and saw a big scorpion. If he pushed it away, it would definitely sting him. If he tried to get up, it would sting him. So he closed his eyes and coolly continued to meditate, thinking, the scorpion got up there somehow, so as he came, he will leave. And so it did.

Another time, Dhyanyogi-ji took his seat to meditate, not realizing that a cobra lay coiled in the corner of the cave. Whenever Dhyanyogi-ji made some noise during puja, the cobra hissed in response. Dhyanyogi-ji heard the snake but he had no intention of leaving. He sensed that the cobra was testing him. He thought, whatever is to happen, let it happen. I do not want to move from here. I have not harmed the cobra, but if it feels I have injured it in any way then let it bite me, and my debt will be repaid. What good fortune to die while worshipping the Lord!

For an hour, both held their ground. The snake gazed intently at Dhyanyogi-ji as though under a spell of devotion to this guru. When he finished his practices, Dhyanyogi-ji quietly climbed out of the cave and arranged for the careful capture and release of the snake into the fields outside the ashram.

On another occasion, Dhyanyogi-ji was in his cave doing an anus-than. Shortly after he began his japa, a six-inch scorpion approached. Dhyanyogi-ji remained on his seat because during an anusthan, he was not supposed to get up until he completed his practices. The scorpion continued to come closer as Dhyanyogi-ji sat silently watching. Seconds before the scorpion reached him, a lizard darted out and attacked the scorpion, preventing it from stinging Dhyanyogi-ji. The lizard and the scorpion struggled in a deadly embrace for almost an hour. Eventually the lizard lost the battle and died after losing the use of all his legs. The scorpion was gravely wounded, losing three or four legs himself, but still wandered off. Meanwhile, Dhyanyogi-ji completed his anusthan. Once again he was protected by God's grace.

Once, a disciple visiting Dhyanyogi-ji at the ashram learned that his guru washed his *asan*, the cloth upon which he sat, only once a year. Yogis do this so that the energy from their meditations can accumulate in their asans. It had been a long time since the cave had been cleaned, and it was time for his asan to be washed, so Dhyanyogi-ji went into the cave and lifted it up. Underneath it were scorpions, centipedes and two baby mice. The disciple had followed him and watched him in amazement.

"You were sitting on this asan all this time with all these creatures under you and the scorpions never stung you?" he asked.

"I don't even know what's down there. I just sit on it," replied Dhyanyogi-ji. "I'm not concerned if they are there. I'm just concerned with my puja. If they consider that to be their home, that's okay with me. They're doing their work and I'm doing mine."

A group of American students came to Bandhwad to do anusthans in 1988, when Dhyanyogi-ji was staying in Ahmedabad. Several of them were rattled by the wildlife in the cave, but during anusthan, all actions are magnified in their impact, so it is particularly important to practice non-violence in thought and deed. However, in an effort to ward off an encroaching scorpion, one student accidentally killed it.

After his anusthan was completed, this man went to see Dhyanyogi-ji and asked if he had incurred any negative karma as a result of the demise of the scorpion. Dhyanyogi-ji explained that the small creatures at Bandhwad were actually saints doing practices. "If they were all there in human form," he reasoned, "they would never be able to fit inside! This is why it is crucial that no harm comes to any living being inside the ashram." However, he went on to reassure his devotee that the accident had been unintended, and that he had removed the karma.

Upon leaving the cave and coming back up the stairs, visitors emerge once again into the bright light of the ashram courtyard. Ahead is a small area where the ashram cows once lived, and to the right, beyond the small Hanuman temple, is a wider temple facing east containing murtis of Ganesh, Radha-Krishna, Durga, the Divine Mother and Lord Shiva.

During the years when Dhyanyogi-ji lived in Bandhwad, this temple wasn't there. Some time after he moved to the ashram, an ancient Krishna temple in a neighboring village collapsed, and the local priest asked if the murtis could be moved to Bandhwad. Dhyanyogi-ji agreed, but since the ashram had no temple in which to put them, he made a sankalpa—a commitment to himself and to God—to build a temple to house the murtis. The residents of Bandhwad donated some fields in which local farmers grew cumin, wheat, millet and beans, so that the income from this land could provide the funds needed to maintain the statues and construct their new temple. With the addition of this property, the ashram now owned about 70 acres. The project was finally completed in 1989.

Visitors to the 5,000-square-foot ashram are immediately struck by its utter simplicity and its unmistakable, overpowering spiritual energy. Many are puzzled that a master with Dhyanyogi-ji's level of attainment chose to live in Bandhwad and devote so much of his life to this humble place. But this choice was a perfect reflection of Dhyanyogi-ji. His gentle appearance and manner belied his compelling inner nature. He was small in physical stature and without possessions or airs, yet he was a giant of a man in a spiritual sense. The example he set in Bandhwad is particularly relevant in current times because he demonstrated that we don't need luxurious accommodations and the stimulation of modern life to find peace and happiness, help humankind and attain enlightenment.

Over the 60 years of his residence, the ashram flourished. Today, a quarter century since he lived there, Dhyanyogi-ji's energy is still palpable. Recently, a visitor said that after making a pilgrimage to India's most sacred spots, he found Bandhwad to be the most powerful place of all.

CHAPTER FOURTEEN

ASHRAM LIFE

Since leaving Durgadih, Dhyanyogi-ji had belonged to no one and no place. Though he lived at Mount Abu for 10 years, nearly a quarter of his life at that point, he never put down roots there. When it was time to leave, he went on his way without looking back.

But all that changed at Bandhwad. From the early 1920s until 1980, Dhyanyogi-ji considered Bandhwad his home. Sometimes he left the ashram to perform an anusthan, to make a pilgrimage to a sacred place of power, or to pursue a humanitarian mission. But never again did he live in solitude, roaming freely through desert plains and mountains as he had for his 30 years as a student.

For the first time in his adult life, Dhyanyogi-ji was part of a village. After 30 years of isolated existence focused exclusively on searching for spiritual knowledge, in which his only interactions were with other yogis, he had gone on to lead an equally lonely life as a sage doing intensive practices. Now, he had been effectively "captured" and lifted into the routines of village life. Other than several hours of meditation and prayer, his daily activities revolved around the people of Bandhwad.

He was a constant, the one who watched over them, who noticed their suffering and provided solutions and salves. After finally breaking away from his family and village in childhood, he had again become the object of great attachment for many.

For the villagers, Dhyanyogi-ji was father, mother, teacher and advisor. They came to depend on him for every need. They brought him their personal problems and sought his advice to fulfill their aspirations. The headman of Bandhwad consulted with him about crises that arose. Dhyanyogi-ji served as the doctor for the village and saved many lives. He had a stethoscope, and kept a small bottle of an Ayurvedic powder that he gave to anyone who was too sick to survive the hour-long trip to Radhanpur. He was more like a faith healer than a medical practitioner, but his "prescriptions" worked.

Dhyanyogi-ji's role as protector went beyond medical emergencies. He had a driver who told a story about how once, on a road trip, they ran out of gas. "He told me, 'Don't look at the gas gauge. Just keep on driving.' Without a drop of gas, we drove another 75 miles!"

The villagers believed that Dhyanyogi-ji watched over them daily, whether he was physically present or not. Once, a young girl fell into the village well and was not discovered until the next morning. By the time some of her neighbors pulled her up, she had drowned. Dhyanyogi-ji was away from the ashram, but they carried her limp body there anyway and placed it in front of Hanumanji's temple. In a short time, she revived. When she was able to speak, she told her neighbors that during the night she had seen Hanumanji, Dhyanyogi-ji, and a ghee lamp burning, so she felt no fear, convinced that she was safe because she was with Dhyanyogi-ji.

As close as they were to Dhyanyogi-ji, the people of Bandhwad had no context in which to comprehend his level of consciousness. Most of the villagers were not spiritually oriented. In fact, they were scared to meditate. But no matter how limited their perceptions, they couldn't help but feel the effects of his energy. One man used to fall spontaneously into deep states of meditation in which he would "see" Dhyanyogi-ji. Whenever Dhyanyogi-ji was away from the ashram, he accurately reported exactly where Dhyanyogi-ji was and what he was doing. Often when the villagers hadn't heard from Dhyanyogi-ji for a considerable length of time, they would ask this person to enter this state and report on Dhyanyogi-ji's well being and whereabouts.

Though most villagers were not spiritually inclined, they had a deep appreciation for Dhyanyogi-ji's efforts to improve their day-to-day lives. He was personally responsible for bringing Bandhwad into the 20th century, arranging for basic services like electricity, running water and road improvements. In times of drought, in 1967 and again in 1973, he became very involved in the care of the cattle, not only because of his particular fondness for cows but also because they were vital to the villagers' livelihood. He collected funds to deepen the lake and to increase the supply of water, and used these projects to give honest employment to the villagers.

School in Bandhwad

Dhyanyogi-ji also changed the educational system in Bandhwad. One morning as he was leaving the ashram he saw two high school students crying beside the road. He stopped the car and asked them what had happened. They said it was the day of final exams, but the local public bus that took them to school had been so packed that the driver had not let them board. They were very upset because their performance on the final exam determined whether they would be able to go to college. If they missed their exams they would lose an entire year. Dhyanyogi-ji told them to hop into his car, and he drove them to school.

After this incident, he resolved that obtaining an education would not be such a struggle for the children of Bandhwad. He established a local school, which he named Samskardham, meaning a place where people gain positive values (samskaras). His mission for Samskardham was that children would learn both scholastic material and spiritual values. Dhyanyogi-ji was adamant that the teachers be continually aware of what they were modeling to their students. He personally oversaw the construction and maintenance of the school buildings during his afternoons.

Practical and innovative in his various roles, Dhyanyogi-ji was clear that the source of his competence was God, Lord Ram or Mother Kundalini, the kundalini energy in the form of a Goddess. He always followed the central teaching of the *Bhagavad Gita*—do work with complete detachment, never see it as belonging to oneself, and leave the outcome to God. "Work is worship," he said, and whether a task was an insignificant chore or a major endeavor, he threw himself into it wholeheartedly. He loved to sing the verse, *"Kar se Karo Ghar Ka Kama, Mukh se Bolo Sita Ram,"* which translates, "Do work with your hands, and with your mouth, go on singing 'Sita Ram.'"

For the most part, it was not his way to discuss how he managed to succeed in his projects, but on one rare occasion, he did. Water was always a problem at Bandhwad. In 1970, the villagers had dug three wells, but all three failed. Dhyanyogi-ji later reported that he went directly to Hanumanji at his ashram residence and said, "If you don't give me water, I'll leave!" That night, Hanumanji came to him in a dream and told him that on the following day he would notice a particular bird not ordinarily seen in this area flying back and forth above the ashram, and he instructed Dhyanyogi-ji to follow this bird. The next day, Dhyanyogi-ji saw that very bird and with its guidance, he directed the villagers where to dig a new well. That well is still working today.

Dhyanyogi-ji's life seemed to have changed dramatically. But just as a river flowing over changing terrain may appear altered, he moved into new situations and stages in his life without any shift in his outlook or manner. He was always content, accepting that whatever happened was the will of God and for the best. "Whatever comes in your life, accept it as *prasad*—as a blessing," he advised. He loved chanting, especially chanting the name Ram, so if he wasn't meditating, or doing something else that demanded his full attention, he automatically started to sing. He ate moderately and spoke only when necessary. He was calm in the face of stress and difficulty, and he never got angry. He showed compassion to everyone and always behaved with generosity and humility. Even those who had disputes with him over his projects because of their political agendas couldn't help loving and respecting him. His greatest dislike was talking or thinking badly of others and he cautioned everyone to avoid gossip. He often sang a verse written by Kabir that translates, "I went out in the world to look into the faults of others, but when I sat down and looked into myself, I was the worst of all."

When Dhyanyogi-ji was in residence in Bandhwad, he followed a fixed routine because a regular schedule helps to still the mind and maintain inner peace. *Brahma-muhurta*, the "hour of Brahma," between 3:00 and 6:00 in the morning, is the ideal time for meditation. During this period, the external surroundings are calm and quiet since the bustle of the day has not yet begun, the body is rested, and the mind is not yet cluttered. Every morning Dhyanyogi-ji awoke at 4:00 a.m. His first thought was of Lord Ram, and he sang songs in praise of God for 10 minutes while still lying in his bed. Then he would rise, bathe and do hatha yoga before going into the cave to do puja and meditation.

Puja is the central practice of worship for Hindus. It is a tangible form of spiritual expression in which the devotee makes symbolic offerings of a seat, food, water, clothes, incense and a lamp to an image that represents the Divine. Once food is offered to the deity, it is considered to be prasad that the devotee then eats as a blessing.

The essence of puja is captured in a story of a man who piously worshipped Lord Ram every day. As hard as he prayed, however, he never had a vision of the Lord. After years of disappointment, he took his statue off the altar and put it in the corner of the room in disgust. The next day, still angry when he went to do his puja, he lit a stick of incense but tied a cloth around his statue's face, saying, "You're not going to smell this!" To his amazement, all the smoke from the incense went directly to the statue, and at that moment, Lord Ram appeared and said, "Finally, for the first time, you believe that I am here in this statue!"

For those with faith like Dhyanyogi-ji, puja is not a metaphorical ritual, but is literally the act of taking care of the living God. A renowned female Indian saint of the 20th century named Anandamayi Ma once said that she wanted her devotees to love her as if she were their child, not their parent. When devotees see God or a saint as an authority figure, she said, they may have ambivalent feelings. They may make demands rather than taking full responsibility for themselves. But if they view themselves as the parent and look upon God as the one depending on their care, their devotion will be strong and committed.

When Dhyanyogi-ji arose each morning to perform his puja, his attitude was that he was literally bathing and feeding Lord Hanuman and Lord Vishnu. He had a small statue of Hanumanji and a shaligram—a fossil that is worshipped as the embodiment of Lord Vishnu. According to the Vedas, shaligrams originated long ago, when Lord Vishnu, in order to defeat a demon who was wreaking havoc in the world, was forced to trick the demon's wife Tulsi, one of his own devotees. Tulsi cursed Lord Vishnu for his deception by turning Him into a stone, and because He understood her despair, Lord Vishnu accepted her curse. Laxmiji herself begged Tulsi to forgive the Lord, and so she did, but Lord Vishnu promised that He would continue to manifest Himself in the form of the shaligram.

Dhyanyogi-ji kept his murti of Hanumanji, his shaligram, and a Shri Yantra, the yantra of the Divine Mother formed by superimposing the symbols for the seven chakras on each other, in a silver box. When he traveled, he always carried this box with him.

After his morning puja, Dhyanyogi-ji meditated until it was time for morning arati. At Bandhwad, the priest hired by the ashram to look after the temple conducted the arati to the murtis of Hanumanji, Shri Radha-Krishna and Lord Shiva, and the villagers came to join in the singing and to receive Dhyanyogi-ji's blessings and prasad.

At the end of the arati chant, everyone remained silent and Dhyanyogi-ji alone sang songs in praise of God. He loved chanting. He said that while prayers are pleasing to the Lord, chanting makes the Lord laugh with delight. When he finished singing, Dhyanyogi-ji stood facing west on the right side of the temple, and his devotees performed an arati ceremony in his honor. With the enthusiastic words "Sadaguru deva ki jay! (Victory to the blessed Sadguru!)" the arati ended. One by one, each person approached him and bowed, touching his feet because the feet of an enlightened being radiate spiritual energy. Dhyanyogi-ji blessed them by softly patting their heads or backs and saying, "Be happy."

When the darshan was over, Dhyanyogi-ji would have tea and afterwards, at 9 a.m., someone would massage him with oil. As Dhyanyogi-ji attracted more disciples, a small group of them would massage him for at least an hour each morning to reduce the enormous amount of heat created in his body by his spiritual energy. The disciples who performed this service received special blessings because the constant touching involved in massaging the guru's body transfers a huge amount of energy to disciples. During the massage, the guru can tune into the subtle body of disciples and help them by burning away past karma, removing blocks in their spiritual evolution, and dissolving the fears and doubts that plague them.

After his massage, Dhyanyogi-ji would glance at the newspaper to keep current with world affairs, and have brief conversations with villagers and visitors before opening his mail. He always responded promptly to letters, even when he received stacks of mail, because nothing was more important to him than helping people with spiritual questions.

Visitors at Bandhwad ashram, in front of the room where Dhyanyogi-ji sat during the day and received visitors

At noon, Dhyanyogi-ji would eat his lunch, and following the meal, he would rest for an hour. Then he sat outside and greeted the villagers who stopped by to say "Sita Ram." At 4:00, he'd have a cup of chai (spiced Indian tea with milk), and then he'd take a walk along the lane that went from the ashram to the road to Radhanpur. He still had his habit of walking fast, born out of his love for running when he was a boy, so most people couldn't keep up with him.

Afternoons were dedicated to the concerns of the village. This was the time when the headman would consult with him about problems inside Bandhwad or political dilemmas occurring within the larger community. Villagers knew they could approach him to discuss an illness, an argument, bad dreams that frightened them, or problems with their crops or animals. Sometimes Dhyanyogi-ji gave advice, sometimes he gave them a mantra to repeat, and always he gave his blessing. In the initial years of Dhyanyogi-ji's tenure at Bandhwad, taking care of the villagers took up the major portion of his time and attention.

This was also the time of day when a visitor who'd heard of his reputation might approach him for guidance. Like the villagers, most visitors were afraid to meditate, but Dhyanyogi-ji would ask them to

Meeting with village elders.

chant "Shri Ram, Jay Ram, Jay Jay Ram."

If for any reason Dhyanyogi-ji had to make a trip into Radhanpur, he would go in the afternoon. Generally he traveled in the traditional way, in a cart pulled slowly by a bullock, but if there were an emergency, he mounted a horse and rode to town. He did this until he was in his early 80s.

As his afternoon of conferences ended and the day drew to a close, the villagers poured in for the evening arati. Afterwards, if there were any disciples visiting from outside Bandhwad, they sat for meditation while Dhyanyogi-ji went to the cave for his evening practices. The hours between 7:00 and 9:00 p.m. are also considered an ideal time for japa, puja and meditation. Then he would have a light supper, often consisting of only a cup of hot mung bean soup, and at 9:00 or 10:00, he'd have a glass of hot milk.

At night, people would gather for *kirtan*, the singing of devotional songs. Certain bhajans were especially dear to Dhyanyogi-ji and when he sang those, a thrill of excitement rippled through the crowd. The audience clapped their hands and repeated the phrases he sang. As they chanted together, Dhyanyogi-ji gradually increased the tempo and they all sang faster and louder until he abruptly stopped and sang the verses slowly and tenderly one last time. While the others continued to chant, Dhyanyogi-ji received massage and dozed outside until 11:00 p.m., when he'd retire to bed after everyone bowed down to him for a final blessing. But even when he slept, he always heard everything going on around him. Many people had the experience of talking nearby to him when he slept, and having him suddenly open his eyes and respond to whatever they were saying.

This was Dhyanyogi-ji's daily routine, with the exception of several occasions when he performed anusthans in the cave and had to follow dietary restrictions and maintain silence. But apart from those austerities, even after he became well known, Dhyanyogi-ji's schedule remained the same. The only thing that changed was that increasingly larger numbers of disciples visited the ashram seeking guidance, more came to meditate each evening, and many more people crowded in for kirtan at night.

From the mid 1920s until the 1950s, very few people outside of other yogis and the people living in this remote area in Gujarat had heard of Dhyanyogi-ji. Aside from his trips to Radhanpur or Palanpur, a small town near Ambaji, he stayed away from public activity. Although word of Dhyanyogi-ji's powers spread through the region, transportation was restricted in those days, so not many were able to meet him. There were several people, however, intent upon their spiritual evolution, who discovered Dhyanyogi-ji and accepted him as their guru.

One of Dhyanyogi-ji's first disciples was the Queen of Limbdi. Limbdi is a city in Saurashtra, also known as the Kathiawar Peninsula, in Gujarat. Mount Abu was a favored summer retreat for the rulers of Gujarat, and the Queen had a summer palace there.

The Queen of Limbdi was an unusual person. She was very small in stature and behaved in the manner expected of a woman of her caste and position, which at that time meant wearing a veil. But she had a sparkling presence. When her husband died suddenly, at an early age, she was left to raise a 5-year-old son. He was the rightful heir but too young to rule, so ordinarily her husband's brother would have been appointed as the ruler of the kingdom. She was a woman, had no formal education, and spoke no English, yet the Viceroy who oversaw Gujarat recognized her intelligence, integrity and fearlessness, and appointed her as guardian of the state until her son reached adulthood.

The Queen's palace was ornate, with Italian marble floors, and wooden pillars made in Paris, but more noteworthy was how creatures who were natural enemies, like snakes and peacocks, lived together in harmony on the palace grounds. At one point, a wing of the palace burned down and when it was renovated, the Queen donated it to the Ramakrishna Mission. She followed precisely the guidelines of *dharma*, and longed to pursue a spiritual path.

One day the Queen was lying in her bed taking her afternoon nap. She felt someone tugging on her pillow. Initially she

Queen of Limbdi with the prince who Dhyanyogi-ji protected several times

125

ignored the sensation because she knew no one could possibly be in her room given the palace security. But the tugging became stronger so she opened her eyes, and to her amazement, standing before her was Lord Krishna. He asked her what she would like from Him. Entirely unprepared for this encounter, her first thought was how others could benefit by indirectly receiving His darshan in the future. Without a moment's hesitation she asked, "Will you stay here while I draw you?" Lord Krishna agreed, and the Queen drew his image on her pillowcase. She kept this pillowcase for the rest of her life, and the people who have seen it have been shaken by the intensity of the energy it holds.

Despite the Queen's spiritual nature, it was unheard of for a woman in her position to travel independently, so it seemed it would be impossible for her to find a teacher and follow her dream.

The Queen's brother understood his sister's dilemma. He was also looking for spiritual guidance, and in his search, he found Dhyanyogi-ji, who was performing austerities in Mount Abu at the time. The Queen's brother wanted to test Dhyanyogi-ji thoroughly, especially before he considered introducing him to the Queen. Once he was absolutely certain that Dhyanyogi-ji was a true sadguru, he helped his sister to disguise herself and secretly sneak visits to Dhyanyogi-ji at night. When the Queen returned to her palace in Limbdi, she invited Dhyanyogi-ji to come there so he could discretely give her spiritual training.

In the early 1920s, Dhyanyogi-ji went to Limbdi and lived there for three months. He gave the shaktipat initiation to the Queen and

Queen of Limbdi chanting her own compositions of bhajans

126

taught her yogic practices. Dhyanyogi-ji said she was one of his most advanced disciples, noting how she mastered the difficult technique of astral travel. He described her as soft and gentle, yet very powerful. She had tremendous faith in Dhyanyogi-ji and followed meticulously all of his instructions for her sadhana.

On several occasions Dhyanyogi-ji used his yogic powers to see into the future and to protect the Prince of Limbdi, the Queen's son. Dhyanyogi-ji knew that there were people who wanted to seize control of the kingdom, who sought to kill the Prince and overthrow the Queen. Dhyanyogi-ji warned her that the Prince's life was in danger. Once, he foretold that the boy's food would be poisoned. At his urging, the royal servants fed the food to a cat and the cat died.

When Dhyanyogi-ji visited the Queen, a side of him appeared that was not revealed elsewhere. She had a collection of classical Indian musical instruments and several times, to the amazement of the Queen and the others present, Dhyanyogi-ji picked up one of these instruments and began to play beautifully and with great skill. His level of performance went well beyond the brief musical training he'd received during his student years. Some speculated that perhaps this was one of his siddhis.

When Dhyanyogi-ji visited her, the Queen opened her palace to all who wanted to come to meditate and be with him, and she did seva for him whenever it was possible. For his part, when the Queen visited him, he extended a little more formal hospitality than was usual in the primitive setting of Bandhwad, offering her a special seat and serving her food with extra care. But the Queen was very humble, and Dhyanyogi-ji was unabashedly thrilled by how, despite her royal background, she was so open and unassuming. Dhyanyogi-ji became visibly excited whenever he saw someone so dedicated to spiritual growth who had the potential to make great strides.

Another one of Dhyanyogi-ji's earliest disciples was a man named Dahyabhai Pandya. Mr. Pandya came from a part of India that became Pakistan after partition, and his family lost everything. Penniless, they resettled in Mumbai. Dhyanyogi-ji had tremendous respect for Mr. Pandya and his family. He and Dhyanyogi-ji had a very close and loving bond. Mr. Pandya and his daughter, Bharti, both received shaktipat. Dhyanyogi-ji later said that Bharti was an extremely advanced soul. Since she was expected to marry and raise a family, she was unable to devote herself completely to her spiritual life to achieve her full potential. Just as the Queen's progress delighted Dhyanyogi-ji, his knowledge that this young girl might not have that chance caused Dhyanyogi-ji pain. Still, for the rest of her life, Dhyanyogi-ji appeared to Bharti daily in her meditations. This is considered to be a sign of rare grace.

Dhyanyogi-ji rarely discussed what he did and where he went when he was away from Bandhwad before the late 1950s, when he began a much more public phase of his life. Sometimes he left the ashram for several days while other times he didn't return for months. Once, soon after he settled in Bandhwad, while on his way back to the ashram on a hot summer day, he was walking through a village where some women were drawing water from a well. It was noon and the heat was unbearable. He was extremely thirsty and asked for a drink. One of the women was very rude and refused to give him any water. Dhyanyogi-ji's self-restraint cracked and he blurted out, "From today, let the water of this well become salty!" Later, he found out that the water in all the wells in the area had turned salty, and he was filled with shame at the realization that while he was working to attain God and help mankind, he had behaved like this. It took him six months of doing a very severe anusthan before he was able to reverse the process and restore the fresh drinking water. This was the first time he had lost his temper since he was a young boy and hit his schoolmate. Both incidents were burned into Dhyanyogi-ji's memory, and he vowed to give up anger. His great remorse for having done anything that harmed another motivated him to repeat these stories. For the rest of his life, he never again allowed emotion to control his behavior.

Dhyanyogi-ji recounted another episode that took place when he was wandering on foot, and stopped to bathe in a river. Among the others bathing nearby was a lady who had taken off her jewelry and left it in a box under a tree on the riverbank. A monkey arrived on the scene and grabbed the box. The bather, unable to act quickly enough to prevent the theft of her valuables, ran out of the river, chasing the monkey, but he escaped up a tree. The woman was traveling alone and had no one to assist her in her dilemma. She called out to the monkey, but he kept swinging from tree to tree, finally stopping to rest on a rooftop, never loosening his grip on her jewels. While she watched helplessly, the monkey sat on the roof, opened the box and began to play with the jewelry. Seeing her despair, Dhyanyogi-ji suggested that she collect some sweets and put them on the other side of the rooftop. The woman followed his advice and offered the monkey the sweets. Immediately, the monkey dropped the jewelry and ran over to eat, and the lady was able to recover her jewelry.

Although it was unusual for Dhyanyogi-ji to relate anecdotes, he told this story as a lesson to illustrate that although we may be distracted by material things, once the soul is offered something that is truly nourishing, the soul will recognize it and go towards it, leaving the worldly objects behind.

In 1933, at the age of 55, Dhyanyogi-ji went to see Guru Gokalibaba who gave him an Ayurvedic treatment called *kaya kalpa* that restores health and youthfulness. Dhyanyogi-ji had been practicing austerities for years, and it had taken a toll on his physical body. For three months, Dhyanyogi-ji lived in a cave while receiving the treatment. Not much is known about Guru Gokalibaba's methods, but Dhyanyogi-ji reported that during the treatment he had a vision of Lord Ram.

In 1940, Dhyanyogi-ji met a very powerful yogi named Upasani Baba who, like many other saints, exhibited unusual, often paradoxical, behavior. Sometimes he hit disciples, but the individuals he struck said they attained samadhi immediately afterwards. Once he chose to remain confined in a cage for four years in order, he said, to work through his karma from a previous life. For a while, he dressed as a woman, for this same reason. When he left his body, he made what was then an uncommon choice and passed his lineage on to a woman saint, Godavari Ma. Only women were permitted to live in her ashram, and they performed *yagnas*, the Vedic fire ceremonies traditionally presided over only by Brahmin men.

Normally Upasani Baba kept silent, but when Dhyanyogi-ji arrived at his ashram, Upasani Baba instructed him to perform an anusthan of the Ram mantra. When Dhyanyogi-ji was done, Upasani Baba said, "Now you go help others."

A few years later, Dhyanyogi-ji joined with a group of yogis who assembled in the Himalayas to recite, between them, 500 *Ram Raksha Stotrams* daily for three months to help stop Hitler and bring an end to World War II. It is puzzling how these yogis, most of whom had neither an address where they could receive mail, nor access to any other available forms of communication like telephones or telegraphs, organized an effort like this. But they had their own ways of communicating.

In 1945, after the war ended, Dhyanyogi-ji walked to Nepal to meet Shivapuri Baba. The journey took him four months at a pace of 12 miles a day. During his six months in Nepal, he met Tibetan yogis, learned about a Tibetan form of meditation called *dzogchen*, and did an anusthan of the Ram mantra at a Ram temple.

Now in his late 60s, Dhyanyogi-ji decided once again to make the pilgrimage that he'd done in his father's name 40 years before. He planned to collect water from the source of the Ganges at Gangotri and carry it to the Shiva temple at Rameshwaram. This time, after descending from the mountains, he had to attend to other matters so he left the water with a disciple for safekeeping. Shortly after this, someone in the disciple's family became very ill. Drinking Ganges water at the time of death is said to help the evolution of the soul. The only Ganges water available to the family was the container Dhyanyogi-ji had brought, so they gave the water to the dying man. When Dhyanyogi-ji returned, the water he collected was gone so he was unable to complete his pilgrimage.

Unfortunately, other than this sprinkling of stories about Dhyanyogi-ji's pilgrimages, very little is known about the time between his arrival at Bandhwad and the late 1940s. During those 20 to 30 years, aside from the spiritually oriented activities he did outside the ashram, the bulk of his time was devoted to his sadhana and the welfare of the village.

There are conflicting reports about when Dhyanyogi-ji went out into the open and began to attract large numbers of students to him. Some of his older disciples say he began giving shaktipat in 1947. Others say his more intensive work with disciples began after he initiated public meditation programs in the late 1950s. But it is certain that in 1958, he began to hold public meditation programs in cities including Rajkot, Ahmedabad, Surat and Mumbai. The more time Dhyanyogi-ji spent in cities, the more widely he became known. This began another radically different period in his life.

When Dhyanyogi-ji first began teaching in public, the force of his energy spontaneously thrust those he met into deep states of meditation. There are countless stories about how touching his body healed people and brought on blissful, transcendent experiences. He soared from Bandhwad into the world like a shooting star, spreading his love and energy wherever people were open to receiving it. The powerful effect he had on spiritual seekers can only make us speculate about the effect he must have had on the people of Bandhwad as they led their ordinary, day-to-day lives. It is still a mystery how he transformed the small village that was once known as a den of thieves into a place where the only one who steals is the One who steals the heart.

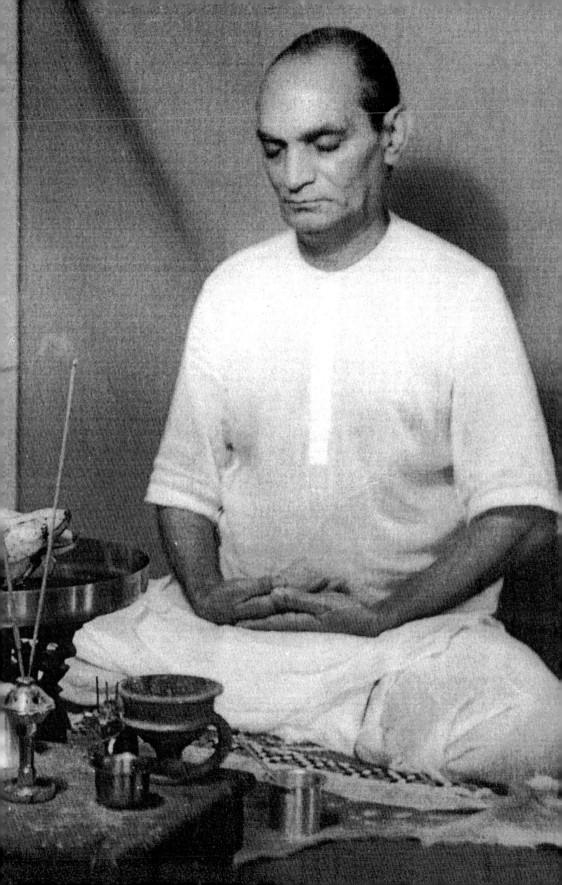

CHAPTER FIFTEEN

"THIS HOUSE IS ON FIRE"

*T*here was a man from Palanpur, a town near the Rajasthan border, who wanted desperately to receive shaktipat. He heard about a saint who had recently come out into the public and was offering the initiation, so he made the arduous trek to the saint's ashram in Bandhwad. When he arrived, he discovered that Dhyanyogi-ji had recently departed. Hearing that the master was en route to Mumbai, the man made arrangements to follow, but when he reached Mumbai, to his great disappointment, he discovered that again, he had just missed Dhyanyogi-ji. This determined soul made inquiries about the yogi's next destination and once more set off to follow his trail, but every attempt he made to meet Dhyanyogi-ji failed. This continued off and on for two years, until he had all but given up.

One day he was walking down the street in Palanpur on his way to a shop, when he saw a car drive by with "Shri Ram" written all over it.

"This is no ordinary person's car," he thought.

He looked in and saw Dhyanyogi-ji inside and started running after the car. The driver didn't notice, but Dhyanyogi-ji did, and thought perhaps they had a flat tire. He told the driver to stop.

The man ran up to the car and asked, "Are you Dhyanyogi-ji?"

"Yes."

"Get out from the car and give me shaktipat!" the man cried.

Even though Dhyanyogi-ji and his entourage were packed and ready to leave, he changed his plans and stayed overnight in Palanpur to give this man shaktipat the next day, saying, "This person is ready right now. Tomorrow, I may not be around or he may not be. This may be our last opportunity to meet."

It was around 1960 that Dhyanyogi-ji's life once again completely changed. Now in his 70's, after nearly 30 years of service in Bandhwad, his desire to help spiritual seekers exploded. Out of this feeling, and with the command of his guru who had appeared to him in meditation, Dhyanyogi-ji emerged from his years in relative obscurity to travel to big cities and begin teaching meditation and offering shaktipat. He was as anxious to give shaktipat as the man from Palanpur was to receive it.

Up until that point, he had given the initiation to only a handful of people. But from this time on, for the rest of his life, Dhyanyogi-ji was motivated solely by his desire to help people on their spiritual quests. He was on fire. No matter what toll it took on him to make himself and his energy available, nothing could hold him back. Although he still looked after Bandhwad, did his puja every day, took pilgrimages, provided for peoples' basic needs and cared for the cows, helping people progress spiritually was his burning mission. Sometimes he talked about his work as if he were a shepherd rounding up his scattered flock. He called his disciples his "lost stars."

Meditation is the cornerstone of spiritual evolution, so Dhyanyogi-ji was committed to teaching the practice to anyone who was interested. He was particularly keen on teaching householders because he wanted to demonstrate that while living in the world, people can live spiritual lives and attain realization. He sensed that the time had come for the message to be relayed that people did not have to give up everything and endure years of hardship in order to reach God. But this message was revolutionary, and was met with suspicion.

In India at this time, meditation was viewed as a private thing, something to be taught and practiced in an ashram by people who had renounced worldly life. Anyone who led public group meditations was suspected of being a charlatan, a mesmerizer trying to control people's minds.

It was even more of a taboo to discuss shaktipat out in the open, let alone to offer it to the general public. Shaktipat initiation was a secret practice, its significance carefully guarded by the yogis. It was something available only to sadhus who attained this blessing after performing rigorous austerities, practicing other forms of yoga, and providing selfless service to their guru.

At one time, Dhyanyogi-ji believed that spiritually advanced souls didn't need shaktipat, that if someone was having a strong experience of the prana, they didn't require his energy to help them along. But he discovered that without the initiation, people kept having the same experiences over and over. Without the formal initiation including the Bhuta Shuddhi mantra for purification that he had been given by his guru, students appeared to reach a plateau and get stuck. He concluded that the blocks caused by their samskaras were preventing their progress. If this was happening to these more evolved seekers, the predicament for others had to be far worse. After this realization, he broke with thousands of years of tradition and began to offer shaktipat right away to people, without any prerequisites at all.

Shaktipat establishes a link between the teacher and the student. The teacher takes responsibility for removing the karma of the student. If an initiate is sick, the teacher may manifest the physical symptoms associated with the student's illness. It was partly for this reason that yogis would only perform the ceremony on someone who had spent years in preparation and was considered pure, someone like Dhyanyogi-ji himself.

But Dhyanyogi-ji was driven by compassion. He had become convinced that without the awakening of the kundalini, spiritual progress could not take place, leaving people trapped in their false notions about life. Therefore, he was determined to offer the initiation, whatever the personal risks. He just couldn't bear to refuse anyone his help, so he trusted in God's grace and the seeker's good karma in crossing paths with him. "Each saint has his or her own way," he explained. "I believe that the very fact that the human body has been attained means that you are ready to go back from where you have come, that you are definitely ready to merge back with God. Therefore I am not of the opinion that anyone needs to pass through some strict regulations before receiv-

Bharti, a very advanced student of Dhyanyogi-ji's, having kriyas during meditation

Kriyas during meditation, Mumbai, 1961

ing shaktipat. After initiation, the kundalini will manifest kriyas as are needed by the person. Hence, I do not see any necessity of conditions for receiving shaktipat."

Dhyanyogi-ji often said that grace is like the sun that shines its warmth on everyone. Rain behaves the same way, falling everywhere, and the benevolent tree keeps its cool shadow open for all animals. Those who are open to God's grace, he said, will reap the most benefits, including, for some, the gift of shaktipat.

"Who am I to decide whether someone is worthy or unworthy? The energy itself decides that. It is enough for me to know that he or she is the child of God. I have started a *parab*, an oasis for the thirsty. Whoever wishes to quench their spiritual thirst can come to my parab without any hesitation."

Despite the incredible generosity on the part of the teacher, it is understood that the disciple is not free of responsibility after shaktipat. Discipline is essential to ensure progress. Dhyanyogi-ji used to say that shaktipat "can be had only by the grace of the guru, and can be preserved only by self-effort."

Dhyanyogi-ji's message was simple. Whenever a disciple consulted him about a spiritual difficulty, invariably Dhyanyogi-ji's advice was, "Devote yourself to meditation and japa and your heart will overflow with love for humankind." He wanted them to see for themselves what meditation could do.

It took time for the public to accept that Dhyanyogi-ji wanted only

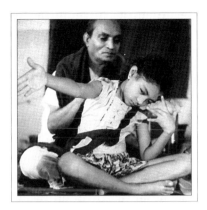
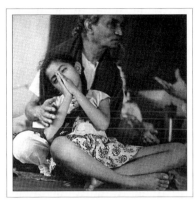

Dhyanyogi-ji assisting with kriya stage of a young disciple

to give and asked nothing in return. In the beginning, many people came to test him, but when confronted with his purity, their misgivings melted away. Once, a businessman confessed to Dhyanyogi-ji that he had attended his first meditation with a revolver concealed in his pocket because of his strong suspicion that Dhyanyogi-ji would hypnotize him. After the meditation program, impressed with the quality of his experience and the saintly conduct of Dhyanyogi-ji, he admitted his apprehensions.

In yogic tradition, a true guru does not identify her- or himself in any obvious external way. The God-realized state is not easily detected, and many people may meet saints without perceiving their greatness. But if they are receptive, Dhyanyogi-ji said, they will feel blissful, their prana will rise upwards, positive thoughts will occur to them, difficult emotions may be released, and a feeling of peace and purity will come. It was this subtle experience that brought growing numbers of people to Dhyanyogi-ji.

Many of those who sought him out questioned why they needed a teacher to accomplish the goals of meditation. "Why should I go to a yogi?" they asked. "Why can't we do things ourselves? Why put our brains on the shelf and follow another?"

Dhyanyogi-ji responded, "There are things beyond our knowledge and beyond our intellect. The yogis don't tell you to mortgage your intellect. They say you should use it, but when you get to subjects that are beyond its capacity, trust someone who knows those subjects and arts."[52]

Although it is possible to achieve realization on your own, he ex-

---

[52]Madhusudandas, *Brahmanada* 44-6.

plained, it is very difficult. A lot of time and energy can be wasted without obtaining many results, and mistakes can be made.

"If you want to go to New York," he said, "you can walk all the way, or you can ride your bike or drive a car. But these days you can also just buy an airplane ticket. That is the fastest and easiest way." The wisest thing, he advised, is to go to a qualified teacher who has the training and expertise, and take advantage of that knowledge. "Then with your own practices you will go deeper and deeper, ultimately experiencing the nature of your own true self."

Some people requested that he perform miracles. Only this, they insisted, would make them have faith in him. But Dhyanyogi-ji refused their requests, explaining, "If someone says to a millionaire, 'Unless you

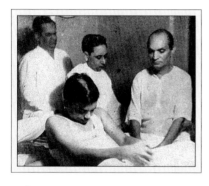

give me $1,000, I won't believe you are a millionaire,' will that millionaire give him $1,000? If someone does not believe him to be a millionaire, what does he have to lose? This is a similar situation. If I perform miracles, you will have faith in me, and if I do not, you will not have faith in me. What have I

Dhyanyogi-ji sitting with disciples in meditation, 1962

to lose? I am not interested in founding a religion, or establishing a cult. Miracles are not meant to be displayed to the world in this way. Come, sit, meditate, experience and judge for yourself."

At these public meditations, Dhyanyogi-ji, by his mere physical presence, exuded a spiritual force that activated the kundalini of those in attendance. This deeply affected the quality of the meditation that followed.

Neem Karoli Baba is another guru from a similar path. One of his disciples described a meeting he witnessed between his guru and a Buddhist master in which the two discussed how they taught meditation. "The Buddhist teacher detailed the steps of discipline in which he instructed his students, and the visualization techniques he used. When it was his Neem Karoli Baba's turn to explain his methods, he called me to him, patted me firmly on the head, and I immediately fell into meditation. This was how he taught meditation."

Ramakrishna employed the same method of teaching when he

touched Vivekananda to give him the experience of samadhi. When a realized being transmits energy to the student, the teacher puts the students in touch with his or her own true energy and divine nature. Then, that energy takes over and leads the person to realization. Nothing external is required.

This was also how Dhyanyogi-ji worked. At times, just by waving his hand in the air, he awakened the kundalini of his students. People 20 to 30 feet away from Dhyanyogi-ji spontaneously entered deep states of meditation. At other times he had students hold one of his sandaled feet in both hands. After a while, he slowly drew back his feet, and the students began having kriyas of purification.

Haresh Chudasama, a successful businessman, remembered how he was affected by Dhyanyogi-ji. Although his wife and her family were devotees, Haresh considered himself a modern man and was skeptical of yoga. Once, Dhyanyogi-ji was visiting Haresh's in-laws in Rajkot, so Haresh kept to himself.

"I wasn't interested in taking initiation. I wouldn't even sit in the room with Guruji," Haresh said, calling him by the name commonly used by disciples to show respect and affection. "I was in the next room, but still, I felt a jolt. A vibration. I fought it. I thought, this can't be happening to me! I even splashed water on myself two or three times! But still, I went into meditation. When I woke up, I fell at Guruji's feet. He was laughing, and he put his hand on my head. Finally, my mind stopped fighting.

"On another occasion, I was visiting Guruji in Mumbai and I had the strongest desire to massage almond oil into his head, as his disciples often did to relieve his burning spiritual heat. I couldn't resist my desire, so I started to do it, although no one had given me permission. I had all these questions going through my mind and I wanted peace. After only a few minutes, Guruji looked up at me, and I collapsed and fell to the floor. For two hours, I meditated, and when I woke up, all my questions had been answered. I felt tranquil. Guruji broke through all of my skepticism!"

Dhyanyogi-ji was determined that no one should be kept from this energy, even people like Haresh who resisted it. He even gave shaktipat and sent his blessings by thought, constantly supporting his disciples in their fervor to realize the self. If he knew where and when his disciples were meditating, he could send them ener-

gy at the fixed place and time. He
did not like to waste time talking
about meditation. Instead, he told
his disciples, "Sit and experience.
This is a cash business."

He later wrote that in order to
give away his energy so freely, he underwent periods where his energy was
transformed and recharged, and these
were not always pleasant experiences
for him. As he described it, kundalini
supported his efforts in an unexpected and remarkable manner by giving
him "bursts of power." He believed
that these intense periods, reminiscent of his most extreme experiences

"Meditation is food for the soul."

during his sadhana, were manifestations of his energy building up even
more, so that he could turn around and give it away without running low
and depleting his own stores.

Before he began his public meditation programs, Dhyanyogi-ji used
to stay with Dr. G. S. Rawal in . The Rawal family was very devoted
and became the founding roots of Dhyanyogi-ji's work. But, as more people
began to hear of Dhyanyogi-ji, a disciple offered the use of a large apartment in Mumbai on Proctor Road for his events. This was referred to as
the Proctor Road ashram. Dhyanyogi-ji described the following events,
which began on Febuary 8, 1965, at the Proctor Road ashram.

*While I sat for meditation, I felt a sharp wrenching in my navel.
I sensed that my kundalini was being pulled or tugged upwards,
and experienced extreme heat spreading all over my body. When
this happened, I went on a relatively restricted diet, eating only
khichari—a boiled mixture of rice and lentils, vegetables and milk.
The kriya manifestations increased daily. I developed a remarkable feeling of heaviness in the head that persisted for days, and I
could not think of any of the usual reasons that would explain this
discomfort, common enough for anyone new to sadhana.*

The wrenching sensation had risen into the windpipe and

I calculated that the prana-vayu *in the chest had overcome the pull of the* apana[35] *in the region of the abdomen. Since I had previously visualized the kundalini in myself in accordance with descriptions given by the yogis, I recognized that it was rising within me and the feeling was familiar. But I could not help wondering, after having spent so many years in meditation and having arrived at this stage in my yogic career, why I was now having the signs and kriyas that accompany the first awakening of the kundalini. I always liked to think myself as being fairly advanced on the spiritual path.*

When I rose from my meditation seat, I had an irresistible urge to write down certain Sanskrit verses that came into my mind. After interpreting the verses with the aid of several Sanskrit scholars, I came to the conclusion that even if I did not have to go through the elementary stages of spiritual evolution all over again for my own sake, I needed fresh "bursts of power" for the sake of my disciples.

This experience continued for seven unremitting days. On the first, I saw a vision of Lord Ram. He was seated, facing me in a meditation pose, against a groundless sky. The next day, I saw the rearing hood of a coiled serpent. A voice within prompted me that this was the power of kundalini. On the third day of meditation I saw a gorgeous woman draped in a white sari lying down facing me in my meditation posture. Resting her head on her palm, she looked at me affectionately. I felt that this woman was the kundalini—the adishakti—*the primordial energy in its ultimate manifestation. When I realized I had been so favored to have such a visitation by this supreme power, my heart brimmed over with grateful contentment and joy, and tears welled up in my eyes and slid down my cheek. I cannot to this day recollect the incident without sensing an acute happiness, unique and far surpassing any pleasure that I have known. The glory of the encounter lies beyond my ability to describe it.*

During this time, I had many classic physical sensations indicating the activity of the kundalini. I felt a sharp jerk or wrench in the navel and the air in my windpipe was emptied as if by sudden suction. The lungs felt drained, leaving me breath-

---

[35]Prana-vayu and apana refer to different aspects of the prana, the vital energy forces that reside in the chest and abdomen areas respectively.

less and gasping. The whole body recoiled, my head was swimming, and I experienced neither hunger nor thirst. Once, when I rose from bed at two in the morning, I felt giddy and I fell, though had no clear memory of it. It was with considerable difficulty that I was able to get up to pass urine. I felt hot, as if the body were on fire. My symptoms suggested a body temperature of 104 degrees, yet the fever did not register on the thermometer. The next day Dr. G. S. Rawal came to examine me when I was nearly unconscious. Dr. K. Pathak, another of my disciples, who took two successive readings of my blood pressure, thought my condition might be due to falling blood pressure, but Dr. Rawal believed that the fluctuating clinical readings were due to a yogic state. My blood and urine were tested in the pathology laboratory but the tests were negative. I felt my physical body to be a distinct identity from myself. I refused the medicines prescribed to stop the giddiness because I believed that the kriya manifestations were the results of kundalini action and would disappear at the subsequent stages without need of any special treatment.

Because the doctor feared the consequences of my physical state, he shifted me from the meditation center to Dr. Rawal's residence. Three or four times a day, my head heated up so much that when a pot of butter and about half a pint of oil were massaged into my scalp, it all just disappeared into the hair roots. Butter was massaged into the soles of my feet with the flat bottoms of a bellmetal utensil, considered to have a cooling effect. For 13 days, my head was regularly dressed with fresh packs of wet mud. Grated gourd was packed on my head in order to keep it cool. A pigment of the henna plant was laid on thick over the soles of my feet for the same purpose over a period of five days. For all that, my condition did not show much improvement.

Dhyanyogi-ji went on to describe how the state he was in affected the people around him:

Anyone who came in contact with me in this condition also went into meditation. There were even instances of people who became unconscious after merely touching me. On one of those days a gentleman came to join us at the center to meditate. When he bowed to touch my feet—a common way of paying one's respect to an elder person or a realized person—I put my hand on his back to acknowledge him. He at once lost external awareness and for 19 days remained dazed, in a continuous state of meditation. Later he told me that he had been barely conscious for the last 10 days and had gone to work in a state halfway between dreaming and waking. He could not remember, for example, where he had parked his car before arriving at Dr. Rawal's house. I advised him that he should resolve, by an act of will, to break the spell, to walk out of the daze. He said, "No thank you, I would not forego the peace and the inner joy for all the world." From that day on, I knew for certain that I transmitted my state of meditation to others by just the act of touching, even inadvertently.

I was still in a state of conscious meditation and physical discomfort when a lady from a well-to-do family came to visit. As she offered her salutations, I responded unthinkingly with a blessing and placed my hand on the crown of her head. Upon returning home, she felt a surging heat in her body and complained of a heavy head. She became nervous and called me to ask if she should send for a doctor. A disciple who had been present at our interview answered the telephone, and since this gentleman knew about these induced reactions, he advised her to drink a cup of warm milk with butter and sleep it off. Drinking milk and butter is a standard manner to deal with excessive heat caused by kundalini activity. She felt tolerably well on waking up, but continued to go into meditation states regularly.

Another person who came to see me at this time was a renunciate who had never succeeded in achieving a state of steady meditation. He expressed the wish that he might be allowed to massage me, thinking that it might help my respiratory circulation. While he massaged me, off he went into a daze and became quite removed from his surroundings. That also reminds me how the entire Rawal family had to take turns at the daily chore of massaging my head, for no one could stay conscious long enough to conclude the ministrations. The regimen usually started with a massage by Mrs. Rawal who soon after went into meditation, and her three sons replaced her in turns only to go off likewise. Mrs. Rawal's states lasted well over 24 hours, and someone had to make a formal prayer that she might wake up from her meditation. She was so sensitive that she could catch the spiritual vibrations from at a distance of even 15 to 20 feet.

Sometime during this confinement to bed, I decided that from now on, I would let no one touch my feet, and I made a special point of avoiding inadvertent contact with my visitors. The Queen of Limbdi called on me and invited me to go and stay with her, but I had to decline, saying that I had no wish to spread this state of meditation among people who did not seek it actively and were likely to be frightened by it.

Groups of people came to visit and went into meditation at the slightest contact. I have a natural depression in the head just below the crown where men from many parts of India still sport a tassel-like bunch of hair longer that the rest. I felt dizzy and flighty, and imagined that I had achieved levitation. I could not lie straight while asleep nor could I raise my head in order to look up. A person practicing Ayurveda, the Indian system of medicine, came to treat me. He felt my pulse and examined me, and diagnosed a cerebral blood clot. While giving this diagnosis all the serious consideration that it undoubtedly deserved, I could explain neither to myself nor to the doctor why I did not feel any of the acute pain in the head that would be expected with that condition, nor how it could be that this state was transmitted to those who came into contact with me. By this time there were about 70 people who, in a spirit of active sympathy and natural curiosity, had voluntarily contracted this meditative state from me. Their experiences were all well documented and proved the authenticity of mine. My view was that this was more than an abnormal clinical condition.

The Ayurvedic physician treating me confessed to ignorance of this kind of spiritual experience, however he prescribed moti basma, *the pulverized remains of an incinerated pearl, to cool off my head, as the feeling of intense heat persisted. I agreed to try this, and the next day, I began taking the pearl powder with butter. Twice a day, I also ate a dish made by frying the root of the lotus in butter, about 20 grams of a sweet dish made of almonds, and another 20 grams of a sweet dish made from gourd. I ate khichari and gruel as my staple diet, and two or three times between meals I drank the water from a tender coconut and orange juice. It is not that I felt thirsty, in fact, I did not at all, but the disciples insisted on pampering and feeding me as they would a child. I tried to digest all that I ate, but could not honestly say that I felt hungry. Four times a day, butter and brahmi oil, an herbal concoction with a vegetable oil base, were rubbed into my scalp.*

Despite all of this effort, my contagious state persisted. Again, a gentleman I'd not met before came to visit me, and when he touched my feet, he felt tickled as if by an insect crawling over him and entered a state of meditation. From then on, he was drawn to meditate. Another person meeting me for the first time also fell into meditation after touching me, but she was skeptical and could not persuade herself that yogic powers were so easily transmitted. She would not accept her meditation experience as genuine unless she saw an inner vision of Ganesh with her eyes closed. On one occasion while massaging me, she said to me, "I can see Shri Ramakrishna and I can see the Guru, but my experience is incomplete. I do not yet see my Ganesh, who heralds the oncoming divinity." All of a sudden she went into meditation and saw a rushing Ganesh swinging into view, and it was as if the keeper of her doubts had finally granted His blessings and released her. She was able to relax into divine meditation. When she came out of meditation, tears of joy were brimming from her eyes.[34]

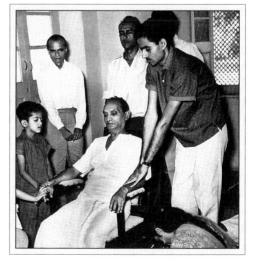

Transmission of energy, Limbdi

Dhyanyogi-ji said that during this period, he could dis-

---

[34]Dhyanyogi Madhusudandas, *Light on Meditation* (Santa Cruz, CA: Dhyanyoga Centers, 1978) 65-69.

tinctly remember incidents like these happening in Mumbai, and others in Rajkot, Ahmedabad, and in the Limbdi palace. He commented that although the individuals were quite different from one another, "in meditative communion, they eventually began to mirror and enrich my own state."

The yogis teach that there is a state

Child having devotional kriyas during meditation at Limbdi, 1964

called *turiya*, which they define as the fourth stage of samadhi. In turiya, a person

is awake but not conscious, so he cannot function normally and requires someone to take care of him. Twice during the years that Dhyanyogi-ji first went out in the open to teach meditation and offer shaktipat, he went into this state. A woman who cared for Dhyanyogi-ji one of these times said it wasn't easy to do. She would fall into meditation while cooking for him!

Kriyas in meditation at Limbdi, 1964

Stories of how anyone in physical contact with Dhyanyogi-ji would drop into meditation were common, even when he wasn't in turiya. Once seven people all entered a deep state while massaging his head, back, neck, hands and legs. Several reported that they fell into meditation after touching a flower or a garland of flowers previously worn by Dhyanyogi-ji. Some people experienced physical tremors the moment they picked up books written by him. In the Limbdi palace, there is a chair that was used by Dhyanyogi-ji on his visits, and disciples went into spontaneous meditation just by touching the empty chair.

But Dhyanyogi-ji wasn't satisfied simply knowing that his energy was affecting people in these ways. Like a research scientist, he kept looking for better ways to interact with the kundalini to help people evolve. He was fascinated with sound as a medium through which he could transfer energy. "Sound creates and sound corrects," he said.

When babies are restless and unable to sleep, a sweet lullaby can put them to sleep. When someone has abused you and spoken badly to you, its effect may last a lifetime. If you are physically injured, the wound is easy to heal, but wounds caused by words are more difficult to heal. Words can be the cause of great wars and quarrels or great love and union. The tremendous power of sounds and words is impossible for us to measure. Yogis say that the whole of creation began with sound, that sound is the cause of creation, its maintenance, and its destruction.

In 1938, I had been doing japa of the Ram mantra and practicing pranayama, when, on the full moon of Phalgun *(a month in the Indian calendar), I heard a loud explosion, like a dynamite blast. My heart began to beat very rapidly. Suddenly I started leaving consciousness, as if I were sinking into the ocean of joy and bliss. All around me, I saw circles of lights. When I was awakened, four hours had passed. My body was light, but I felt a sort of weakness. I wondered whether it was a heart attack or what, so I went to see a doctor. He took a cardiogram and with surprise, given my age of 60, he said, "Oh, Yogiraj, your heart is like a 15-year-old's. It is very strong. You have nothing to worry about."*

After that, for about 15 days I continued to hear a sound like a blast, after which I went into deep meditation. I received an answer from within that this sound was caused by the piercing of the chakras. Since then, I have had a very strong sense of the purpose and potential of sound energy.

I grew up knowing that there were mantras for any and every purpose. During fire ceremonies, I heard the priests recite very pleasing and enchanting mantras. Listening to them, I used to go into meditation. So I have known for a long time that mantras might be the best instrument for meditation.

Since 1958, at the advice of my Guru and by the grace of God, I have been singing mantras at group meditations. My thinking is that if my temperature can rise to 104 degrees from repeating mantras, why shouldn't a listener's temperature also rise? If sound can have an effect on body temperature, why shouldn't it change other things in the body such as blood pressure? If temperature and blood pressure can change by mantra singing, why couldn't brain waves be changed? And if temperatures, blood pressure and brain waves can change, why couldn't kundalini be awakened?[35]

Even if people do not consciously listen or attend to the mantras, sound is energy, and will still have an effect. Dhyanyogi-ji conducted experiments where particles similar to pollen were placed on a cloth covering the opening of a wide-mouthed jar. As he chanted the mantras, the particles took the form of the letter "Aum." Other spiritual scientists interested in this phenomenon have performed similar experiments in the last few decades that demonstrate the same results.

So Dhyanyogi-ji began to construct what he called a *mantrochar*—a series of mantras from the scriptures, sung aloud,[36]—that could be used to awaken the kundalini. He experimented with it to discover which were the most powerful mantras, what were the optimal rhythms and frequency of repetition to help the meditators. Always, he was working to help speed the progress of students and to spare them, whenever possible, the painful delays encountered in spiritual growth.

He sang the mantrochar at public meditations to stimulate the kundalini of the participants and give them a spiritual boost, a small taste of the energy passed along in shaktipat. His voice was rich and resonant.

Dhyanyogi-ji chanting mantras

But the mantrochar was not just music or melody, not just incantation. It was more like the call of a wild bird with a deep voice and a natural vibrato. Dhyanyogi-ji was calling to the souls of those listening. He said the mantrochar was "the sound of God." Dhyanyogi-ji himself was affected by the energy of the mantras as he recited them. Sometimes he swooned or wept from their intensity.

At one point, following his intuition, Dhyanyogi-ji experimented with a special mantrochar that focused on the *bija* mantras, the syllables that form the basis of all sound. He sang these bija mantras in order to create vibrations that targeted individually the components known as the "petals" of the chakras. This was like tuning the subtle body. He said that the impact of hearing this sequence of mantras was almost as powerful as shaktipat itself. It caused both physical and subtle changes.

"As long as the kundalini is dormant in a person, that person will

---

[35]Madhusudandas, *Brahmanada* xiii-xvi.

[36]The mantras chanted in the mantrochars come from the *Vedas*, the *Ramayana*, the *Bhagavad Gita* and the *Guru Gita*.

lead an unfulfilled life, an unhappy life. His perception will be limited. There are many methods to awaken the kundalini but they are very long and difficult. The seed mantra is the root of the chakra. All chakras have their own mantras, their own words, by which the chakras are shaken like a big wind shakes the leaves and branches of the trees. In like manner, by this chanting of the seed mantras, all the petals of the chakras are shaken. This causes changes in everybody's blood pressure and temperature, and activates their kundalini."

The energy he expended in singing these bijas was so great that, just as when he performed shaktipat, it literally thinned his blood. But for him, helping disciples evolve spiritually was worth any sacrifice to his health. To allow his body to recover, he never sang the bija mantrochar more than once a month. In later years he audiotaped this bija mantrochar, but because of its potency—even on tape—he instructed that no one should listen to it more than once a month, and cautioned that they should always listen to it in a group of at least 15 people.

Although we don't have scientific instruments capable of detecting subtle energy, Dhyanyogi-ji said that our brains perceive it. What enters the ear as a particular vibration is registered through the brain to the mind and the prana. The prana sends the message to the physical body, while the mind transmits it to the intellect, the intellect passes it to the ego, from the ego it goes to soul, and the soul reflects upon it and responds. Therefore, the mantrochar deeply and subtly affects the meditations of those present, and initiates a process of cleansing in them. Even the halls and homes in which the meditations were held were noticeably affected by the vibrations of the mantras. After meditation programs, people would enter these rooms and comment on feeling suddenly peaceful and happy.

Dhyanyogi-ji defied the conventional belief that meditation was a private endeavor, in part to reach more people, and also because he believed strongly in the benefits of group meditation. He explained that when people come together to meditate, their concentration improves and their meditations deepen. They balance each others' energy and their wills become stronger.

In group meditation, everyone's mind is turned inward and becomes more and more single-pointed. An extra-powerful current of prana flows outward from the meditators in all directions, and charges the atmosphere. This, mingled with the effects created by the chanting of the mantras by the Guru, creates a charge very much like an electrical impulse; it spreads through the room with the speed of wind and becomes like an activated cell in a battery. For a single individual to create an atmosphere of this intensity by his own power would call for prolonged discipline and tremendous effort. When meditators sit together in a group, the radiation of power from the group's single-pointed concentration gathers and accumulates, and this store of power helps the weaker meditators.[37]

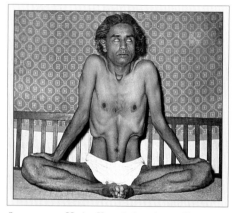

Spontaneous Hatha Yoga kriyas in meditation

At these group events, some people had a pleasant experience while others underwent emotional catharses. Some had a taste of peace and serenity, while others had kriyas, as their prana circulated through the energy pathways known as nadis to remove subtle blocks to their spiritual evolution. Dhyanyogi-ji was masterful at helping students understand and manage kriyas. He said that in order for a road to be built, all the trees in the way had to be removed and this was what caused the physical manifestations.

The most effective way to control and make use of this spiritual energy is shaktipat. With the fully awakened and stable kundalini, the energy paces itself, pulling the student to work on areas that are blocked, but never pushing the student too far. Shaktipat is a bestowal of grace, and it establishes a lasting subtle bond between the sadguru and the disciple. In essence, the guru promises to do whatever it takes to bring the disciple to God-realization. "This is a two-way relationship," Dhyanyogi-ji said. "The disciple must surrender, and the guru must accept the responsibility of taking him to the final stage."[38]

The risks for the teacher are very real. On a number of occasions Dhyanyogi-ji became seriously ill after giving shaktipat. In 1971, he gave shaktipat to 300 people in a two-month period, and he absorbed so

[37]Madhusudandas, *Light on Meditation* 30-1.
[38]Madhusudandas, *Brahmananda* 46.

much on a karmic level that he began to exhibit symptoms of disciples' illnesses. For example, two or three days after a disciple who was afflicted with tuberculosis took shaktipat, Dhyanyogi-ji began to manifest all the classic symptoms of the disease. He developed a cough, a fever, and general weakness in the body. His disciples became alarmed and wanted him to get a chest X-ray. Dhyanyogi-ji seemed unconcerned and said, "Don't worry. Everything will be all right in about 15 days."

One disciple who was a physician was not convinced, and insisted that Dhyanyogi-ji get the X-ray. Dhyanyogi-ji explained that his illness was a yogic reaction to shaktipat and nothing would show up on the X-ray, but the doctor persisted. When Dhyanyogi-ji explained his viewpoint on a certain matter to his disciples and they remained skeptical, he did not insist that they believe him. Rather, he thought, "having spoken with love, let him or her learn from experience." So, Dhyanyogi-ji had the X-ray. When the doctor saw that the results were negative, he fell at Dhyanyogi-ji's feet and humbly said, "This is a new experience for me. The outer signs of tuberculosis are so unmistakable, yet there are no signs of it on the X-ray." Dhyanyogi-ji smiled at him, but it was not the self-satisfied smile of someone who has been proven right. Instead, there was the affection and joy of a father whose child could now understand the truth.

After 15 days, Dhyanyogi-ji's symptoms disappeared.

Some time later, a woman requested initiation from Dhyanyogi-ji and he consented. As it happened, she suffered from hemophilia, and her condition was such that it wasn't appropriate for her to receive shaktipat. However, Dhyanyogi-ji only learned about the problem an hour before the initiation was to occur. Not wanting to disappoint the woman, he said, "Let her come. I will not touch her. I will touch a flower to her from a distance."

But when it came time for the initiation, he ignored his vow and placed the flower directly on her head. As his divine energy flowed into her, the initiate's disease entered his body. The very next day Dhyanyogi-ji began to bleed from his genitals. For four days the bleeding continued unabated. He lost his appetite and experienced the fatigue that comes with a full day's labor. He was so weakened that he discontinued some of his regular hatha yoga practices, including one that focused on his stomach—*uddiyana-bandha*—which he had been doing for many years.

Without this exercise, his digestion was impaired. Even the thought of an extra cup of tea made him feel nauseated. Dhyanyogi-ji said of this incident, "I have not experienced this degree of weakness in 15 years." Although it appeared to have been a mistake when Dhyanyogi-ji touched this disciple and developed a painful illness, after shaktipat, the woman's disease gradually diminished.

Four months later, some disciples from Ahmedabad came to a retreat at the Ambaji temple, only to find Dhyanyogi-ji in poor health, lying huddled, wrapped in a blanket. Ordinarily he never tired of talking with disciples, but this day he panted breathlessly after only a few words and he had a hacking cough. When they asked about his health, Dhyanyogi-ji passed off their questions, saying he had a cough only because it was winter. Soon these devotees realized that he had given this reply to reduce their anxiety. What actually happened was that a saint named Bhashkarananda from Kerala in south India, had come to Bandhwad hoping to receive shaktipat. He came on the recommendation of Swami Shri Vijaykrishnadev Bharati, a learned saint from Kashi, who after spending several months with Dhyanyogi-ji, had given up his own ashrams to help with Dhyanyogi-ji's work.

Bhaskarananda was very devoted. He served Dhyanyogi-ji well, without any self-importance despite his own spiritual accomplish-

Dhyanyogi-ji blessing disciples

ments and reputation. He attended to Dhyanyogi-ji throughout the retreat, day and night, focused only on his seva. Despite his purity, he had one bad habit. He smoked. When his desire to smoke became too strong to resist, he would hide in a corner so that Dhyanyogi-ji wouldn't see him.

One night, he sneaked away to smoke, but in the darkness he didn't notice a dog lying beside him. The animal bit him and Bhaskarananda required medical attention, so his secret was out. As a side effect of the rabies shot he received, he developed a severe fever and cough.

Dhyanyogi-ji gave him shaktipat, even though Bhaskarananda was sick, and then Dhyanyogi-ji fell ill for three weeks. During that span of time, however, Dhyanyogi-ji appeared to be very content.

At one point, his disciples became so worried about his health that they urged him to impose restrictions on who could receive the initiation in order to protect him. But, as he put it, the work of saints is to spread fragrance, like an incense stick, even at the cost of their lives. When Dhyanyogi-ji heard his disciples' suggestion, he argued, "Should I not take the pains of my disciples upon myself?" and issued the warning, "No one should be prevented from coming to me. This house is on fire, let everyone take as much as they can."

His disciples were eventually able to convince him to rest for several months at the ashram in Bandhwad. Later, he began taking six months off every few years in order to recuperate from the wear and tear on his physical body. In spite of the accusations of skeptics and the risks to his physical well being, Dhyanyogi-ji joyfully continued with his work, helping people lost in worldly desires realize the nature of true, permanent happiness. And most important to him, he offered shaktipat, the gift of the lineage that Parmeshwardsji had passed on to him. This was the treasure that Dhyanyogi-ji was burning to give.

Dhyanyogi-ji once said that whenever he met people, he took X-rays of their past, present and future. He wanted to see into their hearts. Some people were like dynamite, he said. He'd touch them once and they'd blast off. Others were like coal; it was hard to get them started, but once they did, they burned very well. Still others were like wood: difficult to get started, and then you had to keep interacting with them to keep them burning. And finally, there were those who were like stone. Dhyanyogi-ji said, "My job is to turn stones into humans, and humans into gods."

CHAPTER SIXTEEN

A FAMILY IN SERVICE

*D*hyanyogi-ji soon had disciples all over Gujarat—in Rajkot, Radhanpur, Porbandar, Surat and Ahmedabad—as well as in Maharashtra, Madhya Pradesh, Bengal, Kerala and his home state of Bihar. He was open to all, and did not limit himself to serving just Hindus. For him, his work in giving shaktipat and teaching meditation transcended artificially created boundaries of caste, religion or race; Kundalini Maha Yoga is a universal science.

Though his name had become known and as many as 500 people attended his public programs, Dhyanyogi-ji said from the very beginning that his following would be small. In 1962, not long after he started his first public meditations in Mumbai, he told a few disciples, "Many will come but very few will remain." This was not a complaint, but a prediction. "Let me have a few disciples, but they should be the best. When you buy wheat and it is full of rocks, then you must spend time sorting out the rocks. I'd rather not do that, but instead spend all of my time improving the wheat."

So Dhyanyogi-ji collected a select group of disciples, and he knew them all personally. Among them were certain people with whom he had even closer, more significant relationships. Once Dhyanyogi-ji was asked, "Who is your most sincere disciple?" Immediately and without hesitation, he answered "Dr. Kedarnath Pathak."

Dr. Pathak was introduced to Dhyanyogi-ji in 1961 by his brother-in-law, Kedarnath Rawal. Rawal was a Sanskrit scholar, well versed in the scriptures. He had lived in Benares, a city filled with yogis and saints, and home to a prestigious university known for its curriculum on Hindu philosophy. There he had contact with many spiritual teachers. But, he said, he had never known anyone like Dhyanyogi-ji. Dhyangyogi-ji's energy, simplicity and practical knowledge impressed Rawal so much that although he had never before taken a guru, he decided to request initiation from Dhyanyogi-ji. When Rawal received shaktipat, the kundalini pierced all his chakras at once, so that he became liberated in that very moment. Of the thousands of seekers who came to Dhyanyogi-ji for shaktipat, only three or four people had this immediate experience of self-realization.

Rawal knew that Pathak was pursuing a spiritual life. When Kedarnath Pathak was barely 15, inspired by the writings of saints like Swami Rama Tirtha, Ramakrishna, Swami Vivekananda and Swami Ramdas, he began meditating on his own. Some yogic techniques shouldn't be attempted without the guidance of a teacher, nonetheless, young Kedarnath was so eager to advance that, for example, he started doing breathing exercises in earnest, after reading Swami Rama Tirtha's pranayama instructions. In spite of his lack of guidance, his meditations were deep, he had some auspicious visions, and he attained brief moments of intense bliss.

At 25, Kedarnath met his first teacher, Anand Lahiri Mataji, a 65-year-old yogini from Kutch. She initiated him as a disciple and personally instructed him in *bhastrika pranayama*, known in the West as the "breath of fire." He experienced dramatic kriyas while practicing this pranayama, bouncing up and down and moving from one end of the room to the other without incurring any physical injuries. Unfortunately, after knowing her for only two years, Mataji took *mahasamadhi* (the conscious withdrawl of the prana from the physical body), and Kedarnath was once again without a guru.

Five years later, Kedarnath met another accomplished yogi named

Asimanand Saraswati. He lived in the wilds, and animals came and sat with him. He could change the speed of an electric fan across his room by a movement of his hands. However, he rarely transmitted his power to his disciples though shaktipat, and he left his body only a few years after Kedarnath met him.

For nearly 30 years Kedarnath practiced on his own, with impressive discipline. Each morning, he said his prayers and meditated. But he was always searching for another guru and anytime he heard of teachers who intrigued him, he went to meet them. In 1960 Kedarnath went to Swami Vishnu Tirtha's ashram to meet this renowned shaktipat guru. On the third evening of his stay, he received shaktipat quite unexpectedly.

"I was leaning on a low wall and facing Holy Mahatmaji. The sun was shining on his face. He started staring into my eyes and thence into my body. I held his stare and gazed into his sparkling eyes. The power emanated from his eyes like cool moonlight, and flowed into mine. Then I could feel it spreading all over my body. The process went on palpably for over a minute, during which I felt happy."

Four days later at dawn, he was participating in a guru puja, a devotional cermony, when Vishnu Tirtha began to chant mantras. "Immediately I began to tremble violently and jump about in *padma-sana* ("full lotus" pose), chanting 'Aum' loudly. I heard the divine sound of a blown conch shell coming from within my body. Feeling profound peace and bliss, I began crying tears of joy. Then I heard the internal divine sound of the low chirping of thousands of sparrows. For the rest of my life I continuously heard this sound during my waking hours. Only during meditation did the sparrows fall silent."

Kedarnath persevered with his sadhana. He meditated regularly and gradually became more detached from worldly temptations and transient pleasures. He said that joy rushed in to fill the void left by these distractions. But in spite of his concentrated mind, deep meditations and obvious progress, his kriyas continued. On May 11, 1962 he had a particularly dramatic bout of kriyas and a flashing glimpse of samadhi. It was soon after this experience that his brother-in-law took him to meet Dhyanyogi-ji at the Proctor Road ashram.

Kedarnath recalled that when he entered the room where Dhyanyogi-ji was sitting, he found Dhyanyogi-ji meditating with his eyes half open, and it seemed to him that Dhyanyogi-ji was observing him closely.

"I felt mildly electrified by his look, and I realized that he was engaged in weighing my past, present and future."

Kedarnath described to Dhyanyogi-ji his years of sadhana, and told him how it had taken him 30 years of searching to find a shaktipat master. When Dhyanyogi-ji heard this, his eyes filled with tears and he said, "I too had to wander and undergo hardships for 30 years to find my ultimate guru." He requested that Kedarnath return the next evening for meditation.

When Kedarnath arrived at Proctor Road the following day, Dhyanyogi-ji asked him to sit for meditation in his usual manner. Immediately Kedarnath began to have kriyas and went into meditation. After observing him Dhyanyogi-ji said, "You have received shaktipat, but your ajna chakra (third eye) is still not open. It is the most difficult chakra to open, but come tomorrow and I shall open it for you."

The next day Dhyanyogi-ji instructed Kedarnath to say a sankalpa before going into meditation so that he would not experience kriyas. Kedarnath recollected his experience quite clearly.

"The only thing I remembered before going into dhyan was that I felt that I had been touched by a flower in the region of the ajna chakra. I lost all awareness of the body as well as of the outside world and forgot myself completely in a resplendent ecstasy and a deep repose. My mind was totally oblivious to the city, and my ears were deaf to its noises. For a while I saw a clear vision of a vortex of blowing wind in the region of my sahasrara. Even this lasted but for a while. My temple was cold and I began to revive from my heavy stupor of samadhi, my leaden lids only half beginning to open. I returned to waking consciousness after an hour. I felt that I had been in a state of samadhi for only about five to ten minutes and I longed to return to that state. I had lost all awareness of time and space."

Others present in the room later reported that Dhyanyogi-ji had, from a distance, merely made a pushing motion towards Kedarnath. Immediately, the hair on Kedarnath's head stood straight up and he went into samadhi. Dhyanyogi-ji confirmed this as a sign of a successful samadhi, resulting from the pressure of pranic currents in the head. From that day on Kedarnath never experienced kriyas again. He could enter samadhi easily in any circumstance.

"Here I was, I had spent three-quarters of my life in the desert of solitude without a guru to guide me, trembling and falling along the way. To climb to the limit of samadhi had always been an ambition of mine since childhood. I owe it to the conferring of grace and power on me—the blessing of shaktipat—by my guru Dhyanyogi-ji, who I believe, enjoys divine sanction."

Over the years, their unique relationship blossomed into a beauty that defies description. Their love was beyond the ordinary, their connection on another plane entirely. Often when Dhyanyogi-ji talked about Kedarnath, tears welled up in his eyes. Kedarnath assisted Dhyanyogi-ji in ways that only the two of them were aware. Even his own family members were not privy to the details of how he served his beloved guru. Kedarnath often quoted Jesus's famous saying, "Don't let the left hand know what the right has done."

Through contact with Dhyanyogi-ji, Kedarnath became saturated with divine love. His every glance, kind word and graceful movement radiated compassion. Publicly he spread Dhyanyogi-ji's message by becoming an ambassador for his guru. He validated Dhyanyogi-ji's words by being a living example of his teachings. The honest simplicity of his life, his devotion to his guru and his service to others deeply affected those who came into contact with him. One American student felt her heart open upon first meeting Dr. Pathak. She suspected that he was an enlightened being because she could viscerally feel his level of purity. When she expressed how blessed she felt in his presence, Kedarnath simply and serenely replied, in what seemed to her a double entendre, "We are all God, if we only just realized it."

There were many experiences during his time with Dhyanyogi-ji that Kedarnath found memorable. "We used to hold group meditations

Dr. Kedarnath Pathak on right, Guru Purnima, 1971

at the Proctor Road Ashram," he said. "One evening, some disciples came early. Guruji was sitting on a wooden chair. He asked several disciples to hold the four legs and handles of the chair, and he asked another to rub oil on his head. To my surprise, the disciples who held the chair and the one rubbing his head with oil all became drowned in deep meditation. Wood is not a conductor of electricity, so we couldn't understand how Guruji passed his divine electric power through the wooden chair to those disciples!"

Kedarnath also recalled the experience of his friend and consultant, a Parsi plastic surgeon named Dr. Sorab Mehta. "My friend was a sincere devotee of Shri Ram," Kedarnath explained. "When I asked him if he would like to meet my Guruji and offer his respect with flowers, Dr. Mehta said, 'Yes, yes, I shall be very happy to see him.'

"One Sunday morning, I took Dr. Mehta to the ashram. Beforehand, I advised him to sit for meditation if Guruji asked him to do so. When we arrived, Dr. Mehta offered flowers at Guruji's feet, and soon Guruji asked him to sit for meditation in the adjoining meditation hall. As Dr. Mehta sat with his closed eyes, Guruji just touched his finger in between his eyebrows. At once, I saw him sinking down into meditation. After some time, the expression on his face became fierce, like going from Dr. Jekyll to Mr. Hyde. Some time later, this expression disappeared and he started softly smiling. With his eyes closed in meditation, he got up, took a walk around the hall, and bowed to the murti of Shri Hanumanji that had been placed on an altar adorned with flowers. Then he sat down again and remained in meditation for an hour more. Since he didn't wake up spontaneously, Guruji softly tapped his head to awaken him. At first, Dr. Mehta was quite drowsy, but once he was more alert, Guruji asked him, 'What was your experience during your meditation?' My friend answered, 'Oh Guruji, I got what I have always wanted! I saw a vast ocean of white and blue brilliant light. Oh Guruji, I saw my body sitting opposite me.'"

Kedarnath had some of his most moving experiences with Dhyanyogi-ji's energy through his work as a physician. In 1966, after being close to Dhyanyogi-ji for several years, Kedarnath went to have Dhyanyogi-ji's darshan at the flat of another disciple from Mumbai named Kanu Patel. When Kedarnath bowed to leave, Dhyanyogi-ji said, "Just move your palm on your patients' diseased bodies and they will be cured."

"As a medical man," Kedarnath later reflected, 'how could I believe this? Days and months passed, and I totally forgot the incident. One day, one of my patients from Parla phoned me to come and see his servant's only son, aged 18 years, who had diarrhea and vomiting. When I arrived the patient was lying on a blanket, below the staircase of the building. His elderly father was sitting near him, in a state of great depression. I examined the boy, and found he was severely dehydrated. His eyes were sunken, his pulse feeble and his tongue dry. All of his extremities were cold. I diagnosed the boy as having gastroenteritis, and I felt that if he received proper treatment, his life could be saved. I advised the father to get his son into Kashirbai Infectious Hospital where he would be given intravenous glucose saline to combat his severe dehydration. I told the father I would give him a note for his admission to the hospital, and promised him that all his treatment would be free.

"The father was reluctant to send his son to the hospital and said to me, 'Doctor, you treat him. I don't want to send him to the hospital.' Tears started rolling from his eyes, and I was deeply moved with sadness at seeing his depressed face and tears. At that moment, involuntarily and without my conscious awareness, the palm of my right hand moved across the patient's abdomen, and I began telling his father, 'It is God who may cure your son, I am afraid I am unable to save him.'

"That same evening, at 6:00 p.m., the father came to me saying that his son was much better and asking me what food he should give to him! I was surprised and overjoyed to hear this good news, and told him to give soft rice, buttermilk, apple juice, and so on, to his son.

"At 8:00 p.m., I started to have loose watery diarrhea and vomiting. I knew I had somehow contracted gastroenteritis, but I could not figure out the cause because I never eat any food outside my home. I did not take any food that night. I took some medicine, but it did not give me much relief. I was thinking of calling a colleague to give me an intravenous glucose saline, but by then it was midnight and I did not want to trouble him. The next morning, I felt better, although still very weak. For the next three days, I kept trying to find out the cause of my gastroenteritis, until I remembered the blessings Guruji had given me that night at Kanubhai Patel's home. At once, I wrote a letter to Guruji telling him all that had happened. He wrote back to me, 'Pathak, the diseases of some patients may be transferred onto your body. Your body will suffer, but you won't die and the patients will be cured. In other cases, the diseases of the patients may not enter your body, and they also will be cured.' I wrote to Guruji, 'If the diseases of my patients are transferred to my body, they are welcome, because someday, my body is going to be lifeless.'"

This was not the only time that one of Kedarnath's patients was mysteriously healed after Kedarnath's moved the palm of his right hand over the patient's body. "I never use this blessed technique, because it is against my principles," said Kedarnath. "What happens is without my knowledge and awareness and is always involuntary. It is all the work of Guruji. He makes me the medicine. It is only his divine power working through me that cures my patients."

Kedarnath had five sons, ranging in age from 10 years old to 27. His eldest son, Harivadan, was also a physician. "One day, Guruji told me that Harivadan would be a great believer in God and Guru," recalled Kedarnath. "This was hard for me to believe, because to my knowledge, Harivadan was an atheist. Once, when Guruji and some disciples were invited to our home for prasad, he left the house to avoid seeing Guruji.

"Guruji often stayed at Dr. Rawal's place in Mumbai, and had left his little murti of Hanumanji for puja with them. Guruji was about to leave for the Bandhwad ashram for the fire ceremony, and Dr. Rawal and his family were going as well, so Guruji told Dr. Rawal to give me the murti so I could do the puja during Rawal's absence from Mumbai. I brought the murti home on a Sunday. As usual, the next morning at 5:00 a.m., I sat down to meditate in front of the murti. After some time, I felt a heavy round article on my lap, but soon it disappeared.

"When I got up from my meditation, I noticed that Harivadan was behaving very strangely. He was walking aimlessly here and there with a vacant look in his eyes. His mother forced him to sit down for breakfast, but he hardly ate a thing. That night, he woke me frequently, saying, 'Papa, I have sinned a lot by behaving rudely to you. Please forgive me.' I tried to calm him, but two days passed in this same way. I was filled with worry and anxiety for my son. Fearing that he must be schizophrenic, I consulted a psychiatric specialist named Dr. Bahadia, who administered electric shock treatments to him for two days. At the same time, I sent a detailed letter to Guruji at Bandhwad. In reply, I got an urgent telegram from Guruji, telling me to stop all the medical treatment, and reassuring me that my son would be alright within a week. I followed Guruji's instructions, and gradually, over the course of a week, Harivadan became normal again.

"Once he was better, I asked my son, 'What happened to you?' He answered, "Papa, I had a dream on Monday morning in which Guruji told me to bow to you and to Hanumanji.' It was his head that was in my lap during my meditation! Furthermore, he told me, 'As I bowed to Shri Hanumanji, beautiful white rays of light came from Him and entered my body through my eyes, and then I don't know what happened.'

"After a few days, I received a letter from Guruji, telling me that he had given shaktipat to my son from Bandhwad. After this event, Harivadan became a great believer in Guru and God, and Guruji started staying at my place in Mumbai."

Once Dhyanyogi-ji began staying the Pathak's, he would remain for long periods of time, something he didn't normally do. He commented once, "The entire family loves me, so I love to stay here." He said that he got some of the best *chapatis* (flat bread) at the Pathak's residence, because Mrs. Pathak took such great care of his meals.

Shortly after Kedarnath received shaktipat he took his two youngest sons, Sandeep and Deepak, aged 10 and 12, to meet Dhyanyogi-ji. Deepak was a little reluctant. He was in the sixth grade and was more interested in playing with his friends than in meditating, but he would never do anything to displease his father.

When they entered the room where Dhyanyogi-ji was sitting, Kedarnath instructed his sons to bow down before his guru. "Even though bowing is customary in India," recalled Deepak, "I had been attending a Roman Catholic school, so I'd never bowed down before and I was inwardly uncomfortable. Guruji blessed us and gave us prasad, and would have excused us, but my father said, 'They are here to meditate.' Accustomed to my father's spiritual ambitions for us, I said to myself, Here we go again!"

Dhyanyogi-ji instructed the boys to do some deep breathing while he stood in front of them. Immediately Deepak started to have kriyas and saw a vision of the sun. After about 20 minutes Dhyanyogi-ji woke the boys up from meditation and said, "These children have extremely good samskaras. Their kundalini has just awakened in my presence."

Later Deepak described his experience of this first encounter with Dhyanyogi-ji.

"The energy pouring out of Guruji's eyes was so profound that I could not look into them for more than a few seconds," he remembered. "At that time, he had collected all this energy and had done only a handful of shaktipat initiations, so his energy was more than most people could handle. The love he poured out was so immense that I have never felt or experienced anything like that from any person to this day. He truly gave unconditional love. I fell deeply in love with him that very first day."

When Dhyanyogi-ji began staying with the Pathaks during his visits to Mumbai, he spent time with Deepak and Sandeep, teaching them hatha yoga and meditation. A year after they'd met, when Deepak was 13 and Sandeep 11, Dhyanyogi-ji was preparing to leave Mumbai and go with the Rawals to Matheran, a quiet hill station between Mumbai and Pune. He asked the boys to do puja to his Hanumanji murti during his absence.

Deepak protested, saying, "I don't know how to do puja. I don't even know the *Hanuman Chalisa*."[39]

"Do whatever you know," Dhyanyogi-ji replied. "You can read the *Chalisa* from a book."

"One day, while performing the puja," Deepak recalled, "I was overcome by a strong urge to close and latch all the windows in the room. As Sandeep and I did the *Chalisa*, we heard a loud bang as if someone had opened the window from the inside and the window had flown open. Outside the window stood Hanumanji in his full form! In Catholic school, I was taught that Hanumaniji didn't really exist. 'How can God be in the form of a monkey?' But here I was, having His darshan, for sure!"

Kedarnath was present on this occasion, and he wrote the following much more detailed account of it: "Guruji had gone to Matheran and asked Deepak and Sandeep to perform puja at the Proctor Road ashram. One Sunday morning, I was at the ashram with a few other disciples. The ashram was on the fourth floor, so we had to keep all the windows tightly latched to protect us from the strong winds. All of us were surprised to notice that both boys were performing puja with their eyes closed. They prepared a flower garland, sandalwood paste, and ghee-soaked cotton for the arati.

"After some time, one side window opened with a great noise, though it had been firmly latched. We all ran to see what had happened, but at that same moment, Deepak and Sandeep, their eyes still closed, ran to the window holding a small pot filled with water. They washed the threshold of the window and both of them made gestures as if call-

---

[39]The *Hanuman Chalisa* is a 40-verse devotional song about Hanuman, well-known in India, that Dhyanyogi-ji sang as part of his daily worship.

164

ing somebody from the sky. After some time, they again sat down in front of Hanumanji's murti and went into deep meditation.

"As I was curious to know how both of them could do all of this with their eyes closed, I got up and lifted the upper right eyelid of my son's eye. To my surprise, I saw only the white sclera of the eyeball; the rest had rolled upward above the eyelid and could not be seen.

"Some time after the meditation, both boys got up, went over to the open window, bowed and made gestures of goodbye. When they were fully awake, I asked them, 'What were you doing like lunatics with your eyes closed?' With great surprise and joy, they said, 'Didn't you see Shri Hanumanji coming from the sky and entering the hall through the window? We performed His puja!' All of the rest of us present were unfortunate, because we could not see Shri Hanumanji with our physical eyes, but Deepak and Sandeep saw Him with their spiritual eyes."

Several years later, Kedarnath arose from his meditation one morning and said to Dhyanyogi-ji, "I have five sons. I would like to give you one for your work."

Dhyanyogi-ji accepted this offer, saying, "When the time comes, I will take Deepak."

This turn of events was daunting for the now 15-year-old Deepak Pathak. But Dhyanyogi-ji had touched his heart deeply. Not only was he impressed by Dhyanyogi-ji's humility and his compassion, "his emotion to lift others in the spiritual sense," as Deepak worded it, he was amazed at Dhyanyogi-ji's strength. He listened with awe when Dhyanyogi-ji told his students, "Don't worry. Give all your worries to me."

"Guruji had reached a level of perfection," Deepak said. "That's why he had the strength and the ability to say to hundreds that came to him not to worry, not to have any fear, but to give these to him. When you meet a person for a few minutes or a few hours, everything is nice and pink and rosy, but the more you live with the person, the more different circumstances you experience and witness with the person, the more you know who the person really is. I watched Guruji for years and I know he was a true saint."

At first, Dhyanyogi-ji was like a wise, loving, and protective grandfather for Deepak. He began to expose the young man to some of the spiritual wonders of India by bringing him along on pilgrimages.

When Deepak was 16, he and his mother went with Dhyanyogi-ji

Mrs. Pathak performing puja to Dhyanyogi-ji

to Vrindavan, the ancient city in northern India that was the birthplace of Lord Krishna. While there, they paid a visit to one of the powerful temples. Krishna temples often feature a statue of the form of Baby Krishna lying in his cradle, and part of the act of worship is to rock the cradle. Deepak's mother wanted to rock the cradle in this temple, but the priests kept insisting on larger and larger donations before they would allow her to do it. Finally, annoyed with the priests for being so greedy, Dhyanyogi-ji told his mother, "You have rocked your children enough. You need not worry about rocking the Krishna statue."

Deepak also recollected a trip he took with Dhyanyogi-ji to visit a disciple. "We left at 2:00 in the morning to drive from Ahmedabad to Mahabaleshwar, a resort in the mountains in Maharashtra, to visit a disciple who owned a power loom factory that operated 24 hours a day. The driver was driving so slowly that although we had hoped to stop in Mumbai for the night, it was evident that we wouldn't make it. It was obvious from his driving that the driver was exhausted. Guruji said, 'This guy is going to kill us! We'd better stop!' But where could we go?

"Then Guruji remembered that he had a disciple named Keshu who lived nearby. He told us, 'This man has been calling me asking when will I come to see him. Well, we're in his town now, so let's find him.' He looked up the address, since the disciple had no phone, and we drove to Keshu's house.

"Guruji got out of the car and called up to his disciple, from the street, 'Wake up, Keshu! It's me. I've finally come.' Keshu looked out the window, rubbing his eyes.

"'It's me! Open the door,' cried Guruji.

"Two carloads of exhausted people poured into Keshu's apartment, and fell asleep on the floor. This was not an uncommon occurrence. Without notice, we'd arrive at a disciple's home at odd hours and a group of us would be welcomed by the disciple, thrilled to have Guruji bless his home."

Sometimes Dhyanyogi-ji would bring Deepak with him when he went home to the ashram. Bandhwad was such a remote place that there was nothing else to do there except spiritual practices, so Deepak began his sadhana.

When Deepak tried to analyze things or sought more background information about the practices, Dhyanyogi-ji answered "Don't get lost in all that. Just meditate. Repeat Ram's name."

"Guruji would always brush off my questions about the details of meanings of things saying, 'Don't ask why, just *do* it. The important thing is to *become* Brahma, not to know how many hands and heads he has. You don't need to know all these details, you just need to have a basic understanding, feeling and attitude. It's the energy that touches your heart and brings you to divinity.'"

In 1969, when Deepak was 20, he did a particular anusthan in which the student writes the mantra "Ram" 125,000 times on little slips of paper and then feeds the mantras to fish. The trick to getting the fish to ingest the mantras is to make a dough, wrap the pieces of paper in it, and then dry the packets in the sun. Once they are baked, they can be tossed into the water. Fish are attracted by the dough, and when they eat it, they eat the mantras as well.

After he wrote the mantras, Deepak had the desire to feed them to the fish in the Ganges River at Rishikesh. He asked Dhyanyogi-ji to go with him and Dhyanyogi-ji said he would.

Unfortunately, Deepak had been misinformed about the proper method for wrapping the mantras. He had been told to just use dry flour to coat the slips of paper. "When we got to Rishikesh," Deepak remembered, "Guruji asked me, 'What's this?!' and told me what I was supposed to have done. As it was, the flour just blew away and the fish wouldn't touch the mantras!

"Guruji had written some mantras himself, so we prepared these in the correct manner and offered them. Guruji reassured me saying, 'The significance of the anusthan is writing the mantras. Feeding the fish is a way to offer the anusthan. But the important part was the writing, so don't worry.'"

As he got older, Dhyanyogi-ji began to prepare Deepak to do his seva. When they traveled, Dhyanyogi-ji woke at 3:30 in the morning, so someone had to wake up even earlier to make his tea and bring him hot water for bathing. Dhyanyogi-ji would wake Deepak to do these chores by softly, but persistently, chanting his name, "Deepak, Deepak, Deepak." Deepak said that this is one of his sweetest memories.

Though Dhyanyogi-ji could be indulgent—he characteristically took on the mistakes of others and fixed whatever karma might have resulted from them— he never tolerated sloppiness. He impressed upon Deepak that that when any soul reaches enlightenment, it has a tremendous impact on all of humanity. He taught Deepak that the work they were doing was about service, attaining realization for the welfare of all humankind.

Deepak's most profound experience happened while doing an anusthan in the cave along side of Dhyanyogi-ji.

"Guruji was sitting to the right of me. I heard a loud sound from where he was sitting. I opened my eyes and saw that Guruji had completely changed into the form of Lord Hanuman. He remained this way for a little while, then changed back." This was not an inner experience. Deepak was fully awake when it happened, and it convinced him that Dhyanyogi-ji was no different from Lord Hanuman himself.

"He was everything for me. His word was God to me. I just did it. No whys, ifs, or buts. It wasn't that he was forceful. It's just that he saw what was good for you and told you. I learned that if I did what he said, it would benefit me."

In the context of his extremely close relationship with Dhyanyogi-ji, Deepak's faith and humility grew very deep. An astrologer once told him that he would never achieve anything great, but he would never miss doing his puja every day. This reading pleased Deepak, who had come to identify with his seva. True to his father's word, Deepak's life became dedicated to service to his guru.

Standing left to right: Harivadan, Nayan, Dr. Kedarnath Pathak, Mrs. Jaya Pathak, Nitin, Deepak.
Seated left to right: Raju (Harivadan's son), Dhyanyogi-ji, Sandeep.
Mumbai, circa 1968

CHAPTER SEVENTEEN

"The world is my home"

Now that Dhyanyogi-ji was out in the open, life was busier. He continued to perform anusthans in Bandhwad, to take care of the village and its people, and in several cases, he intervened in local sociopolitical struggles. For instance, in December 1971 there was fighting on the border of India and Pakistan, not far from Bandhwad. Dhyanyogi-ji called together a group of yogis to recite *Ram Raksha Stotrams* at the border. They chanted the mantras non-stop for several days until the fighting stopped. While Bandhwad remained his base of operations, he traveled much more, going wherever he had students or where people arranged for him to give meditation programs. He had become a public figure.

In our Western culture, when people command the attention and adoration that Dhyanyogi-ji was now receiving, they change. They usually acquire wealth and live more extravagantly. Their desires increase. They hire a staff. They show signs of pride. But Dhyanyogi-ji was still humble. He enjoyed the fact that so many people were experiencing the effects of divine energy, and he did whatever he could to bring on those effects by using his own energy, but these were selfless acts. He took pleasure in God's manifestation and in the growth in consciousness of others.

In describing Dhyanyogi-ji's humility, his disciple Pranav Parekh wrote, "He could remove the fear and feelings of inferiority of the poor, and melt the pride of the rich. He expressed love for people of all classes, but made it clear that saints and sages can be bound to no one. They cannot be tied by the silk thread of the rich, nor do they run away from the rags of the poor."

Dhyanyogi-ji appeared indifferent to his external circumstances, never showing any preference for being at the Queen of Limbdi's palace or with wealthy disciples in Mumbai over staying in a hut in some small village. One of his disciples in Radhanpur had a tiny betel leaf and nut stall, which was no more than six feet square, with a shop in front and a little storage space in back. Whenever he went to town to visit this disciple, Dhyanyogi-ji would nap at the back of his stall on the bare floor. The disciple was dismayed that he could not offer a silk pad, a fan or another amenity to his beloved master, but Dhyanyogi-ji would reassure him saying, "I feel like I am in a royal palace. Don't be sad. I can sleep here the best."

Pranav and Sushila Parekh lived in a one room flat in Ahmedabad. "Our place was so small that Guruji couldn't stay with us," said Sushila. "It made us sad. Everyone else had houses, so Guruji could stay with them. It seemed to us like all the people with money got to have him as their guest."

Dhyanyogi-ji was very close to the Parekhs and they did a lot of seva for him. Pranav was a skilled writer. He was the author of *Pathway to the Self*, the Gujarati biography of Dhyanyogi-ji that covered the first 93 years of his life (1878-1971), and he compiled Dhyanyogi-ji's teachings into two books entitled *Madhupark I* and *II* (Madhupark means "collection of sweetness"). Dhyanyogi-ji often worried about the Parekhs, since their financial status was not good.

"Guruji had given us a copy of the *Ramayana*," Sushila continued. "When he was in town, we'd ask him to visit us. He'd come in the late morning, and I'd have lunch ready. I'd give him his seat, and he'd say, 'Start,' and I would read to him. Then he would eat and take a nap, and leave.

"One time he must have heard our thoughts about wishing that he would stay with us. We'd invited him for the day again. I had made

Pranav & Sushila Parekh

ladoos (a sugary, buttery confection infused with cardamom and rolled into a ball), a sweet that Guruji loved. I had prepared 12 ladoos because whenever Guruji came, other disciples accompanied him. I estimated that about 10 to 12 people would be coming. When Guruji arrived, before he came into the house, he called to me. His driver was suggesting that he drop off Guruji's luggage at the place where he'd be staying, but Guruji said no. 'These people have a desire for me to stay here, so tonight, I'm going to spend the whole night here.' Others had asked Guruji to stop at their houses so they could see him, but he had said no, he was spending the day at our place only. So 40 people poured into our little flat! I had only cooked for 10 and Guruji kept saying that everyone should be sure and eat before they go, and people kept coming! We kept serving and we didn't run out of food.

"Our little flat was located in a compound of flats with a central courtyard. Whenever Guruji visited someone, he'd always hold a meditation program at their house, so this time, he said we'd have the meditation in our courtyard and sent someone off on a bicycle to notify all the local disciples. Several times during that afternoon, others said to Guruji, 'We have room, stay with us.' But he continued to say that he would be staying with us, sleeping outside under the trees. I told him that we would sleep outside and he could stay in the flat, but he said no, he slept outside in Bandhwad all the time and liked it. 'It's like Panchavati,' he said. Panchavati is the place on the Godavari River where Ram, Sita and Laxman lived for a while during their early years of exile from Ayodhya. 'I will have everything I need. The world is my home.'

"Guruji slept outside that night and my husband slept by him. The next day, he was supposed to leave. I tried to convince him to stay one more night, but he said no, he had fulfilled my desire. After he left, I opened the container for the ladoos and there were more in it than I had originally made!

"We were such little people, yet Guruji showered his grace upon us!"

When it came to his disciples, Dhyanyogi-ji bent over backwards to help them. Rather than demanding their loyalty, he stressed his commitment to them. Rather than holding court, calling others to come see him, serve him, he was always trying to avoid burdening anyone else. He took long journeys to visit them, saying he didn't want to inconvenience them.

"If they visit me, they'll have to spend five rupees for the bus and another five for food. I'll visit them instead." Dhyanyogi-ji actually once scolded a disciple named Bindra for "wasting your money to come and see me."

Guru Purnima is the full moon that is the most auspicious time to honor the guru. On that day, rather than staying in either Ahmedabad or Mumbai and letting his devotees come to him to receive his blessing, Dhyanyogi-ji would celebrate in one place in the morning, and then travel to the other city so that his disciples there would also have the chance to see him.

Humility so permeated Dhyanyogi-ji's nature and bearing that he often went unnoticed. Several times, when Dhyanyogi-ji was sitting with disciples who were swamis themselves, visitors who had come for his darshan bowed to the swamis and sat down without bowing to Dhyanyogi-ji. One such person said that when he realized his mistake, he wondered, "Is this simple, unassuming man the mahatma I came to see?"

Triveni, a long-time devotee of Shri Ramakrishna, had always desired to have a first-hand experience of samadhi like the one Swami Vivekananda had by the grace of Shri Ramakrishna. As a teenager living in India in the early 1940s, her longing for a spiritual life was so strong that many evenings she tied up her hair and dressed like a boy so that she could attend the arati in her village. She immigrated to America as a young woman, but returned to India years later, in the early 1970s, to make a spiritual pilgrimage, and more than anything, she hoped for a true spiritual experience.

Triveni began her stay in India at the home of a friend, and it was there that she saw Dhyanyogi-ji's photograph. She asked about him, and after being regaled with stories about this great shaktipat master, she was determined to go to Bandhwad to ask for his blessings for her pilgrimage.

She arrived in Bandhwad late in the evening and learned that Dhyanyogi-ji was away from the ashram. When she woke the next morning, filled with anticipation, she went to look for a bucket of water to wash herself. She saw an old man brushing his teeth and joined him. He offered her an herbal twig to be chewed upon for cleaning the teeth, and after thanking him, she paid him little mind. Her attention was focused on her upcoming meeting with the master.

After tea, she went to meet Dhyanyogi-ji and recognized him to be none other than the old man she'd ignored earlier that morning! But even more than her embarrassment, she noticed how, contrary to her first impression, she now felt deeply affected by Dhyanyogi-ji's energy. He invited her to massage him that morning, and after doing so, she had an excellent meditation. After receiving his blessings, she left Bandhwad and traveled to the Vishnu temple in Badrinath, high in the Himalayas. While there, she had the transformational experience she had longed for, and she was sure it must have happened through Dhyanyogi-ji's grace. For years afterwards, she chuckled at how he had initially fooled her completely with his humble demeanor.

With this utter lack of ego, everyone found him approachable. The peacocks and peahens at the ashram who never let anyone get close to them would strut right up to Dhyanyogi-ji to be fed. Their chicks would climb on him, sit on his head, and otherwise pester him. He had the ability to attune himself to the level and temperament of anyone. Although he was often very serious, even austere, children never felt any fear of him, and would abandon their games to come and sit in front of him, not caring if he were discussing aspects of yoga incomprehensible to them. From a three-year-old child to an 80-year-old, with the poor and with the rich, he honored and respected every person, and they, in turn, were deeply affected by being treated this way.

For many, separating from Dhyanyogi-ji was unbearable, and on several occasions, disciples attempted to hide him from others in their desperation to keep him from leaving them. It was common for his departure to be a scene of open anguish and tears.

As much as they wanted to be with him, Dhyanyogi-ji also loved to be with his disciples, and was very unhappy if anyone was unable to see him for any reason. If someone arrived at the ashram late at night, he came down from his room, no matter what the hour, to greet them and make certain they felt welcome, that they had something to eat or drink. When a disciple left the ashram, he personally bade them farewell at the main gate, often with his eyes filled and his voice choked as he said his goodbyes.

Like Lord Krishna, Dhyanyogi-ji had a special place in his heart for cows. Cows are believed to have great spiritual energy and seva to the cow is highly prized by saints in India. Dhyanyogi-ji named the cows in the ashram after India's sacred rivers that were said to originate in Heaven. According to ancient lore, they were formed when Indra, king of the gods, freed the cows from their celestial corral, and they rushed down upon the Earth, overflowing with milk for their calves. One of the calves in Bandhwad, born with six teats, was called Narmada, after the sacred river that flows west from the Vindhya Range to the Arabian Sea. Dhyanyogi-ji's favorite cow was named Ganga, after the most holy of India's rivers. He always called her Gangli, a term of endearment. Ganga was particularly attached to Dhyanyogi-ji and once jumped from the second floor of a building to be closer to him.

During the 1973 famine in Gujarat, while Dhyanyogi-ji was doing famine relief work, he cared for 1,700 cows whose owners were unable to feed them. The director of the World Shipping Corporation, a woman from Mumbai, donated a large sum of money to feed the cows. Very impressed with Dhyanyogi-ji's work, she came to visit him in Bandhwad. Attracted by the beauty and gentle disposition of the ashram cows, she asked to have several for her farm outside Mumbai. Dhyanyogi-ji offered to give her two of his own cows from the ashram, and it was agreed that they would travel to Mumbai by train.

Two days prior to their scheduled departure, an extraordinary and inexplicable thing happened. The cows stopped eating and actually began to weep. Gently patting them, Dhyanyogi-ji cried along with the anguished cows. His relationship with them was as close as with disciples. He consoled the cows saying, "It is a question of my word and honor, so you'd better go."

Finally, with great difficulty, the cows reluctantly boarded the truck. But once at the station, they would not get on the train. Dhyanyogi-ji went to the station and they all cried together until at last, with his encouragement, the cows boarded the train. For the first few days after reaching Mumbai, again they would not eat, but gradually they adjusted to life without their beloved Dhyanyogi-ji.

Dhyanyogi-ji's love for cows inspired one disciple to an act of self-lessness. This man was called Mauni Baba, because he had remained in silence for 12 years. He had come to live at Bandhwad to serve Dhyanyogi-ji, when one of the ashram calves became very sick and it looked like it would die. Mauni Baba prayed for the calf, offering all the benefits from his years of silence to go to saving its life.

Later, while visiting in the United States, there were several times when Dhyanyogi-ji reported that the cows in the ashram came to him in dreams and complained that they were being neglected. He immediately wrote to the ashram, telling them to take proper care of his cows.

Whether it was cows or disciples or all of humankind, Dhyanyogi-ji was there to serve others. He never asked for help. He'd do his dishes, fold his blankets, and look after everybody else. One wintry January morning in 1971, Dhyanyogi-ji was staying with a disciple named Mukut in Ahmedabad, but Mukut did not wake up in time for morning medi-tation. Dhyanyogi-ji woke up at his normal time and found his devotee sleeping. It was very cold that morning, so Dhyanyogi-ji went to Mukut very softly with his own woolen blanket, wrapping him in it gently so as not to wake him up. When Mukut awoke and saw Dhyanyogi-ji's blanket wrapped about him, he was overcome with shame, but also filled with amazement and love that his beloved guru, rather than scolding him for his laziness, had tenderly cared for him.

Dhyanyogi-ji never complained when he was hungry or sick, and he always avoided hurting anyone's feelings. He had never forgotten the consequences of his actions the two times he had lost his temper. In 1966, at a festival dedicating the temple spire in Bandhwad, Dhyanyogi-ji said in the presence of a disciple, "I could forget everything. I do not even remember my hometown and my family. I have forgotten other sweet and bitter things. But I cannot forget the incidents of the boy in Suryapura and the woman at the village well."

Having learned through these experiences how destructive his anger could be, Dhyanyogi-ji unflinchingly bore his discomfort. Once he was invited for lunch by a disciple in Mumbai. At the time, he was still relatively unknown and he traveled on public transportation if he could afford it, or else he'd walk to his destination. On this day, he arrived at the disciple's home at the appointed hour and the woman began to talk with him at length, never mentioning anything about food. After three hours had passed, he assumed she had forgotten about lunch. He gave the woman his blessings and left, hungry and penniless.

He remembered another disciple who lived nearby and had also invited him several times for lunch. In the past, he had not been able to accept the invitation, but Dhyanyogi-ji was sure that if he arrived at this disciple's house, the family would give him something to eat. He walked for 45 minutes to get there. The disciples were overjoyed to see him at their door. When the teacher comes like this, unexpectedly and uninvited, it is considered an especially great blessing. The family chatted at length with him but again, no food was offered. It was by now 4:00 p.m., and as Dhyanyogi-ji later said, "the stomach was howling!" He gave his blessings to the family and left.

At this point, he practically ran to Dahyabhai Pandya's house, which he treated like home. He rushed to the door and said, "Just heat up and give me whatever food you have. I am very hungry."

Mrs. Pandya protested, "But Guruji, I have no sweets to offer you. Please wait while I make some."

"No," Dhyanyogi-ji said, "I am not going to wait. Just serve what you have!"

Once, when some disciples were traveling with him they could not locate any milk. The only thing that Dhyanyogi-ji ate for dinner was a glass of milk, so they searched all over the village but no one had any milk to spare. Finally, an elderly woman in her 90s learned of their predicament and came to them, saying, "You cannot allow your guru to go to bed hungry. Please take this milk for him. I also have only milk at night, but today I will offer it to your guru." The disciples were relieved and happy that Dhyanyogi-ji would have his cup of milk.

After Dhyanyogi-ji finished his evening practices, his disciples gave him the milk. Immediately he asked, "Where did you find this milk?" The disciples were reluctant to reveal the source, but finally told him about the elderly woman. Dhyanyogi-ji scolded them, saying, "How can you expect me to drink this milk when an old woman will go hungry tonight? Go and return the milk to her. I cannot let anyone suffer on my account."

Like a mother indulging her children's bad habits, Dhyanyogi-ji sometimes made allowances for his disciples. One of Dhyanyogi-ji's drivers smoked cigarettes. Often, after they had been driving for some time, he had the urge to smoke, but didn't mention this to Dhyanyogi-ji. Sensing his driver's craving, Dhyanyogi-ji said, "Let's stop for *chai*," although he had no desire for tea. He just wanted to give the driver an opportunity to smoke.

Instead of criticizing a temple servant who was very forgetful, Dhyanyogi-ji affectionately nicknamed him "Paramahansa," a term of respect for enlightened beings in such a high state of consciousness that they are unable to bring their minds down to the mundane level.

At times he used his disciple's failings to teach them a lesson. One instance of this happened when he was traveling with his driver, Valji, and Maffa, a man who massaged Dhyanyogi-ji at Bandhwad and who occasionally served as his attendant. When they traveled together, Dhyanyogi-ji would give pocket money to Valji and Maffa. Maffa used to save his money because he viewed it as something valuable—a gift from his guru—but Valji spent his money freely. One day on their journey, Maffa got some extra cans of Ganges water, but Valji claimed that there was no room in the car to carry them. This upset Maffa, and he went to Dhyanyogi-ji, complaining that Valji wouldn't carry his water, and moreover, that Valji had carelessly spent all the money that Dhyanyogi-ji had given him.

"Don't be like a horse," Dhyanyogi-ji said. "When a horse is eating, it is more interested in kicking the other guy off, whereas if an elephant is eating, he doesn't worry about others but just concentrates on enjoying his meal. Be like an elephant and share."

Dhyanyogi-ji ate very pure foods, and although he preferred that his students do the same, he never pressured them to change their diets. He believed that the kind of change that comes with pressure and preaching would not last long. Instead, he led his life such that people would be inspired to follow his example. An understanding gained in this way, he said, was long lasting. He said, "Where there is love, there are no rules. How can love be bound by rules?"

There were times, however, when he would speak firmly to his closest students, particularly if they were serious about their sadhana. More than anything else, Dhyanyogi-ji wanted his devotees to have a spiritual practice, so if a disciple was faltering on that path, letting laziness or lack of discipline interfere with meditation, he would say something. Once, when one of his disciples was reluctant to meditate regularly, Dhyanyogi-ji said to him, "You meditate within the four walls of a comfortable house, and yet you cannot commit yourself to meditation. How are you going to meditate in a forest or outside your home?"

If, on the other hand, a disciple was practicing, Dhyanyogi-ji showered such a person with blessings. J.V. was one of Dhyanyogi-ji's earliest disciples in Ahmedabad. He was very devoted and had strong faith in the Gayatri mantra. He had been doing japa of this mantra for many years and had received subtle blessings from saints and mahatmas. After receiving shaktipat, Dhyanyogi-ji paid him several visits on the subtle level. J.V. said that Dhyanyogi-ji manifested in various forms during these visitations. Sometimes J.V. saw a vision of beautiful glowing light; other times, he heard Dhyanyogi-ji's melodious voice.

"I was starting to sing the section of Guruji's mantrochar that invokes Hanuman," J.V. said. "I began the verse, but couldn't remember the second line. I kept repeating the first line hoping to jog my memory, but the second line continued to elude me. Suddenly, when I'd gotten very frustrated, I clearly heard Guruji's distinctive voice chanting the next line. I looked up and saw him standing before me, and was surprised to notice that he seemed startled to see me! Puzzled by this, I later tried to make sense of it, but I couldn't figure it out. A few days later, Guruji came to Ahmedabad and I asked him, 'Why were you so startled to see me the other day?' He smiled and said, 'On that particular day, you were wearing yellow. It looked like you had renounced the life of a householder and become a sadhu.' It was true. That day I had been dressed in yellow."

Another incident took place in the early 1960s. One of Dhyanyogi-ji's disciples was passing away. The time around this transition is critical for the soul. If the person's mind is on God, the soul gets a tremendous boost and can even attain enlightenment. Ganges water washes away karma and brings the soul closer to God, so it is ideal to drink a little water from the Ganges at the time of making the passage between life and death. There was no Ganges water in the house where Dhyanyogi-ji's disciple was dying. According to a family member who was present, Dhyanyogi-ji manifested water—this time, from his right toe—and gave this water to the disciple to drink.

As much as Dhyanyogi-ji was the mother, comforting and guiding her young, at his core, he remained the ascetic. His spiritual work was what mattered most to him. He once said, "You can insult me but don't insult my path, Kundalini Maha Yoga. I'm not important; the teachings are important."

Gulabsingh Bapu told a story about an experience with Dhyanyogi-ji that paints a clear picture of how much Dhyanyogi-ji considered himself a servant of the *guru tatwa*—the guru principle—rather than a master. Dhyanyogi-ji had driven many hours from Ahmedabad to visit Bapu and other disciples in Rajkot. He arrived at Bapu's home in the mid-afternoon, but as soon as he got out of the car, he surprised everyone by saying they had to take him, immediately, to a town called Morbi, several hours away by car.

"But why?" asked Bapu. "You have just gotten here! Won't you at least take some tea first?"

"No, we must go right away," Dhyanyogi-ji insisted.

Once in Morbi, Dhyanyogi-ji directed Bapu to an old house shaded by an ancient-looking tree. He knocked on the door and an elderly couple appeared. Apparently, they didn't know him because they asked who he was and what he wanted.

Dhyanyogi-ji put them off, saying, "I'll tell you later," and asked, "You were in Rishikesh a few years ago, right?" The mystified couple nodded.

"And do you remember what happened there?"

The couple explained that they were both professors of religion, but despite all of their scholarly knowledge, they had never had any spiritual experiences. So several years before, they decided to make a pilgrimage to Rishikesh. As they were wandering in the mountains, they came across a sadhu. They touched his feet and told him, "We have been living in our minds only, without any inner experience. We have intellect, but no intelligence. Will you initiate us?"

The sadhu said, "I will do it, but the time is not right." He promised them that he would give them initiation at the proper moment.

Hearing this, Dhyanyogi-ji picked up the thread of their story and told them, "Yesterday, this sadhuji left his body and he came to me on the subtle plane and told me to initiate you. I have come to give you initiation." And he proceeded to give them shaktipat on the spot.

Dhyanyogi-ji never gave explanations. He just shrugged off any questions people asked, implying that he was merely the instrument for something that needed to be done.

In 1966, Dhyanyogi-ji went to stay for a month with a family of disciples who lived in Matheran. Here he worked on writing his first book, *Message to Disciples,* which included an account of his enlightenment experience. Most Indian householders only practiced external forms of worship, and Dhyanyogi-ji wanted to inspire his students to meditate. Several years later, he wrote *Light on Meditation*[40] in which he went into even more detail about Kundalini Maha Yoga.

When he was away, disciples longed to see him. Normally, that kind of attachment to another person can be a stumbling block on the spiritual path. But this isn't the case when it is the soul thirsting for God. "Being attached to your teacher will not bind you," explained Deepak Pathak. "It will liberate you. The pain at separating from God and Guru is not like worldly pain, it is not binding. Unconditional love and pain go together. That is why Mirabai[41] cried for Krishna."

Dhyanyogi-ji spoke tenderly to his devotees when they were missing him. "I am always with you," he said. "You are all my own soul. You will always receive my love. I am giving you this assurance without a doubt that I may not be there physically at some important event in your life, but I will surely be there subtly and help you. You will experience my presence every moment."

---

[40]*Light on Meditation* was published first in Gujarati in the late 1960s and translated into English in 1972.
[41]Mirabai was an ecstatic devotee of Krishna, who defied the societal constraints on noblewomen in 16th-century India to follow her spiritual path. She wrote hundreds of devotional poems and ultimately merged with Lord Krishna.

Folk dancing (garba), Bandhwad, 1966

CHAPTER EIGHTEEN

A CAUSE FOR CELEBRATION

*T*he same combination of determination and divine guidance that over three decades had transformed Dhyanyogi-ji into a great meditation master, had a powerful effect on his followers and the community of Bandhwad.

The villagers had a chance to demonstrate their devotion to Dhyanyogi-ji in 1966, when he hosted a five-day festival to dedicate the new spire for the ashram's Hanumanji temple. Nearly a decade had passed since the old spire had collapsed in 1953. At that time, Dhyanyogi-ji took a vow not to eat any rolled or fried foods at his meals until the spire was restored. He never asked anyone for money to reach this goal, but slowly and steadily collected any donations offered year after year. This meant he ate no bread, a staple of the Indian diet, for about 13 years. Now, with the help of the

Dedication of new temple spire at Bandhwad, 1966

people of Bandhwad, he was about to bring his vow to completion.

With all of our modern conveniences, it may be hard for us to comprehend just how difficult it was to organize such a huge event in rural India. As many as 15,000 to 20,000 guests were expected to attend the celebration, which featured a yagna. In a yagna, special offerings are made to a chosen aspect of the divine through fire. Fire ceremonies of this size were rare in the Bandhwad area because of the logistics involved and the enormously expensive preparations. To begin with, the festival was held during a time of year when the heat is oppressive, the thick air is filled with fine dust, and food and pure drinking water are in short supply. In 1966, food rationing was in effect, and supplies of grain and sugar were not available in the free market. The local roads were not paved, and it was eight bone-jarring miles to Radhanpur, the closest town that had basic supplies readily available. Radhanpur was also the last train stop for guests arriving from destinations such as Mumbai, Ahmedabad, Rajkot and Porbandar, so transportation to Bandhwad had to be arranged from there. To top it all off, in 1966 there still was no electricity in Bandhwad, so temporary lights powered by a portable generator had to be strung.

Despite these obstacles, Dhyanyogi-ji and the villagers began their preparations, confident that God would help them provide for their guests. The villagers did not work in their own homes and fields for two months, using their time instead to help prepare for the festival. They worked day and night in the courtyard of the temple, and they offered to Dhyanyogi-ji all the corn and sugar they had acquired with their own ration cards.

The work began at the break of dawn, with the call of the cuckoo and peacock. Every morning the girls of the village formed a long, unbroken line, carrying pots of water on their heads. Those who had to do the cleaning set themselves to their tasks, and the cooks began the work of cooking. The villagers provided their own bullock-drawn carts for transportation from Radhanpur, and the Queen of Limbdi sent a jeep and a driver named Labhu to help out. Because space was so limited in Bandhwad, arrangements were made to house guests in the temple of the Divine Mother at Devgam, three miles from the ashram. This was the temple that housed the murtis of the Divine Mother that had been discovered years before in Zalor, around the same time that the statue of Hanumanji had been found in Arjansar, and it was close to

Dhyanyogi-ji's heart. The temple was supported by a wealthy community, so its priest always tried to accommodate the needs of the more humble Bandhwad.

As the festival guests were jerked and bounced around on the rough roads, they sometimes wondered why their guru had chosen this isolated village over so many others in Gujarat. Once they arrived, however, and experienced Bandhwad's unique brand of hospitality, they quickly began to appreciate its charm. It was the time of year when scorching heat could raise blisters on the feet, yet they were greeted by the girls and women of the village dressed in their best clothes and dancing the *garba*, a traditional dance done to praise the Divine Mother. They joyfully clapped and sang as they twirled gracefully in an enormous circle of swirling color.

The entire village was floating in merriment. Guests offered to pay for their own transportation and other services, but the villagers politely declined. When one disciple from the city developed a shooting pain in his waist and found he could not sit or breathe well, he worried about what he would do in this remote place where one could not buy flowers for worship, much less medication. Finally, he went to the local barber, who relieved his pain with a total body massage for three consecutive days, using oil from his own home. When offered payment, the barber replied, "What for? You are the guest of our guru."

In the cities, disciples also displayed a sense of devotion and service towards Dhyanyogi-ji, yet it cannot be denied that behind their good works there was often a hidden desire to obtain something in return. But the simple and frank people who inhabited Bandhwad did not even know what shaktipat and kundalini were all about. Their only wish was to act according to their *Bapuji's*[42] wishes and not do anything that might hurt him. Their selflessness left some disciples from the city looking inside themselves and questioning their own intentions.

Dhyanyogi-ji himself impressed his guests with his organizational skills and his close attention to small details. He constantly worried about their meals and lodging arrangements, and he took personal responsibility for any lapse in service.

Thousands of guests were served full meals each day of the five-day festival. They consumed 320 pounds of whole milk each day, and 900 bags of sugar were used for tea alone.

---

[42]Bapuji is another name showing honor and love for a teacher or elder. It means "Beloved father."

Vishnu Yagna (fire ceremony)

Because this special event honored Hanumanji, one of the foods offered to the guests was His favorite treat—ladoos. In addition to being served at meals, ladoos were to be given to departing guests as prasad. As the sweets were prepared, they were stored in a locked room. Soon after their production began, however, Dhyanyogi-ji and the villagers discovered that red ants had invaded the room and were crawling all over the ladoos. At that moment, according to Kedarnath Pathak, Deepak turned to Dhyanyogi-ji in horror and asked, "Now what can we do?"

"Guruji told Deepak not to worry," remembered Kedarnath. "He closed the doors of the room, and while chanting some mantras, he sprinkled some water around the room and tied a string outside the room's door. After some time, the doors were opened and to the surprise of all of us, we could not find a single ant. When the yagna was over, Guruji went back to the room and sprinkled sugar powder everywhere and the ants appeared again to taste the sugar offered by Guruji. How blessed were those ants to get prasad from Guruji!" Dhyanyogi-ji also placed bags of sugar in the ashram yard for the ants to feed on—to return to them the food that was denied them earlier, he said.

Such occurrences were not uncommon during the festival, which was saturated with Dhyanyogi-ji's presence. Many people had unusual experiences just sitting in his company. One girl had a wound on her knee that would not heal. Dhyanyogi-ji asked her to sit directly in front of him, about three feet away. As he held his thumb opposite her injury, a ray of white light emerged from his foot and shot into her knee. The white light completely dried the wound, and it finally healed.

Dhyanyogi-ji's presence also intensified the meditations of some of his disciples and gave them glimpses of the

Final offering at fire ceremony

true nature of their guru. Late one afternoon, Dhyanyogi-ji rested on a couch in his sitting room, adjoining the peaceful courtyard of the Bandhwad ashram. A few disciples took turns fanning him while the rest sang bhajans. Two girls became so entranced by the chants and the atmosphere of devotion that they entered meditation. As they went into a deeper state, they began having visions of corpses. These visions were, of course, alarming, but didn't startle them out of their meditation. One girl's head rested peacefully on Dhyanyogi-ji's left leg for three hours, but he didn't show a bit of discomfort or annoyance.

Occasionally he would try to wake them by softly calling, "Daughter, be awake. Daughter, be awake." Eventually he took a bowl of water, recited mantras over it and told the girls to drink it. That did the trick, and both of them woke up, filled with a momentary uneasiness about what they had seen.

After dinner, some disciples gathered in front of Dhyanyogi-ji on the verandah outside his sitting room. Bathed in the light of an oil lamp near the spreading neem tree, they conversed softly, in hushed nighttime voices, and someone asked Dhyanyogi-ji about the girls' unsettling visions. Why had they seen something as gruesome as corpses in their meditations? Before he could answer, one of the girls, who was named Saroj, cried out, "I see Dhyanyogi-ji in the chimney of that oil lamp!"

Dhyanyogi-ji smiled and replied, "Now you will not be afraid, even a little. I am with you. Go anywhere in the dark without fear." Suddenly, everywhere the girls looked they saw comforting visions of Dhyanyogi-ji.

But some disciples were still perplexed. "In meditation we should have good visions," one disciple said. "Why would we have frightening ones instead?"

"It means there was a calamity somewhere involving the loss of lives, or it signifies that such an event is going to take place in the near future," Dhyanyogi-ji said.

Next, a boy named Gautam was massaging Dhyanyogi-ji's back when suddenly he cried out, "I see Lord Hanuman in Guruji's back!" Gautam then told the group about a prediction he had received in meditation. "Guruji will continue his humanitarian and spiritual work for 18 years," he said, "and will be more popular than he is today."

Then Saroj spoke again. "Guruji, I see a cow and Lord Krishna on your forehead," she said.

Bemused by this ongoing cascade of spiritual insight, Dhyanyogi-ji chuckled to himself. He decided to have a little fun with his disciples. A girl who was massaging his feet suddenly whipped her hands away, exclaiming, "Your feet are very hot. I've been burned!"

Dhyanyogi-ji laughed and replied, "It cannot be. My feet are cold. Check again."

She was afraid to touch him again, but Dhyanyogi-ji insisted, so she started kneading his feet. A puzzled look slowly crossed her face. She looked up at him and grinned, saying, "Yes, Guruji, your feet are ice cold!"

The other disciples tittered in the near-darkness, not exactly sure what their guru was up to this time.

"Why did you lie before?" Dhyanyogi-ji asked, shooting the girl a mischievous glance.

"I did not lie," she said matter-of-factly. "Your feet were definitely hot."

"And how are they now?"

"Now they are very cold."

"You are lying again," Dhyanyogi-ji said. "My feet are hot, but you say they are cold."

Before he even finished his sentence, the girl dropped Dhyanyogi-ji's feet as if they were burning coals and wailed.

"I feel your feet are hot again!"

"That's so," Dhyanyogi-ji said. "See, I know how to play games, too!"

Two days after the game of "hot and cold," Dhyanyogi-ji was again sitting in his favorite spot on the verandah, outside his sitting room. It was about 9:00 p.m., and the moon cast a silvery glow over the ashram. As usual, an oil lamp illumined the courtyard. A gentle breeze caressed tired faces as everyone settled down after the day's festivities. Two disciples were seated on the ground before Dhyanyogi-ji, massaging his feet, while another stood quietly by fanning him to keep the insects away. Someone else massaged his hands, while another disciple rubbed oil on his head, oil that had a cooling effect according to Ayurvedic medicine. Kartik, a boy from Mumbai, sat near Dhyanyogi-ji's feet.

"Kartik, do you like it here?" Dhyanyogi-ji asked the child.

This seemed a rhetorical question since there was nothing in this magical place that one would not like, especially an adventurous boy away from the difficulties of daily life in Mumbai.

"Yes, Guruji, I very much like it here," Kartik answered.

"Don't you miss your father?" asked Dhyanyogi-ji.

A disciple interrupted, saying, "Here, he has a 'father' who surpasses his father in Mumbai. Why should he miss him?"

From the questions Dhyanyogi-ji was asking, everyone began to suspect that their guru was up to something again.

"Well, you may not miss your father," Dhyanyogi-ji continued, "but today I am going to send you to him, even though you are sitting here in Bandhwad."

At first, the other disciples thought he was joking again. But then Dhyanyogi-ji called Kartik to him and gave him a sankalpa to repeat. He placed his hand firmly on the boy's head.

The *balyogi* (child yogi) closed his eyes, entered a meditative state and began an astral journey. His facial expressions revealed changing emotions. One moment there was a smile on his face, the next moment an expression of curiosity. After 20 minutes Kartik opened his eyes.

Dhyanyogi-ji rubbed Kartik's back affectionately and asked, "Well, son, did you visit Mumbai? You came back so quickly."

Everything grew quiet, as if the air itself wanted to hear what the boy had to say.

"Yes, Guruji, I have been to Mumbai," Kartik said.

"Then give me some money," Dhyanyogi-ji responded.

"Money for what?"

"You traveled in my train of meditation," he said. "I shall have to tell your father that you have begun to travel without a ticket—and at such a young age! It is not fair."

The disciples burst into laughter.

"Well, it doesn't matter," Dhyanyogi-ji continued. "At least tell us what you saw in Mumbai."

Kartik began to tell the story of his astral travel. "Guruji, the moment I closed my eyes, I began to see Mumbai. I wanted to see my father, so I went directly to my home. I wanted to have a long talk, but my father was asleep in his striped night shirt."

He lowered his head a little and looked up shyly at Dhyanyogi-ji.

"Guruji," he confessed, "I made one mistake while I was there."

"What happened?"

"You have told us to observe whatever we see in meditation and just let events happen, without taking action. We shouldn't desire anything. But, seeing my father asleep, I wanted to know if he remembered me or not. I also had a wish to read his mind. The moment I had this desire, I lost sight of Mumbai and returned to Bandhwad."

The next day, Dhyanyogi-ji sent a letter to Kartik's father, Janakray, asking him to describe in detail what he was wearing the day Kartik visited him. He also asked him to write about what he was doing that day after 8:00 p.m. Janakray's response confirmed what Kartik had described that evening.

A few days later, Dhyanyogi-ji sent another young disciple on an astral journey. Sensing that Saroj, the child who had massaged his feet, was a bit homesick, he asked her, "Do you wish to see your father?"

Saroj instantly replied, "Yes!" She had heard about Kartik's adventure, and the thought of trying it herself excited her. Dhyanyogi-ji decided to tease her a little.

"Well, you will not do as Kartik did," he said. "You shall have to pay the fare before boarding the meditation train." Everyone laughed.

Saroj described what happened next: "First, Guruji put his hand on my head. Then he made me hold his legs. He instructed me to close my eyes and repeat a sankalpa. I didn't like the restless nature of my mind, but automatically, it steadied.

"For some time there was darkness. Soon a light came into view in the distance, and then Ahmedabad was before me. I reached the housing complex, but the gate to the housing complex was locked. I jumped over and went to search for my family, but no one was home. Then I went to the printing press where my father works and found him there. I called to him, but he was so absorbed in his work he did not hear me. Finally I called loudly, and his attention was drawn towards me. We exchanged news of Bandhwad and Ahmedabad. That was enough. Then I returned to Bandhwad."

Later when Thakor, her father, was asked to describe his experience, he said it was true he was busy at the time and there was no one home. But he insisted he had not spoken to his daughter, and nothing unusual had happened to him that day.

The children's experiences with astral travel piqued the curiosity of other disciples attending the festival and generated much discussion with the guru.

"How did they travel in complete darkness?" one disciple asked.

"All these events cannot be seen by ordinary eyes," Dhyanyogi-ji replied. "They saw with divine eyes, and therefore they got a clear suggestion of direction even in the darkness."

"If Saroj and her father talked to each other," another disciple wondered, "why doesn't Thakor remember the conversation? If he has no memory of it, what is the evidence of its truth and existence?"

"There is nothing to be doubted," Dhyanyogi-ji answered. "There was communication between the subtle bodies of Saroj and Thakor. It is natural that the physical body of Thakor may not be aware of that."

"If the physical body does not know what the subtle body is doing," the disciple asked, still not convinced, "then how does Saroj know what her own subtle body does? If Saroj knows, why doesn't Thakor?"

"Not everyone has the same experience in meditation," replied Dhyanyogi-ji. "Advanced disciples have more experiences than beginners. Saroj is ahead of her father on this path, so she is aware of her subtle body. Those who lack progress fall short of experience.

"This is called seeing things at a distance," Dhyanyogi-ji continued. "As one progresses on the path of meditation, one's experiences change. In Kundalini Maha Yoga, one can easily get the achievement of having one's desires fulfilled." This is one of the eight siddhis, or paranormal powers, of yoga.

"But why is it that only children have these experiences?" asked one disciple.

"If adults could be as pure, humble and uninhibited as children, they could certainly have these experiences," Dhyanyogi-ji said. "But who is ready? Adults are too engrossed in worldly concerns. Complete surrender is essential."

Astral travel is a technique that usually requires years of intense practice to perfect, but Dhyanyogi-ji gave the experience to the two children with just a few words and a simple touch. With this unique gift, he demonstrated to them the power of meditation and other yogic practices. Dhyanyogi-ji often taught that meditation is like carving in stone. Other modes of worship are as impermanent as writing on a sheet of paper, which can be easily rubbed out, but letters carved in stone are eternal. These were some of the experiences and teachings disciples received throughout the five-day festival.

To celebrate the dedication of the new spire, Dhyanyogi-ji planned to end his vow of abstaining from rolled or fried foods. For this special occasion, the Queen of Limbdi sent her son by plane from Mumbai with tortilla-like bread that she had made herself. At the time she was very sick, and her doctor had ordered her to rest. But her love and devotion for her teacher were so great that she made the bread anyway. The Queen rarely cooked for anyone, so this was a great honor for Dhyanyogi-ji. For the first time in 13 years, he put bread into his mouth.

The Queen's driver, Labhu, who was helping to transport guests to and from the event, was a cheerful and devout man. He became so focused on serving Dhyanyogi-ji that he only came for darshan twice a day. Dhyanyogi-ji showed great concern for him, always inquiring about him at mealtimes, and once he defended him against unjust accusations of laziness.

Labhu had been detained while doing an important errand, and did not show up at the appointed time to pick up a sadhu who needed a ride. When Dhyanyogi-ji saw the sadhu scolding Labhu, he sharply reprimanded the sadhu.

"Why do you scold him without reason?" Dhyanyogi-ji said. "Do you realize how much effort he has made to serve you without concern for his own needs? I personally sent him on the errand that delayed him. Do not rebuke him."

Days later, when this same sadhu was preparing to leave the festival, he approached Dhyanyogi-ji, who was standing in the Radha-Krishna Temple.

"Bapuji, I am leaving," the sadhu said.

"Wait just two minutes," Dhyanyogi-ji said as he disappeared into the ashram storehouse. It is traditional for the host of a fire ceremony to offer a gift to all his departing guests. Soon Dhyanyogi-ji returned and handed the sadhu a brass water pot.

The sadhu removed the cover and peered inside. Finding the pot empty he said, "Bapuji, an empty pot cannot be given as alms."

Dhyanyogi-ji, always tolerant, did not flinch. Without saying a word, he reached into his pocket and put all the money he had into the sadhu's pot. Satisfied, the sadhu prostrated at Dhyanyogi-ji's feet and departed.

Another man came to Dhyanyogi-ji and said, "Bapuji, I want bamboo for a manger. May I take it? It is in the backyard."

Dhyanyogi-ji replied, "Why did you come to ask for it? Go and take as many as you want."

"Bapuji, I must ask because they are yours."

"Oh my friend, what is mine here? Whatever there is, it is God's. You go and take it."

No one left the festival empty-handed; their desires were fulfilled on a material or spiritual level, each according to their needs.

Dhyanyogi-ji's close disciple Pranav Parekh became very emotional when it came time to leave Bandhwad. With tears in his eyes, he fell at Dhyanyogi-ji's feet.

"Tomorrow we shall be leaving," he sobbed. "How will we live without you?"

"Why do you worry? I am always with you," Dhyanyogi-ji reassured him. "Go! I will come to your house in a subtle form."

"But Dhyanyogi-ji, how will we know you have come to our house?"

"You will know. Just go home, and then tell me what happens."

Pranav didn't feel worthy of Dhyanyogi-ji's favor. He returned home, but he was like a person whose eyes cannot adjust indoors because they have been temporarily blinded by the sunlight. He couldn't work, and didn't talk with anyone. Yet even in that condition, Dhyanyogi-ji's words were like a sweet stream in a desert. Pranav passed the next few days with an intense longing that Dhyanyogi-ji would visit him on the subtle plane. What form would he assume? he wondered. How would he know it was Dhyanyogi-ji? He pondered these questions and waited. Fortunately, he did not have to wait long.

After lunch on Sunday, June 17, Pranav took a nap. He fell fast asleep the moment he lay down. After half an hour, someone shouted loudly enough to wake him: "Pranav!" He got up and looked around. There was no one in the room. When he asked his wife Sushila, who was close by, if anyone had called him she replied, "No." He was bewildered. There had been a shout loud enough to wake him from a deep sleep, yet his wife had heard nothing.

Two days later, he was awakened by a loud shout: "Pranav!" He looked around, but no one was there.

A week later, Dhyanyogi-ji came to Pranav's house for dinner. Later that night he heard the same loving voice say, "Pranav." Again, no one was in the room. A month later, he heard the voice twice—shortly after 4:30 a.m., and again approximately four hours later. The voice continued to call to him over the next two weeks.

The next time Dhyanyogi-ji came to visit, Pranav anxiously told him about the mysterious voice. "Dhyanyogi-ji, please explain these experiences," he said. "What is this? Who might have called me?"

Dhyanyogi-ji listened quietly and attentively, then suddenly he laughed. Pranav was ashamed that he had burdened his guru with details of these strange visitations.

"Will you ever be satisfied?" asked Dhyanyogi-ji with a smile. "You invite me to your house, and when I come and call out to you, you ask me who might have shouted your name."

Pranav was speechless. In that instant, he realized that Dhyanyogi-ji had not forgotten his promise to visit him in a subtle form. Plunged momentarily into divine ecstasy, Pranav spontaneously went into a meditative state. Soon after this incident, Sushila also began having similar experiences, and Dhyanyogi-ji's subtle presence remained with the couple for months, again fulfilling their desire to have him as a guest in their home.

The festival in Bandhwad ended with an address in Dhyanyogi-ji's honor. The words captured the deep feelings the disciples held in their heart for their teacher:

"Why should we worry, when we have with us a sadguru like you who knows how a person can be free from the cycle of birth and death?"

Batasondevi, Dhyanyogi-ji's sister

CHAPTER NINETEEN

RETURN TO DURGADIH

*A*fter the last guests had departed from Bandhwad and life had returned to normal, Dhyanyogi-ji still had one last task to perform before the yagna would be complete. The head priest who had presided over the fire ceremony during the festival told Dhyanyogi-ji that in order to obtain the complete fruit of the *Vishnu Maha Yagna* he should perform certain rituals for his ancestors. Otherwise, the full benefits of the ceremony would not be realized.

To fulfill this requirement, he decided to go on a pilgrimage to the sacred city of Gaya, in his home state of Bihar. Gaya is extolled in the scriptures as the ideal place for the practice called *shraddha* that honors ancestors. He gathered together 16-year-old Deepak Pathak, along with Deepak's mother and aunt, and the four of them set off together in a hired car.

Their first stop was Ahmedabad, where Dhyanyogi-ji met with another shaktipat guru, Swami Vishnu Tirtha, the master who had first given shaktipat to Deepak's father, Kedarnath Pathak. This was an unusual meeting because there were very few living shaktipat masters.

Swami Vishnu Tirtha invited the group to come to his ashram in Devas. Dhyanyogi-ji met with him for two to three hours, during which time the two masters had a wide-ranging discussion about meditation, shaktipat and yoga, and Dhyanyogi-ji gave the swami a copy of his book *Message to Disciples.*[43]

Once the pilgrims were back on the road, Dhyanyogi-ji realized that he had no idea which of his ancestors should be included in the final part of the ceremony. He had, after all, left his family many years before to pursue a spiritual life. In moving forward on his chosen path, he had severed his ties to the past and never looked back. So dedicated was he to his new life that he had forgotten how to speak Bihari, his native tongue. He now exclusively used the language of his adopted home state of Gujarat. Although he acknowledged his spiritual debt to his parents in various ways throughout his life—to his mother who had given him life and to his father who had supported his spiritual desires—Dhyanyogi-ji had had no contact at all with his family or other people from Durgadih for more than 60 years. He didn't know who was still alive and who had died while he was away. Now he would have to return to his birthplace to find out so he could complete the shraddha ceremony.

When the car crossed the border into Bihar, the once-familiar terrain jarred Dhyanyogi-ji's memory and he recalled that the closest town to Durgadih was Bikramganj. They stopped there, hoping to come across some shopkeepers from Durgadih so they could ask them about Dhyanyogi-ji's parents, brothers and sisters. They did indeed find a few, but so much time had passed that no one knew anything about Dhyanyogi-ji's family. Everyone they talked to from Durgadih, in fact, was so young they hadn't even been born when Dhyanyogi-ji left. They were able to discover, however, that a Mishra family still lived in the village, and it appeared as if some of Dhyanyogi-ji's nephews might be there. Finally, they came across someone who was able to tell them that Dhyanyogi-ji's parents and brothers had all died. Dhyanyogi-ji was already aware of this, but still he turned to Deepak with tears in his eyes and said, "All my brothers are gone." Deepak was at a loss as to how to comfort his guru.

Dhyanyogi-ji asked a man from Durgadih to guide them to the Mishra family's house. As he entered the village, a torrent of childhood memories flooded him. He started reflecting on the time when, at the

[43]Swami Vishnu Tirtha is no longer alive, but his disciple, Shivom Tirthji, now continues his work.

age of 11, he secretly left his parents' home in the middle of the night.

Although Dhyanyogi-ji had virtually forgotten his roots, the Mishra family had never forgotten him. There had been no communication with their Kashinath since he left the village to complete his pilgrimage to Rameshwaram, but over the years family members had continued their search for him, hoping to assuage Ramdahin's grief for his lost son.

Ramdahin nearly died from the constant weeping caused by separation from his son. He was tortured by thoughts of Kashinath's welfare, as any parent would be: "Where will my Kashinath be today? Will anyone give him dinner? Who will prepare his bed? He would never ask anyone for anything. And if he does not ask, who will give it to him?"

The family, trying to maintain Ramdahin's sense of hope, looked for Kashinath in places they felt a young sadhu might frequent, exploring caves in the mountains, monasteries, the huts of saints and pilgrimage sites. They traveled to four of the most famous pilgrimage destinations—Varanasi, Allahabad, Nasik and Puri—expecting they would eventually find him.

Their search was fruitless, and after Ramdahin died the memory of Kashinath faded. As time passed and more of his relatives died, those still alive assumed that Kashinath might also have died. They actually performed shraddha for him. They had no idea that Kashinath had assumed a new name and was now leading a vigorous life devoted to serving humankind.

When Dhyanyogi-ji and the others arrived at the Mishra's house, Dhyanyogi-ji told the people living there who he was. His family members were extremely skeptical because they had been deceived by others, who, masquerading as Kashinath, had tried to claim his inheritance. One unscrupulous swami in particular had gained the family's trust, but was later exposed as an imposter. Believing this swami to be their long-lost favorite son, they had opened their home to this man, offering him cherished possessions with the hope that he would finally stay. But after several days, some of the village elders began to suspect that he wasn't who he said he was, and they peppered him with questions that only Kashinath could answer. His answers revealed the deception, and they ran him out of town.

Now Dhyanyogi-ji found himself in the uncomfortable situation of having to prove that he was the real Kashinath. He began by saying he did not want anything from the family except the names of his relatives who had died. He explained that he needed the names to perform shraddha for them in Gaya. Once he had them, he would leave right away. Immediately people began to bombard him with questions to see if he was telling the truth.

"No one was ready to believe my story," Dhyanyogi-ji later recalled. "I felt like an accused criminal, standing in a cage. All of a sudden someone would appear in front of me and ask, 'Do you know me?' Of course I did not recognize him after so many years, so naturally I said, 'No.' Then they would murmur that there was certainly something wrong: How could it be that he does not know?"

By this time, a crowd had gathered around him. Someone came forward and asked, "How many sisters do you have?"

Fortunately, Dhyanyogi-ji clearly remembered that he had two sisters, and with some relief he confidently answered the question. Then someone else asked for their names. "I do not remember the names of my sisters, but I am certain that I had two sisters," he said. The murmuring began again. How could anyone forget the names of his sisters?

An elderly man, about Dhyanyogi-ji's age of 87 years, made his way through the crowd and stood directly in front of the stranger. "I wondered what question this man would ask," Dhyanyogi-ji said. "He addressed me politely: 'Swamiji, will you show me your right arm?' I held out my arm. He pushed the sleeve up past the elbow and closely examined the scar of the wound that I had received while playing in my childhood. Then, without saying a word, he turned and motioned for some of the men to join him in a corner."

"I think this is definitely Kashinath," the old man said to the others. "When I was small I played with him. The scar on his elbow is exactly the same. Yet we must be cautious and continue to investigate. We don't want to be deceived again."

Dhyanyogi-ji recognized it was time to take the initiative and speak on his own behalf. "I clearly remember three or four incidents from my childhood," he told the crowd. "I am going to tell them to you. I'm not concerned whether you believe them or not. You can see I have a car, and I have good, respectable people with me. I have not come to claim property. I don't expect anything from you."

He sensed that these words satisfied the villagers, so he continued to speak. "I'm going to Gaya to give oblations to my ancestors," he said. "I do not know who has died in my family, and I have returned to Durgadih to find this out. If you object, please say so. Rest assured that when I know this information, I will continue on to Gaya."

Hearing Dhyanyogi-ji's heartfelt tone, the people in the crowd began to trust him. One person spoke up. "Let Babuji sit. He has been standing for over an hour."

Dhyanyogi-ji sat down and began recounting a few very old memories. "Some of you must remember that long ago, a sadhu threatened to commit suicide unless my father paid him 200 rupees," Dhyanyogi-ji said. "He said he would jump down from a pipal tree and kill himself. He even climbed the tree. My father feared that the sadhu might commit suicide in his courtyard. However, my brothers climbed the tree and, holding his arms, said, 'Come on! Let us help you. We can push you to the ground if you want to commit suicide.' The sadhu got confused, climbed down and went his way."

Three or four men in the group confirmed the story, and then Dhyanyogi-ji continued. "Let me tell you a story about one of my ancestors," he said. "British hunters came to the lake at Maunibava's ashram to shoot the birds feeding there, but because of his firm desire that the hunters spare his innocent birds the guns did not work. Is this true or false?"

"True!" the crowd responded.

As the atmosphere became friendlier, Dhyanyogi-ji started saying whatever came to his mind, however trivial it might appear. "We had a cow named Rupiya who was white as marble and never stopped giving milk," he said. "She used to give milk the day before she gave birth."

"Babuji, it is true."

While the villagers listened intently to Dhyanyogi-ji's memories, his sister arrived. Dhyanyogi-ji had sent his nephew, Vaikunth, with Deepak to fetch Batonsadevi from her home in the next village, 10 miles away, where she had moved when she got married.

Batonsadevi and Dhyanyogi-ji had been especially close as children. She was so overwhelmed when she heard the news of her brother's return that she fainted and remained unconscious for a full half-hour. When she came around, her excitement was replaced by skepticism. After so many disappointments over the years, she dared not hope Vaikunth's story was true.

"Oh, Vaikunth, are you telling me the truth or making a joke?"

"No, it is true," Vaikunth replied. "That's why I came to get you."

All at once the years melted away, and the fondness she felt for her lost brother welled up inside her. This longing erased all her doubts, even though she had not yet laid eyes on the man who was claiming to be Kashinath, and she ran toward the waiting car.

"Where is my brother?" she cried. "I must see him now!"

When they arrived in Durgadih, she collapsed at Dhyanyogi-ji's feet, sobbing. Batonsadevi did not question him, or express any doubt about his identity. She was certain Dhyanyogi-ji was her brother. When the crowd saw how closely they resembled each other, they decided he was not an imposter.

Dhyanyogi-ji later described this first meeting with his sister in a letter:

"There was such a crowd that I could not talk with my sister with ease. The many years that had passed since I had seen her caused a gap between us. I could not understand her. She could not understand what I spoke because the language there was Bihari. When she met me, she began to cry."

Soon others who had known Dhyanyogi-ji well began to arrive. First was a cousin, Magani. As a child, Dhyanyogi-ji had been fond of giving people nicknames. He called a friend who was extremely thin "Sudama," for example, after the poor, emaciated friend of Lord Krishna. Despite Magani's protests, Dhyanyogi-ji had insisted upon calling him "Mathani," which is the word for a butter-churning stick. Now, as his cousin approached, Dhyanyogi-ji instantly recognized him

Kailash Mishra, last nephew of Dhyanyogi-ji (died 1999), in front of pond in Durgadih, built with funds raised by Dhyanyogi-ji

and slyly called out, "Mathani, do you remember me?" Everyone laughed because they had not heard this name for many, many years. Magani had come to test the stranger, but as soon as he heard his old nickname all his doubts about Dhyanyogi-ji dissolved.

Another man came running and fell at Dhyanyogi-ji's feet, trem-

Group photo in Durgadih, 1966 **Front row, from left:** *Deepak Pathak's mother and aunt*
On chairs: *Batasondevi, Dhyanyogi-ji* **Next row, from right:** *4th is Deokrishna Mishra*
(grandnephew), 6th is Kailash Mishra (nephew), 9th is Vaikunth (grandnephew)
Top row, left: *Deepak Pathak*

bling and crying uncontrollably. It was Kailash Mishra, Dhyanyogi-ji's nephew. Dhyanyogi-ji comforted him saying, "Why do you cry? The person to whom you gave final rites has returned alive. Why should you cry?"

For a moment everyone was speechless, then the murmuring began again. They were astonished that Dhyanyogi-ji knew that final rites had been done for him even though he was still alive.

"Yes, uncle, it is true," said Kailash, who felt ashamed. "It was a mistake, but there was no news about you for a very long time."

"You have removed my gold ring that I gave you," Dhyanyogi-ji said. "It is not on your hand. Why?"

By now word of Dhyanyogi-ji's presence had spread, and before Kailash could respond to his uncle's question, another old acquaintance approached. It was Indrajit Pandeya, the childhood companion who had planned to run away with Kashinath to become a sadhu. It had been decades since the two had seen each other, and at first Indrajit did not understand his old friend's first words to him: "Did you lie to me?"

"Babuji, what do you mean, what are you referring to?" Indrajit answered, puzzled.

"Why did you tell me that you would run away with me in the middle of the night when we were young boys?" replied Dhyanyogi-ji. "I trusted you completely, so I left my house expecting you to come with me. But you stayed home, saying you would join me later."

Embarassed, Indrajit bowed his head and said, "But, Babuji, I got married. So I could not get out of the house." The crowd broke into laughter.

Next, Dhyanyogi-ji's grandnephew Radhakrishna, arrived. "This Babaji is my uncle," he said. "No one should argue with him."

Someone else spoke up, declaring, "This is Kashinath."

"No!" exclaimed Radhakrishna. "He is no longer Kashinath, he is now Vishvanath. When he left he was Kashinath—Lord of Kashi, the holiest city in India—but he has returned to us as Vishvanath, Lord of the Universe. When my father lay dying, he called me to him and said, 'Radhakrishna, you will certainly meet him.' Confused, I asked him, 'Who?' He answered, 'Your uncle, who has become a saint. He is still alive and he will certainly return.'

"'But how can that be?' I asked him. 'Didn't everyone search endlessly for him? If they could not locate him during that search, how will I possibly find him?'

"He said, 'Dear son, you will not have to search for him. He will come to you.'"

Radhakrishna gazed at Dhyanyogi-ji with tears in his eyes and said, "Today my dream has come true. How fortunate I am that my *sadhuchacha* (saint-uncle) has come home."

The crowd was now convinced that this was indeed Kashinath. The next day Dhyanyogi-ji's relatives and the villagers of Durgadih honored him by doing puja to his feet. After they finished, he departed for Gaya so he could finish performing shraddha, the spiritual task he had come home to complete. During this special ceremony, balls of boiled rice called *pindas* are offered for each ancestor. Four pindas are made for each relative. One pinda representing the deceased is divided into three sections. Each piece is then mixed with one of the three remaining

Pilgrimage taken as part of Dhyanyogi-ji's first trip home after 50 years.

pindas, which represent the deceased's father, grandfather and great-grandfather. Finally, the pindas, water and sesame seeds are offered to the ancestor with special mantras. This frees the soul from earthly bondage, and helps the soul continue to evolve spiritually.

Dhyanyogi-ji performed shraddha for his ancestors on the ghats lining the banks of the Phalgu River, then he and the other pilgrims continued all the way to Ayodhya and Chitrakoot before returning to Mumbai and Bandhwad.

But his business in Durgadih was not yet complete. In 1968, he returned there for a *bhandara*, a large feast held as a part of his observance of shraddha. During this return visit, he gave the village some money for digging a small reservoir, to supply water and to provide employment for the villagers. He also gave money for improving the local school.

The restoration of the Hanumanji temple in Bandhwad, the visits to Durgadih and the pilgrimage to Gaya re-established Dhyanyogi-ji's ties to

Durgadih middle school, under construction "by the grace of Guruji"

Durgadih upper primary school, constructed with funds raised by Dhyanyogi-ji

his family and his birthplace. He even became fluent in his native Bihari once again, less than a week after his return. His pronunciation was exact, even though he had not spoken the language for more than 60 years.

When Dhyanyogi-ji returned to Mumbai, his sister was there waiting for him because she was scared to lose contact with him again. Later that year, again fearing that there might not be another opportunity to spend time with her brother, Batonsadevi traveled to Mumbai to visit for two weeks. It pleased Dhyanyogi-ji that she began a daily practice of meditation during the course of her stay.

During this visit, the siblings and some other family members went on a brief pilgrimage to Nasik and Tryambak. The holy city of Nasik is located on the Godavari River in the hills of the Western Ghats, about 115 miles northeast of Mumbai. Some of the pivotal events of the *Ramayana* took place here. Ram, Laxman and Sita lived in Nasik while exiled from Ayodhya, and Ravana carried Sita away from here to Lanka. The city's rich spiritual tapestry draws thousands of pilgrims, and it is one of the four sites of the spectacular Kumbha Melas. Twenty miles west of Nasik lies Tryambak, home of Tryambakeshwar temple, which houses one of India's 12 jyotir-lingani.

Only three months after completing the pilgrimage to Nasik and Tryambak, a simmering tragedy drew Dhyanyogi-ji back to Bihar.

GANGOTRI

BADRINATH

RISHIKESH

DELHI

Ganges River

AYODHYA

PRAYAG
(ALLAHABAD)

VARANASI
(BENARES)

DURGADIH

ORCHHA

CHITRAKOOT

GAYA

MOUNT ABU
AMBAJI
GANDHWAD

AHMEDABAD

Vindhya Range

Narmada River

LIMBDI

NIKORA

TRYAMBAK
NASIK

UMBAI

HYDERABAD

Tibet

Nepo

Chi

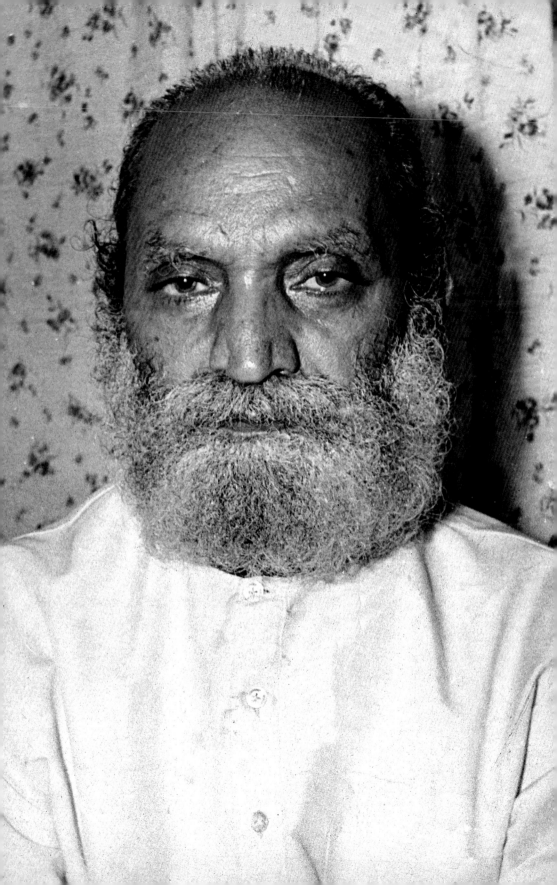

CHAPTER TWENTY

FAMINE RELIEF

From Bihar, an ancient land of windswept plains and plateaus, came stunning news. A famine of unthinkable proportions had settled in after a year without rain, and the situation was growing desperate.

Dhyanyogi-ji had been actively involved in humanitarian work for 40 years, but his projects had been limited in scale and restricted to the area surrounding Bandhwad. Now he expanded the scope of his work as he tried to relieve the raw human suffering that confronted him in the land of his birth.

Bihar, which covers more than 67,000 square miles, is one of India's most populous states as well as one of its most rural and depressed. Bounded by Nepal on the north and Orissa on the south, it was once considered the seat of Indian culture and civilization. The name Bihar comes from the Sanskrit word *vihara*, which refers to the many Buddhist communities that thrived there in ancient times.

Today Bihar is largely an agricultural state. Three-quarters of the population is involved in farming in some way, producing rice along with other staples such as corn, wheat, barley and legumes. The crops are dependent on the southwest monsoon rains that drench the landscape from mid-June until October. Normally, anywhere from 40 to 60 inches of rain may fall during this three- to four-month period, but nearly half of it doesn't arrive until July and August.

It is hard enough to scrape a living from the land—even in recent years, Bihar has ranked last in the country in per capita income, and almost half its people are considered by the government to be living below the poverty level—but when the rains fail, the results can be disastrous.

During Dhyanyogi-ji's lifetime, periodic regional droughts and famines were a fairly common occurrence in India. When grandparents recounted their life stories to their grandchildren, one way they marked the years was to talk of the famines they had lived through. Modern agricultural practices such as the increased use of irrigation, the stockpiling of grain for emergencies and a more efficient food distribution system have blunted the impact of food shortages, and these recurring, widespread famines are for the most part a thing of the past.

But in the mid-1960s, starvation was still a very real threat for many of Bihar's poor. The famine that struck in 1966 and 1967 came to be known as "the last of the great famines."

For about two weeks in August 1966, the rains were strong enough to allow the transplant of seedlings. But then they stopped, and there would not be another rain helpful to crops for almost another year. Fields that should have been lush green turned hard and brown, worthless for a winter sowing. Some families cut their crops early to sell as fodder, others were growing so hungry they went ahead and ate the plants though they were not yet mature. Cows, buffalo and other animals, bloated with hunger and searching for something to fill their bellies, roamed the dried, cracked fields and consumed whatever was left.

By the time October rolled around, the situation was growing increasingly desperate. The southern and northern districts of Bihar had been hit the hardest. People were so hungry they ate any seed they had on hand, and sifted through dusty fields all day for whatever they could scavenge, usually no more than a handful of seed. They foraged for anything edible they could find from trees, roots and shrubs. According to one account, even poisonous tubers were fair game—they were boiled, mashed, soaked in the river overnight to leach out the toxins, then boiled again before they were eaten.

By December, local politicians were sending word of the famine back to New Delhi, asking for aid. At first the central government did not grasp the seriousness of the situation, and then the relief efforts became embroiled in politics and corruption. Some people complained that help was not being given to those who needed it most, but to those who had the most land and best political connections.

But politics also turned out to be the saving grace of the people of Bihar. There was an election coming up in February, and politicians took the opportunity to demand relief for their constituents. Once it was understood just how serious the famine had become, it started receiving extensive news coverage. Pictures of the people of Bihar, now beginning to resemble living corpses, were beamed around the world, and this resulted in a massive mobilization of resources both within India and abroad. Grain, medicine and money flowed into the district. Ultimately, because of these humanitarian efforts, the number of deaths would be limited to thousands rather than millions.

The renowned Indian relief workers Ravishankar Maharaj and Ranchodas Maharaj were among those who assisted with the relief efforts for the famine. Ranchodas Maharaj was a saint from Gujarat who was said to be more than 400 years old. Ranchodasji was in Bihar organizing eye camps—temporary outdoor clinics that provide free cataract surgery—when the famine started. Like Dhyanyogi-ji, he was a devotee of Lord Ram, and there is speculation that there was a connection between their spiritual lineages. In May, 1965, Kanu Patel, one of Dhyanyogi-ji's disciples, had gone to receive darshan from Ranchodasji. He explained that he had received shaktipat from Dhyanyogi-ji and described his spiritual progress. The old sage told Kanu, "I am the setting sun, and he is the rising sun." By 1967, the two men had still never met, but Ranchodasji contacted Dhyanyogi-ji to ask for help feeding people. Normally Dhyanyogi-ji did not participate directly in large relief efforts, believing he was put on this earth for another purpose—to attend to spiritual health and end spiritual suffering. But when famine or other forms of physical suffering occured "close to home," he felt it was his duty to help in any way he could, just as one would care for an ill person at home. So he told Ranchodasji he would come to Bihar.

On May 21, 1967, Dhyanyogi-ji departed from Mumbai on the

Howrah Mail Train bound for Calcutta, accompanied by disciples from Mumbai and Gujarat. Two days later, after a hot, tiring trip, the weary group reached Sasaram at 5:30 a.m. There they were joined by Dhyanyogi-ji's sister, Batonsadevi, and his nephew Dadan, the son of Radhakrishna Mishra. They did not rest for long. At 4:30 p.m., they climbed into a caravan of jeeps and trucks and started for Adhaura Mountain, 59 miles away. Along the way, they kept their spirits up by singing Gujarati bhajans.

They spent more than two weeks at Adhaura Mountain, which is part of the Amarkantak Hills at the eastern end of the Vindhyachal Range. About 140 villages were scattered in the area, but many of them had been partially abandoned or deserted because of the famine. It was particularly difficult to reach the mountain top villages because of the steep, dangerous access road to the summit of the 3,000-foot mountain. At any moment, the relief vehicles could plunge off the road into deep valleys.

The living conditions at Adhaura were difficult. The Gujarati disciples were used to the extraordinarily hot weather of the Indian dry season, but they were not accustomed to the combination of debilitating heat and hot, dry winds. During their 17-day stay, some of them suffered from sunstroke. The disciples lived in a 40-foot by 20-foot grass hut that sheltered them, but just barely. In the evenings, they chose to spread their beds outside to take advantage of the cooler night air. Dhyanyogi-ji was offered a one-room brick shelter, but he, too, chose to sleep outside, on a small couch.

Even by Bandhwad standards, Dhyanyogi-ji and his crew of volunteers were isolated at Adhaura. The disciples from Mumbai missed such luxuries as daily mail and access to a telephone. There were days when they all had to go without baths, or make do with a single bucketful of water. When they could get water for bathing, it was usually stinking and turbid. Drinking water was, of course, carefully rationed, and milk and ghee were scarce. Powdered milk was obtainable for the very high rate of 12 annas—three-quarters of a rupee—per pound, but buying it entailed a walk of several miles, and even then there was no guarantee it would be available. Oil was available, but it was oil from mustard seeds, not the more desirable sesame oil or oil from ground nuts.

Despite these difficulties, the disciples did realize how fortunate they were compared with the victims of the famine, whose suffering could not be comprehended. They had lessened their own inconvenience by thinking ahead. They brought a few items with them, including extra rice, sweets and canned milk for Dhyanyogi-ji's tea. And when Batonsadevi first saw how her brother would be living, she immediately returned to her village, Kachainiya, to gather some rice, wheat, ghee and other staples.

Dhyanyogi's room was sturdier than the grass hut the disciples lived in, but the doors could not be fastened, much less locked. The wind played with them, and they flapped open and shut with an endless thumping. On his second day in Adhaura, a pack of dogs—known there as "Vitthal Bhagwan," an incarnation of Lord Vishnu[44]—got into his room and ate the cache of sweets and 11 pounds of rice. It was a devastating setback, but instead of becoming angry or upset Dhyanyogi-ji smiled and said, "Would God approve of us eating sweets and luxuries while there are people here in need of every single piece of grain? So Lord Vitthal ate it up for us!"

For the people who lived in Bihar, the famine exacerbated already intolerable conditions. Backward and depressed, Bihar was not only a poverty-stricken place, it was rife with inter-caste violence, banditry and widespread corruption. The starving Biharis were victimized by corrupt local officials and neighbors who profited from their desperation. Even Dhyanyogi-ji's feeding stations were at risk of being looted. As his disciples lay sleeping, the guru maintained a quiet vigil over the storehouse of grain near his quarters. His presence frightened off at least one group of masked men.

Every day, long lines of gaunt figures made their way to Dhyanyogi-ji's food kitchens at Bifora, Bamani and Chamani. Between them, the kitchens fed 500 people a single noontime meal each day. Feeding people who are starving is a tricky business because they often cannot keep any solid food down. Their food intake must be carefully monitored until body functions have been restored to normal. People who came to Dhyanyogi-ji's kitchens were fed a bland diet of boiled cracked wheat mixed with powdered milk and—when the cooks were able to find some—molasses. Daily portions were strictly limited to avoid diarrhea and other complications, possibly even death.

---

[44]The dogs were known as Vitthal Bhagwan because of a story about the saint Eknath. Eknath had visions of God in which God told him that he needed a teacher if he was to become fully enlightened. He accepted the young boy Jnaneshwar as his guru, and after practicing under him, he reached his goal and started to see God everywhere. Once a dog snatched a piece of bread that Eknath was about to eat. Eknath ran after the dog saying, "Wait! Let me put butter on your bread, Lord!"

Dhyanyogi-ji developed special guidelines for his feeding stations, for he wanted to nourish souls as well as bodies. He asked people to chant Ram's name before eating. This was nearly impossible for those whose malnutrition was the worst, but he expected everyone to participate as best they could. He also insisted that his disciples maintain their daily spiritual practices, no matter how grueling their work schedule, because he was concerned about the emotional and spiritual toll the famine was having on them. In the morning, disciples meditated on their own. In the evening, they took walks with Dhyanyogi-ji that were full of wisdom and laughter. Then they meditated together as a group, ate dinner, and sang bhajans before retiring.

After 17 days at Adhaura, word came that the monsoon rains were approaching. The monsoon is always preceded by a short period of unsettled weather that ranges from dust storms and brief rain showers to violent electrical storms. Dhyanyogi-ji knew that when the torrential rains finally arrived, much of Bihar would be flooded and travel on the muddy mountain roads would become treacherous, if not impossible. If the relief team stayed in Adhaura until the rains began in full force, they could be stranded there for at least two weeks. Dhyanyogi-ji decided it was time to move.

At 6:00 a.m. on June 8, 1967, Dhyanyogi-ji and his disciples bade goodbye to Adhaura and started for Sasaram. It took about 10 days to find a suitable place to resume their relief efforts. During this time, Dhyanyogi-ji returned to Durgadih for a few days and made a brief, two-hour visit to Batonsadevi's house in Kachainiya. Since being reunited with him, Batonsadevi and her relatives had developed a renewed sense of love and admiration for Dhyanyogi-ji. At times they complained to the Gujarati disciples, "You snatched our Baba away."

"Yes, he is ours," the disciples would reply.

Dhyanyogi-ji was always at the center of a tug-of-war between his disciples of varying backgrounds and classes. The people of Bandhwad complained about city people from Mumbai taking away their Bapuji, or father. In Ahmedabad, common folk grumbled about rich disciples keeping them from their Gurudev. Dhyanyogi-ji watched this friendly rivalry with amusement.

Once, when his sister served him a lot of rice with his meal—the typical Bihari way of eating—Dhyanyogi-ji teased her, saying, "Oh dear, I am not a Bihari. I am a pure Gujarati. Why did you give me so much rice?"

On June 19, 1967, a new relief center opened in Kudera, along with two others nearby. Although he had only been in Bihar a month, Dhyanyogi-ji had established a reputation for efficiency and honesty. Impressed with his integrity, the Bihar relief committee approached him and asked if he would assume responsibility for five additional centers.

Living conditions were much better in Kudera. Dhyanyogi-ji and his disciples stayed in Hanuman Mills, which is centrally located on a highway near the railway station. They had access to telephones, electricity, a telegraph, mail delivery and other modern conveniences. They even had a cow to supply fresh milk. The disciples held a special 24-hour Ram chant to bless their new beginning, and they resumed their daily meditations.

Dealing with the specter of famine and death every day did take its toll on the relief workers, but Dhyanyogi-ji continued to look out for them, sometimes in unusual ways. One day, while the Kudera feeding station was serving dinner, a politician passed by in his car. He saw bedraggled crowds of people milling about, and instructed his driver to stop. Looking around, he approached a woman named Kamala, who was one of Dhyanyogi-ji's disciples.

"What is going on here?" he demanded.

Kamala, exhausted from her hard work, had little patience for such arrogance and lashed out a curt reply that she instantly regretted. The politician left quietly, but Kamala berated herself, feeling that she had not behaved appropriately. She worried about what her guru would say. As her dismay grew, Dhyanyogi-ji appeared before her. "Don't worry," he said gently. "I am coming tomorrow at 12:00." Then he disappeared.

Kamala was relieved to hear the kindness in Dhyanyogi-ji's voice. In her distress, she had assumed her guru was actually standing in front of her, but when she thought about it later she realized what he had said: "I am coming tomorrow at 12:00." After some investigation, she learned that Dhyanyogi-ji was in fact visiting another village, and her encounter with him had been a vision. He had appeared in his subtle body to reassure her from afar.

The next day, he kept his promise and returned to Kudera, where he remained for three months. While he was there, he had two life-threatening experiences.

One morning at about 11:00, Dhyanyogi-ji headed into the

forest carrying a jug of water. As he crossed the railroad tracks, his foot slipped between the rails and he dropped the water jug. At that very moment a train appeared, approaching rapidly. But instead of panicking, Dhyanyogi-ji remained calm and, at the last moment, he was able to remove his foot and get out of the way in the narrowest of escapes. Not a drop of water had spilled from the jug.

Just a few days later, Dhyanyogi-ji faced death a second time when he began having difficulty breathing, and a messenger went to fetch some medicine for him. The doctor prescribed four tablets of a potent drug, recommending that only half a tablet be taken at a time. The person misunderstood the instructions and gave Dhyanyogi-ji all four tablets at once, a mistake that could have killed him. Dhyanyogi-ji began to perspire profusely as he reacted to the overdose, and had to change clothes as many as 16 times. Other symptoms started to appear, and his disciples grew alarmed and immediately called the doctor. When the doctor heard what had happened, the first words out of his mouth were "Is the patient still alive?"

Dhyanyogi-ji ate some almond *shira*, a sweet made from sugar, ghee, almonds, cardomon and cream of wheat, and that appeared to ease the effects substantially. He was soon out of danger.

By the end of September 1967, there were torrential rains across all of Bihar. Relief work began to wind down, and the food kitchens started closing. Dhyanyogi-ji prepared to return to Gujarat. Just before he left, his grand-nephew Radhakrishna came to see him.

Radhakrishna was the father of Dadan, the young relative who had been assisting in the famine relief work. On a previous visit to Durgadih, Dhyanyogi-ji had repeatedly and mysteriously suggested that his nephew call Dadan back from his post in the army. Though Dhyanyogi-ji gave no reason, Radhakrishna took his suggestion seriously and made Dadan resign his post and return home.

Now Dadan and Dhyanyogi-ji had just spent four months working side by side during the relief effort, and they had grown close. Dadan had come to deeply respect his uncle and his work, and Radhakrishna felt that his son could benefit from spending more time with him. "You can take Dadan to Gujarat with you, if you like," he told Dhyanyogi-ji. But Dhyanyogi-ji turned down the request and told Radhakrishna that he should take his son home.

Only a few months later, Dadan contracted a fatal illness and died. He had been so inspired by Dhyanyogi-ji during their time together that his final words were *"Sadaguru deva ki jay,* Dhyani Maharaj Madhusudandasji *ki jay. Matapita ki jay."* ("Victory to the Sadguru, victory to Dhyanyogi. Victory to Mother and Father.")

In a condolence letter to his grand-nephew, Dhyanyogi-ji wrote, "The soul of this yogi only came for a short time. Do not lament over it." Now everyone understood why Dhyanyogi-ji had insisted that Dadan be called home from the army.

A similar incident occurred when Dhyanyogi-ji heard the news of the death of his disciple Shri Tryambaklal of Ahmedabad. He said, "When I went to his house on the occasion of his grandson's sacred thread ceremony, I felt that his end was near, and so I often insisted upon his coming to Bandhwad and passing his remaining life in worship and song in praise of God."

As the relief work ended, the people of Bihar decided to honor Dhyanyogi-ji by giving an address expressing gratitude and love: "This dry district of Palamu, covered with palm trees, has obtained new tender shoots by your holy touch and is singing a song of your praise with thousands of its tongues...You are among the shining stars by whose light the direction of human knowledge will remain marked for an endless time."

On September 27, 1967 Dhyanyogi-ji left for Mumbai, and the relief centers closed.

A year later, Dhyanyogi-ji was preparing for his annual anusthan during Navaratri when he heard more bad news. Another famine was tightening its grip on the country, this time in the Banaskantha district of Gujarat, which surrounds Bandhwad. Once again, there had been no rain during the monsoon season, and once again the situation was growing desperate. Scenes from Bihar were repeated in Gujarat—the cracked soil, the withered crops, and starving people begging for a morsel of food.

This time, however, there were also starving cattle everywhere. In India, it is not unusual for people to worry about the welfare of cows because they are essential parts of the rural economy, pulling carts, plowing fields, producing milk and providing dung for cooking fuel and fertilizer. Because they are so difficult and expensive to replace, it is vital to protect them in times of drought and famine. They are also considered sacred.

Dhyanyogi-ji distributing food during 1967 famine

Dhyanyogi-ji could not bear to see them suffering so he opened a feeding station known as the "Field of Service to Cows."

Dhyanyogi-ji had no idea where to find food or money to feed the cows. He acted totally on faith, and the villagers acted on their faith in him by bringing him their animals. Without their cattle, they would be lost forever. Dhyanyogi-ji comforted them by saying "Lord Hanumanji will take care."

Those words always came true. Somehow it seemed that just when donations were most needed, they would suddenly appear.

The same relief organizations that had helped in Bihar began sending supplies to Gujarat. For the first time in 30 years, Dhyanyogi-ji put aside his anusthan and, on October 7, 1968, opened a free kitchen at the Bandhwad ashram. As in Bihar, people were fed one meal a day. This time they were served a loaf of *bajara* (a bread made from millet) and *dal* (lentil soup) or a vegetable dish.

In a way, the situation was worse here than in Bihar, for the misery of famine continued into the following year. During this time almost 150,000 people ate at the relief center in Bandhwad, as well as 240,000 animals, mostly cows. The center gave away more than 83,000 pounds of corn and provided another 100,000 pounds of corn at cost. Nearly as much was subsidized at a quarter of its usual price. The villagers also received millet seed and cash for buying other kinds of seed, and children were provided with enriched food and powdered milk. Almost 6,000 people were given free medical care. More than 300 woolen blankets and 500 cotton sheets were distributed, along with more than 1,300 items of clothing. And for two years, the center ran a free water station on the highway.

Word of the relief work being done at Bandhwad soon spread so widely that strangers began approaching Dhyanyogi-ji while he was

traveling with offers of support. Many of these donors were living examples of Francis Bacon's belief that "in charity there is no excess." One
day, Dhyanyogi-ji's car was parked in the area of Ahmedabad referred to
as Three Gates. The car had a poster attached to it that said "Famine
Relief Center, Bandhwad." A 10-year-old boy walked up to the car and
offered all the change he had in his pocket, which amounted to just half
a rupee, to a disciple who was waiting there for Dhyanyogi-ji to return.
When Dhyanyogi-ji heard what the boy had done, he was just as pleased
as if someone had offered him a fortune.

"To me this is equal to 50,000 rupees," he said. "We could eliminate starvation with such pure charity. It is good that this boy is spiritually refined at such a young age."

Another time Dhyanyogi-ji was in Mumbai giving a meditation
program when a stranger came up to him and asked, "Are you Dhyani
Maharaj?"

"Yes, I am."

"Are you running a famine relief center?"

"Yes."

"Then take this 100 rupees," the man said, placing it at Dhyanyogi-
ji's feet. "Use it in relief work."

"What is your name?" asked Dhyanyogi-ji.

"What is the need for a name?" Though he would not identify himself, the stranger did eventually confess that he had been unemployed
for six months and had eight family members to support. "But I cannot
bear to see the miseries of famine, so I give this money," he said.

"These 100 rupees of yours are very pure," Dhyanyogi-ji told him.
"To me, they are equal to thousands of rupees. The famine will be con-
quered with such charity."

In another incident, a traveler approached Dhyanyogi-ji when he
was riding on the train from Surat to Broach and placed 500 rupees
at his feet. He also refused to identify himself, saying only, "Use this
money for famine relief work."

Monetary donations were essential for the operation of the relief
centers, but money couldn't solve every problem. Sometimes what was
needed was the intervention of a higher power. One day 2,600 cows arrived at the relief center's feeding station. The supply of cattle feed was
already nearly exhausted, and by the next day there would be nothing

left. Dhyanyogi-ji asked people in the surrounding villages for any extra hay, but they had none. Night fell, and he reluctantly went to bed. Ill at ease and restless, periodically he'd come down from his room and ask, "Is there any hay?"

At midnight, a strong rumbling roused everyone from their beds. Sleepy-eyed disciples made their way to the ashram's courtyard, where they found three trucks loaded with hay! They ran to the drivers, asking "Where did these trucks come from? Who sent them?"

"Why are you concerned with who sent us?" they replied. "Our employer has ordered us not to disclose his name. Just unload the hay from our trucks. We must be on our way."

Hoping to end the prolonged drought, Dhyanyogi-ji arranged for a continuous, 24-hour chanting of "Ram" that would last for five days. On the fifth day, at 11:00 p.m., a soaking rain began to fall on Bandhwad and the surrounding villages. In a spontaneous outburst of joy, the villagers began jumping and dancing, making their way to the Hanumanji temple. Here they unfurled a new flag to put on top of the temple as a symbol of their faith and devotion to God and Guru.

With the arrival of rain, the parched land sprang to life and produced a bumper crop for the farmers. They saw that the largest crops appeared wherever cows had been kept during the famine. The villagers credited Dhyanyogi-ji with their good fortune, saying, "It is because of Bapuji that we have rain. He is responsible for our big crop. He did japa and tapas for us, and we reap the benefits."

The relief center closed on November 11, 1970. In the coming years there would be similar though less devastating droughts, and Dhyanyogi-ji responded to each of these with the same love and compassion.

His *karma-bhumi*—field of action—had now expanded beyond the borders of Gujarat.

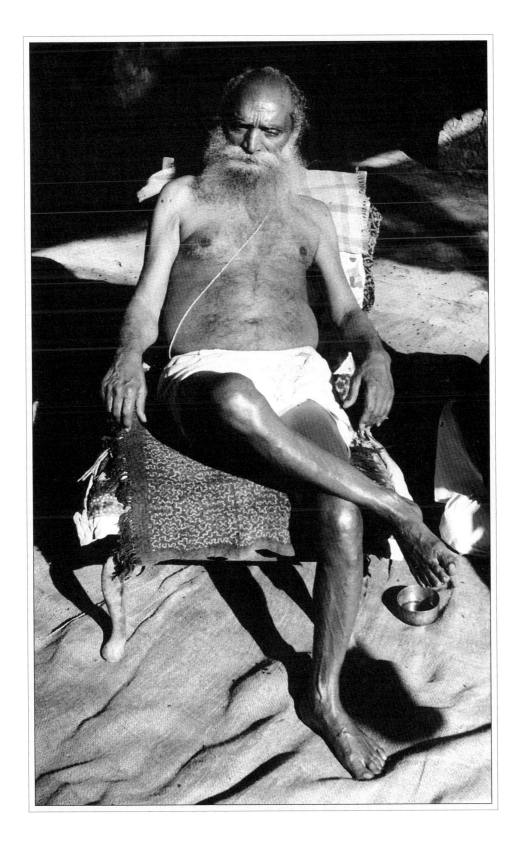

CHAPTER TWENTY-ONE

GRACE LIKE DIAMONDS

By the end of the 1960s, word had spread about Dhyanyogi-ji's humanitarian projects and his bold venture of openly teaching meditation and giving shaktipat. He had two books in print that explained kundalini, revealing things that were once well-kept secrets among the yogis. Wandering sadhus repeated the stories they'd heard about him when they shared meals in temples or their paths crossed on mountain trails.

As his reputation grew, hundreds of people approached him with all manner of requests. For some, he was a wise elder to whom they turned for advice about their personal problems. Others saw him as a great mahatma and sought him out for inspiration or guidance in their sadhana. A select few recognized his uniqueness even among enlightened beings. For them, meeting Dhyanyogi-ji and receiving the shaktipat initiation proved to be just what they needed to fulfill their deepest spiritual longings. His energy blasted through whatever remaining blocks they had to attaining realization.

But no matter what circumstances brought people to Dhyanyogi-ji, he met them wherever they were. In some cases, that meant being "on call" for dealing with the difficulties in life that make us all turn to prayer—emotional trauma, medical emergencies, heartbreaks, financial disasters and legal problems.

Dhyanyogi-ji told the story of a devotee who came to him when his son was imprisoned for a murder he hadn't committed. Mr. Joshi was a politician and he suspected that the opposing party was responsible for his son's arrest. Ordinarily a stoical man, Mr. Joshi broke down in tears when he told Dhyanyogi-ji the stituation.

"Don't worry." Dhyanyogi-ji told Mr. Joshi. "Your kundalini is awakened and She is taking care of you. I will help you also, and everything will be fine in the end."

He instructed Mr. Joshi to do a 40-day anusthan. As the 40 days came to an end, the judge's mother fell sick. He took a month's leave so he could go and take care of her, and another judge came to take his place. When the proceedings began, the people who were leveling the accusations against Joshi's son started to forget things, and make statements that contradicted their original written depositions. The judge threw the case out of court and Joshi's son was freed.

The moral of this story, in the words of Dhyanyogi-ji, was, "There is always protection. The kundalini is always protecting you, and trying to fulfill your desires so that you can be free of them."

In another case, a businessman from Rajkot was embroiled in a lawsuit. It looked as if he would lose everything, and he came to Dhyanyogi-ji sick with anxiety over what might happen to his daughter. Once again, Dhyanyogi-ji told him not to worry. Three days later, his opponent's lawyer called and told him there were flaws in the case so they were dropping the suit.

Sometimes, Dhyanyogi-ji used his yogic powers in very obvious ways to help disciples. For example, there was a disciple in Ahmedabad who lived in a luxurious home shaded by coconut palms and deciduous trees. The house was filled with finely upholstered furniture, plump pillows piled high on floors covered with silk carpets, and lighting provided by imported chandeliers. Despite these material comforts, Mr. Desai[45] was very unhappy because of a strange misfortune that plagued his family. Every first-born male child in his extended family died. The family asked Dhyanyogi-ji for a blessing.

---

[45]This is a fictitious name, used to protect the privacy of the parties involved.

Dhyanyogi-ji entered the house, and in silence, took a few steps. He then said that there was a place in the kitchen where they should dig eight feet down, and he gave them the exact dimensions.

Mrs. Desai was ready to follow Dhyanyogi-ji's instructions, but her husband hesitated, reluctant to ruin their beautiful marble floor. "It's up to you to choose if you want to be happy or have your marble floor," Dhyanyogi-ji said, "but this is what you would have to do."

Finally, Mr. Desai agreed to do what Dhyanyogi-ji suggested. In the exact spot that he had indicated, they uncovered the skeleton of a body that had apparently been buried there long before. They had been cooking all their meals in this room where the energy of this unhappy soul was trapped. Once they removed the skeleton and dealt with it appropriately, the family never lost a first-born son again.

Often when people came to him with problems, Dhyanyogi-ji gave them mantras. Reciting the correct mantra reduces the intensity of the karma at the root of a problem. "There's a mantra for everything," he said. If someone was having financial difficulties, health problems, or a couple wanted children, Dhyanyogi-ji often asked the disciple to sit by him, and sound by sound, phrase by phrase, he would teach the mantra to the disciple. The disciple would repeat after him until he had spoken the mantra three times. This repetition empowered the mantra. There are scores of testimonials from people who, after using their mantras, found jobs, received money in the mail that they'd long been awaiting, and gave birth to babies after years of futile attempts.

But most of all, there was a seemingly endless stream of stories in which disciples were inexplicably cured of serious medical conditions after seeking the help of Dhyanyogi-ji. Haresh Chudasama's wife Krishna discovered a lump, but the family could not afford a biopsy, let alone surgery. In desperation, Krishna's mother traveled from Rajkot to Bandhwad. Dhyanyogi-ji gave her a rose and told her to give it to Krishna, with the instructions that she smell it every day. In four days, the lump was gone.

A disciple from Mumbai told how Dhyanyogi-ji helped his wife during a medical crisis. Mr. Roy's[46] business took him to Delhi for months at a time. Once, when he was on such a trip, his wife became extremely ill. She went to a doctor who found a tumor the size of a tennis ball blocking her uterus. She was in a great deal of pain, and the doctor said that if they didn't operate within 24 hours, the threat to her health

---

[46] This is a fictitious name, used to protect the privacy of the parties involved.

would be even more critical. Mrs. Roy called her husband immediately. He told her that he wanted to speak with Dhyanyogi-ji before they consented to the operation.

"Unless Guruji gives permission for the surgery, I am not prepared to have you go through it. Stay calm and have faith in Guruji, no matter what the surgeon says."

Mr. Roy contacted Dhyanyogi-ji and explained the situation to him. "Don't worry," Dhyanyogi-ji said. "There is no need for you to rush to Mumbai. Just ask your wife to meditate and she will be okay."

The Roys were conflicted. On the one hand, the doctors were saying that Mrs. Roy was in danger and they had to operate right away, while on the other, Dhyanyogi-ji was coolly telling them just to meditate. Still, they had strong faith in Dhyanyogi-ji, so Mrs. Roy started meditating.

A week passed, but the pain continued and Mrs. Roy was unable to meditate well. The couple consulted Dhyanyogi-ji again and this time he told her husband, "If she can't meditate, don't worry. You meditate."

Mr. Roy was due to return to Mumbai in two weeks. While he remained in Delhi, he meditated without fail. When he got back home, he took his wife to the doctor, and to their amazement, they discovered that the tumor was gone. There was no sign of it at all. "This is impossible," insisted the doctor with a trace of resentment. "You must have gone somewhere else and gotten it removed!"

Physicians were baffled again in the case of a woman who entered a very painful labor in the eighth month of her pregnancy. Her family approached Dhyanyogi-ji to request his blessing and assistance with this difficult, premature birth.

Dhyanyogi-ji had studied and mastered the science of yantras, so he knew about one particular yantra that looks like a maze and is essentially a map showing the baby how to find the way out of the womb. He drew the yantra with sandalwood paste inside a special metal plate and told the mother to gaze at it.

It so happened that two physicians from Mumbai were visiting Dhyanyogi-ji on the day that this family came to see him, so he asked the doctors to examine the woman. Both agreed that the baby was in a reversed position in the womb, and that this was what was complicating the labor and causing the mother such excruciating pain. They told Dhyanyogi-ji that either the mother or infant would survive, but not both, and urged him not to take on the responsibility for such a risky birth. Instead, they suggested that he send the woman to the nearest town that had medical facilities available.

In a situation like this, Dhyanyogi-ji never challenged the advice of physicians. He typically deferred to the "experts," left the decisions up to the disciple, and then let the incident unfold. So he told the family what the physicians said, and encouraged them to "please, go ahead and take her to the hospital."

But the young mother spoke up. "I don't want to go anywhere. Whatever is to happen, let it happen by the grace of Guruji. He is my doctor."

Dhyanyogi-ji consented, saying with some caution, "Okay, let us wait for 12 hours."

In the meantime, the woman gazed at the yantra and followed Dhyanyogi-ji's instructions. By the time the 12 hours had passed, the baby had completely turned around, and the mother had a normal birth.

Dhyanyogi-ji always seemed tickled in these situations as he watched people realize that there was more going on in the world than what their rational minds told them. He teased the doctors saying, "Can your scientists explain how all this happened?"

But Dhyanyogi-ji didn't believe that his primary role was to be a healer. Once, after curing a young girl of a particularly serious disease, a line of people who wanted to be healed formed at the door of the place where he was staying. Dhyanyogi-ji left through the back door, saying, "This is not my work." He responded to his devotees' requests out of compassion, but his main concern was to help them spiritually benefit their souls, not merely fulfill their desires.

Once, anguished parents of a teenaged girl came to Dhyanyogi-ji. In Gujarat, during the nine days of Navaratri, it is traditional to dance the garba late into each night. Their daughter wanted to join the festivities, but her parents didn't feel it was safe for her to be out all night, so they told her she couldn't go. Adolescents typically express strong emotions when their freedom is curtailed, but this girl's reaction was extreme. In a reckless moment, she took her own life, leaving her parents torn apart with shock and grief. Over and over, they asked themselves, "Why did she kill herself? It was such a small thing."

The couple wanted Dhyanyogi-ji to communicate with their daughter and find out where her soul had gone, but Dhyanyogi-ji told them

Ahmedabad, circa 1970

that this wouldn't help them or their daughter. Instead, he told them to chant "Shri Ram, Jay Ram, Jay Jay Ram" for 24 hours because this would bring peace to her soul and help it to evolve as it moved through the next stages of being.

The girl's parents followed his instructions, but their distress was unrelenting. They still longed to find out what happened to their daughter, so they looked for someone else who could call on the dead. When they found such a person, they contacted their daughter's soul, and received a message from her.

"Please forgive me. I made a big mistake," she said. "It was such a harsh reaction to what was really only one night of my life. I know I caused you pain and grief.

"But I also want you to know that the procedures they did at the hospital to try to revive me were horrible. When a soul is leaving the body, attempts to revive only complicate and confuse the soul and make the passage very difficult. I wanted to leave the body. No one should have touched me and poked me with needles as they did.

That caused me even more agony and trouble with the passage.

"But please thank Guruji a thousand times! The chanting you did at his advice brought me tremendous relief and helped me with my transition. Through the energy of the chanting, I have evolved and I am now at peace."

When disciples came to Dhyanyogi-ji, even if they were asking for his help with worldly problems, he focused on a very different level. Most people found that following his guidance pushed the limits of their faith, but the results were startling. These were first-hand experiences of grace. And when this kind of grace comes into people's lives, it can change them completely.

Dhyanyogi-ji used to say that just meeting a saint, having his or her darshan, was a blessing that indicated a person's previous karma at work. To take full advantage of this meeting, people must also put forth their efforts by doing sadhana. Otherwise, they will miss the depth and significance of the opportunity they've been given—the chance to make spiritual progress.

To bring home his message of valuing spiritual evolution above all else, he used to tell a story about a wealthy man who had four sons. Although this man had plenty of money to pass on to his children, he wanted them to gain knowledge about life, so he sent them out into the world to seek their own fortunes.

First, the boys came upon a coal mine. Content with this discovery, the first son stayed and mined coal. The others believed there was something worth more than coal out there, and continued on their way.

Next, they came across a silver mine. The second son was dazzled by the fortune he could make with silver, so he staked his claim there. The remaining sons still felt that there was something more valuable than silver so they resumed their quest. After some time passed, they discovered a gold mine. The third son believed that at last, he had found the treasure his father had in mind.

But the fourth son sensed that there was something still greater. He was determined not to settle for anything until he reached this goal. He continued to search and to dig deeper and eventually he found a diamond mine. His perseverance brought him the richest rewards.

Dhyanyogi-ji constantly reminded his students not to be distracted from the final goal of enlightenment—not to be satisfied with the coal, silver and gold of temporal, material and emotional gains—but to continue seeking until they attained the most precious diamond of self-realization. When people asked only for worldly boons, he taught, they were shortchanging themselves because he had diamonds to offer.

But it was not so easy to apprehend and appreciate who Dhyanyogi-ji was and what he could give them. In the *Bhagavad Gita*, the scripture in which Lord Krishna teaches his disciple, the prince Arjuna, about the essence of yoga, there comes a point when Arjuna requests that the Lord reveal His true form to him. Lord Krishna is willing, but explains that Arjuna would be unable to perceive His cosmic form with his physical eyes because they are limited. To see the divine, it is necessary to have spiritual vision. So Lord Krishna gives Arjuna the "divine eyes" required to see behind the "veils of maya" that keep us from seeing things as they really are.

Without divine eyes, we notice only worldly things, never glimpsing the permanent and "real" aspects of life, like the existence of the soul, the interconnectedness of all beings, the workings of karma, the true nature of someone like Dhyanyogi-ji, and the true nature of ourselves. When we do spiritual practices, we gradually free ourselves from the temporary attachments that divert us from recognizing these truths. That, Dhyanyogi-ji explained, was the importance of putting forth effort. But ultimately, he said, it is only through grace that we can acquire the capacity to see beyond maya.

This was the jewel that Dhyanyogi-ji offered. By his grace and through the shaktipat initiation, he enabled people to peek beyond maya. Then, the obstacles to spiritual growth began to be destroyed and the soul could find its way home.

For those who understood this, meeting Dhyanyogi-ji was, in and of itself, the goal. But even among those who came to Bandhwad expressly for spiritual guidance rather than help with worldly problems, most still operated out of ego and this blinded them. Furthermore, no matter how much they had attained spiritually, their attachments to their beliefs and ambitions prevented them from being able to hold onto the energy they received from Dhyanyogi-ji.

Dhyanyogi-ji used to say, "When it rains, hold your umbrella upside down!" Energy is showering down upon us, he explained, and if we hold up an umbrella to protect our egos, we'll miss out on its benefits. If we

Yreka, California, 1978

hold our umbrellas upside down, we will be drenched in the energy and can soak in as much as possible.

According to Eastern thought, most of us lose the spiritual energy we collect from enlightened masters because of how our samskaras direct us to interpret and respond to events. That's the paradox of spiritual practice—we do practices so that these habits formed in previous lifetimes can be burned away, enabling us to increase our energy, but those very habits interfere with our doing practices! Put in Western terms, we need to free ourselves from the tyranny of our egos. The ego wants to retain control over our lives, wants to feel special, and sets itself apart from others. It resists the kind of discipline and sacrifice necessary for spiritual practice, because these deprive the ego of the attention it craves.

In 1970, there was a sanyasi from Kashmir who came to see Dhyanyogi-ji for spiritual guidance. He had his own ashram and many disciples. He was a scholar and a master of the scriptures who had performed austerities and Vedic practices for 40 years. But after traveling 60,000 miles, criss-crossing India and meeting different saints, he had never met anyone able to awaken his kundalini, and in all that time, he didn't feel that he had made significant progress. When he heard about the great shaktipat guru from Bandhwad, he eagerly set out to meet him. Upon his arrival, he was shocked to see little children sitting in meditation. He fell at Dhyanyogi-ji's feet and began to cry. With great humility, the sanyasi asked for shaktipat initiation.

When he heard the sanyasi's request, Dhyanyogi-ji said, "I'll initiate you later. First, massage my head." Occasionally, when Dhyanyogi-ji met someone, he immediately invited that person to massage him so he could pass on some energy right away.

After massaging Dhyanyogi-ji for 20 minutes, the sanyasi fell down unconscious and remained in that state for two hours. When he woke up, Dhyanyogi-ji asked, "What happened to you?"

The sanyasi, completely overcome by the intensity of Dhyanyogi-ji's energy, replied, "I don't know anything!" He had lost consciousness, and this had never happened to him before. The last thing he remembered was noticing a lot of heat in his body, but then his awareness dissolved and he fell down. He couldn't remember how he'd gotten there or where he was staying, so Dhyanyogi-ji had someone take him home.

This disorientation persisted for three days. Once he returned to normal, he went to Dhyanyogi-ji and again expressed his desire to receive shaktipat. The following day, Dhyanyogi-ji gave him the initiation and the sanyasi went into meditation for 24 hours.

When he woke up, he felt that he had gotten what he'd come for and was eager to return to his ashram as soon as possible. To his dismay, Dhyanyogi-ji told him that to fortify his current state and make it permanent, he should stay in Bandhwad a little longer.

"But I am in a hurry. I must go back to my ashram and give shaktipat to my disciples so they don't have to go through years of painful searching as I did."

"First strengthen yourself," advised Dhyanyogi-ji. "Then you can share your energy." But the sanyasi stubbornly refused. "No, I cannot wait."

Dhyanyogi-ji told the saint that the experience he'd just had did not indicate that he had attained the ultimate goal. He'd had a glimpse of the final state, but it would not last. He had to progress further before his energy was fully under his control. Such stability was a requirement for safely and effectively awakening the kundalini in others.

"Stay with me for six to 12 months and I will train you," said Dhyanyogi-ji. "Then you'll have enough energy and I myself will ask you to perform shaktipat."

Despite Dhyanyogi-ji's promises to take care of him, the sanyasi only grew more adamant. A dignitary was scheduled to visit him, and he argued that he couldn't miss their meeting. Dhyanyogi-ji continued to urge the sanyasi to take more time, but his words fell on deaf ears and finally, he gave up.

"Go if you wish, but it would be better if you stayed and gained balance and reached a higher level before you teach. I cannot be responsible for whatever happens with your energy if you leave."

The sanyasi's ego prevented him from holding out for the diamond mine. He was more concerned with visions of helping others and greeting his important guest, so he returned to his ashram.

A few days later, the sanyasi was bitten by a rabid dog. He sent a letter to Dhyanyogi-ji right away, asking him what to do.

Dhyanyogi-ji joked, "You were in a great rush to go and show what you had attained. Instead the dog showed you something! You didn't listen to me, so now you'll have to listen to the dog. Waste no time in beginning your practices or else the poison will spread."

The sanyasi recovered from the dog bite, but not from the loss of energy that resulted. Although he had the wisdom to continue his practices in order to rebuild his energy, he never again experienced what he had while with Dhyanyogi-ji.

There was a handful of devotees who were so sincere and surrendered in their spiritual quests that they were able to absorb Dhyanyogi-ji's energy. Kedarnath Pathak was one. After 30 years of sadhana, his

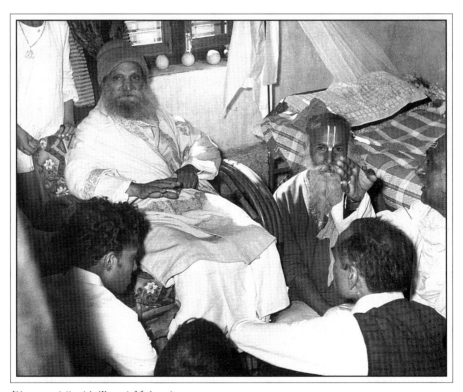

Dhyanyogi-ji with Tapasi Maharaj

ajna chakra had still not opened, but the moment he received shaktipat from Dhyanyogi-ji, the chakra was pierced and he attained realization. Tapasi Maharaj, one of Dhyanyogi-ji's companions at Mount Abu, was another. For the nearly 40 years since he was with Dhyanyogi-ji, he had continued to do austerities without reaching the ultimate state. In 1970, he began to hear stories about his old friend and he realized that the yogi who had once been his peer had become a master. Remembering Dhyanyogi-ji's purity and perfection, he suspected that Dhyanyogi-ji could help him. He went to Bandhwad, requested shaktipat initiation and became Dhyanyogi-ji's disciple.

In that same year, Swami Vijay Krishnabharati, a great saint from Benares, also came to see Dhyanyogi-ji in Bandhwad. Swamiji, as he was called, was 62 years old and had spent his entire adult life doing sadhana. He was open enough to receive Dhyanyogi-ji's energy and detached enough to hold onto it. Although he also had his own ashrams and many disciples, his ego was untouched by them. He didn't grasp onto any of it. He cared only about attaining self-realization.

Outside Dhyanyogi-ji's sitting room
Top Row: *Kantibhai, caretaker of Bandhwad; Swami Vijay Krishnabharati; the ashram cook; Dhyanyogi-ji; Dr. Kedarnath Pathak; Deepak Pathak; Gopaldas, a visiting sadhu*
Seated: *Mukat Rawal & family; Kamala; Raghunath, the Bandhwad village merchant*

Before he met Dhyanyogi-ji, despite his level of evolution, Swamiji was not at peace. He'd had remarkable experiences and visions of God, "but the goal of a sanyasi," he said, "is fulfilled only when the eternal blissful state of God is merged with the soul.

"I was very keen to find refuge at the feet of a great master. It was my excellent fortune that I met the well-known Vedanta scholar and writer, Swami Shri Sureshwaranandji. He lived at the banks of the Narmada at Karnali, but was visiting Benares. I met him and discussed my situation with him, seeking his advice. He spoke to me about a complete and perfect yogi who was worthy of adoration, and united with Brahma. He was talking about Dhyanyogi-ji.

"Sureshwaranandji had met many saints and mahatmas, 'but as far as I know,' he told me, 'at the present time, if you are looking for a being who is immersed in the absolute state of bliss, has undergone all possible sadhanas, and is the embodiment of compassion, Dhyanyogi-ji is the only one.' Sureshwaranandji invited me to come to Karnali and said that he would take me to see Dhyanyogi-ji. Hearing all this made my heart feel an incredible level of joy.

"Soon after this, I went to Karnali. Swami Sureshwaranandji wrote to Guruji requesting him to shower his grace upon me, and I continued on to Bandhwad for darshan of Guruji. My first sight of him gave me a deep and profound sense of complete bliss. I saw in him the united form of soul and God, transcending all things of this world. I felt intuitively that my search and travels here and there were now over. I had come to my final resting place.

"I spent a few days in the purifying and uplifting land of Guruji. Finally the great day dawned. On October 20, 1970, Guruji bestowed upon me the shaktipat initiation according to the scriptures. I felt something spinning at a very great velocity on the top of the head, and my entire body was filled with light. That night, I felt as if I was intoxicated, and all night long I spontaneously heard the Bhuta Shuddhi mantra in my mind. The next day, I started to do the 10-day Bhuta Shuddhi anusthan as Guruji had told me, but I could hardly say the mantra without passing into deep states. I can surely say that all the experiences I had prior to meeting Guruji were quite insignificant in comparison to the ones I had after shaktipat. I was convinced that I would now have the ultimate experience of my soul merging with the formless Brahma, that I would enter the state of nirvikalpa samadhi at the feet of my all-compassionate master."

Swamiji had known that in order to reach self-realization, he needed to be able to mix the five pranas, the five forms that energy takes in the body. Vedic scholars debated about the plavnik pranayama, that supposedly merged the pranas, but Swamiji had never met anyone who knew the technique, let alone mastered it. Plavnik was one of the practices that Dhyanyogi-ji had perfected during his years as a student, and after their meeting, Dhyanyogi-ji took Swamiji down to his cave, charged with the energy of his years of practices, and showed Swamiji how to do the plavnik. Swamiji was so advanced that as soon as he performed this pranayama, he fell into samadhi. He awoke in a state of bliss, crying tears of gratitude.

"I experienced waves upon waves of energy and infinite joy. Various experiences of light and sound manifested at exquisite levels. I had never had such experiences before. The very essence of all scriptures was revealed to me with this teaching and Guruji's ability to show me how it was done. To such a being, my Guru, I offer everything up."

Filled with the sole desire to serve Dhyanyogi-ji, Swamiji dropped all of his other activities, and dedicated his life to helping further his guru's work.

Rambhai, a devotee from the district of Mehsana, north of Ahmedabad, told the story about when he first consciously began to appreciate Dhyanyogi-ji's spiritual stature. He had received shaktipat from Dhyanyogi-ji years before, and he always went to see his guru whenever Dhyanyogi-ji visited his city.

Then, in 1970, Rambhai and a companion embarked on a difficult trek into the remote forests of northern India in search of a rare herb. In the middle of the wilderness, they came upon a sadhu's cave. People rarely traveled in this wild and inaccessible area, so the sadhu invited them in. As they sat talking and drinking tea from metal cups, Rambhai glanced around the cave. To his amazement, there, hanging on the rough, earthen wall, was Dhyanyogi-ji's photograph! The sadhu noticed his visitor's reaction and asked, "Why are you staring at that photo?"

"That is a picture of my own personal Gurudeva! I am shocked to see it here, in such a remote place." exclaimed Rambhai.

Bandhwad, late 1960's

The sadhu laughed. "You don't know what you have attained," he said. "There are only three beings like him in India, and probably in the world, at this time. Have faith and devote yourself to him. With a guru like Dhyanyogi-ji, you don't need anyone else or any other blessings."

Carl Kuntz, the first American disciple, in front of the Hanuman temple at Bandhwad ashram.

CHAPTER TWENTY-TWO

THE FIRST AMERICAN DISCIPLE

*A*t the close of the 19th century, Swami Vivekananda brought Indian philosophy to the West. His wisdom touched the lives of many spiritual seekers, and by 1970, Indian culture and spirituality had captured the attention of whole generations of people in the United States and Europe. In the 1960s, Irina Tweedie, an educated Englishwoman in her mid-50s, went to India to search for the meaning of life after the death of her husband. She wrote about her experiences in *Daughter of Fire: A Diary of Spiritual Training with a Sufi Master.* At the height of their success, the Beatles went to Rishikesh to study meditation with Maharishi Mahesh Yogi, founder of Transcendental Meditation, after which their recordings began to reflect the influence of classical Indian music. Ravi Shankar, the great sitar master, appeared at the "Woodstock" rock festival. Richard Alpert left his position at Harvard and traveled to India where he met his guru, Neem Karoli Baba, who gave him the new spiritual name Ram Dass. Their meeting transformed Ram Dass's life. From then on, his work centered on meditation and service, and he started an organization in America committed to humanitarian works called the

Seva Foundation. As he put it, in the early 70s "spiritual growth rooted in Eastern mysticism was definitely 'in.'"[47]

The first Western seeker roaming through India to come across Dhyanyogi-ji was Carl Kuntz, a civil engineer from California. Carl had caught the wave of interest in Eastern meditation practice and was drawn to visit India in 1970. Hindus might say he'd had many previous lifetimes in India, and that his karma with Dhyanyogi-ji had pulled him back to find his teacher again. Whatever the reason, Carl felt curiously at home in this very faraway place with its foreign traditions, and ultimately, he played a critical role in bringing Dhyanyogi-ji's work to the west.

Upon his arrival in India, Carl started looking for a teacher. He began by visiting Sathya Sai Baba's ashram, Prasanthi Nilayam, in the village of Puttaparthi near Bangalore in South India. Sai Baba is a saint with an international following. He is noted for performing miracles, like materializing sacred ash out of thin air. His ashram, despite its simple accommodations and remote location, grew from a primitive compound that could only be reached by bullock cart, into a huge complex, including a university and hospital, accessible by all means of public transportation. It was at Sai Baba's ashram that Carl first heard about Dhyanyogi-ji.

"In the late 60s, I was in California studying with a disciple of Yogananda," Carl remembered, "when I decided it was time to go to India to find a guru. Just when I had this desire to go to India, my work commitments suddenly evaporated. They say there are no coincidences! So, on October 1, 1970, I ended up at the San Francisco airport with a one-way ticket to New Delhi.

"I'd heard many amazing stories about Sai Baba, a saint known for creating miracles, so I began my journey by visiting his ashram. When I got there, in the midst of the noise and chaos that greeted me, I heard this voice say, 'Can I help you?' It wasn't a western voice; my new friend was an Indian named Markandrai Vyas, who had just arrived from Gujarat.

"I said, 'Sure.' Markandrai very graciously helped me get my baggage and go to the American part of the compound. Over the next ten days we got to know each other very well, and talked a lot. He kept telling me about this guru who gave people shaktipat. 'By the touch of his hand, he raises your kundalini up to your crown chakra and you become enlightened.' That sounded pretty good!

"I had an interesting experience with Sai Baba and many other

[47]Ram Dass, *Grist for the Mill* (Berkeley, CA: Celestial Arts, 1987) ix.

wonderful encounters in India, but my true objective in coming to India was to find a teacher. Sai Baba didn't work with individuals, and by now, I'd been in India for three months and had to leave soon, so I traveled to Ahmedabad and looked up Markandrai.

"After a few days' visit, he told me that his guru was in town. We went to see him in this big house with hard terrazzo floors. When it was time to meditate, my hosts gave me a very thin dishtowel to sit on. I basically meditated on my ankles!

"After the meditation, Dhyanyogi-ji asked Markandrai about me. I was the first Westerner with whom these people had really come in contact, so they were very curious.

"'What did he experience?' Guruji asked.

"Not wanting to embarrass the guru, I said, 'Well, I felt a *little* energy.'

"For several days, we returned and meditated with Guruji and each time he would ask about my experience. And each time I would say, 'Well, I felt a little energy.'

"Then Guruji told me, 'You'll have to come to Bandhwad to my ashram and I will teach you yoga.'

"I replied, 'I'm about to leave India. I can only come for a week.'

"He said, 'Come anyway.'

"After four or five days, Markandrai took me up to Bandhwad. It was this little village with no running water, no electricity and we were living on temple grounds. But it was very peaceful. The sense of peace was pervasive, especially after being in the commotion of Indian cities. Markandrai couldn't stay, and no one else in the village spoke English at all. Not even a word. But fortunately Deepak Pathak's brother Nayan was there at the time. He was off from college and was doing an anusthan. So he was my translator.

"People came up and asked me questions through Nayan. Nayan translated them, I answered, and Nayan would translate my answers. They were curious about things like, 'How much money do you make?' 'Are you married?' 'What is your caste?' and so on. After a while Nayan stopped asking me the questions and just answered for me.

"We settled in and after a couple of days Guruji asked, 'Would you like shaktipat?'

"'Yeah, that would be good.'

"'First, you need to do some purification. I'll give you this Ram mantra, and you need to do it for at least six weeks before you'll be ready for initiation.'

"My plans to leave India completely vanished. I had found my teacher.

"So I said, 'Okay.' I did the mantra, and had a good experience. I adjusted to the customs of the village and found life pleasant.

"The day of shaktipat finally came, and we prepared for the initiation. Swami Vijay Krishnabharati—Swamiji, as we called him—was there. They gave me a long list of things I needed for the ceremony and Swamiji and I went to Radhanpur on a shopping spree. After several hours, we'd only gotten about half of what we were supposed to, but that would have to do.

"Then I sat for initiation. I'm the sort of person who gets things slowly, but I'm sure that night changed my life.

"After initiation, I started traveling with Guruji. We went to Ahmedabad, to meditation groups and so on. Probably one of the most special times was when he felt that he needed to go to his family home, his father's house, and do some service. So Guruji, Markandrai, another man, a driver and I set off to cross over a thou-

Dhyanyogi-ji at Mount Abu (photograph taken by Carl)

sand miles of the country in a jeep. We had some delightful experiences, going to a lot of very special temples, bathing in the Ganges at Benares, visiting Allahabad and Bodhgaya, the place of Buddha's enlightenment.

"At Bodhgaya, we stayed at a Hindu temple and because some political dignitary came by, they had a feast. I remember that they brought around all of these different dishes—I counted 23 different items. After an hour and a half, everyone else was finished, but I was still only about halfway through because I didn't know what was what. Some things were very hot, some things were very salty, so it took me a while to figure it out!

"We went to Rishikesh and had a lot of experiences of the old India, on a lot of back roads, visiting many very sacred temples in out-of-the-way places.

"Several times priests looked at me and turned to Dhyanyogi-ji. 'We don't allow any Westerners in the temple. How do you explain why you want to bring this person with you? What caste is he?'

"Guruji answered, 'He's California Brahmin. He's okay.'"

Carl postponed his departure from India several times in order to make the most of his opportunity to spend time with Dhyanyogi-ji. In May 1971, when the temperature in Bandhwad climbed to 120 degrees, he decided to go home. But Dhyanyogi-ji was about to travel to Ahmedabad for the dedication of a new ashram that local disciples were giving him, so once again Carl extended his stay to go on this one last journey with his guru.

Dhyanyogi-ji's devotees in Ahmedabad had been eager to establish a local ashram. It was over 100 miles from their city to Bandhwad and traveling that distance on dirt roads shared by trucks, bicycles, carts pulled slowly by camels and bullocks, grazing cows, shepherds with their flocks of sheep, and women balancing urns or piles of kindling on their heads, took at least five hours by car for those who could afford it, and even longer by bus. The discipleship had grown, and his students wanted a more convenient place to meet and a personal residence in Ahmedabad for their teacher. They also hoped to establish an educational institution to serve the spiritual and social needs of their community.

The Governor of Gujarat donated a beautiful piece of land on the bank of the Sabarmati River, near Hansol village, just outside the city limits of Ahmedabad. The location was appealing because many saints had ashrams on this river including Mahatma Gandhi, who had lived in his ashram, not far from Hansol, from 1917 until 1930. It was from here that Gandhi and 80 of his followers departed to make their historic, month-long, 240-mile march to the sea, where they made salt to protest the British monopoly on its production and sale.

When the disciples from Ahmedabad approached Dhyanyogi-ji in Bandhwad and asked if he wanted another ashram, he hedged. "What's wrong with this one?" he asked. "I'm not interested in bricks and stones. That is not an ashram. An ashram is the heart of the disciple."

However, the disciples pressed on, so on June 13, 1971, Dhyanyogi-ji, accompanied by Carl, came to Shri Madhusudandas Dhyanyoga Niketan, as the new ashram was called, to give his blessings for the groundbreaking ceremony. The ritual consisted of digging the initial hole for the foundation of the building, and performing a puja to Mother Earth to show respect and gratitude. The local temple of Ranamukteshwar arranged for the villagers to raise the energy at the new ashram by chanting the name of Lord Ram for the 48 hours before Dhyanyogi-ji's arrival. The excitement built until, at last, Dhyanyogi-ji appeared. One hundred young girls with pots of water balanced on their heads—each girl representing the Divine Mother in her pure, innocent form—met him at the main road and escorted him through the village to the ashram, while joyful crowds played music and sang bhajans. Political dignitaries, businessmen and spiritual teachers from all over Gujarat and Mumbai had been invited to join the disciples in this festive procession.

When they reached the ashram grounds, the puja began. Dhyanyogi-ji invoked special energies to express reverence before digging into the earth. The hole was dug in what would be the northeast corner of the foundation. Inside, precious stones and a silver turtle and snake were buried, to represent stability, strength and permanence.

When the ritual was complete, everyone gathered before a stage where local devotees honored Dhyanyogi-ji and the Governor of Gujarat with garlands of flowers. The spiritually minded governor gave a short speech, expressing his support for the new ashram.

"When I was given an invitation to come here," he began, "I remembered that in ancient times the saint Dadhichi had an ashram on this holy bank of the River Sabarmati, and about 55 years ago, Gandhiji

CHAPTER TWENTY-TWO

Dhyanyogi-ji with state governor who donated the land for the Hansol ashram

established his ashram here as well. Today you are here doing another good work.

"Meditation does not mean that one should move away from the world. My understanding is that by meditating, we make ourselves fit for the service of poor and needy. Meditation helps us to merge our will with the will of God. If we join our will with the Divine Will, we will be able to hear the message of God. The voice of the soul is the voice of God. Gandhiji was engrossed in God, so he could hear the voice of God.

"Dhyanyoga—meditation—is not imaginary. God is subtler than an atom. If an atom is broken, you get energy. Ancient sages have declared that one gets energy if he is able to break his pride. By breaking ego, spiritual energy is obtained. Some have said that they experience joy by meditating. The instrument of meditation is not gross and material. It is the mind.

"I am very glad that you are doing a good deed here with the guidance of Dhyanyogi-ji. Please take full advantage of this ashram and what it can offer you."

At this, the governor sat down and Dhyanyogi-ji came forward. He lifted his rich and resonant voice and began singing some mantras of invocation. Immediately, the mood shifted. Many of his disciples passed into meditation and some started having kriyas. But after only a short time, Dhyanyogi-ji stopped chanting and began talking in a very serious way about the importance of meditating.

"This is an occasion of great joy," he said. "The Governor has thrown much light on what I intend to say.

"The subject of dhyanyoga is difficult, yet simple. For the last 20 years, I have been teaching that it is a mistake to believe that meditation is not a subject for householders. Householders think they can't meditate, and saints say that it should only be taught to those who are 'fit.' But I

Group meditation at Hansol ashram after construction was completed, 1978

think everyone has the right to perform positive actions. And once you begin to observe spiritual practices, and restrain your senses, you will automatically become pure and holy. The great beings discovered and taught the key to realization—shaktipat. At first, people did not believe in it. But now they have begun having faith. Now they are eager.

"Here, we make no distinction between theist or atheist, young or old, this caste or that caste. Among our disciples there are people who belong to all communities. After coming here and meditating, they have simplicity, sincerity and sympathy.

"You may have noticed that even a small child sits for meditation. He sees light. His nature changes. A change takes place in his intellect. Honest emotion is created. During group meditation, many people simultaneously hear and are affected by the same mantrochar. Their minds experience peace. This is the nature of the medicine of meditation. It spreads everywhere invisibly. Our aim is to encourage people to practice meditation while staying in the world. Our work is not to make people become sadhus. There are plenty of sadhus."

Then Dhyanyogi-ji spoke about how Indians were losing touch with their spiritual heritage and being seduced by the illusions of modern life, while Westerners like Carl were leaving behind the comforts and excesses of modern life to find, instead, a way to achieve peace of mind.

"In foreign countries there is abundant wealth," he said, "but there is no mental peace. The American gentleman who is with me says Americans have no mental peace. What is the use of wealth that does not grant peace?

"Our people have come to feel ashamed of chanting. We prefer to follow the practices of Westerners. So when we hear Americans chant, we are surprised that they are adopting the very practices that we are rejecting. People in America have begun giving up eating meat, while here in India they have begun serving meat in hotels. Mr. Carl says that he likes the vegetarian food here. As is your food, so does your mind become. If you eat impure, tamasic food, your intellect will not be pure. It is shameful on our part that we are making meat-eating our own habit.

"In America they have a pill to help one fall asleep. After taking it, one can lie down for a few hours, but it has negative side effects. Similarly, the body relaxes after intoxication, but again, there are side effects. On the other hand, the yogis from our country went to foreign lands in the West and taught people to chant. The Westerners enjoyed chanting and found that through this practice, they slept better and their bodies relaxed. Not only that, but chanting creates honest emotions in the mind. There are no negative side effects. With less effort you get better results."

Finally, Dhyanyogi-ji explained how the loss of emphasis on spirituality had brought about devastating consequences for India.

"When there is calamity, it is the energy of the soul that protects," he said. "Our country suffered for 1,200 years during the Mogul invasions, yet it was able to endure that misery. During that same period, other countries came into being and were destroyed. In India, spiritual roots were deep, so we could face the difficulties. But as time passed, the religious elements of our culture receded and India lost her freedom to the British."

Dhyanyogi-ji said that as Westerners came to India to find deeper meaning in their lives, they reminded Indians of what Indians once knew—their true spiritual natures. Then he raised his hands in blessing, his palms facing the crowd, and sang a prayer for world peace and the welfare of all beings.

Sarve Bhavantu Sukinah
Sarve Santu Niramayah
Sarve Bhadrani Pashyantu
Ma Kaschid Dukhabhag Bhavet.
Om Shantih, Shantih, Shantih

In everything, let everyone be happy.
Let them be healthy.
Let them see prosperity,
And never be afflicted with suffering.
Om Peace, Peace, Peace

CHAPTER TWENTY THREE

SWAMIJI

For Carl, the completion of the groundbreaking ceremony signaled the time for his departure for America. By his next visit in 1973, Shri Madhusudandas Dhyanyoga Niketan had been built, its setting transformed. Now there was a residence for Dhyanyogi-ji, and cottages for disciples, each with a bedroom, sitting room and stairs leading down to a private meditation cave below. Between the rows of cottages were colorful gardens filled with ginger, mango trees and mogra. Each morning, the air was filled with the calls of peacocks, as they strutted around, dragging their trains of brilliant tail feathers. Playful ground squirrels, doves, sparrows and a noisy flock of green parrots also shared the lovely, serene ashram, and frequently, a troop of Langur monkeys made their way across the grounds.

As much as he supported the construction of a center devoted to spiritual work, Dhyanyogi-ji was true to his word that he didn't need another ashram. He visited when he could, but he didn't alter his schedule to stay on there. Instead, he asked Swami Vijay Krishnabharati to live at the ashram to provide spiritual guidance, and he empowered Swamiji to give shaktipat.

A shaktipat guru can, through his sankalpa—his will—enable another to perform shaktipat. In essence, the other becomes an instrument through which the guru operates. In such a case, it is the guru's energy that is being transferred during the initiation, even when someone else's hand is touching the head of the initiate. With Swamiji installed at Hansol ashram, Dhyanyogi-ji ensured that his energy would always be present, whether he was physically there or not.

A remarkable thing had happened. For 50 years, Dhyanyogi-ji alone had carried the torch of the lineage. Certainly many people had done significant seva, but only Dhyanyogi-ji had done the actual spiritual work. Now that had changed. Someone else was helping to ignite the kundalini in other souls. And though, in theory, a guru could empower anyone to perform this role, only someone who had greatly strengthened him- or herself in a spiritual sense could survive being the vehicle for the magnitude of energy that is passed during shaktipat. Most of us would collapse if we were exposed to that intensity over time. Swamiji's purity and state of evolution made him the perfect vessel through which Dhyanyogi-ji's energy could function.

Swamiji was born in 1908 in the state of Kerala. No one knew his exact place of birth or family background. Like Dhyanyogi-ji, he left home as a young boy in pursuit of God-realization. After taking sanyas, he went to Benares. It was here that he met his first guru, but again, like Dhyanyogi-ji, he spoke very little about this early time in his life, making only occasional references to his many years of sadhana.

"When I first arrived in Benares," Swamiji recalled, "I initially did the complete anusthan of the Shiva mantra, as a result of which I had visions of Shiva, Parvati, Ganesh and Kartikeya. Later on, I repeated the mantra 2,800,000 times, after which I had darshan of the Divine Mother. She revealed the absolute meaning of the mantra to me, and resolved many of my doubts.

"Once I fell very ill with a temperature of 105 degrees. The doctors were of no help. I finally surrendered to the Mother. After this, a 10-year-old girl came to my room and said, 'Open your mouth, take this medicine. Your fever will go away forever.' I refused to take the medicine, but she forced open my mouth and gave me some. Since that day, I have never again had any fever. Such is Her grace.

"I had many such experiences with Her presence over the years. In

1942, when I was 34, I began to meditate at the ashram where a saint named Shri Narsimha Bharti Yogiraj had entered 'live samadhi' 500 years ago. Live samadhi is when a realized person feels that his or her work on the earth is done, and they choose to cut themselves off from the world and remain in samadhi to continue working on the subtle plane. Such a person may enter a cave and request someone to seal off the entrance so that no one can enter or leave.

"The place where Shri Narsimha Bharti Yogiraj was buried was in ruins. One night, I had a vision of the saint. I asked him how to repair the ashram and get it started again. He said, 'Everything will be well. Don't worry. Just worship the form of Lord Narsimha.' Lord Narsimha was the incarnation of Lord Vishnu with the head of a lion and body of a man— the form Vishnu had taken to protect his disciple, the boy named Prahlada, from his own father, the demon king Hiranyakashyap. I followed the saint's instructions and prayed to Lord Narsimha, and after three months, a gentleman offered a large sum of money to rebuild the ashram.

"As a result of the externally-oriented work I was doing to reestablish the ashram, my practices were reduced and irregular. One day, I saw the Mother. She scolded me for my negligence. I was sad and hurt and started crying. She gave me Her vision again—She whose heart always melts for the devotee. In my vision, She gave me a lot of love. She let me sit in Her lap, as if I were Her very own child, and She asked me to repeat Her eight-lettered mantra. She said, 'Continue to do this japa and never again miss your daily practice.'

"With Her grace, I attained a lot of peace. I continued to have many profound experiences, but still, I had not reached the final goal of merging the soul with God. I knew this could happen only through the path of yoga. In 1952, now 44 years old, I met the very famous Hadiya Baba in Prayag. He initiated me into *asana, neti, dhauti, basti, nauli, pranayama, shakhaprashalni*, the 10 *maha mudras*. Through all these yogic practices, I attained profound levels of purification of the physical and subtle bodies, both externally and internally. But very soon after that, Hadiya Baba left his body at 105 years of age and I was again without guidance and was in despair."

Swamiji said that he once spent time in an ashram on the Narmada River. The Narmada is considered to be so holy that once a year, the Ganges River, after having absorbed the sins of all who bathe in Her, comes to the Narmada to cleanse Herself. From this ashram, he did the pilgrimage known as Narmada Pradakshina, in which the pilgrim walks from the mouth of the river at Bharuch on the Arabian Sea, along one side of this 800 mile-long river, all the way to the headwaters and back to the mouth of the river on the other side. When he completed this pilgrimage, said to guarantee liberation, he settled in a cave and did austerities.

During these years, Swamiji continued to run the Narsimha temple he had restored in Benares, and he was also given an ashram in Orissa, the state south of Bengal on the east coast of India. Still, his goal eluded him.

"Later on I met a Punjabi mahatma in Benares who gave me shaktipat and thus initiated me into raja yoga. I had many beautiful experiences after that, including a vision of Lord Krishna, yet the eternal inner peace was missing. I constantly felt incomplete."

Then Swamiji met Shri Sureshwaranandji, the scholar who told him about Dhyanyogi-ji. After meeting Dhyanyogi-ji in 1970, and receiving initiation, "my search and running around were truly and finally over," Swamiji said. He was 62 years old. When asked to explain what Dhyanyogi-ji meant to him, he said, "To use any adjectives to describe and praise my guru, who is united with Brahma, would be shameful, because even the Vedas stop when it comes to describing the principles of Brahma. All you can do is fold your hands and bow. Similarly, my dear ones, how can I bind my guru in a limited way with my words? All I can say is that the good karma of previous lives has surfaced and brought me to my guru. I just pray that my focus always remains on the two liberating feet of my guru and as the *Bhagavad Gita* says, 'I am your disciple. Keep me in your refuge forever.'"

Once Swamiji met Dhyanyogi-ji, he wanted to devote himself exclusively to his new teacher. Nothing else mattered to him. He gave away his ashrams. Some of his disciples came to him, imploring him to return to Benares, if only to visit. But Swamiji knew that if he went back, they would try to keep him there, so he refused, saying "No, my work is here now, doing Dhyanyogi-ji's seva."

Swamiji stayed on at Bandhwad for two years. At one point, he felt inspired to follow in Dhyanyogi-ji's footsteps and tour the places central to Dhyanyogi-ji's life. He visited Dhyanyogi-ji's cave in Mount Abu, had darshan at Ambaji, and traveled across India to Bihar to see Dhyanyogi-ji's birthplace.

It was in 1973 that Dhyanyogi-ji spoke to Swamiji about helping
with the spiritual work of the lineage. At first, although Swamiji was 30
years younger than Dhyanyogi-ji (he was 65 and Dhyanyogi-ji was 95),
he told Dhyanyogi-ji that he was an old man and couldn't take on that
responsibility. But at Dhyanyogi-ji's request, he moved into the Hansol
ashram and remained there for the rest of his life.

Swami Vijay Krishnabharati had an unusual rapport with the animals that lived on the ashram grounds and was frequently seen feeding
forest parrots seeds from the palm of his hand. He always dressed simply
in an orange dhoti, and there were usually lengths of orange cotton dry-
ing on lines hanging across the back of his hut. Like Dhyanyogi-ji, he
had a fixed daily routine. Every morning, Swamiji awoke at 3:00 a.m.
and began his yoga practices and meditation. At dawn, he had tea and
took an hour's walk, never straying from the ashram grounds. Later in
the morning, he sat in the chair on his porch and read the scriptures.
After lunch, he took a short nap. Late afternoon was the time when
visitors could come. Ordinary men, sadhus and devotees of many saints
and sects came to hear him speak on his main topic of interest—*guru
bhakti*, devotion to the guru. Swamiji insisted that his guests join him
in drinking his very sweet chai, asked them about their spiritual aspirations, and talked to them with great love about Dhyanyogi-ji.

One family, in particular, became very close to Swamiji and over
time became his primary devotees. "When I was a boy," Mr. Menon
recalled, "my family members and I used to go to the Sabarmati River
by evening every Sunday. One day, on our way, we peeped into the ashram and saw a huge crowd of people—ladies, gents, as well as children.
We thought it might be a marriage ceremony. We suddenly saw a sadhu
in his saffron dress inside the compound and he saw us. I asked him
whether we could come inside the ashram and meet him. He said yes, so
we went inside. Bowing, with our hands folded, we asked him about the
ashram. He told us that it belonged to Dhyanyogi-ji, who was there con-
ducting shaktipat that very day. We went and bowed before Guruji."

Rajan, another family member, picked up the story. "After this,"
Rajan said, "we became regular visitors of the ashram. I was 8 years old
at that time. I remember that the next time we went, Swamiji took us
down into the cave under the building where Guruji stayed, and we recited the *Hanuman Chalisa* with the others seated there. Then Swamiji

played a tape of the mantrochar and we sat calmly. If we opened our eyes, Swamiji told us to close our eyes and attend to the meditation. When the tape concluded, some people were laughing in a high pitch and someone else was crying. Swamiji clapped his hands three times to awaken the group and we opened our eyes. Some people were lying on the floor and others were rocking forward and backward. Those who opened their eyes got up and went up to Swamiji and bowed before him and Swamiji gave them blessed fruit. Then we did arati.

"When the arati was over, Swamiji walked upstairs and out across the compound to his room and sat on his cot. We followed him and sat on the floor before him. Tea was prepared and offered to us all and Swamiji explained to us that what we had witnessed in the cave was meditation, and that the voice we heard on the tape of mantras belonged to Guruji.

"From then on," Rajan continued, "we came to this meditation program every Sunday at 3:30 p.m. I'd also go to see him in the morning, and he taught me more than a hundred yoga asanas and showed me the proper way to do various pranayamas."

"We were able to have the darshan of Guruji many times," Mr. Menon recalled, "but we became even closer to Swamiji. Later, when I was married, my wife Shanta used to prepare food at home and send it to Swamiji."

Rajan began to do personal seva for Swamiji in his cottage. "He was very particular about keeping his quarters neat and tidy," Rajan remembered. "He mopped the floor, swept, washed his clothes, and decorated each of his divine photos with flowers, and he would let me help. I remember that by looking at the food served to him, Swamiji could tell who had cooked it and if it had been prepared correctly."

Swamiji was the boys' primary spiritual teacher. "Once, when I was still in school," Rajan recalled wistfully, "my friends and I went to the movies and didn't mention it to Swamiji. The next day, he said, 'A sparrow came to my veranda and uttered something about a movie yesterday,' and he looked into my eyes. There was no way to hide! I admitted it straightaway! He wasn't angry. He just smiled and advised my friends and I not to go to movies because it would affect our studies. Believe me, our movie craze vanished into thin air after that!

"Still, I remember in my third year of college, after exams, my friends took me by force to a movie. After so many years, we never felt the desire to go for a movie. Why should we? When we were so blessed as to experience the real movie, why would we be interested in the unreal one?"

Swamiji pointed out to the children that no matter how much success people attain in their worldly lives, their spiritual progress is what counts. He'd make his point by asking them the rhetorical question, "Why do all the top people—politicians, judges and doctors—all bow down to a saint?"

"He encouraged us to take our spiritual life seriously and not to dwell on our worldly desires," Rajan said. "He used to say, 'Your practices are your bank balance. Keep investing in it. This will reap a huge return later,' and, 'Guru mantra is like a train ticket in your hand. You don't have to worry if the conductor comes and asks for it. You are always safe, unlike a person traveling without a ticket.'"

Like Dhyanyogi-ji, Swamiji was sometimes strict—like when he was teaching the boys spiritual values—and other times indulgent, but always kind.

"With visitors," Rajan recalled, "Swamiji asked them many questions to get to know them. He remembered everyone's names and made them feel at home. Everyone felt like Swamiji was only his. Unknowingly, lots of questions, suggestions, plans and dreams in people's hearts would be answered or guidance would be given automatically while they sat in satsang. So many times, Swamiji would just give a smile and raise his eyebrows while looking at a particular person. No one else understood what this meant. Only that person would know and feel it."

Disciples tell a host of stories of how at times when they were in a crisis, they mentally turned to Swamiji for help, and just at that moment, someone turned up to steer them to safety. When the disciples next saw Swamiji after these rescues, he asked them in all innocence, in a manner reminiscent of Dhyanyogi-ji's, "And what happened when you were away?" Others told of experiences in which Swamiji healed them.

"At one time," Mr. Menon remembered, "I became very ill. Swamiji told my wife Shanta that he could cure my sickness within 41 days and told me to come stay at the ashram. Every day, I had to go to the Sabarmati riverbed and pluck an entire satyanashi plant, the root of which was to be prepared as medicine with milk. Swamiji was extremely kind to us. He gave me a Shiva mantra and asked me to do an anusthan of japa of this mantra."

Once Swamiji took residence at Hansol, he rarely spoke to outsiders. When he did, it was only to talk about spiritual matters. For the next 22 years, until he left his body in 1995, he virtually never left the ashram, except during the last years of Dhyanyogi-ji's life, when Dhyanyogi-ji was bedridden and no longer came to the ashram. Then, once a month, Swamiji went to the small flat in Ahmedabad where Dhyanyogi-ji stayed so he could have Dhyanyogi-ji's darshan. To get there, he hired an auto rickshaw, an open, three-wheeled, metal motor carriage that liberally emitted diesel fumes. It was about as comfortable as sitting in an oversized child's wagon. The engine put-putted at a maximum of 10 to 15 miles an hour to take him the 10 miles from Hansol to Ahmedabad, and the trip took the better part of an hour, assuming the rickshaw didn't break down along the way. But Swamiji never sought any other means of transportation. He was just grateful for each visit he had with Dhyanyogi-ji. He had walked away from his ashram, his possessions, and his disciples without a moment of looking back. Now, he had nothing but five dhotis, a few cups for tea, basic cooking utensils and a platform upon which to sleep, but he was completely at peace.

PART 3

"Some saints are like bees,
who always keep on humming,
while others are like the wind—
they spread their fragrance
all around."

CHAPTER TWENTY-FOUR

A SPIRITUAL HEIR

By 1972, Dhyanyogi-ji had two ashrams and thousands of disciples, several of whom had attained the final goal of liberation. He was six years shy of having lived for a century, but he still had tremendous energy and enthusiasm for his work. Given his age, however, it was inevitable that eventually he would have to slow down and turn everything over to someone else. But there was no one new in sight who had a sufficiently elevated level of spiritual samskaras to transmit the energy of the lineage through shaktipat and guide others on the path to liberation. Although Dhyanyogi-ji had installed Swamiji in his place at Hansol, apparently he was not the one destined to become Dhyanyogi-ji's spiritual heir. Some of his students began to wonder: Would this ancient lineage end with Dhyanyogi-ji?

To those who knew him, Dhyanyogi-ji was one of a kind. It was inconceivable that someone else could assume his role and carry on the lineage. But privately, Dhyanyogi-ji was searching for the person who could take his place after his mahasamadhi. Several times during the years when he was out in public, he appeared excited about a new disciple. Perhaps it seemed to him that this might be "the one." But each time, his initial enthusiasm faded.

In the fall of 1972, another possible successor to the lineage appeared, this time in a suburb of Mumbai. She was just a slip of a girl, shy and quiet, with her mother's dark eyes, and on the surface it hardly seemed possible that she could be the one chosen to carry on Dhyanyogiji's work in the world.

Her father was Pravinji Jani, a Gujarati business professional who worked for a pharmaceutical company and lived in Ghatkopar, a Mumbai suburb. Pravinji was an intellectual man with fiery eyes who tended to be more concerned with worldly life than spiritual matters, until several spiritual experiences began transforming him. One of the most powerful of those experiences occurred in 1959, when his wife, Jashu, was about to give birth to their second child. The labor was difficult, but the family didn't have enough money for them all to go to Mumbai, and men aren't allowed in the labor rooms in India. So Pravinji stayed at home with their 2-year-old daughter Asha, and a neighbor woman accompanied Jashu to the hospital.

Pravinji was very worried about Jashu, and both he and Asha had fevers. He put Asha in her cradle, covered her with mosquito netting, and began rocking her. After a while, they both fell asleep. At 3:00 in the morning, as he was dreaming deeply, Pravinji had a vision of the Divine Mother. She was sitting, laughing, her form completely illuminated by *deepmala*—an arc of ghee lamps—and in front of Her lay a magnificent lion. The lion roared three times, and at that very moment Asha cried out in her sleep. Pravinji got up and started rocking the cradle. He was concerned about his wife since there was still no news. Then, around 5:00 a.m., the neighbor who had taken Jashu to the hospital woke him: "Get up! You have a son!" Then, once again, Pravinji saw the Mother Goddess. She said, "I came to tell you," and he started crying. He named the new arrival Umesh, another name of Lord Shiva, husband of Uma, the Divine Mother.

This was the beginning of a new level in Pravinji's relationship with the Mother. After this, he became very involved in doing practices to Her. He wanted to find a good-quality, well-fashioned murti for his worship, so he turned to his uncle, Gaurishanker, who worked in Mumbai's jewelry market, for advice. Gaurishanker led Pravinji to the silver jewelry shops in the crowded, winding alleys of Mumbai, and there they searched from morning to evening. Pravinji asked to see statues of the Mother, and as the shopkeepers brought them to him, he held each one in his hands, sensing their unique energy. But nothing felt right. Finally, they entered a place where the shopkeeper, when asked if he had any murtis of the Divine Mother, said, "I have only one."

"The moment I saw it," Pravinji said, "I said, 'Yes! This is it!'" From that moment on, he incorporated the murti into his daily worship. Even now, whenever he has a problem, he sits before Her and always gets a reply.

Pravinji had strong support at home for his devotion to the Divine Mother. Jashu was earthy and strong, a powerful maternal figure herself, who was also deeply devoted to the Mother. She sometimes sang by heart a 118-verse scriptural song to the Mother called the *Anandanogarba*, which means "garba (or prayer) of bliss." This home atmosphere led to a deepening of Pravinji's prayers. Tears came to his eyes whenever he thought about the form of the Mother. He had such an intense relationship with the murti that he was not interested in finding a guru.

One day Pravinji was visiting a hospital when he learned that the Shankaracharya from the sourthern monastery was residing nearby. "I felt a strong attraction to go and see him." Pravinji recalled. "I went there and was told that he had just left to visit someone. The next day, I was still in the area and went to see him again. This time, his secretary told me that my dress—a Western style men's suit—was inappropriate, so I would not be allowed to see the guru. I explained that because of my professional responsibilities I couldn't come in a dhoti, the attire a Hindu man wore in the temples. After some arguing, the secretary agreed to let me stand in the darshan line so I could at least see Shankaracharya from a distance. But after the saint saw three or four people, he signaled from his seat to me. I was surprised and confused that he seemed to be calling me, and checked with a gesture. 'Are you calling me?' He nodded yes, so I went to him. I told him that I did not need money, a son, position, all I needed was devotion and bhakti. He asked me whom I worshipped, and I told him the Mother Goddess Durga. He asked, 'What practices do you perform?' He recited a prayer in praise of the Mother that I started reciting with him. At that point, he turned to his secretary and picked up a beautiful pomegranate, stating that I was a pious

Brahmin and he gave me the pomegranate as prasad. After that, he left the room and saw no one else in the queue.

"This incident affected me emotionally so strongly that I started crying like a child, and then suddenly an idea occurred to me: Why should I not bring my statue of Mother Goddess for his blessings? I went back to his room, and he was surprised to see me and asked, 'Again?' That time, with folded hands, I told him that I have a *Pran Pratisthith* (empowered) statue of Mother Durga and requested him to do a puja. He readily agreed, stating that I could come the next morning.

"The next day, clad in a dhoti, I took my entire puja (all of my murtis) along with my whole family. When he first came, he held my statue of Ganesh in his hand and put it on his forehead, and when he looked at Mother Goddess, he spontaneously saw Mother and said, 'Amma, Amma, Amma,' and performed the puja. He asked if I had been initiated by anybody for a mantra, and if so, what mantra was it? I told him that I did the Navarna mantra but had not been initiated by anyone. Then he said, 'Come, I will initiate you.' He was my first guru. My spiritual path was further strengthened."

A few years later, a relative in Rajkot, a town in Gujarat, gave Pravinji a copy of one of Dhyanyogi-ji's books, *Light on Meditation*, and advised him to learn to meditate. "I was going to England on business, and would be away for two weeks, unable to do puja," recalled Pravinji, "so I thought it would be good to get initiated so I could meditate while I was away." Pravinji learned that Dhyanyogi-ji visited Mumbai quite often and that when he did, he stayed with Dr. K. Pathak or Dr. G. Rawal. Pravinji called Dr. Pathak to find out the time when Dhyanyogi-ji held darshan.

At their first meeting in July 1972, the hairs on Pravinji's arms stood up. "I told Guruji that whenever I meet a holy being, either this happens or tears come to my eyes, and Guruji told me it was a good sign. He asked me to sit with him for the meditation that evening, and I did. Immediately after the meditation was over, he asked, 'Has your head become heavy?' I told him it had, and he said, 'Fast tomorrow and I will initiate you. And don't come alone because you won't be able to drive after this.'" At this time, Dhyanyogi-ji always instructed people who were coming for shaktipat to have someone accompany them since the energy was strong.

When Pravinji received shaktipat the next day, he remained in a meditative state for two-and-a-half hours.

Two months later, in September 1972, came the nine-day festival of Navaratri, an extremely happy time in Pravinji and Jashu's home. The house was filled with energy from the intense spiritual practices performed during the day, followed by evenings redolent with chanting and clapping to the rhythm of bells and the organ-like tones of the harmonium. Each evening Manubhai, the family priest, and his brother, a priest named Rasikbhai, came to the house to do puja. The atmosphere was as festive as a wedding, fragrant with flowers and the smell of good food.

Each year for the last 12 years, Pravinji had performed a strict anusthan during Navaratri. His wife assumed any social obligations so that he could concentrate on his practices and minimize his contact with the outside world. This year however, Jashu was away on a pilgrimage, so Pravinji said to his 13-year-old daughter, Asha, "You'd better not undertake an anusthan this year as your mom is not here." Asha agreed, but the next day she asked Pravinji if she could do a small anusthan of Durga, one that would only require a few hours daily.

Asha was a shy and undemanding girl, and not particularly interested in studying. Her parents attached no significance to her introverted nature, and had never noticed anything unusual about her. But as the days of Navaratri passed, Pravinji noticed that when Asha did her mantras "her face lit up and tears poured down her cheeks." He was surprised at how powerfully she connected with the energy of the practice.

Statue of Durga with which Asha Devi had her first experience of divine union

On the final day of the anusthan, as the fire ceremony was going on, Asha entered a meditative state. She recalls having a vision of a dazzling light, "like the light of 1000 suns," seeing the statue of Durga her father had on the altar for worship, then having a vision of the live Mother and merging with Her.

"We were both crying during the final fire ceremony," Pravinji remembered. "Later, she went to the home of a relative to distribute prasad from the ceremony. When arati was sung, her body began to shake."

For weeks afterwards, Asha continued in this unusual state. During the day, she sat in meditation as if in a world of her own. When Pravinji recited prayers, she went into an even deeper state. At night, while in meditation, she danced for hours without tiring. Her graceful movements were in perfect classical Indian tradition, although she had never received any training. Sometimes she took on the personality of Baby Krishna, crying and rubbing his eyes, or of the teenaged Krishna in the form of Govinda, playing his flute with the Gopis. In her constant state of meditation, she ate and drank very little and completely stopped attending school. At this point, Pravinji said, "I realized that Asha's kundalini must have awakened. I had seen powerful manifestations of kundalini in someone else, and the same thing was happening to Asha."

Asha did not easily come out of the deep states she was entering, so after Navaratri ended, her father called the family priest to confirm his assessment of the situation. Manubhai came to their home, gently took hold of Asha's little finger and asked, "Who are you?" She pushed him away and said, "I am Durga." For weeks, Asha continued to enter these deep states of meditation without warning.

Later that fall, Pravinji learned that Dhyanyogi-ji was back in Mumbai. "I went to pay my respects and let him know that I had safely returned from London. I casually mentioned to him that I was sure that my daughter's kundalini had spontaneously awakened."

Dhyanyogi-ji asked Pravinji where he lived. As it happened, Dhyanyogi-ji had been invited for lunch the following day by a disciple in Ghatkopar. "Since you are visiting so nearby," Pravinji asked, "would it be possible for you to visit us?" Dhyanyogi-ji agreed but Harivadan, Deepak Pathak's eldest brother, stipulated that they could only stay for five minutes.

The next day, Pravinji urged his daughter not to go into meditation because Dhyanyogi-ji was coming. Nonetheless, an hour before Dhyanyogi-ji's arrival—just when he was leaving from Mumbai—Asha went into meditation. Here is Pravinji's account of the astonishing events of that day:

"When Guruji arrived at our house, Asha was sitting in front of the puja room door in a very deep meditative state. She gave him a thunderous smile and said, 'Ha, ha, ha,' in a deliberate, throaty voice. For a while Guruji just stood there in front of her, and then, without touching her, he walked inside.

"The rest of the family greeted him in the puja room and we performed a guru puja. Afterwards, Guruji began to ask questions like how long Asha had been like this. We tried to wake her so he could speak to her. She woke up and we brought her in to see Guruji. He gave her orange juice and said, 'This is a very good sign.'

"After saying this, he sat silently. His five-minute visit turned into 45 minutes. He left our house for his lunch, but later in the afternoon, called from the house where he was having his tea and asked, 'What is Asha doing now?' I told him, 'She is in meditation.' He asked me to try to wake her up and to tell her he would like to meet with her if she was willing to come. When I woke her, she readily agreed to come with me, and I drove her to where Guruji was.

"As soon as we entered the house where he was sitting, she again went into meditation. After a few minutes, we brought her back to 'normal.' Guruji told her that he would like to speak to her, so we went into the adjacent room and he inquired about her experiences during Navaratri.

"'When you see the Divine Mother, what form do you see?' asked Guruji.

"Asha gave him a description of the Divine Mother Goddess Durga.

"Then he asked her if Durga came alone or with anybody else, to which Asha replied, 'Sometimes She comes with a tiger, and other times She comes with a lion.'

"'Aren't you scared of this?'

"'No,'

"'Why?'

"'Because Mother is smiling all the time, so I'm not scared.'

"Guruji continued. 'Do you see Mother Goddess as if in a picture or like a human being?'

"'Like a human being,' she answered.

"After this, Guruji hugged her and said, 'You are a great soul who has come to do divine work.' At that moment, Asha said, 'I want to come

Jani family: Umesh, Jashu, Dhyanyogi-ji, Kalyani, Asha, Pravinji

with you to your ashram.'"

Deepak Pathak had accompanied Dhyanyogi-ji to the Jani's that fateful day. His recollection highlights different aspects of this first encounter between Asha and Dhyanyogi-ji:

"When Guruji and I entered the apartment, we saw a girl of 13 sitting on the floor with her eyes closed and a divine look on her face. As soon as Guruji entered, she burst into a loud laugh, which startled everyone and sent a chill down my spine. Guruji stood where he was, motionless, with an expression of great joy on his face. Her meditative state was very deep, and it differed from anything else that I had ever seen or experienced with the hundreds of other persons who had come to see Guruji.

"The girl's father told us that she was in that state most of the time. Guruji calmly said, 'She is a very highly evolved soul.' A little later, he said, 'In my lifetime, I have not seen anyone so young reach such lofty spiritual height. With the right guidance and help, she can be a great spiritual leader and perform great works in life.'

"After a while we left to visit another disciple close by. Guruji invited Asha, along with her family, to accompany him back to Mumbai. During the trip, he put his hand briefly on her head and asked her to see what was happening at his place. She did so and what she described was later confirmed in a phone call."

After that first meeting, Pravinji took Asha to the Pathak's every day to see Dhyanyogi-ji, and picked her up on his way home from work. Wherever she happened to be, she often went into meditation, sometimes dancing for hours in that state. Even if she was just sitting in the living room at home, if someone said a divine name, she'd slither off the couch like a snake, and move down the hall into the family's puja room. When she reached the altar, she would raise up the front of her body as if doing the cobra pose in hatha yoga—except, instead of her hands staying on the floor, they would be parallel to her body.

Several days after they first met, Dhyanyogi-ji performed shaktipat upon Asha, the rest of her family, and a family friend named Kusum Sheth. Dhyanyogi-ji said, "Asha does not need the initiation to awaken her energy, but to connect her to the lineage this is a necessary step." She remained in her usual state of meditation for about two hours, after which Dhyanyogi-ji woke her and asked, "What did you see? What did you experience?"

Asha said, "I saw Lord Hanuman."

"My work is now done," Dhyanyogi-ji said.

During this time, Dhyanyogi-ji seemed to be in an unusual state of contemplation. He was very happy and talked almost all the time about Asha. He said, "I have not met anyone like her in all my life. For a person at so young an age to attain such a level! The potential seed has been found. If God wills, if the lineage chooses, and if the samskaras of this being stand up, there is hope that my work can continue."

Asha stood out among all others, Dhyanyogi-ji explained, because the divine energy that flowed in her was so strong. Such intensity is necessary for one soul to be able to raise the souls of others, and indicates a tremendous level of spiritual evolution.

"When I first met Guruji, he was waking me up from meditation," recalled Asha. "He gave me juice and prasad. When I came to my senses, I didn't see him as Guruji; I saw Shiva. Later that day, when I visited him, it wasn't like meeting someone for the first time. I wanted to stay with him always. I fell in love with his eyes, his energy, his love and compassion.

"Right then and there, I told him I wanted to go to his ashram with him. I had no intention of doing his work or giving shaktipat. I just wanted to be with him.

"I had always wanted to leave home, to become a bird and fly away, to go to Vrindavan, the sacred city of Krishna, but who could I tell this to? My cousin and I never wanted to study. We were always thinking, 'Let's go to the Lord.' We would say, 'Let's give up everything and go to Vrindavan.'

"Now that I'd met Guruji, I wanted to fly away to Bandhwad and be with him."

When Asha asked Dhyanyogi-ji if she could come stay with him, he initially expressed concern. She had been raised in comfort, while he lived in a poor, rural village. He wondered if she would be able to adjust and be happy there. "But if your parents permit it," he told her, "I have no objection."

Asha's family and friends had entirely different concerns. The society she grew up in did not sanction such a choice. If she went to live with Dhyanyogi-ji, people might suspect that her father sent her away because he was unable to support her, and this would bring shame upon him. Asha's mother worried because she was so young, and the family had just met Dhyanyogi-ji. With all the negative incidents that happened with young girls, even true teachers were not easily trusted. Manubhai objected to the idea. One of Pravinji's relatives advised him to hold onto Asha for selfish reasons. He told him, "Keep this energy in your house. Don't let it become too public, and you'll get the maximum benefit."

Pravinji believes it was divine guidance that led him to agree to let Asha go in December 1972. "I got connected to this path intensely after my son's birth, but once, in a deep meditative state, when she was manifesting the Divine Mother, Asha told me, 'You have worshipped me in three births and that's why I came as your daughter.' In retrospect, it was divine will operating: First, Asha's kundalini on the verge of spontaneously awakening, then my meeting with Guruji, his visit to Ghatkopar, her express desire to go with him to Bandhwad, and my standing firm against all opposition to let her go." He kept remembering what Dhyanyogi-ji had said about his daughter—that her soul had come into the world to do great work. If this were true, he must be able to stand up to everyone and endure his own loss. Both he and Jashu thought that once Asha's kundalini was under control, she would come back home.

"I thought, if she has good energy and can do good, let her go," Pravinji recalled. "I never anticipated that my daughter was about to be trained to succeed Guruji as head of the lineage."

"Grace is the master key to self-realization"

CHAPTER TWENTY-FIVE

ASHA DEVI IN BANDHWAD

Both Asha and Dhyanyogi-ji felt that their meeting was a re-union of two souls connected through lifetimes. When she first arrived in Bandhwad, Dhyanyogi-ji asked her, "Where have you been all this time? I have been waiting for you all these years." He showed her the ashram and said, "All this is yours." He began calling her "Asha Devi," which means "Asha Goddess," a sign of his respect for her divine nature.

Asha Devi recognized Dhyanyogi-ji as the one she had longed to be with and told him, "I wish I had met you earlier." But Dhyanyogi-ji said that if she were any younger, her family never could have allowed her to come live with him. No one would have understood their connection.

Asha Devi was drawn to Dhyanyogi-ji's humble ways. He "never painted his face or wore a big mala" like other sadhus, she said. "He was very plain and simple" yet held tremendous knowledge in many fields, including music, mantras, meditation and yantras. This impressed her. She also noticed that Dhyanyogi-ji never forced teachings on his disciples. He suggested practices that would help them or be good for their spiritual growth, but he always left it up to the students whether to follow the advice. When mistakes were made, he would correct them in a loving and gentle way. He was extremely cautious not to hurt anyone in any way, and this was something that touched Asha Devi deeply. His heart was "soft like butter," she said. "If I started crying, he would cry as well. Yet if he needed to be strong to give a teaching, he could be as strong as armor."

"When I first met Guruji," Asha Devi said, "he was recovering from a little accident. Someone had slammed the car door on his thumb. I heard that when it happened, he didn't cry out. Very coolly and quietly, he said, 'Would you please open the door. My thumb has been caught inside.' When the door was opened, his thumb was completely swollen and bleeding. You could see the bone. Yet he exhibited no pain. On the contrary, the person who had slammed the door appeared to be in greater pain, and Guruji had to spend energy calming him down. That is the quality of a saint—in spite of being in pain, he or she is concerned about the pain of others and works to reduce and remove that pain."

Asha Devi asked Dhyanyogi-ji several times if she should wear only orange or white clothes, which would be an outward sign that she had renounced the world for a God-centered life. He always replied that it wasn't necessary. The level of detachment and understanding that comes with a life of spiritual service is an inner state, he ex-

Asha Devi at Bandhwad

plained, one that doesn't occur just by changing the outer appearance.

Asha Devi came to believe that, in fact, Dhyanyogi-ji's greatest teaching was his life. He did not give large, public talks as some teachers did; rather, he conveyed what he had to offer in a few words and by simply *being*. "His essence was as vast as the ocean," she said, "though his students were able to catch and understand only a drop of his true nature." To remain in his presence, Asha Devi learned, was to be filled with such joy that everything else was forgotten.

Yet, on a worldly level, the transition from the bustle of Mumbai to Dhyanyogi-ji's quiet little village was an enormous adjustment for someone so young. Before her arrival, she had pictured herself doing *guru seva*, taking care of Dhyanyogi-ji. She had been a little intimidated, thinking of all the chores she would have to do. "Guruji had said to me, 'You have to do this and you have to do that,'" recalled Asha Devi. "I said, 'I'll do everything.' I imagined there was a river there, and it would be my job to get water for him each day." Instead, she found herself in meditation most of the time.

"Fortunately, others were there to get the water for Guruji because I was in no condition to do any seva. Instead of taking care of the guru, he took care of me. He spent hours waking me up, showing infinite patience and love."

Dhyanyogi-ji made sure her physical and emotional needs were met as well. He consulted Asha Devi's parents on her likes and dislikes, including her favorite foods—rice, potatoes, vegetables and yogurt—and made a special effort to provide them for her. Her parents came to see her whenever they wanted, and she went home to see them. Whenever he traveled to do meditation programs or visit disciples, she was always by his side, and when he traveled to Mumbai, they often stayed in Ghatkopar with her family. The Janis became very close disciples. Jashu was exceptionally devoted to Dhyanyogi-ji, who often said that the 'best food he was given was at the Jani's.'

"When they came to stay here," Pravinji said, "people would come and we would sing bhajans until late into the night. When Asha came home for her first visit after going to Bandhwad, she had already written a beautiful bhajan called 'Guru Mari,' in devotion to the guru. Before this, she never had that beautiful singing voice and had never written bhajans. When visitors went into kriyas, she would sometimes touch

Dhyanyogi-ji and Asha Devi in the Jani's puja room

them and they would calm down again."

Pravinji recalled several memorable incidents from these visits, when Asha would manifest the Divine Mother. "When Asha and Guruji came, our family would perform guru puja, and my wife would have made sweets for prasad. Asha would go into meditation and start eating all the prasad! We'd have to stop her and tell her that others needed to have some too! On one particular visit, we were going to do the fire ceremony for the *Chandi Path*. First, Asha crawled inside the little temple in our puja room without disturbing any of the statues or images, and then, before we lit the fire, she sat in the copper *kund*, the basin where the fire would burn (approximate one foot square). During the ceremony, when we repeated the word '*Swaha*,' and made our offering to the fire, Asha would put the offering in her mouth instead.

"She woke in the middle of the night and said she wanted something in particular to eat, and we'd cook it for her because she was manifesting the Mother. Once, Dr. Rawal had organized a *Chandi Path* fire ceremony at his home, and I went there with Guruji, Asha Devi and

In samadhi, with head on burning fire kund

one of my aunts. As was usual at this time, Asha Devi went into meditation, with her head resting on an altar that was very near the copper fire

kund. The priest refused to start
the ceremony, worried that Asha
Devi might catch fire. I told him
not to worry. 'My Guruji is here
so he will take care of things.
I take the full responsibility if
anything happens.' So the priest
started the puja, in which ornaments and clothing were offered
to the Divine Mother. One of
these ornaments was a *mangal-*

*Fire ceremony at Janis; Asha's foot is in the fire
kund and her mother is seated next to her*

sutra (wedding necklace). Asha Devi picked it up and started revolving it
in her hand as if it were a *sudarshan chakra*—the wheel that Lord Vishnu
holds—and then she threw it. The mangalsutra fell into my aunt's hand,
and her hand starting shaking. After some time, the Mother, who was
manifesting in Asha Devi, said that the gift was not meant for my aunt
but for Dr. Rawal's wife so it was given to her.

"Another time, she and Guruji visited during Navaratri. She was
in our main room where the puja was being done. She laid her head on
the kund, and began to beckon with her finger. My uncle Gaurishanker
sometimes manifested the Divine Mother in the form of Bahucharaji,

Durga's younger sister. At
the moment when Asha
beckoned, my uncle went
into that state and came
running to her from the
other room!"

For the next four years,
Dhyanyogi-ji's primary focus
was caring for and training
Asha Devi, upon whom the
future of the lineage now
depended. He worked in-
tensively with her day and
night to teach her to control

*Dhyanyogi-ji said this was a unique photo that caught
the light of Asha Devi's heart chakra. Mumbai, 1973*

her energy. If she did not master her prana, she would not be able to function on the physical level to do his work because she would be in meditation so much of the time. Furthermore, if she continued to remain in these very deep states for too long and over too extended a period of time, with her prana rising to the sahasrara chakra at the crown of her head—a condition that caused her neck to swell up—she would not survive. So Dhyanyogi-ji had to work constantly to bring her prana down, and to teach her methods for staying in her body. Kusum Sheth visited Bandhwad and witnessed how Dhyanyogi-ji worked with Asha Devi during her kriyas. Once, she was there when Asha Devi's prana was ascending with tremendous intensity and Dhyanyogi-ji was actively working to bring it back down to the heart chakra. Kusum said that to an onlooker, it appeared that Asha Devi was in great physical discomfort. "Guruji just worked with her, massaging her and pouring out love for hours. If she grabbed onto his shirt, or lay in his lap, he'd sit there,

completely still, for the whole night, his eyes pouring shakti onto her. Sometimes, she would have very intense kriyas and he'd sit for hours without moving, like a motionless flame."

It frequently took Dhyanyogi-ji several hours to bring Asha Devi out of meditation. He sat with her and softly called her name to wake her gently and gradually. If he woke her too abruptly, it might damage her subtle body, so the process required tremendous patience. Often her energy was so intense when she was in that state that she moved her hands around wildly. Once she hit him with such force that an ordinary person would have passed out, but Dhyanyogi-ji remained totally calm and continued to work with her for another three hours until she finally woke up.

When Asha Devi slept, she usually passed into a state of samadhi. Dhyanyogi-ji made certain that someone was always next to her to protect her in case she began to move around while in meditation. Often Dhyanyogi-ji himself was that person. Once, she remained in Dhyanyogi-ji's room in meditation for 36 hours and during that time, he never left her alone.

Asha Devi's arrival in Bandhwad changed all the routines and rhythms to which the villagers and disciples had been accustomed. His new disciple occupied Dhyanyogi-ji's attention most of the time, and their relationship was unique. Although she was a girl of 15, and Dhyanyogi-ji was 94, he viewed her as his spiritual equal. He often said, "She is a very old soul in a very young body," and he immediately treated her with that attitude of respect. One day in Ghatkopar, he put a fruit called *chiku* in front of a photo of the Hanumanji at Bandhwad. At the end of the day, he told her to eat the fruit and then said, 'Now you can give shaktipat.' Although she had received initiation only a month before, Asha Devi began giving shaktipat side by side with Dhyanyogi-ji as soon as she reached Bandhwad. He was her teacher, and therefore he gave her instructions and guidance, but he never did anything to subjugate her will or her intuition to his own. This was completely unprecedented in the experience of those who had spent years around Dhyanyogi-ji.

Pravinji recalled how Dhyanyogi-ji granted Asha Devi's wishes without question. One instance occurred during a visit to Bandhwad, several months after she moved there. "I was meditating in the cave when Asha Devi, in meditation, crawled down the stairs like a serpent. She was manifesting Hanumanji and she crawled over to the altar and removed Guruji's silver murti of Hanumanji, a gift given to him by Deepak and his father. Then, she gave the murti to me and applied sindoor, the orange powder applied to Hanuman and Ganesh, to my forehead, and told Guruji, in a commanding voice, not to take the murti back. It was not Asha doing this, it was Lord Hanuman through the medium of Asha."

As might be expected, Dhyanyogi-ji's special treatment of Asha Devi caused some uneasiness, resentment and jealousy among his other disciples. Many of them found it difficult to accept the degree to which he was entrusting her with his work. She was so young and uneffusive, so different from their wise and fearless Guruji who represented ultimate authority for them. They couldn't fathom the idea that this child would someday take his place. But Dhyanyogi-ji remained firm about his decision to work with her.

For the most part, other disciples treated Asha Devi with respect because that is what Dhyanyogi-ji expected of them, but there were times when they could not hold their tongues. During one of her father's visits, things came to a head. Pravinji remembers what happened that night:

"Asha Devi was upstairs on the floor of the room where she often meditated or slept so that he could watch over her. She was in a half-meditative state when she apparently heard people below in the courtyard berating her to Guruji. People could not understand or accept this young girl leaving her home to come and live with Guruji without the supervision of her family. They had no concept of the spiritual state she was in, nor did they comprehend the depth of faith that her mother and I had in Guruji, God and our daughter. I had received letters accusing me of being unable to take care of my own daughter, or not caring to do so, and therefore sending her away. Hearing this crowd insulting her was terribly painful and she began to cry. She cried so hard that Guruji and I started to cry also. Guruji asked me, 'Should I tell them to go away?'"

With that simple reply, Dhyanyogi-ji communicated his grief over the situation, and his compassion for all his disciples. He wept for Asha Devi at overhearing such talk, for Pravinji's distress at being perceived as a bad father for allowing his daughter to live at the ashram, and for

Asha Devi in bhav samadhi

the envious disciples who were expressing their pain and ignorance in such a hurtful way.

Dhyanyogi-ji tried to reassure his devotees, telling them, "I know what I am doing and what she will do in the future. The choice of the heir in the lineage is not just my personal wish. It comes from above. My guru has appeared and told me to train and prepare her for the future. She is ready and worthy."

Over time, the people of Bandhwad came to accept and love Asha Devi, but in the beginning they were unprepared for

Asha Devi in bhav samadhi manifesting Baby Krishna

Asha Devi embodied the level of detachment that comes with advanced meditative states. She could go into meditation anywhere, always spontaneously. Dhyanyogi-ji had to assign helpers for her in the bathroom because she'd often "pass out" there. In deeper states, she often remained for hours in the Hanuman temple, but she was also known to make her way to the village dump and sit in meditation there.

In this condition, she was able

Asha Devi in bhav samadhi at Bandhwad, manifesting Krishna playing his flute

Manifestation of Maha Kali while in meditation, Guru Purnima, Mumbai, 1973

to "tune in" to the wants and needs of those around her. One longtime Indian disciple recently recalled inwardly desiring a pair of Dhyanyogi-ji's sandals for his daily puja, but he was too shy to ask for them. One day, while she was deep in meditation, Asha Devi brought a pair of sandals to him, fulfilling his wish.

Asha Devi's training at Bandhwad further developed and highlighted her rare abilities. While she lived there, Dhyanyogi-ji performed certain spiritual practices with her daily. Sometimes those practices were part of a broader lesson that could last for weeks or months. He also gave her some unusual exercises—for example, he would bury an object and then ask her to meditate to find it. Once he even asked her to "read" the serial numbers on a bill tucked inside a person's pocket, and she recited the numbers accurately, as if the bill were right in her hand.

Asha Devi also received teachings on a subtle level. Shri Krishna, Shri Ram and other deities spontaneously appeared to her in meditation. Other people indirectly observed these encounters with the Divine through Asha Devi's outward

Guru Purnima, Mumbai, 1973

Asha Devi blessing Dhanyogi-ji at Guru Purnima, 1973

Dhyanyogi-ji's birthday celebration at disciple's home in Chanasma. Dhyanyogi-ji's sister is sitting beside Dhyanyogi-ji and Asha Devi.

Asha Devi blessing Dhyanyogi-ji at the birthday celebration in Chanasma

Dhyanyogi-ji with disciples in Chanasma; two are his nephew's sons (Radhakrishna, 2nd from left and Bansidha, 5th from right)

behavior, and saw first-hand how God was working through her. One incident that stands out occurred during Guru Purnima in 1973. The Guru puja was held that year at the Pathak home in Mumbai. During the ceremony, Asha Devi began to move into the inner puja room with her eyes slightly closed. Dhyanyogi-ji and a few other disciples followed her. She stopped right in front of the altar, upon which was a murti of the Divine Mother. Dhyanyogi-ji asked her, "What do you see?" She said, "I see Mataji," and she began to manifest Kali Ma.

"In this state," Deepak recalled, "she came up to Guruji and began to pat his head and give him blessings. Guruji lowered his head to receive them. This was very surprising to me and to the other disciples present. We had seen Guruji bless everyone. For us, he was the supreme. But now we saw someone blessing him! Afterwards, we realized that, of course, this was the Divine Mother and not the physical aspect of the girl who was blessing him. Guruji called her 'Asha Devi,' which means Asha Goddess. For us, truly, Guruji had changed this girl into a Devi."

Witnessing such things led many disciples to open their hearts to Asha Devi. Several of the women devotees took her under their wings and looked after her during the day in Dhyanyogi-ji's absence. Others noticed

285

how the energy around Dhyanyogi-ji had more than doubled after Asha Devi's arrival in Bandhwad. Some people had profound spiritual experiences, or were healed as a result of this tremendous increase in energy.

They also saw that Dhyanyogi-ji and Asha Devi had a bond like no other. Their special connection was most apparent during times of difficulty, such as when, in 1973, a serious famine had once again cast its shadow over the rural, desert-like communities dotting the countryside near the ashram. In desperation, the people turned to Dhyanyogi-ji for help protecting their families and the cattle that were their livelihood, and he spent months traveling long distances to find feed and gather donations to take care of them all. He had to drive to remote areas where only a four-wheel drive vehicle could move through the heavy sand in the desert heat. He'd rise early in the morning and never returned to the ashram until late in the evening.

"Asha Devi would go into deep states of meditation and with eyes closed, find her way to the Hanumanji temple," recalled Rambhai, a frequent visitor to the ashram. "One night at about 10:00 p.m., during this famine period, she was at the temple and Guruji kept calling to her, but she wasn't responding. Finally, she said, 'Why do you keep calling me? I'm happy.' Guruji was saying to her that there was trouble. Because of the drought, there was no grass for the cows to eat. But Asha Devi, still in samadhi, answered, 'The grass will take care of itself and you'll get the money you need for our work. If you need money, it will come. Why are you worrying? Just do the work you were put on earth for. You have so many disciples who love you wholeheartedly. Your word is so dear to them. They hold it so highly, like gold. You'll have no problems. All your troubles will go away.'"

Around that time, while Dhyanyogi-ji was away from the ashram searching for resources to help with the famine, Asha Devi began to develop a serious pain in her abdomen. When her pain became unbearable, the devotees attending her decided that they should get her to a doctor as quickly as possible. They took her to Radhanpur, where the local doctor examined her and concluded she had appendicitis and needed surgery as soon as possible. Radhanpur didn't have the facilities for an operation, so she would have to go to a larger town where there was better medical care.

In the meantime, Dhyanyogi-ji returned to Bandhwad. When he heard what happened, he rushed to Asha Devi's side, and together they

Ministers of state visiting ashram during famine relief work, behind them is the grain gathered

traveled to the town where the surgery could be performed. The doctor gave her a tranquilizer to ease the pain for the journey, but it had no effect, so the trip only added to her suffering. When they arrived at the hospital, the doctors there confirmed the diagnosis and scheduled the surgery for the next morning.

Asha Devi was frightened. This was a completely new experience for her. It was the first time she had ever seen a doctor in a strange town or been to a hospital. "Let's go back home," she kept saying to Dhyanyogi-ji. "I do not want to undergo this surgery."

A few hours before the operation, she went into a very deep meditation. During that meditation, Dhyanyogi-ji appeared to her, surrounded by light. With the little finger of his right hand, his nail glowing, he cut her abdomen open, inserted his hand and moved it around.

Not long afterwards, Asha Devi could hear Dhyanyogi-ji trying to wake her up from her meditation, just as the doctors were preparing her for surgery. As soon as she was awake, she began throwing up a lot of blood and other fluids. Then she reported that the pain had disappeared. She insisted she was completely recovered, and no longer needed surgery. At her request, the doctors repeated the tests and were surprised to discover that the results now appeared to be perfectly normal. Such was the healing energy of Dhyanyogi-ji and the bond of unconditional love and care between guru and disciple.

CHAPTER TWENTY-SIX

A MEETING WITH LORD RAM

Several months after the famine settled over northern Gujarat, a pivotal event gave the disciples a glimpse of Asha Devi's true identity.

The drought had decimated the food supply, and there was no animal feed to be had except for what could be brought in at exorbitant prices. Dhyanyogi-ji had been doing what he could for the relief effort through his ashram at Bandhwad, feeding more than 1,700 cows every day. Farmers who could no longer care for their cattle simply left them at the ashram, where they were boarded for free. Most saints who did this service kept the milk, but Dhyanyogi-ji took care of the cows and let the owners take the milk.

Disciples from Mumbai and other places where conditions were not as desperate paid the bills with their donations, but Dhyanyogi-ji was doing much of the legwork involved in keeping the operation running. His daily routine included running around in 100-plus temperatures, trying to buy cheap hay at the more fortunate villages. After a while, the exhaustive schedule began to take a toll on his health. He began running a low fever and a boil developed on his upper back. A doctor tended to him, advising him to apply moist hot packs to the boil, but he did not stop working despite the pleas of concerned disciples. He weakened further and eventually fell seriously ill.

At 9:00 p.m. on December 7, 1973 Dhyanyogi-ji was reviewing relief accounts with some of his disciples while hot packs were being applied to his back. Suddenly, he began to feel the heat in his body rise higher and higher. Despite the chill of the desert night, his temperature rose to a dangerously high level of 105-106 degrees.

In his book *Death, Dying and Beyond*, Dhyanyogi-ji wrote about the events that occurred that night: "The heat kept increasing and I wanted to tell the people around me that I was feeling funny, but I found that I could not say anything at all. My mouth and tongue would not work. Then I remembered that many years before, a yogi had predicted that I would encounter death at around the age I now was. I wanted to let people know something was happening, but I could not speak at all. My legs went numb and I was starting to lose muscular control over my body. I felt I needed to urinate and got out of the bed, but I had to hold the wall to support myself when I walked to the bathroom and came back."

Dhyanyogi-ji felt that he was dying, and he wanted everyone to chant Lord Ram's name. The *Bhagavad Gita* says that if you remember God at the moment of death you will attain liberation. Dhyanyogi-ji had already attained a very high state, but he knew how strong the pull of maya could be. He wanted his students to use the chanting to help them concentrate, and calm their minds and emotions, so everyone began chanting "Ram."

The disciple treating Dhyanyogi-ji's boil noticed that his guru was losing consciousness. He started shaking him and saying, "Guruji, what is happening to you?" Then the disciple lost consciousness himself. Another disciple came and tried to rouse Dhyanyogi-ji, but he also lost consciousness upon touching Dhyanyogi-ji. The same thing happened to a third person—anybody who touched him lost consciousness.

Dhyanyogi-ji lost control of his legs and could no longer move them at all. People were now running around and calling, "Guruji, Bapuji, Guruji!" But Dhyanyogi-ji could scarcely hear them and could not answer back. Then he lost control over his hands. They became heavy like wood, and he could not move them. His sight failed.

"I could see light all around, but I could not discern any figures. The things around slowly got dimmer and dimmer until I could not see them at all.

"Then, even touch sensations started to fade out. If people handled my body, I could hardly feel it and finally could not feel anything at all. Now I knew for certain that I was dying. There were many things I wanted to tell people, but I could not utter even a word, so all these things were going through my mind. In the unsettled accounts for the famine work, there were people who needed to be paid and people who were going to pay me. I wondered how the work would be carried on and started worrying about how the cows were going to get fed and the milk distributed.

"And I also had unfulfilled desires to start a school and a hospital. There were no schools for 30 miles around Bandhwad, and in the rural area near my birthplace in Bihar there were no hospital facilities for a hundred miles. Also I wanted to build a temple and improve the ashram. I thought of how I had delayed in completing these projects, and began to repent because now I knew that I was going away forever and would never have a chance to finish them. So I was thinking, uselessly, that I should have put more effort into them before. I began scolding myself for my laziness, but then I remembered that death was coming, so I began to chant to myself the name of Ram. By then, all sense functions had disappeared. I could not see, hear, touch, or feel anything."

Later, Dhyanyogi-ji learned that at this point some disciples gave him a strong stimulant that is often given to revive a dying person, but it had no effect at all on him.

After losing all external sensations, Dhyanyogi-ji began seeing the actions he had done in his past several births, as though watching a movie. Usually people going through a death experience see only the actions of their present lifetime played out before them, but someone with Dhyanyogi-ji's advanced spiritual nature may review many lifetimes as they are crossing over. Some of his karma was good and some of it was not very good, but he had faith that because he had spent time in prayer and service in his most recent lifetime he would go to God.

Dhyanyogi-ji's breathing became labored, and then he lost all voluntary control over his breath. "I forgot about everything else and mentally chanted Ram, the name of God. I reconciled my concern with the pending accounts and the other unfinished work by thinking that whatever happened would be what God wished. It was beyond my control, so I let God take care of it and I only thought of the name Ram. I felt then as if somebody pushed me very hard, and I came out of my body."

The disciples who were present said it looked as if a shadow came out of Dhyanyogi-ji's body. Everyone started crying bitterly.

"Once out of the body, I could see the room, the body lying there and the people crying. It was pleasant not to need to walk, but instead to be able to float around in the air like a bird. I could see and hear perfectly. People were all crying and I wanted to tell them not to cry, that there was no point in crying and that they should chant God's name, but there was no way I could communicate with them. Even the cows were crying. One cow in particular, Ganga, even now I can see how bitterly she was weeping. I am so attached to that silent animal's love that even now it makes me feel like crying to remember her grief.

"Once I was pushed out of the body, there was no pain or discomfort. The boil did not hurt. The fever was gone. I was separate, different from the body that I could see lying there. I felt an emotional attachment to that body, yet I felt distinct from it.

"Then in the space where I was floating, I saw two beings come towards me who said, 'Now it is time to join us. You have to go to a different place.' I wondered what that other place would be like, but when I saw the faces of the beings, they were very pleasant, blissful, and quiet. I had no fear of going with them.

"We floated through space, and I could see on one side a row of people weeping and crying, and on the other side, a crowd laughing and happy. On both sides were all kinds of people, men and women of all countries and colors, people of every religion.

"I wanted to ask a question of the beings who were talking, and I found that I could speak to them. So I asked why one crowd of people was crying and the other seemed happy. They told me that the crying ones were in fear of the results of their bad karma and the troubles it would lead them into. The others were anticipating happy rebirths in heavens or among men.

"Then I asked the beings why I could now talk to them, but I could not talk to the people back on Earth and tell them not to cry and be sad at my dying. They told me that when I was still in the body I could not talk because the life energies were all concentrating in the heart, so the *indriyas* (senses) could no longer function and the body became very cold. They said I could not speak because no energy was going into those channels that control and empower speech. As for our conversation now, they explained that only beings on this plane could hear or see us.

"They asked me if I was afraid, and I told them that since seeing them I was not afraid of anything because I felt a oneness with them. But I wondered where I was going. They said I would see when I got there, but assured me that it would not be unpleasant.

"Finally we arrived at a place shining with many colored lights which seemed to me like some kind of audience room of God. I asked where we were, and they told me that because I had called on Lord Ram all my life, they were taking me to Him. The lights became more and more brilliant until they were brighter than the sun. Yet the brilliance never seemed unpleasant, even at its most intense level.

"Then I saw the form of Lord Ram and I prostrated. Ram smiled and blessed me. But then he said, 'It is good that you came here, but you cannot stay. You must go back right away because if you stay here even a little longer, they will burn your body on Earth. You died with unfulfilled desires to help people, so you must go back and fulfill them.' He showed me a vision of a large crowd of people and said, 'Look at all those people who are waiting for your help.'

"I said I did not want to return. I wanted to stay there.

"'So long as there are any desires in your mind,' Ram said, 'you cannot attain liberation. So you must return to fulfill those desires to help all those people you see before you.' Then he told the messengers to quickly take me back to my body.

"As I was coming back down, I saw people preparing to make arrangements for disposing of the body. Asha Devi was sitting in her room upstairs in deep meditation, and my body was lying on the first floor. I watched her crawl down the stairs, still in meditation, take my head in her lap and open my eyes.

"I suddenly felt pushed back into the body, the same way I felt pushed out of it, and now I could see and speak again. When my eyes first opened, I saw light streaming from Asha Devi's eyes and falling all over my body and enlivening it. All my senses worked again."

When Dhyanyogi-ji re-entered his body, his first concern was for the three or four people lying unconscious about the room. He tapped them gently and rubbed their backs to bring them back to consciousness. Then he instructed them to chant Ram's name. The fever and the boil were both gone, and his body felt very light. For the next eight days, he felt extremely detached from his body. His mind kept returning to the state of floating freely. Inwardly, he thought of his body, "What is this thing?" When eating, he wondered who was doing the eating, and when drinking water he marveled at how "this machine" —his body—worked. He had little

desire to eat or drink anything, but his disciples made him eat a little mung bean soup each day so that his energy would come back. After the eight days, his normal bodily feelings returned and he resumed his activities.[48]

Dhyanyogi-ji's disciples were thrilled to have their guru back. Some of them had witnessed Asha Devi's extraordinary role in reviving him, and those who hadn't seen it with their own eyes soon heard about it. They realized how indebted they were to her for bringing him back to them. They also began to realize why Dhyanyogi-ji was so intent on being with her and so focused on her training. Their misgivings about the girl who had so suddenly been thrust into their lives began to fade as they sensed the significance of the bond between them.

As for Dhyanyogi-ji, his death experience gave him a new appreciation for the spiritual power that lay within Asha Devi. He said that it was the energy flowing through her eyes that had pulled him back into the body, and now he was more determined than ever to prepare her for the future.

ॐ

---

[48]Dhyanyogi Madhusudandas, *Death, Dying and Beyond* (Santa Cruz, CA: Dhyanyoga Centers, 1979) 16-23.

CHAPTER TWENTY-SEVEN

PILGRIMAGES WITH ASHA DEVI

*D*uring the period from 1973 through 1976, Dhyanyogi-ji gave two or three shaktipat retreats, gatherings for people to receive initiation, which were attended by 200 to 300 people. These retreats were the embodiment of his deep feeling that he should give shaktipat to anyone who asked for it, without any tests or training to filter out those who were truly deserving.

Asha Devi recalled one such retreat at Vishnagar in Gujarat state. The meditation was set up in a kind of courtyard, where residents could look down and watch what was going on below. As the shakti began creating kriyas in the meditators, the people receiving shaktipat began laughing, crying and moving about

Asha Devi performing shaktipat initiation

in unusual ways. One of the neighbors, a woman watching from her perch high in the courtyard, constantly made fun of the group, but after two or three days she was so overcome by the energy that she, too, went into meditation.

Performing opening ceremony of disciple's factory in Vishnagar

The pair regularly went to Ahmedabad and Mumbai to give public meditations and offer shaktipat. At these programs and at the retreats, Asha Devi sat next to Dhyanyogi-ji and worked with him side-by-side. She was timid, speaking only rarely, but when she chanted, her voice sweet and haunting, Dhyanyogi-ji's eyes filled with tears, and she touched the hearts of those who heard her.

Guru Purnima retreat, Mumbai, 1975. **Front row from left:** *Mother Queen of Limbdi, her son, now King of Limbdi, and his Queen.* **2nd row from left:** *3rd man (in cap): Dahyabhai Pandya, Shivkumar Daga (disciple who later financed Dhyanyogi-ji's trip to America), and Jayendrasinghiji, the Mother Queen of Limbdi's brother who introduced her to Dhyanyogi-ji in Mount Abu around 1920*

Dhyanyogi-ji and Asha Devi also visited disciples and went to various pilgrimage sites throughout India. Although in meditation much of that time, Asha Devi had some fond memories of her travels with Dhyanyogi-ji.

Yogis are directed by their intuition and tend not to have rigid itineraries, so frequently Dhyanyogi-ji's plans were spontaneous. He might, for example, head out of Ahmedabad to visit a dev-

Queen of Limbdi offering respects at Guru Purnima; Sandeep Pathak in back left

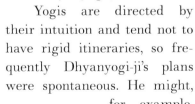

Asha Devi in bhav samadhi

otee in Mumbai, only to decide, on the spur of the moment, to turn the car around and drive to Bandhwad. Sometimes he'd leave at once, even if it were late in the evening, to make a journey to see a devotee who lived hours away.

In their travels, they encountered both the earthly and the mystical, physical travails as well as spiritual treasures. At times, it appeared as if they were being watched over by some unseen force. In 1973, Dhyanyogi-ji took Asha Devi to Ambaji and Mount Abu, the place where he had reached his final goal. Several other disciples, including Carl and Sushila Parekh, who helped to take care of Asha Devi at Bandhwad, were along for the trip. It was searingly hot as they drove, but no matter where they went a cloud always seemed to follow their car around, providing them some welcome shade.

Sometimes the places they visited were not particularly safe, and Dhyanyogi-ji would pile suitcases against the door of their hut and sit on them, staying up all night to guard the door while Asha Devi slept. During this period, Dhyanyogi-ji lovingly tended to her when she could not care for herself because she was so often in a deep state of meditation. It could take him anywhere from a half hour to three hours to rouse her, causing them to miss meals and change itineraries. Always deferring to the powerful kundalini energy moving within her, he never grew frustrated with her when her meditations threw them off schedule.

Ghatkopar, 1973

"In those days it often happened that we were supposed to go at a certain time, but we couldn't leave because I was in meditation," she said. "I was unable to wake up, so we had to delay our trip. But Guruji was very balanced, like a saint. Very loving. He didn't get angry."

Wherever they went, memorable things happened. Once, they went to a disciple's home in the desert town of Bikaner in Rajasthan to rest for about a month. On the second day they were there, they met a man whose great-great-grandfather used to walk to the

Jagganath Temple in Puri every year for darshan—a distance of about 700 miles—always beginning his journey on a particular full moon. The Jagganath Temple is a very powerful temple dedicated to Krishna.

As the pilgrim got older, the arduous trip became hard for him physically, so he prayed, "Lord, I am getting old. I can't walk any more. Please forgive me. I can't come to the temple anymore." The Lord answered, "Don't worry. I'll come to you."

"But how will I know it is you?" the man asked, and the Lord replied, "You'll know when you do arati. Take a clay pot and offer sweet rice with cardamom and cloves to a photo of the murtis at Jagganath, just as you have done at the temple. After the arati, you will see that the pot has been cut into four equal pieces. That's how you will know that I have come. This blessing will continue for seven generations in your family."

The king of the province heard about the phenomenon and believed that there must be a trick, so he went to the home of the man to test it. "Maybe it splits because it's a clay pot. Let's try it with a brass pot. If it still breaks into four pieces, I'll accept that the legend is true." The man didn't approve of testing the Lord in this way, but since it was the king, he had to comply. He used a brass pot and at the end of the arati, it fell into four pieces. Then the devotee told the king, "Never do this again. Don't test the Lord!"

Dhyanyogi-ji and Asha Devi met the seventh generation of the family that had been bestowed this blessing. The last descendant performed the arati right before their eyes, and when he finished the clay pot was split into four pieces.

"They told us his son could not do it," Anandi Ma recalls. "The father could do it, but the son could not."

The three years that followed Dhyanyogi-ji's death experience were primarily dedicated to Asha Devi's spiritual training. Dhyanyogi-ji took her on a number of pilgrimages, during which he instructed her to do certain austerities, with the aim of gaining control of her prana so she could channel her energy into helping others.

In 1973, Dhyanyogi-ji took Asha Devi into the Himalayas for the first time. At several points in Dhyanyogi-ji's life, he had set out to do the anusthan in which a pilgrim carries water from the Ganges to the Shiva temple in Rameshwaram, on the southern tip of the continent. For one who has not already attained the ultimate state, this task ensures enlightenment. Dhyanyogi-ji had a specific desire to collect the water from Gangotri, at the headwaters of the Ganges. In 1906, as a young man, Dhyanyogi-ji had completed this anusthan in the name of his father to repay his debt to him. Forty years later, he attempted it again, but was unable to complete the pilgrimage. In 1966, he again began the anusthan, this time accompanied by Deepak, as well as Deepak's mother and aunt, but landslides along the mountain roads prevented them from reaching Gangotri. Now, Dhyanyogi-ji felt it was important for Asha Devi to perform this anusthan.

Included in the journey were Dhyanyogi-ji's sister, Batonsadevi, his nephew Kailash,[49] and Kailash's son Deokrishna. Also along on the trip were Asha Devi's mother, Deepak Pathak and two other disciples.

September was the ideal time to set out for the Himalayas because the rainy season was over, and it was not too cold and snowy for travel in the mountains, but there were unexpected obstacles right away. The group flew straight from Ahmedabad to New Delhi, then headed north. Dhyanyogi-ji's plan was to travel to Gangotri and on to Gaumukh to collect the purest, just-melted glacier water. However, as before, the journey was too treacherous and they were unable to make it all the way to Gangotri. They stopped at Devprayag, and then climbed on to the tiny village of Badrinath, just a few miles from the border of Tibet.

At an altitude of 10,000 feet, Badrinath appears to sit near the roof of the world. The settlement itself lies on the right bank of the holy river Alakananda, a branch of the Ganges, in a breathtaking valley surrounded by two magnificent, snowy, windswept mountain ranges known as Nar and Narayan. Towering above it all at 21,643 feet is the pyramid-shaped peak Neelkanth, known as the "Garhwal Queen."

Badrinath was the home of Lord Vishnu in his incarnation as Narayan, and is one of the four most revered pilgrimage sites in the Himalayas, together with Yamunotri, Gangotri and Kedarnath. Its name derives from "Badri Van," the forest of wild berries that sustained Lord Vishnu when he took refuge there to meditate. Thousands of pilgrims have walked Badrinath's ancient streets, prayed in its temples and ashrams, and caught their breath at the simple beauty of this place that has been called "heaven on Earth."

In the center of the village is a brightly painted temple dedicated to

---

[49]Kailash Mishra was a Sanskrit scholar. He was the last blood relative of Dhyanyogi-ji who spent time with him. Kailash Mishra died in 2000.

Lord Vishnu, the destination of many of the Hindu pilgrims who come to Badrinath. Before entering the temple, they bathe in the Tapt Kund just below—a thermal hot spring whose waters are said to be curative as well as spiritually cleansing. Each day, inside the temple, priests wrap the striking, black stone murti of Vishnu in gauze-like cloth, and by day's end, as crowds of pilgrims crush into the temple for arati, the fabric virtually vibrates with spiritual energy.

Dhyanyogi-ji's band of pilgrims was happy to reach the peaceful environs of Badrinath, but once there, problems continued. One disciple opened his suitcase and discovered that the glass had broken on a picture of Dhyanyogi-ji that he carried with him to use in his puja. He was frightened that this was a sign that something bad would happen, and he went to Dhyanyogi-ji in tears. Dhyanyogi-ji explained that the glass had broken because some negative karma had been avoided. He reminded the disciple of a story in the *Ramayana* where the demon king Ravana attacked his brother Vibhishana. Ravana was at war with Ram, and his brother, realizing that Rama was the incarnation of the Lord, had taken the side of Ram and begged for his refuge. This betrayal sent Ravana into a rage. But when Ravana threw his weapon at Vibhishana, Ram came between them and protected Vibhishana, taking the blow himself. Similarly, Dhyanyogi-ji had taken on some karma for this disciple, and the damage manifested in the broken glass in the picture. Dhyanyogi-ji told his disciple not to worry, but to just go and change the glass. He reassured him that everything would be okay.

"We changed the glass and took the picture, with its new glass, into the temple at Badrinath," Deepak recalled. "It was crowded, but we managed to put the picture on the wall on one side. We had paid our respects and were about to depart, when a lady in a white sari came and bowed to Guruji's picture. She was the only person in the crowd who did this. There were so many people there that we were forced out of the main temple. We went outside and looked for the lady in white to ask if she knew Guruji. Why else would she have bowed down? But there was no trace of her. We hadn't seen her face, but there was no lady in a white sari anywhere near the temple.

"Later, we went back to our guest house and told Dhyanyogi-ji what happened. He said the lady we had seen was Laxmi Herself."

Not only were the disciples humbled that the Divine Mother had come to pay her respects to Dhyanyogi-ji, they were overcome with gratitude that, through his grace, they had been blessed to receive Her darshan.

After this incident, the group encountered no further obstacles. They headed back to Delhi, then flew directly to Madras.

They made their way by car about 250 miles south to the Shiva temple in Rameshwaram. One by one, they poured their vessels of Ganges water over the Shiva Lingam. After they completed this most auspicious pilgrimage, some other disciples from the area met them and took them to visit several significant spiritual places. In Madurai, there is the 17th-century Meenakshi Sundareswarar temple to the Divine Mother, famous for its colorful, intricate carvings on 12 soaring temple towers and its hall of 1,000 columns.

The group continued south to Kanya Kumari at the southern tip of India, where there is a powerful temple devoted to the Divine Mother in the form of a young girl. Here, Asha Devi had a vision of the Mother. From the edge of the town, they looked south across the water to Vivekananda's Rock rising out of the sea. The great sage meditated on the rock, and today there is a statue and memorial to him there.

In 1974, Dhyanyogi-ji and Asha Devi set out by car on a trip that would take them on a wandering path. Joining them were two women disciples who helped take care of Asha Devi's needs, Dhyanyogi-ji's nephew Kailash, and Kailash's son Deokrishna. They began in Bihar, where they attended the groundbreaking ceremony for the new hospital that Dhyanyogi-ji was building there, and continued on to Allahabad, Vrindavan, Ayodhya and Varanasi. As was often the case, Asha Devi spent much of the time in meditation. Whenever she went into a temple, she would have a vision of whichever saint or deity it was dedicated to—Shiva, Ram, Krishna or the Divine Mother.

Their ultimate destination on this trip was Rishikesh. Here they would spend six months while Dhyanyogi-ji guided Asha Devi through specific practices and anusthans he wanted her to master, including a Hanuman anusthan.

By this time, in the mid-1970s, the population of Rishikesh had grown. It was now considered a gateway to the trekking and temples of the Himalayas, but the city itself was still a place of great natural beauty, steeped in ancient lore, with much to offer spiritually. The

Groundbreaking ceremony for hospital in Bihar

Ganges River in Rishikesh is very fast-moving, and the water remains much purer there than in other spots. The simple rope bridge that young Kashinath crossed almost a century before has been replaced by a suspended bridge made of iron. Along the beach are makeshift huts where sadhus stay. Cows stroll or lounge along the water's edge. In the mornings, pilgrims can be seen making offerings of milk to the river, and puffed rice to the fish that live there. Ashrams line both sides of

Local police of Bihar honoring Dhyanyogi-ji

the Ganges with ghats leading down to the water, and the town is filled with hotels for pilgrims and shops selling items for pujas. At Triveni Ghat, two gorgeous sculptures greet those making their way down to the water for a dip. One depicts a scene from the *Mahabharata* in which Arjuna rides to the battle in his chariot with Lord Krishna as his charioteer. The other is a commanding representation of Lord Shiva, with the Ganges River flowing through his hair. Beside him stands his consort, the Divine Mother Parvati.

Each evening at sunset, as pinks and purples streak the sky and melt into the horizon, the distant sound of bell chimes calls people to the river for arati. Women sit together and chant, while priests set floating lamps on the water and watch them drift downstream in the dimming of the day.

It was to this magical place that Dhyanyogi-ji often retreated when he needed to take a break to restore his energy after a long spell of giving shaktipat and taking on the karma of his disciples. In the mountains surrounding Rishikesh, he could find the solitude he needed to rest in a meaningful way. There, he would do more malas and practices, and take Ayurvedic medicines.

Asha Devi soon began receiving the fruits of practicing in this special place as well. At one point during her ansuthan here, she saw the form of Hanumanji with the entire universe contained in Him.

After they had been in Rishikesh for a few months, Deepak came to visit Dhyanyogi-ji. Soon after, they were joined by Asha Devi's parents, her 7-year-old sister Kalyani, Kusum Sheth, as well as 20 to 30 other disciples. The group decided they would travel on to Badrinath. They spent a week there, then hiked seven miles to a holy place called Vasudhara, home of a spectacular 475-foot waterfall where strong winds spray the water so powerfully at times that it seems as if the flow has been cut off entirely. Legend has it that if a person stands by the falls and the water drenches them, it means they are pure of heart.

"On our way back from Badrinath, there was a landslide," Pravinji recalled. "Huge boulders were falling onto the road. The bus stopped and began to go in reverse. Guruji said that he was scared. I loved that about him, that he would say things like this. He was very, very down to earth, without pomp and show. He could have said, 'As long as I am here, or Lord Hanumanji is here, why worry?' But instead, he told us that he was worried. This didn't belittle him—it showed how humble he was."

In 1976, Dhyanyogi-ji once again took Asha Devi to Rishikesh, where she was to do another three-to-four month ansuthan. Once again

Ganges River in Rishikesh, 1974

disciples accompanied them to take care of the cooking and laundry, so they could completely withdraw from the world.

This intense training helped to prepare Dhyanyogi-ji's most advanced student for what came next—their journey together to America.

309

CHAPTER TWENTY-EIGHT

"I AM OUT TO SEARCH FOR MY LOST STARS"

*D*hyanyogi-ji's first American disciples, Carl Kuntz and Betsy Enochs, served as his East-West connection. Carl and Betsy met when Carl returned to California, after spending six months in India with Dhyanyogi-ji in 1971. Once home, he wanted to find like-minded people with whom he could meditate. Since Dhyanyogi-ji had no disciples outside of India, he looked into other yoga groups with similar philosophies, and began to meet with a group of devotees of Swami Yogananda. It was here that he met Betsy. They became friends and he regaled her with stories of his time with Dhyanyogi-ji.

For the past several months, unbeknownst to Carl, whenever Betsy closed her eyes to meditate, she had been having visions of "a yogi, dressed in white, giving me blessings." One evening, Carl invited her to come look at his photographs from his trip and she saw a picture of Dhyanyogi-ji for the first time. She cried out, "This is the person I've been seeing in my meditations!"

Betsy went on to pour out to Carl her recent experiences. "As soon as I gaze into my third eye center, I see him," she told him, "but I had no idea who he was." She was very excited to discover that she was seeing an actual living person. Convinced that he must be her guru, she wanted to know more.

Carl told Betsy all about his anusthan at Bandhwad, and gave examples of Dhyanyogi-ji's playful ways of pushing him deeper into his practice. "I was supposed to do five *lakhs*—that's 500,000—repetitions of the Ram mantra," Carl said, "and just when I got close to completing this number, Guruji told me, 'I think you need to do six lakhs!' Each day I did mantras for six hours and meditation for a few more hours, and for 21 days I had to remain in complete silence. That was both a blessing and a curse. As difficult as it was, I did have an amazing experience as a result. Of course, it wasn't the one I was expecting. I thought I'd have a vision of Lord Ram, but to my surprise, I had a vision of Lord Ganesh instead."

When Betsy heard the name Ram, she grew even more animated. During her visions of Dhyanyogi-ji, she had heard the sound "Ram," but she didn't know what it meant. Now that she learned that this was the name of the incarnation who had started Dhyanyogi-ji's lineage of shaktipat masters, and was Dhyanyogi-ji's chosen form of worship, she felt closer still to Dhyanyogi-ji.

Several months after this, in December 1972, Betsy experienced a spontaneous awakening of her kundalini. "I had been sitting in meditation for about two hours," she recalled, "when suddenly, I felt a stirring at my tailbone, and then a very hot energy moved up my spine to the area of my heart. I had no idea what was happening or what was to become of me. I tried to use my will to force this energy back down but to no avail. A little while later, I heard thousands of tinkling bells. My heart was beating very fast and I was afraid it would stop completely."

In January, Betsy had the same experience again. "For some weeks after my first experience with the kundalini, I spent most of my free time meditating. While in meditation, I heard sounds associated with the different chakras. One particular day, the sounds were very loud, like a roar. I prayed to Guruji to help me get through this experience. I faintly heard someone breathing very rapidly—at the time I did not realize that it was *me*. I surrendered as best I could. Then I saw a brilliant white light at the third eye center, followed by a deep blue color, and some symbols including a circle encasing a purple star. My inner

Asha Devi and Betsy Enochs

sense told me that this was the star of India, representing for me my goal of enlightenment."

Betsy's visions and kriyas continued for the next eight months. In the summer of 1973, she also began to have experiences in her dreams. "I felt certain that whenever I offered the least conscious resistance, kundalini would work on me in my sleep. Once, I received shaktipat initiation in a dream. I saw Guruji and when I knelt to touch him, he told me to first have a bath. After I bathed, he touched my head and sent a tremendous electrical shock through my body. I awoke still feeling the currents of energy in my spine."

Carl was planning to return to India, and Betsy decided to go with him. In late September 1973, she finally met Dhyanyogi-ji. After spending a week with Asha Devi and him at Bandhwad, she received shaktipat initiation in person on October 11, Asha Devi's birthday. "Asha Devi placed her hand on my head," she remembered, "and after some time I felt very hot and my head felt very heavy." A week later, she received the initiation again, this time from both Asha Devi and Dhyanyogi-ji.

Just as Dhyanyogi-ji had taken Carl under his wing a few years before, often referring to him as his own son, he welcomed Betsy into his family of disciples. She lived in Bandhwad with him for three months, during which time she put in great efforts to grow close to him and understand more about his teachings. She was interested in learning devotional music so Dhyanyogi-ji helped her to learn some bhajans in

Bandhwad, from left: Betsy Enochs, Asha Devi, Dhyanyogi-ji, Deepak Pathak, Mani, Bharti, Carl

Gujarati. He took her, along with Carl, Asha Devi, Deepak, and several others, on the trip to visit Mount Abu and Ambaji, so she could see the sacred places that had been central to him during his years of sadhana.

A strong connection developed between them.

It was after Betsy left India that Dhyanyogi-ji's intention to go to America surfaced. Carl had repeatedly offered to host Dhyanyogi-ji if he would come to America to teach meditation, but Dhyanyogi-ji had not expressed any interest. There had been talk of his going to the United States when, in 1970, he was asked to speak at a World Spirituality Conference, but the conference had been cancelled. Later, he was invited to go to Africa, but that trip never materialized either. When Betsy's visit was nearing its end, she, along with Carl, urged Asha Devi and Dhyanyogi-ji to come to California. A month later, Dhyanyogi-ji had his death experience, and, in retrospect, this foreshadowed his coming to America. It was then that Lord Ram gave Dhyanyogi-ji a vision of a crowd of people waiting for his help, and many of the faces he saw were Westerners. "All of the people I saw are my family," he later wrote, "and I have to help them."[50]

At this point, in January 1974, Carl was still in India. He and Deepak had gone to visit Dhyanyogi-ji in Bandhwad just days before his death experience. The two were working on the project of retranslating Dhyanyogi-ji's book, *Light on Meditation*, to make it more accessible for English-speaking audiences.[51] Although Carl and Deepak saw the boil on Dhyanyogi-ji, they had no idea how serious his condition would turn out to be. He sent them away to do an anusthan, so they weren't present when Dhyanyogi-ji left his body.

During Carl's visits to India, he and Deepak had become good friends, and Carl invited Deepak to come and live with him in California. Deepak had always dreamed of studying in America, and since his family and Dhyanyogi-ji were supportive, he decided that he would go. In the summer of 1974, before he left, Deepak went to see Dhyanyogi-ji to receive his blessings. "The saddest part of leaving India was that I would not be able to see Guruji for a few years, at least," recalled Deepak. "I went to visit him in Rishikesh, where he was in retreat, working with Asha Devi. When it came time to leave, I was heartbroken, but he said, 'You go to America, and I will come.' This made me very happy. If Guruji could come to America while I was there, this would be the

---

[50]Madhusudandas, *Death, Dying and Beyond*, 22.

[51]Carl was largely responsible for retranslating Light on Meditation. The book was first published in Gujarati in the late 1960s and in 1972, it was translated into English for Dhyanyogi-ji's disciples in South India, who could not read Gujarati. Dhyanyogi-ji wasn't satisfied with the translation because it had a formal, British tone, and he wanted it to be simple to read, comprehensible to anyone interested in yoga.

greatest blessing of all!"

So, in the fall of 1974, Deepak Pathak, now 24 years old, went to California, moved in with Carl, and enrolled at San Jose State University. For the next two years, Deepak studied microbiology, Carl resumed his work building houses, and the two settled into the routines not uncommon to bachelors—watching *Hogan's Heros* and *Star Trek* on TV, and living on staples like Rice-A-Roni. Still, unlike most of their peers, their lives were anchored in daily meditation, and every morning Deepak faithfully did his practices.

On one typical evening in the spring of 1976, Carl was at home with his roommate. Deepak had a relaxed, unceremonious style, and in his characteristic way, he mentioned to Carl that Dhyanyogi-ji was coming. Carl responded in kind. "Oh. That's nice. How long is he staying?"

"Three months or so," answered Deepak. "He's just checking things out." This offhand exchange was their acknowledgment that their lives were about to be turned upside down.

Looking back, the stage was set for this next step in Dhyanyogi-ji's work. He had trained Asha Devi for four years, Swamiji was installed at Hansol to continue Dhyanyogi-ji's work in India, and Deepak, Carl and Betsy provided a home base for him in America. A disciple named Shivkumar Daga donated the money for their travel expenses, so on September 2, 1976, Dhyanyogi-ji, along with Asha Devi and a devotee from Patan named Vinod Patel,[52] flew from Mumbai to New York, where they stayed with some Indian disciples living in New Jersey for two days, and then went on to California.

Carl was accustomed to spontaneity where Dhyanyogi-ji was concerned—at his guru's suggestion, he had repeatedly changed his schedule, extended visits, and taken on projects with little or no notice—so he quickly came up with living arrangements for his guests. He had just finished building a house in Scotts Valley, California near Santa Cruz. The house was in a clearing surrounded by redwood trees, a perfect setting for Dhyanyogi-ji. Large enough to accommodate Dhyanyogi-ji, Asha Devi, Vinod, Deepak and himself, there was also a spacious room downstairs well-suited to be a meditation hall. Carl stopped working so he could organize Dhyanyogi-ji's activities, and Deepak was completing his final semester of school, and would soon be free to serve as translator.

---

[52]Dhyanyogi-ji wanted someone to accompany them to do seva and Vinod and his family wanted to serve Dhyanyogi-ji, so Vinod came to America with him and did seva for several years. Ultimately he relocated to the United States.

Before Dhyanyogi-ji arrived, Deepak worried that they hadn't made enough contacts with spiritual centers. He feared that Dhyanyogi-ji would come all the way from India for nothing, and he wrote to Dhyanyogi-ji about his doubts. Dhyanyogi-ji answered, "When I come to America, even if only one person receives shaktipat, I will consider my work done."

Dhyanyogi-ji and Asha Devi, the day they left India for America

Woodbury, Connecticut, July, 1978

CHAPTER TWENTY-NINE

IN AMERICA

*A*s it turned out, there was no need for concern about whether Dhyanyogi-ji's trip to America would be worthwhile. Although he was against publicity, word spread fast that there was a yogi in the United States who could give shaktipat and provide guidance to individuals who were having intense interactions with the kundalini. Several of his disciples had relatives living in the United States, who arranged for him to lead meditation programs in their living rooms. When Dhyanyogi-ji was home, there were nightly meditations at the house in Scotts Valley. The more people he met, the more requests he got to visit somewhere new, and he accepted every invitation.

The first group that formed around Dhyanyogi-ji was in the Gujarati community in San Francisco. Many of the Indians who came to meet him had not been following any spiritual path. One example was Chaturbhai Patel, a man in his late 70s, who lived in Foster City, south of San Francisco. Kaka (Uncle), as he was affectionately called, had never meditated when he lived in India, but when he retired and moved to California to be with his children, he decided he would explore the spiri-

Chaturbhai Patel working with Dhyanyogi-ji

tual realm of life. He went to see Dhyanyogi-ji and received shaktipat.

"I knew nothing of yoga or kundalini shakti, until I met Guruji," Kaka once said. "I am a son of an ignorant farmer, but look what Guruji has given me! I can feel pulsating shakti in my body and all around me everyhere. When I first met Guruji, five minutes of meditation seemed like five hours. But after being with him for a while, five hours of meditation felt like five minutes." It was Kaka who did the initial translation—by hand—of the original Gujarati biography upon which this volume was based.

Soon after his arrival, Dhyanyogi-ji was invited to Los Angeles. He and a small entourage of disciples drove there and presented programs at the East-West Center and the College of Oriental Studies. Then the troop packed Dhyanyogi-ji's pots and pans, copies of the books he'd written, his personal belongings and their own, into Carl's car and Carl drove them across the country, stopping wherever he'd been asked to teach, even in places like Reno, Nevada, where only one person attended the meditation program. He visited Denver, Chicago, Cleveland, Newark, Buffalo, Boston, Connecticut and Maine. The next year, Dhyanyogi-ji purchased an old station wagon and that became the official vehicle for his tours.

After people received shaktipat, Dhyanyogi-ji gave them spiritual names. The names indicated the traits that the student would develop as they followed their spiritual path. Soon after meeting him, a young man named Will Hartzel became his personal assistant. Dhyanyogi-ji gave Will the spiritual name Laxman, the name of Ram's brother who accompanied Ram into exile, and exemplified selfless devotion.

"In 1977, I was living in a remote part of northern California," recalled Laxman. "I'd been on a spiritual path my whole life, but I really wanted a teacher. I spent many hours talking with my friends Rajiv and Hansa about how great it would be to have a spiritual teacher. Then we met some people who'd told us about an Indian master in Santa

Cruz. They said he was wonderful and that we should meet him. Rajiv and Hansa went to see him and came back with glorious reports, so I went down and met him at Carl's house. There was to be a meditation downstairs, and people were chanting. As soon as Guruji came in, I felt electric current rush through me. He walked past me and I felt energy and warmth and light. I was overcome by it. I experienced a feeling of familiarity, of home, an instant powerful connection.

"Guruji was leaving to go to L.A., so I decided to follow him down there. This gave me a little time to prepare for shaktipat, which I received in Pasadena. It was powerful and intense. When Guruji touched the top of my head, I had a vision of light, colors, and I felt an electric charge going through my body. More than that, it was a reconnecting of something extremely deep and powerful in my life that had been buried until now. Guruji told me later that we'd known each other in another life.

"My friends and I made frequent pilgrimages to Santa Cruz. Guruji was just starting the Bija Mantra meditations, and I was helping out. After one Bija meditation, Guruji was preparing to leave to go cross-country for the first time. I was asked to come to a meeting with him. This was highly unusual and therefore intriguing to me. I didn't have a clue what it was about. When I got there, I was asked if I would drive Guruji, Asha Devi and Deepak for an unknown period of time—just drop everything and go. It was a difficult decision to make, but also easy. I was fully surrendered to the will of Guruji. I had bitten the entire bullet. I said that I would. I made the seven-hour trip home to Hurd's Gulch, California, put my stuff in storage, and drove back to meet Guruji. Before I knew it, a couple of years had gone by."

For nearly two years, Laxman traveled with Guruji. His role included a range of tasks—washing dishes, driving the station wagon, doing guru seva, and introducing Dhyanyogi-ji at public meditation programs. He recalled one typical evening traveling with Dhyanyogi-ji.

"Guruji had been invited to give meditation programs in New York City," Laxman said. "We were staying in Jersey

Dhyanyogi-ji and Laxman

Sacramento, 1979

City, but the programs had been arranged for Manhattan, in an office building on 42nd Street, about half a block from Times Square. That was the first time I had ever been to New York City, and I was not prepared for it! In those days, 42nd Street was where they had theaters where there was live sex on stage—I kid you not. Some of the people on the street looked pretty rough, and this is where we were holding meditation programs!

"When we arrived, it was my job to park the car. I dropped Guruji off and found a parking spot several blocks away. After the meditation was finished, I went back to get the car. That area of New York City is mostly one-way streets, and somehow or another I managed to come around and be going in the wrong direction. There was Guruji on the sidewalk in front of the building, but I couldn't get to him because I was on the other side of the street facing the wrong direction. The streets were so congested that if I drove around the block, it could have taken half an hour to get back to him. I was horrified at the thought of leaving him just standing there in the midst of the Times Square scene. Suddenly there was an open gap in the traffic and, on impulse, I decided to cut cross four lanes of traffic. I whipped this enormous U-turn and pulled right up at the curb where Guruji was waiting. I received robust compliments from the local New York devotee who thought this was a great move!

"When I pulled up to the curb, Guruji got into the front passenger seat but he wouldn't leave until he was sure that everyone who had come to the program had a ride home.

"While we waited, I noticed a man walking towards us. He looked like he was pretty down and out. Coming from rural California, I wasn't used to seeing people who lived on the city streets, and I worried about what would happen if he confronted Guruji. This was one of the greatest examples I saw of how Guruji impacted people who might appear to be very dense and dark, but who, in fact, were able to receive the essence of who he was. The man staggered up to the car window, looked in at Guruji in all his regalia, and said to him, 'I don't know who you are, but you're all right!'"

Some Americans were taken by surprise by Dhyanyogi-ji's unusual appearance. He had a long white beard and, to a Westerner, his clothing—knee-length white shirt and ankle-length dhoti—must have appeared to be a flowing, white robe. After a lifetime in Indian heat, he was usually cold in the United States, so he wore a ski cap pulled over a towel on his head. But whatever the initial reactions, it was only a matter of time before those who met him were enchanted. There was something about him that people recognized and responded to, even if they didn't quite understand why.

Dhyanyogi-ji had relocated around the world to a place with a radically different climate and culture, going from the dusty little village of Bandhwad and Indian roads where the top speed was 30 mph, to the bustling cities of America and highways with 70 mph speed limits. It was almost as if he had traveled through time, not just space. But he seemed to feel as at home in America as he did in India. He had to adapt, of course, to the weather and the language, but he suffered no apparent culture shock, no awkward adjustment. When people marveled at how he so quickly and effortlessly picked up English, he said, "He who knows the One Thing need not know another." From his state of God-realization, all knowledge was available to him.

Dhyanyogi-ji waking Asha Devi from meditation, Scotts Valley

Just as in India, he attracted all kinds of people to him and watched over them with tenderness and tolerance. Those who came to him for spiritual instruction were impressed by his simplicity, generosity and spiritual power. They were thrilled to have a genuine yogic master in their midst. One devotee commented, "It was like he walked right out of the Vedas."

The love affair between Dhyanyogi-ji and the Americans he met was mutual. He often said he was moved by the hearts of the Americans. They delighted him with their openness. Here, just as in India, he felt driven to spare people the agonies of his long years of sadhana, eager to demonstrate the potential of the awakened kundalini. He saw sincere desire and willingness to learn, practice and evolve in his American students, and this thrilled him.

In his enthusiasm to teach, he adapted his methods to cross the cultural barriers. During the previous decade, Dhyanyogi-ji had written *Light on Meditation* and *Message to Disciples* to explain the workings of the kundalini and to inspire people with his own story. In his four years in America, he published four more books directed to his new American audience: *Brahmanada*; *Death, Dying and Beyond*; *Yoga Dipika*; and *Shakti*. In India, his attitude had been sober and serious, while in America, he used humor more, tailoring his approach to his new students. His meditation programs in India had been held in silence, but in America he gave talks and answered questions because he recognized that Westerners were used to verbal, intellectual exchanges. He enjoyed Americans' curious and analytical questions, so different from the reactions of Indians, who tended to take things more at face value, and he was indulgent and patient in the face of people's doubts.

There are countless stories about how he responded to skepticism. Marsha Newman, who became one of his closest students, first met Dhyanyogi-ji when she accompanied a "gullible" friend to a meditation program at Carl Kuntz's house in Scotts Valley "in order to protect her from being hoodwinked by some charlatan guru." During the

Kriyas in meditation, 1976

meditation, Marsha thought to herself, if he is a real guru, he can probably read minds, so I'll talk to him in my mind. Silently, she spoke to Dhyanyogi-ji. "If you are true, please come over and put your hand on the top of my head." But Dhyanyogi-ji didn't move from the chair in which he sat.

"I thought, oh well, I may as well just relax and close my eyes," Marsha recalled. "I was aware of people around me having kriyas. It was very noisy, like a zoo. Then I heard this rustling in front of me and I opened my eyes. I thought, 'Oh my God, he is going to do it!' but instead, he took my glasses off. He walked over to the side of the room and placed them on a ledge and then he walked back over to me and put his hand on my head.

"That was last thing I remembered—then I went into a very deep meditation. When I woke up, the room was empty except for my friend Maryann. I knew something extraordinary had happened. I had never meditated like that in my life! I started crying, out of a recognition of something.

"Maryann said, 'I know, I know,' and she told me to come upstairs to meet Guruji. I remember that he was sitting on Carl's turquoise couch with a small circle of disciples around him. Maryann motioned me to sit down. I asked her what I should do and she told me that I could just talk to him. So I whispered, 'Thank you for my meditation.'

"One of the disciples there from L.A. asked, 'What did she say?' and Guruji replied, 'She tested me.'

"I remember that he stood up over me and he looked so tall—he was only a little over 5 feet tall, but I sensed his power—and he smiled and said to me, 'Now what do you want?' I said, 'I want initiation.'

"I was given some prasad and it tasted so good! All the colors looked brighter, and there was magic in the world again.

"Four days later, I came for shaktipat. I was waiting for Guruji in the living room of Carl's house. Chaturbhai Patel was there quoting scriptures while this L.A. disciple was doing yoga, and I felt very uncomfortable. 'I do not understand this culture,' I thought, and I got up to leave. I went out to the stairway that led down out of the house, and at that moment, Guruji appeared at the bottom of the stairs. I felt electricity in my body. 'Did you recognize me?' he asked. 'I don't know,' I answered, 'I just love you.' Then he said, 'Well, I just recognized you. You were my disciple in a former life.'"

At that moment, Marsha went back inside the house and took shaktipat. Dhyanyogi-ji gave her the spiritual name Moti, which means "pearl."

"Those were the most powerful days I've ever had," said Moti. "These memories don't fade. They are the light posts that light up my life."

Dhyanyogi-ji had fun with Americans. Once, he challenged someone at a meditation program to take his temperature and then take it again. The astonished man watched as Dhyanyogi-ji's temperature fluctuated several degrees, while Dhyanyogi-ji giggled. On many occasions, he did what was referred to as the "bija mantra experiment." "After

Moti (Marsha Newman) and Kusum Sheth

two weeks of programs, the final event was when Guruji sang the bija mantras," remembered Laxman. "Sometimes he'd have people take their temperature and blood pressure before and after the meditations. Most people's temperature went up, but some people's went down, as much as eight, 10 or 12 degrees. He also did experiments with people touching his head. He'd ask them to take their temperature before receiving darshan, then touch his head for a couple of minutes. Their temperature would go up four or five degrees. He seemed to like to do this with new, skeptical people. He'd get this twinkle in his eye—would they like to see some proof?—and I'd run off to get a thermometer."

Dr. Lee Sannella, author of *The Kundalini Experience: Psychosis or Transcendence?*, was a psychiatrist interested in "spiritual emergence," who started a clinic that would do groundbreaking, scientific investigations into the nature of kundalini. Dr. Sanella heard about Dhyanyogi-ji and went to meet him. "I attended meditations, satsangs, anything he offered," Sannella said. Dhyanyogi-ji asked him to design some experiments to demonstrate the power of the kundalini energy. "He had a profound curiosity in the scientific side of meditation," recalled Sannella. "It was difficult to objectively show how the energy was working, but the bija mantra was certainly a device for transmitting energy. He kept us enraptured and enthralled when he chanted it."

When Dhyanyogi-ji asked his new disciples to massage him, he joked with them saying, "Energy, free of charge!" In his more serious moments, he explained, "A touch can do a lot. A single touch can transmit energy and give a person realization. That is the flow of energy through the Great Beings." Most yogis at his lev-

el avoid physical contact with other people. In contrast, Dhyanyogi-ji's attitude was, "God has given me energy, and I reached the goal. But it is there for others. If you get a million dollars but you don't use it, so what? You need to invest it, to start a business to grow it and help people."

"He never withheld himself at all," Dr. Sannella remembered. "He had a remarkable relationship with his devotees. He treated all of us the same and never showed favoritism."

Sannella had studied with nearly 30 different gurus and other teachers during his lifetime, including Swami Muktananda, Robert S. de Ropp, Shunryu Suzuki-roshi in San Francisco, Maezumi Roshi, abbot of the Zen Center of Los Angeles, Bernie Glassman, Guru Raj from South Africa and the Self-Realization Fellowship. "Of all the gurus I was with, he was the most constant, straightforward, available, loving human being, and I remember him very dearly. I always had a very close tie with him, and it never changed. When I heard of his death, I was very sorry, but I knew that he would always be my teacher and that he would be one of my shepherds when I die."

Occasionally, as in Moti's case, Dhyanyogi-ji seemed to recognize people who came to see him. He became especially excited when he encountered someone he had seen during the vision from his death experience. Certain faces had appeared repeatedly in his meditations so when he actually saw them, he was openly joyful. A disciple from California named Mildred told a story of one of these reunions. Mildred was a meditation teacher and she had a picture of Dhyanyogi-ji in her studio. One day, a new student came to class and noticed the photograph. She told Mildred she felt she knew this man.

"I invited her to come to the meditation program we were holding the next morning," Mildred said, "because I knew that Guruji would be there. When she and a friend arrived, the program had actually been cancelled, but Guruji said he'd do it anyway. So he did—for just the two of them. After the meditation, he asked me to massage him and then he invited this newcomer to massage him also. This surprised me because I knew that in India, people waited five years for this privilege. At one point, the student left the room and Guruji said to me, 'She's one of the faces!' and he was beaming.

"He was always looking for his lost stars. In January 1977, at the first group meditation in L.A., he asked, 'Who saw a blue light during the meditation?' Twelve people raised their hands. Two-and-a-half years later, Guruji came to visit me and told me that the people who'd seen the blue light that night were people whose faces he'd seen in his vision."

There are many stories like these, uncanny stories of people who felt they'd seen Dhyanyogi-ji before they met him in the flesh. Some, like Betsy and Mildred's student, reported that they had seen his face in their dreams and meditations. A retired couple living in Carson City, Nevada named Jill and Frank Thomas had a particularly unusual experience. One day, a dark-haired, thick-bearded man appeared at their door asking if they might have some bread and milk to spare for him to eat. The Thomas's home was only a mile from a prison, and the man's scruffy appearance scared them. They offered him money in hopes that he would leave quickly, but he wouldn't take any money, so finally, they gave him

Jill and Frank Thomas

the food, and he thanked them and left. Later that week, they attended a public meditation with Dhyanyogi-ji and met him for the first time. After the program, they were browsing at the book table where there were photographs of Dhyanyogi-ji for sale. One of these was a picture of Dhyanyogi-ji as a much younger man. They were thunderstruck as they both simultaneously recognized him as the man who had come to their door earlier in the week.

Another of these remarkable meetings occurred in Boulder, Colorado in 1978. A young man from Brazil was among a group that received shaktipat. After the ceremony, this man told Dhyanyogi-ji that during his meditation, Sanskrit letters appeared before his closed eyes. He was completely mystified since he had never even heard of the Sanskrit language before. Dhyanyogi-ji asked him to draw the letters he'd seen. When he did, Dhyanyogi-ji identified them as mantras from the *Upanishads.*[55] Dhyanyogi-ji asked the young man about his background, and he said that he came from a tribe that lived deep in the Amazon jungle, and that most of his people had never left the forest. His grandfather was the medicine man of the tribe. He had hoped to take over as medicine man, but his grandfather had told him no, that his teacher was in America. His grandfather had gone on to describe Dhyanyogi-ji's appearance to

---

[55]The *Upanishads* are a class of Indian scriptures written after the Vedas and Brahmanas, and before the development of the six formal philosophical systems and the Puranas.

him, and on that word alone, the young man had traveled to America, searched for and found Dhyanyogi-ji.

Some of the people who met Dhyanyogi-ji in the United States were Indians who had read *Light on Meditation* in the original Gujarati edition and had been trying, unsuccessfully, to contact him while he was still in India. Early in 1976, Pravin and Daksha Doctor were living in New Jersey when an acquaintance gave them Dhyanyogi-ji's book. "When I read his words: 'This house is burning, everyone take what they want,'" Pravin said, "I felt a pang in my heart at his kindness." Pravin was eager to meet Dhyanyogi-ji, so he wrote to his uncle in Mumbai asking him to call the Pathaks.

"We couldn't catch Guruji at that time," Daksha recalled. "Then, months later, a friend of ours told us that he had just met a saint in Jersey City. Our friend had a back problem and he told us that the saint had patted him on the back and the pain immediately went away, and this saint's name was Dhyanyogi Madhusudandas. Guruji had been five minutes away from our home, but we had missed him! We called him and said we would come to California to see him, but he said, 'Don't come here, I'm coming back to New Jersey this summer, so you arrange some programs and I'll see you then.' Pravin's brother lived in L.A., so we called him and told him about Guruji and asked him to go and meditate with him. He invited Guruji, Asha Devi and Deepak for lunch. Meanwhile, we wrote a letter to Guruji. Apparently, he wrote back to us but we never received his note. When he was at my brother-in-law's house, we called to speak with him and told him we had never gotten

his letter. He said, 'Ok, I'll write again.' And he did. And again he said that he would come to see us, so we didn't need to come out there. He was so kind.

"We arranged programs and a place for Guruji to stay," Daksha continued. "I remem-

ber the first time I met him. Pravin was massaging his feet and I began singing a bhajan. I lost control and went into meditation. I remember something smelled very good, like incense, but no one else smelled it.

"At that time, there was a couple who were our neighbors. They were unable to have kids so they talked to Guruji. He blessed a coconut, gave it to them as prasad, and they had a baby girl. When he came back in 1978, they went to see him again. I was with them and I remember that they asked Guruji what they should do with the coconut now? He spoke with them so nicely, saying, 'You have a brick of gold. What would you do with that?'"

Bhailal Suthar had read Dhyanyogi-ji's book in 1973, when he lived in India. He went to Ahmedabad to try and meet Dhyanyogi-ji, but was unable to find him there. "My wife told me that when you want to meet him enough, he will come." In 1974, Bhailal moved to America. "Five years later, in 1979, we were living in New Jersey," he recalled, "when someone called me and told me that Guruji was right here in New Jersey! I called and spoke with Deepak, who said that they were about to return to California, but would be back soon. I invited them to come and stay with me, and as it turned out, they did.

"Guruji had a divine personality. I remember that before meditation, he would take a stick of incense and walk from one end of my apartment to the other, intoning mantras. He looked like he was from another planet. I almost went into trance watching him."

Then there were those who reached out to Dhyanyogi-ji without having any previous conscious connection with him at all. These were cases of people who were having difficulties, on the worldly or spiritual planes, and someone suggested that they contact Dhyanyogi-ji.

Bipin Pancholi, a friend of Pravin Doctor's, was a young veterinarian who had moved to America from Ahmedabad with his wife and three small children. It was very difficult to get the credentials he needed to work here and establish his new life. Pravin urged him to call Dhyanyogi-ji and ask for a blessing, but Bipin felt awkward. "I had never talked to a saint," he said, "so I asked Pravin what to say." After receiving some coaching from Pravin, but without any idea what he was really doing, Bipin phoned Dhyanyogi-ji. Dhyanyogi-ji said that he had blessed a garland of roses for Pravin, and he instructed Bipin, "Get a flower from that garland and a picture of me and everything will be all right." Daksha remembered that they gave Bipin a flower but since they didn't have a photo, they took a flyer for the recent meditation programs, cut out the picture of Dhyanyogi-ji and gave that to him. According to Bipin, his life immediately turned around. He found a position and his practice blossomed. This was the beginning of an enduring relationship between the Pancholi family and Dhyanyogi-ji. The Pancholis remain deeply involved in Dhyanyogi-ji's work.

Tom Thompson, a meditation teacher living in Woodbury, Connecticut was another American who wrote to Dhyanyogi-ji out of the blue. Tom's problem was spiritual in nature. He had some familiarity with kundalini and the concept of purification. But after taking initiation from another guru, he was alarmed by the intensity of the kundalini process that followed. As he described it, "I felt like I was in a dream, like my reality was continually altered. It wasn't necessarily bad, but it was pretty bizarre. I had a wife and baby to support, so I had to function and take care of them. Although I had an intellectual understanding of what was happening to me, the intellect and the experience are very different, and I was frightened. In retrospect, my ego was cracking. I had held a pretty rigid belief system, and kundalini was not going to let that continue!"

Tom's guru was back in India and not in good health, so Tom didn't know where to turn for guidance. Then he heard about Lee Sannella's book, which explained the differences between psychological problems and reactions to the kundalini. Tom read it cover-to-cover, and began to feel some hope. He wrote to Dr. Sannella. "Lee was very kind and supportive." Tom recalled, "He told me that there was a shaktipat guru traveling in the United States named Dhyanyogi-ji, who was a very high saint, and suggested that maybe he could help me.

"So I wrote a letter to Guruji," Tom went on, "and told him about my problems and invited him to visit me. I felt so arrogant doing this—like who was I to ask a sadguru to come see me, as if he had nothing better to do? But I was desperate. The moment I mailed that letter, I wanted to do anything to get it back! I remember thinking, what will I do if he says yes?!

"Guruji wrote back to me saying, and I quote, 'I would be pleased to accept your offer to stay in your house for a short visit,' and he signed the letter, 'My blessings with love, Dhyanyogi.' He said he could come on June 28-29, 1978, that several disciples would be accompanying him, and

Performing shaktipat

Performing shaktipat with peacock feathers

that I should arrange two meditation programs."

Tom remembered clearly how the visit unfolded. Initially, like many who hosted Dhyanyogi-ji, he felt unprepared. He didn't even know exactly how to prepare. He just opened up his heart and home without the slightest idea of what was coming next.

"We took most of the furniture out of the house so there would be room to meditate," Tom said. "We just left a chair for Guruji to sit in, and a bed for him to sleep in. I remember the scene when this big station wagon pulled up, with a footlocker on top, holding all of Guruji 's belongings. He was in the back, with two disciples—Moti and Laxman—sitting in the front. Asha Devi had gotten sick a few days before, so she and Deepak had remained behind in Boston.

"In the afternoon, I talked to Guruji about what had been going on for me. He affirmed that it was kundalini. 'Don't worry, there's nothing to fear,' he told me. 'I'm always with you.' He patted me on the head, and immediately I started getting better. Then I took shaktipat from him. I felt conflicted over who was my guru now, since I had taken initiation from two, so I asked Guruji about that. He said that all true gurus are the same. So I kept them both."

Tom had a group of friends with whom he'd been meditating. They all helped with Dhyanyogi-ji's visit, they all took shaktipat, and, Tom said, "We all fell in love with him." That was the start of a group of disciples who met regularly to practice Dhyanyogi-ji's teachings, a group that still meets 25 years later.

"I remember the extraordinary effect he had on my father, who was there when Guruji came," Tom said. "My father was never supportive of my

Dhyanyogi-ji and Asha Devi performing shaktipat

Dhyanyogi-ji with Shivkumar Daga (who financed his trip to America) and Vinod (who came along to do seva) at Disneyland

interest in yoga. He thought that religious figures were con artists, so he assumed that I was being conned by Guruji, until he met him. It was very moving for me to see how much my father was in awe of Guruji. It was the first time I saw him treat anyone with respect like that.

"In a way, what I remember most of all was what it was like just being with him, the moments of his visit that were simple, not 'powerful' or public. I remember going into his room that first morning, and seeing him sitting on the edge of the bed feeding grapes to Kelly, my one-year-old daughter. I remember sitting next to him when he was lying on his bed, and he asked me about the rural town in Connecticut where we lived. 'When is monsoon season here?' he asked, 'Where are the irrigation ditches?'"

Many of his disciples commented on Dhyanyogi-ji's playfulness during his time in America. He liked seeing new things. His disciples brought him to Disneyland, where he rode on some of the gentler rides like "It's a Small World." He visited the Sears Tower in Chicago, and the World Trade Center in New York. He declared that Mt. Shasta was a holy mountain.

Others remembered quiet moments with him when he said something that revealed his nature in its simple glory. "One afternoon, I was sitting with Guruji while he went through his mail," recalled Tulsi, a disciple from Northern California. "I was feeling full of bhakti, and he looked up at me and said, 'What you feel is what I feel.'"

Moti described the range of Dhyanyogi-ji's personality. "He went from being like Santa Claus to being very serious," she recalled. "It

Dhyanyogi-ji blessing Asha Devi in Hawaii

CHAPTER TWENTY-NINE

Hawaii, 1978

was like he was in touch with God. His was no ordinary pair of eyes. It was like he was looking into eternity. Sometimes he would cook and serve food to us with the greatest humility. But if someone were silly or pompous, he would make a wry comment. Once, I had a summer free and spent it traveling with him. We visited some Indians in New Jersey and I remember how he would give lots of pats on the head, his hand always fluttering. When he was in a room, it would fill up with energy so intense that I thought I would explode. Sometimes I thought it was too much for American people, that we had no self-control in his presence.

"For me, meeting Guruji was like walking out of a black and white movie into color. He was more real than life. He became the point of all comparisons, the center of my life. Yet once he asked me, 'Will you remember this old yogi from India when I'm gone?'"

Despite the enormous impact he had on his disciples, Dhyanyogi-ji continued to remind them that he was just one of many saints employed on a "sacred staff." He was merely a conduit for the guru tatwa—the archetypal energy that worked through him and other sadgurus. In Hinduism there are many forms of God, so every individual can find a form to which they can relate. Similarly, there are many teachers, each following a different path, each appropriate for different students.

One of Dhyanyogi-ji's disciples had a near-death experience. When he died, he found himself standing before a judge, with Dhyanyogi-ji as his counsel, pleading for his life. The judge was Lord Buddha. The disciple won the case, and was returned to his body. After he recovered, he went to see Dhyanyogi-ji, and asked him, "Why was Lord Buddha the judge? Shouldn't it have been Ram, since I am on this path?" Dhyanyogi-ji replied, "That's just who was on duty at the time."

Between 1976 and 1980, Dhyanyogi-

335

ji crossed the United States four times by car, making public appearances almost every day that he wasn't en route. Laxman, Deepak, and Asha Devi always accompanied him, and between 1977 and 1979, Kusum Sheth, who was now in the United States, toured with them.

Kusum became a key person in doing Dhyanyogi-ji's work. She served Dhyanyogi-ji with deep love and faith, and her organizational skills were put to good use in planning meditation programs. Side by side with Asha Devi and Deepak, she cooked, washed dishes, and translated for Dhyanyogi-ji during his talks. Often, when she brought him his morning tea, he said, 'What can I give you? If I had a village in my pocket now, I would give it to you.' In 1975, before Kusum emigrated, she went to see Dhyanyogi-ji in Ahmedabad. At the end of her visit, Dhyanyogi-ji and Asha Devi brought her to the airport to return to Mumbai. When they were dropping her off, Asha Devi told Dhyanyogi-ji to give something to Kusum. He took off his sandals, gave them to Kusum, and walked barefoot back to the car.

Kusum remembered one time when, while she was cooking some cumin seeds, she got a second degree burn from a pot of ghee that had been sitting on the stove. "All day, I kept my hand in ice to relieve the pain. Asha Devi kept telling me to ask Guruji for help, but I didn't want to bother him. Finally, when it was time for bed and I could no longer keep my hand cold, I went to him. He poured some water in a Styrofoam cup, stirred his pinkie in it, and told me to drink the water. Immediately, all the pain left. My hand still blistered, but there was no pain.

"Guruji said, 'In the current day and age, America is going to play a vital role in the development of spirituality worldwide.' So instead of sitting in a cave, enjoying his bliss, he worked—all the time. There would be morning meditations with questions and answers, afternoon satsang followed by private appointments with disciples, and evening meditation with another session for questions and answers. He'd let people sit in with him during his own puja and meditation. Even if he suffered, he didn't say a word. When he rested, people would disturb him and he'd receive them with a smile. He only slept from 1:00 to 3:30 a.m. at night. But he was like shakti condensed into physical form."

An assortment of American devotees joined the tours over the years. Most commented that they were exhausted by the demands of Dhyanyogi-ji's work and stunned by his stamina. "I am so old and yet I'm not tired," he teased them. "How come you are tired while you are so young?" Most people assumed Dhyanyogi-ji was in his 70s, judging by his appearance and energy level. He never discussed his age, and few knew that he turned 100 in 1978.

"I remember one time when a group of us went for a long walk with him," Tom Thompson reminisced. "It was very hot out. When we got home, we were all hot and thirsty. Guruji said, 'What do you want to do

"Walk, don't run, to keep up with me!" —*Dhyanyogi-ji to disciples in Santa Cruz, 1978*

now?' Someone jokingly answered, 'Let's take another walk.' Dhyanyogi-ji thought this was a great idea! We all gasped in horror and told him no, we were only kidding! Another time, we were walking in a cornfield and he kept walking faster and faster until the rest of us were running to keep up with him. He disappeared into the corn and we were looking for him until we saw him, up on this hill ahead of us, looking down on us and laughing."

When asked about their memories of Dhyanyogi-ji, many of his disciples marveled at how fast he walked, and how difficult it was to match his pace. "We'd go walking on the beach in Santa Cruz," Laxman said,

Dhyanyogi-ji's birthday, Clayton, California, 1979

"and pretty soon Guruji would be by himself, the rest of us trailing behind. The strangest part was, he didn't leave any footprints! There was no way to understand it. We were in absolute awe. Guruji was magical. Your mind tries to find an explanation. You find that you're questioning reality. But how can you discount something when you're actually seeing it?"

Still, the constant travel was challenging even for him. He continued to follow his usual schedule, waking up for meditation before dawn. He always took a walk at 4 p.m., and Asha Devi and Deepak tried to ensure that he received an oil massage twice a day. But when they were on the road, staying at different places each night, maintaining this routine was very difficult. Sometimes they were unable to find a store that sold the Indian groceries necessary to prepare the food that Dhyanyogi-ji preferred. At first, they occasionally stopped for French fries or tea at a restaurant, but soon it became apparent that Asha Devi was so sensitive to the energy in the food that eating from non-vegetarian kitchens was causing her to fall sick. Dhyanyogi-ji decided that they would only eat food cooked by themselves or people who they knew followed the traditional yogic guidelines for purity. After this, they would frequently stop on the side of the road and use a camping stove to make their afternoon chai or warm food that was prepared for them in the morning, before they left.

An additional complication was that they were always at the mercy of their hosts, and sometimes this was an austerity in itself. Once, Dhyanyogi-ji, Deepak, Asha Devi, and Kusum Sheth were invited to stay at the home of a woman we'll call Mrs. Jones. Mrs. Jones was very fastidious, and the group's level of activity in her kitchen made her very uneasy. She allowed the disciples to cook for Dhyanyogi-ji, but insisted that the rest of them eat elsewhere. Late each night, she demanded that they all leave. Dhyanyogi-ji would ask, "Where can I go with two girls in the middle of the night? Let us stay here tonight, and in the morning we'll leave." Mrs. Jones would grudgingly relent, insisting, "In the morning I want you out!" When the next morning came, however, she would apologize profusely, and beg them to stay on. This went on for two weeks.

"It could be like a hurricane to be around Guruji," Laxman recalled. "Right next to him, it was calm and wonderful, but further out, it was a whirlwind of commotion, controversy, conflict and miscommunication. All I could do was to try and focus on my service."

Of course, most hosts were not so conflicted and were very grateful to have Dhyanyogi-ji bless their homes. Still, having guests with specific requirements, and long and honored traditions, can create strain on both ends. But just as Dhyanyogi-ji's physical vigor never seemed to weaken, his tolerance and unconditional love seemed to melt whatever tensions arose. He put out his energy constantly, regardless of the toll it took on him. Night after night, he gave meditation programs, came home at 10:00 p.m. and tried to go to bed by 11:00, since he woke up each morning at 3:00 a.m. But if someone appeared with a question, even after he was asleep and snoring, he would instantly wake up with the answer. Lee Sannella put it simply. "He just made himself available to everybody, all the time."

"Guruji was a real yogi," said Tom Thompson. "He was awake, present, he practiced what he preached, and his energy was tremendous. Many years later, a woman named Bhavana came to our yoga center to meet and take initiation from Asha Devi, by then known as Anandi Ma. Bhavana told us that she had known that Guruji was here in 1978, and deeply regretted the fact that she hadn't come to meet him when she'd had the chance. But at that time, she said, she had thought that he couldn't possibly be a true guru. 'If he was a *real* guru, what would he be doing in Southbury, Connecticut?' Now she understood that it was precisely because he *was* a true guru that he was in Southbury, Connecticut. When disciples asked, he came."

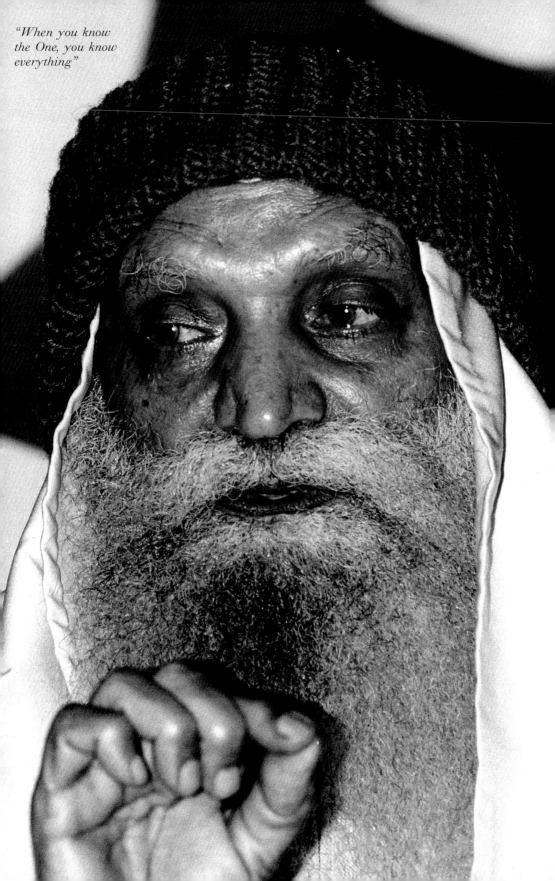

"When you know the One, you know everything"

CHAPTER THIRTY

"WHAT CAN I GIVE AWAY?"

While he was in America, yet another level of Dhyanyogi-ji's work manifested. Again, he broke with tradition when he began to offer a series of retreats in which he taught the esoteric practices he considered to be among the most powerful ones he had mastered, in a format and depth he had never attempted before. Previously, he had focused on teaching meditation and mantra japa. Occasionally he gave out bits and pieces of his knowledge of yoga to specific individuals, but there were advanced techniques he had shared only with Asha Devi, Deepak, and perhaps the Queen of Limbdi or a very few others. With the exception of Asha Devi and Deepak, he had certainly never taught so much to any one person, let alone to a group.

While Indian followers typically accepted whatever he offered, assuming that he'd give them what they needed, Americans constantly asked for more. Now Dhyanyogi-ji was inspired to reveal techniques that were once carefully guarded, and his American disciples were hungry to learn. Their interest fired his excitement. Just as he had burned to give shaktipat when he first emerged into public, now he was so impatient to impart spiritual knowledge that at the first retreat he was heard to say, "What can I give away? What can I teach?"

The impetus for these retreats came in December 1976 when a major earthquake was predicted. One of Dhyanyogi-ji's students from New York called and pleaded with him to come to New York until after the threat of the earthquake had passed.

"Oh my dear, but there are so many people here," Dhyanyogi-ji replied. "and I have come from India to lead them on a spiritual path. I am very happy to be here with these people. If they go into the ocean, I will go with them. I have come here to teach meditation so if necessary, I will go in the ocean and teach them there!"

Dhyanyogi-ji didn't go to New York. "I stayed in L.A. for two months," he later recalled, "and there was no earthquake. But we were all together. Soon after that time, I was in meditation when my guru spoke to me. He told me to teach my disciples some of the techniques that he had taught me so that they can be protected from calamities like earthquakes, floods and wars by these very powerful practices, and so that they can do good work for society and remove unhappiness from the world."

Parmeshwardasji's words took form in what Dhyanyogi-ji called the Vajra Panjar retreats. Vajra Panjar means "The Shield of the Thunderbolt." It is a phrase from a verse in the *Ram Raksha Stotram*, the collection of mantras that Dhyanyogi-ji and his fellow yogis had used to help bring peace during World War II and later, during skirmishes between India and Pakistan. The *Stotram* was the heart of these retreats, in which Dhyanyogi-ji taught what he called "the cream" of what he had learned during his years as a wandering sadhu.

A story was published in a Calcutta newspaper in June 1974 that described someone's experience of the *Stotram*.

A fierce fire accidentally started which covered a great part of Calcutta. At 2:00 a.m., the phone rang. I awoke and answered. I was told that the building in which my husband's office was located was surrounded by fire. My husband was away on a business trip. At such a time of difficulty, I had no one to turn to except Shri Ram. I began to recite the Stotram *continuously.*

The fire continued to spread throughout the next day. The

three stone buildings were literally burnt. Millions of rupees worth of damage was done.

On the third day after the fire was brought under control, my husband, with the help of the fire department, went inside the building. Everyone was shocked to see the office. It was completely saved; everything was in perfect order. I just cried and said, "Oh, Ram, your grace is indeed so infinite." I was overwhelmed, and tears began to flow from my eyes.

I remembered the incident in the Sundarkand *chapter of the* Ramayana, *when the entire city of Lanka was on fire, but Vibhishana's house was saved, because he was a devotee of Ram. Similarly, by the energy of the* Stotram, *my husband's office was not damaged. Indeed, the power behind the* Stotram *and the grace of Ram to this day bring tears in my eyes.*[54]

Demonstrating a headstand at age 100 at VP III, 1978

The retreats were designed to promote personal and planetary protection at the physical and subtle levels, by strengthening and healing the body, and helping disciples to attract and hold increasing amounts of energy for spiritual evolution. "They say that necessity is the mother of invention," Dhyanyogi-ji said. "I never thought of teaching these sacred practices, not even in India. But because of the earthquakes in California, I began to teach, and I told my disciples, 'Don't worry. If a big quake comes, we'll all be together.' That's why I myself never ran away."

Dhyanyogi-ji explained the Vajra Panjar (VP) teachings in a letter to his students at the first retreat in October 1978.

My Dear Brothers and Sisters:

The time has come for worldwide dissemination of knowledge traditionally given by a Guru to only a few select, sincere disciples who would come to his ashram and renounce worldly life.

---

[54]Translated by Dileepji from a Calcutta newspaper dated June 3, 1974.

The scientific progress of human civilization has occurred at a staggering rate during the past few decades. As a result, a large majority of people have come to believe in and worship the physical sciences to such a degree that they have lost sight of the subtle, more powerful forces at work in the whole universal manifestation. There is an imbalance that needs correction.

I am contributing my humble efforts toward creating a balanced lifestyle in human existence. Vajra Panjar, Part 1 is a step toward that end. In this series of retreats, I will impart some very important knowledge regarding ways to attract and channel subtle forces for the betterment of ourselves and society at large.

You are all very lucky. You are lucky to have the desire and opportunity to learn something that most traditional Westerners would reject as useless because it is apparently intangible. In my opinion, it is very valuable.

It is my strong desire that all who attend this retreat will continue with great dedication to master these techniques and after mastering them, use them for yourself, and selflessly for the health, happiness and prosperity of everyone you can reach.

May God bless you all,

Guided by his intuition, with Asha Devi teaching by his side and Deepak and Kusum translating, Dhyanyogi-ji taught hatha yoga postures, pranayama, and tratak—gazing techniques used both to develop concentration, and to strengthen the eye's capacity to absorb and impart energy. He instructed his students in mudras, which are physical poses used for spiritual practice or for healing.

Dhyanyogi-ji discouraged his students from do-

*Yagna at VP III, 1978; **front row from left:** Deepak, Asha Devi, Kusum Sheth, Dhyanyogi-ji; visible behind them are from left, Rudy, Liz Ely and her baby, and Shanta*

346

ing energy healing. "The yogis say that until you should
become strong, obtain energy for yourself, and are very
stable in that, you should not
be concerned with helping
others," he explained. "If
you have a gun that could
be used for your defense and
you don't know how to use
it, you could kill yourself. If
you don't have the strength
to hold the gun and use it,
what value is it for you?"
However, since many of his
disciples were already doing healing work, he taught
techniques to protect them.
He was concerned that they
didn't fully understand that
they were both giving and

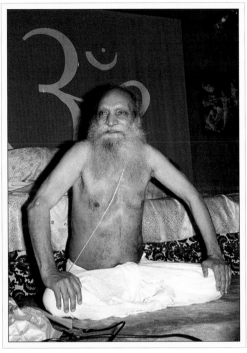

Dhyanyogi-ji preparing to demonstrate advanced pranayama, VP II, 1978

receiving energy. The healing methods he offered included measures
to safeguard the healer. He also gave out mantras that were known to
have tremendous powers of protection.

Dhyanyogi-ji chanting and Asha Devi in bhav samadhi, VP II, 1978

All of these different
teachings built on each other,
so that by the end of the series,
practitioners of Vajra Panjar
had the tools to effect change
on the inner and outer levels. Dhyanyogi-ji said that his
dream was that 100,000 people
would learn the Vajra Panjar
practices and use
them to work for
world peace. At
one of his first re-

Deepak, Dhyanyogi-ji and Asha Devi at VP I, 1977

treats, Dhyanyogi-ji explained his vision. "If a man can heal another man with his will power, then why not 10 men? If 10 men, why not 100 people? It's possible. If healing work benefits a hundred, then why not a thousand? Yogis say it is possible. If we can cure what doctors can't cure, if some of our techniques cure some serious diseases, why not then cure others? If we are able on a mental level to do more, then it is not impossible. To do this, we must increase our will power to help the world. If I can help people strengthen that will power, it will benefit humankind. If one person brings 10, then these bring 10 more, eventually we will have 100,000, in one-pointed meditation together. Then nothing will be impossible in this world."

His students were anxious to find a way for Dhyanyogi-ji to stay in America, so Michael Hannon, a close disciple from Los Angeles who was an attorney, formed a non-profit organization that could sponsor his teachings. Dhyanyoga Centers was founded in 1977.

The other major development in Dhyanyogi-ji's work in America was the creation of two ashrams. Whenever he transmitted his energy or his students gathered to practice, spiritual energy would begin to accumulate, but without a permanent space, there was no opportunity for that energy to build. In 1977, Carl needed to sell the house in Scotts Valley. The woman who bought the house had never studied yoga or meditation, but she reported to Carl that a most peculiar thing was happening—she kept seeing a yogi dressed in white walking around in the basement, in the room where the meditation programs had once been held. Dhyanyogi-ji's energy was continuing to work, but it wasn't benefiting his students. After leav-

Dhyanyogi-ji planting, Soquel ashram, 1978

ing Scotts Valley, Dhyanyogi-ji stayed with Moti in Santa Cruz when he wasn't on the road, until finally, in 1978, a disciple named Robert Pugh offered to lease a piece of property in Soquel to Dhyanyogi-ji to establish his first American ashram. There was a big house, a small residence for Dhyanyogi-ji, and a barn that served as a meditation hall. Fifteen people moved into the house and followed a schedule of daily meditations and on-going spiritual practice.

From 1978 to 1980, Dhyanyogi-ji resided at the ashram when he wasn't traveling, and kept in touch by telephone when he was. A resident named Kanta described one episode that indicates the close ties he had to the ashram. One night, the disciples at the Soquel ashram were talking after their evening group meditation, and the subject turned to how several people were noticing odd things, like apparitions, out of the corners of their eyes.

"I'd seen this lady in a housedress walking back and forth on the porch," Kanta said, "but I had never mentioned it to anyone else. That night, one of the guys asked, 'Has anybody noticed a guy in white up on the hill behind the house?' and someone else said, 'You see him too?' Then someone said she'd seen the lady on the back porch, and now I knew that somebody besides me had seen her, and we all began to get pretty shaken up, thinking, 'Oh man, there are *ghosts* here!'

"Moti didn't like ghost stories and she started to get really scared. Just then, the phone rang, and it was the house line. Now usually if Dhyanyogi-ji called, he'd call on the Dhyanyoga Centers' line, and he wouldn't call himself—Deepak or someone else would call for him. But this time, his voice answered when Moti picked up the phone. He asked, 'So what's going on?' and she said, 'Oh Guruji, it's terrible! There are ghosts! Everyone is seeing them. The ashram is haunted!'

"Guruji told her, 'Don't worry. The ghosts

Working in the garden at Soquel ashram, 1978

are attracted by spiritual energy and they can help you. They can prevent accidents.' He went on to explain about how they could be of great service. 'So just ask for their help,' he said.

"Suddenly everyone relaxed. Now that we'd heard from Guruji, it all seemed very ordinary. Our fear vanished. In a moment, just as we were creating anxiety among ourselves, he had shifted the energy."

Kanta recounted another memory highlighting the heightened communication existing between Dhyanyogi-ji and the ashram residents. She was sweeping the floor in the ashram kitchen when she heard Dhyanyogi-ji's voice in her head saying, "Kanta, could you check the mail?" Kanta thought it was just her imagination, and disciplined herself to keep to her task. Again, she heard Dhyanyogi-ji's voice asking her about the mail, and again, she dismissed it. Finally, she heard Dhyanyogi-ji call her from another room. She went to where he was sitting and this time he said out loud, "Kanta, would you please check the mail?"

Her experience was not uncommon. Shanta Gabriel remembered that one night Laxman woke up thinking that Dhyanyogi-ji needed a flashlight. Thinking that this was just his imagination, he went back to sleep. The next morning he learned that three disciples had all woken up in the middle of the night with this thought, until finally someone paid attention and went and brought Dhyanyogi-ji a flashlight.

"The next night," Shanta continued, "there were 50 people at the ashram for the meditation program. Normally, Asha Devi and Deepak would take care of Guruji, but that night, they were away. I was sitting in the back of the room and I kept getting the message, 'Guruji is cold. Close the door.' I was so far from the door that I'd have to walk across 20 meditating people and go around the hall to get there, and I wondered if the whole thing wasn't just my imagination. But the message was persistent and I remembered the flashlight incident, so finally I did it. I walked over all these people and wandered around and closed the door. At the end of meditation, before arati, Guruji got up and walked back to me and put his hands on my head and blasted me with energy and I was 'gone'—my reward for paying attention.

"These stories demonstrate the level of connection we had with Guruji," Shanta said. "Heart connections. He was inside us."

At the same time, another ashram was being formed in northern California. Laxman, Rajiv and Hansa, who had met Dhyanyogi-ji at Carl's house in Scotts Valley, lived in a tiny rural community called Hurd's Gulch, located 45 minutes west of the small town of Yreka, California, 20 miles south of the Oregon border. They had been making the long trek to Santa Cruz to see Dhyanyogi-ji, but in the summer of 1977, they invited Dhyanyogi-ji to give meditation programs in Hurd's Gulch. "I remember that I was nine months pregnant, it was the summer, we'd been having a drought, and Hurd's Gulch had no water or electricity," said Lisa Cooper, who owned a bakery in Yreka where a flyer for Dhyanyogi-ji's programs had been posted. "Hurd's Gulch was literally in the middle of nowhere, yet to our amazement, 75 or 80 people came to see Guruji." After the programs, Lisa, her husband Larry, and many of the others who took shaktipat at this time made the long drive to Rajiv's and Hansa's home every week for group meditation, and the following year, they all attended the first Vajra Panjar retreat.

A-frame at Swargadham, 1979

During this period, the disciples in the Yreka area decided that they wanted to live together, have an ashram, and create a place where Dhyanyogi-ji could hold retreats. Larry and Lisa Cooper co-owned 200 acres of land in Dutch Creek, California, a half an hour northwest of Yreka, in the Klamath National Forest, so they suggested this as a possible site. The group asked Dhyanyogi-ji to look at the property, and he told them, "it was very good land, but only for spiritual work." In the summer of 1978, the group pooled their resources so they could buy out the Cooper's co-owners, and with the understanding that the ashram would be gifted to Dhyanyoga Centers (which had no money with which to buy property). Dhyanyogi-ji named it *Swargadham*—Place of Heaven.

There was an A-frame house on the property that was expanded to provide some housing, showers, a community kitchen and a meditation hall. The ashram bought a small trailer for Dhyanyogi-ji, Asha Devi and Deepak to stay in when they visited. Some of the disciples lived in tents and trailers, and a few families built themselves simple homes on the land. There were lots of kids, some goats, and a cow named Jamuna. The property was a mile and a half down a dirt road, and drinking and bathing water came from a creek that ran through the land and flowed

355

Residents of Swargadham, 1979; Hansa is on bottom left, Rajiv middle top, Larry Cooper is leaning in on the right

into the nearby Klamath River.

Transforming land with only cold running water, no electricity, and very primitive structures into a retreat center that would accommodate over a hundred people demanded a huge group effort. Larry Cooper and Mike Hannon approached Siskiyou County to get the approvals needed for building a large dome to serve as a meditation hall and a bathhouse, and for digging a septic system to accommodate 150. Ashram residents worked together on the physical construction and interpersonal challenges involved in such an undertaking, and Swargadham became Dhyanyogi-ji's second ashram.

"I have a sweet memory of walking from our little cabin to the A-frame in the early morning, before dawn," said Larry. "I'd see the lights from the kerosene lamps coming from the little structures and tents, as we all were getting up to go to meditation."

By 1980, Dhyanyogi-ji's three-month visit to America had been extended to four years. He had initiated 5,000 people and groups were gathering at his ashrams and at people's homes in the places he had visited.[55] As much as Dhyanyogi-ji was absorbed in his work in America, he was still concerned with India and his disciples there. He didn't discuss his thoughts publicly, but there were several times when his involvement there came to light.

Before he left India, he had become aware that women who lived near his birthplace in Bihar were dying in childbirth because there was no medical facility in that area. He felt he could not let this continue so he began to collect funds to build a hospital to serve this very poor community. Finally, in 1979 Robert Pugh donated the bulk of the money needed.[56]

Dhyanyogi-ji with Robert Pugh, Soquel, 1979

[55]Groups formed in Woodbury, CT, where Tom Thompson and Janaki Pierson had organized programs, in Cleveland, OH, Denver, CO, Jersey City, NJ, Chicago, IL, and northern and southern CA.

While the hospital was under construction, a child from the village was playing at the site, and had scrambled up to the roof. At that moment, Dhyanyogi-ji was in Palm Springs, California on a walk with disciples. Those with him remembered that while they were walking, he suddenly fell to the ground. It was most unusual for Dhyanyogi-ji to stumble, but he offered no explanation other than, "I had to save someone." Several weeks later, a letter arrived from Bihar notifying him that the boy who had been playing at the construction site had lost his footing, plunged down from several stories high, and could have died, but miraculously, had sustained no injuries whatsoever. According to the child's report, as he was falling, he felt as if a giant hand caught him and placed him gently down on the ground.

Sushila Parekh recounted a story of when her husband, Pranav, had a serious heart attack while Dhyanyogi-ji was in America. The doctor attending to Pranav said that he might not survive the next two days, and his relatives were pouring into the hospital to say goodbye. Someone sent a telegram to Dhyanyogi-ji, and meanwhile, they placed a photo of Dhyanyogi-ji by Pranav's hospital bed. Pranav began to do bastrika, the forceful, rapid pranayama, and continued doing it for 45 minutes, to the dismay of some of his visitors. But Sushila told everyone not to worry. "Guruji is here, and he is our doctor."

After Pranav stopped the pranayama, he opened his eyes and bowed to Dhyanyogi-ji's photo. He fell asleep and dreamt that Dhyanyogi-ji came to him and said, "I'm sorry. Your telegram arrived when I was eating lunch, so it took me a minute before I got your message. But now everything will be fine."

The doctor had predicted a two-month stay in the hospital, but within a week, Pranav was home. Pranav was told that it would be six months before he could return to work, but he was riding his scooter back there within a month. "Even though Guruji was in America," Sushila said, "we were saved by him."

At the very same time, a disciple from Chicago described being saved by Dhyanyogi-ji. Rudy had a near fatal motorcycle accident as he was driving through Colorado and "took the high side of a switchback turn, skidded off the road, and fell 300 feet on a Harley without a helmet." As he flew over the side of the road, Rudy was sure this was the end. "But just before I hit the rocks below, I remembered Guruji saying,

---

[56]The hospital functioned from 1975 until 1994, when it closed its doors due to lack of funds. Now, medical services are offered at the Nikora ashram.

'If you're ever in trouble, just call my name three times and I'll help you.' He even had us practice saying, 'Guruji, Guruji, Guruji.' And the words just came to me, just like that.

"They tell me I was unconscious for about 18 hours. What I remember was that Guruji was right there, with his face right in front of me. Periodically he would fade out, although it felt more as if I was being pulled away. Then I would come back, and he would still be there. The last thing I remember—now, this happened years ago, but I can remember it as if it happened yesterday—was that it felt like someone had grabbed me by the hair and yanked me, and Guruji's face was a bright light, like a star, and he was receding in the distance. I was really agitated, because I could actually see the light of his face through my feet, and I was wondering, hey, where am I going? What's going on?

"But all that time during that 18 hours, I definitely—this was not my imagination—was with Guruji. There were disciples that happened to be with Guruji when this happened, and they told me that Guruji just bolted up and said, 'We have to call Rudy. He's in trouble. He's calling me.' He just knew."

After he regained consciousness, Rudy was given a box of his belongings that had been found at the scene of the accident. He always carried a picture of Guruji, but it wasn't in the box. He asked his friends to go and find it.

"From what I understand, it took them about 45 minutes to walk down to where I'd landed. It was slick, rough, slag rock, and when they got there, they couldn't find Guruji's picture. One of my friends, Steve, knew how much it meant to me, so he was not going to give up, except that it was getting dark. It had been drizzling for about half an hour and the rain was starting to pick up. The other guy, Jim, said, 'Hey, we've got to go, man.' But Steve said, 'I've got to find that picture for him.' Finally, they gave up. Steve turned around and started climbing back to the road. Then, right up under a rock outcropping, standing straight up, Guruji's picture was looking right at him."

Disciples asked Dhyanyogi-ji how he knew Rudy needed him, and he answered, "I am like a spider at the center of a web. When the web vibrates, I feel it."

CHAPTER THIRTY-ONE

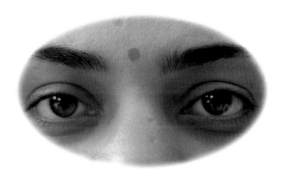

A DOOR CLOSES

At the age of 102, it seemed that Dhyanyogi-ji would never slow down. But in the spring of 1980, something shifted. Dhyanyogi-ji had given a Vajra Panjar retreat in Desert Hot Springs, California, a small spa town near Palm Springs, 450 miles south of Soquel. Following the retreat, Moti recalled, "Guruji woke from his afternoon nap feeling very abstracted, not focused on this plane. The room where he was staying lacked proper ventilation, so we speculated that his confusion might have been caused by the wall heater in his motel room." He had, after all, been in good health just hours before. No one had noticed anything wrong, other than his seeming a bit tired. But days went by, and still, he didn't regain his energy.

For the next month, his health continued to go downhill. Asha Devi and Deepak were not alarmed at first. They had witnessed Dhyanyogi-ji's illnesses in the past. When he'd been performing shaktipat without any breaks, he would eventually need to stop and recharge himself. They understood that this kind of outlay of energy had its cost on his body. But in the past, three to six months of rest and Ayurvedic herbs had always restored his strength. So although they were pained to see Dhyanyogi-ji like this, they believed his state was temporary.

Some of the closer American disciples made similar assumptions. "When you were massaging him," Moti said, "or even just touching him, he was transmitting energy to you all the time. We were receiving direct shots of prana. We were very lucky to find someone who was giving away that energy. Despite the toll it was taking on him, he continued because we benefited."

But most disciples were disturbed by the transformation in Dhyanyogi-ji. They considered him beyond normal human limitations, so it was upsetting to see him this sick—or worse, not to see him at all.

There was another layer of meaning rumbling beneath the surface of his illness. Everybody was feeling it, but nobody wanted to name it except Dhyanyogi-ji himself. He called Deepak and Asha Devi to him and said, "I am getting old now, and I don't think I will be able to continue as I have been. You must now prepare yourselves to continue my work. I want you to start singing the mantrochar during meditations. I am not concerned about anything except that the work for human welfare must continue." Asha Devi and Deepak assured him that they would do as he told them.

He instructed them to give a message to the disciples at the upcoming group shaktipat ceremony. Those present that summer day remembered their shock when Deepak read the announcement from Dhyanyogi-ji saying that he was formally passing the lineage on to Asha Devi. "I am giving her my energy," the statement read. "Everything I have is now hers."

Seva, a devotee close to Dhyanyogi-ji, wrote about her experiences around this time. "On the evening of the last night during the Vajra Panjar III retreat, after attending meditation, I was feeling a little spaced out because the energy had been so intense. It was about midnight before I felt tired enough to sleep, but as soon as I lay down, I began to go into a deep meditation. My body felt like it was on fire. I started doing pranayama and entered a state of bliss where I began to talk to Guruji and mentally picture him. I expressed my desire to be with him, and told him that the separation from him was breaking my heart. Suddenly, the form of Asha Devi appeared, and I started to cry to

Guruji and told him that I loved Asha Devi very much, but I still wanted to be with him. I could see that he was tearing away the attachment I had for his physical presence, and I was fighting it. I kept crying, 'No, Guruji, please don't leave me.' This went on for some time, and then he became very upset with me and said, 'You must understand that you are to serve Asha Devi now.' And Guruji gave me a vision of Asha Devi as Divine Mother."

It was common knowledge that Asha Devi would head the lineage at some point. But none of his devotees—including Deepak and Asha Devi herself—were prepared to face that Dhyanyogi-ji was talking about retiring. For both practical reasons and out of sheer denial, people occupied themselves with finding a physical cure for him.

Dr. Allen Lee, a disciple from Clayton, California, a small town nestled in the hills 90 miles north of Soquel, had a very comfortable home, and he offered it to Dhyanyogi-ji as a place to rest in seclusion. Asha Devi, Deepak and a few close disciples went with Dhyanyogi-ji to Clayton for a month. During their stay, the disciple who hosted the meditation programs in Sacramento, California, a physician named Dr. Ely, came to visit. After seeing Dhyanyogi-ji, he told Asha Devi and Deepak that he thought that he had congestive heart failure. This scared them, and they moved Dhyanyogi-ji to Dr. Ely's home so that they could consult with a colleague of Dr. Ely's who was a cardiologist. A full battery of tests was done and everything appeared normal. After examining Dhyanyogi-ji, the cardiologist pronounced, "Your heart is like that of a 15-year-old. It's strong. Except for some minor things, normal for someone of your age, there is nothing wrong with you."

Though he was resting, taking Ayurvedic herbs, and all the doctors that saw him insisted he was fine, Dhyanyogi-ji's physical condition continued to deteriorate. He stopped eating and drinking. He stopped answering his mail, something he had always done faithfully. While in Sacramento, he spoke to Deepak privately and asked him to write his will. Deepak was reluctant, believing that the illness was temporary. But Dhyanyogi-ji insisted that he wanted to "just express his desires," so to pacify his mind, Deepak agreed. "Dhyanyogi-ji told me not to tell Asha Devi," Deepak recalled. "There were no legal formalities. Dhyanyogi-ji just signed his statement. As it happened, the will became unnecessary; Dhyanyogi-ji later took care of all of his concerns in person."

Increasingly discouraged and worried, Asha Devi and Deepak brought Dhyanyogi-ji back to the ashram in Soquel. Soon after they arrived in Soquel, they were again confronted with the deeper significance of his illness. Once more, Dhyanyogi-ji called Deepak to him to speak about the future. At the time they had discussed his will, he had told Deepak that he wanted Deepak and Asha Devi to marry. Now he explained that although he had been working with Asha Devi to control her energy, there would still be times when she would go into bhav samadhi. When she did, she needed someone to bring her out of that state in the correct manner, or there was a danger that her subtle body could be damaged. She needed someone to live with her who had the skill and sensitivity to awaken her properly because every night she went into meditation while she slept, so she needed to be awakened every morning. Only someone who was very knowledgeable about kundalini and had been specially trained could do this.

"Would you be willing to marry Asha?" Dhyanyogi-ji asked. "She needs someone to take care of her and help her to function in the world. Although she has been with me for a while, she has been in meditation for the greater part of the time and is still not much aware of the external world. You, on the other hand, have been with me for the past 17 years. You have traveled with me and been with me as no one else has, and you are very familiar with my thoughts and feelings. Together you and Asha should continue my work. This is my wish, should you choose to accept."

"Guruji, if this is your wish," Deepak answered, "and it is in the best interests of Asha Devi and your work, and especially if it will not hurt her in any spiritual way, I would be open."

But internally, Deepak reacted strongly. "Dhyanyogi-ji's words were a joy and a shock. I had a great feeling of sadness. Dhyanyogi-ji the lion was talking of stopping his roar, at least physically. But I hoped that maybe all would still change."

When Dhyanyogi-ji told Asha Devi about his desire that she and Deepak marry, she dissolved into tears. Traditionally, marriage demanded that a person put aside the spiritual life to allow family life to take precedence. This was precisely why Dhyanyogi-ji had so fiercely objected to plans for his own marriage long ago. Asha Devi pleaded with Dhyanyogi-ji to give her initiation into sanyas, as she had done years before.

But Dhyanyogi-ji again refused her request, saying, "You have already attained that state." He reminded her that Vasishthaji, the sage who started their lineage, was himself a householder. Both Ramakrishna and more recently Anandamayi Ma were saints who had married and still continued to be wholly absorbed in matters of spirit, and each made immeasurable contributions towards uplifting humankind.

He went on to tell her that in her case, being alone is not practical. "Also, I have always taught that one should be in the world. This is not the age for sanyas. Now it is more appropriate to be a householder, do sadhana and evolve. You and Deepak can set that example."

Dhyanyogi-ji knew that the suffering he had undergone as a sadhu was beyond what most people would or could endure. The heart of his work in giving shaktipat and making esoteric teachings available to the general public was to show people that at this time in history, they can live ordinary lives—work, raise families, shoulder worldly responsibilities—and still attain enlightenment. The reason he had made himself so available to his students in India, and now in America, was so that they could see that their goals were within their reach. If Asha Devi and Deepak married, they would be living proof that people don't have to run away to the forest to reach God. Now, as always, his concern was for the benefit of humanity. He was unsentimental about the changes that were taking place; he just wanted to be sure that the work of the lineage would move forward.

Asha Devi and Deepak had faith in Dhyanyogi-ji, and absolute commitment to doing his work. There was no question that they would do as he requested. But they were both aware that their marriage was another step towards his retirement. It was agonizing for them to imagine losing their day-to-day relationship with him. So they both returned their focus to restoring Dhyanyogi-ji's health.

These conversations between Dhyanyogi-ji, Asha Devi and Deepak were taking place, of course, behind the scenes. The American disciples knew only that Dhyanyogi-ji was very sick and no longer appearing at programs, and they didn't know when he'd be back. No one could understand what was happening, and the sense of uneasiness grew. Some wondered how such a great being could be so ill. Since his arrival, Dhyanyogi-ji's American disciples had been accustomed to turning to him for explanations for strange and troubling occurrences. Now, there was no information forthcoming and Dhyanyogi-ji himself was the source of their distress.

Often, when people can't account for things, they begin to dread the worst. Disciples feared that he had "digested American karma." Rumors of black magic began to circulate. There was talk that someone in India was causing Dhyanyogi-ji's illness. The yogis have experienced that when people use their energy—even with negative motives—and have faith in their energy, it will have some impact. Even Hanumanji was affected by negative energy. In the *Ramayana*, there is a description of a demoness using her energies to trap and kill Hanumanji while He was flying over the ocean to Lanka. Hanumanji felt the energy and was able to recognize and destroy it, but if Hanumanji was affected, then certainly it was likely that a human would be affected.

Another possibility was that Dhyanyogi-ji was taking on negative energies to protect someone else from harm. Those who had studied the lives of saints knew that holy beings sometimes work out negative aspects of other people's lives by taking the suffering onto their own bodies.

The most likely explanation still seemed to be that Dhyanyogi-ji's illness had been caused by the karma he had taken on giving shaktipat, but the uncertainty of if and when he would recover was still hanging over everyone.

In the late summer, Janak and Tulsi, residents of the Yreka ashram, drove the 400 miles to Soquel so that Dhyanyogi-ji could teach them how to do puja. "His energy felt the same," Janak said, "but his personality seemed unfamiliar. Usually he'd ask how things were going, but this time, although he was still friendly, he was more matter-of-fact, a little impersonal in his surface conversation."

According to Moti and Shanta, two of the very few who helped care for him, Dhyanyogi-ji was preoccupied and internal. If they asked questions, his answers were brief. He seemed to prefer keeping quiet, so as they took turns massaging him, they silently repeated the Ram mantra and prayed.

Meanwhile, having discovered that Western doctors were baffled by Dhyanyogi-ji's illness and had no treatments to offer, Asha Devi and Deepak searched for an Ayurvedic physician, since Ayurveda takes spiritual energy into account. They learned, however, that the quality of Ayurvedic care that Dhyanyogi-ji had received in India was not available in America. It was now months after the initial episode. Dhyanyogi-ji was still not eating and he seemed weaker than ever. They felt they had no other choice than to take him back to India.

Their situation was even more distressing when Dhyanyogi-ji expressed his extreme reluctance to leave. Although he had announced that he was passing on the lineage, his commitment to his work in America was strong. Despite his physical pain and his awareness that the help he needed was in India, he wanted to remain in the United States. The night before he left, he told Moti that he didn't want to go, and he said the same to Shanta the next day, at the airport in San Francisco as she pushed him in a wheelchair toward the departure gate. This created even more conflict and distress for Asha Devi, Deepak and the others close to Dhyanyogi-ji. Yet there seemed nothing else to do but to take him home.

Dhyanyogi-ji left California with visible regret in October 1980, vowing he would return. On the trip to India, he had a stopover in New York, at Kennedy Airport, where local disciples came for his darshan. Daksha Doctor went to the airport, bringing blankets so that he could rest during his layover. Along with others, she massaged him. "I felt so bad that he was suffering so much," Daksha recalled. "As I massaged his right palm, I prayed to Lord Ram to please give me all his pain. All of the sudden, just as I made my prayer, Dhyanyogi-ji pulled his hand away and gave me his left hand instead. He broke my sankalpa. He wouldn't let me take it on. It seemed I had made a terrible mistake."

Dhyanyogi-ji's disciples were shaken by the sudden onset and relentlessness of his decline. The change in him from one day to the next and the threat of a more permanent loss upset everybody. In hindsight, it may be that the cause of all the upheaval was that this was the moment that he was actually passing the lineage along to Asha Devi. This may have been the deeper source of everyone's confusion and anguish as they helplessly witnessed the course of events during Dhyanyogi-ji's last few months in America.

Deepak wrote, "It seemed that with the onset of the illness, Dhyanyogi-ji felt that even if he got better this time, it was evident that at some point in the future, Asha Devi and all his disciples had to learn to be without him.

"Mothers take care of their infants, but once children begin to walk, they move on their own, under the watchful eyes of their mothers, of course. The guru cannot be used as a walking stick forever. The disciple has to learn to walk alone, with the understanding of the teachings and the subtle help of the guru and the lineage.

"It was time to put away the walking stick and learn to walk without the physical but only the subtle support."

नेकामश्याम सुंदरं - भवाम्बुधे च मंदरं

फुल्लकंज लोचनं - मदादि दोष मोचनं

लम्ब बाहु विक्रमं - प्रमे प्रमेय वैभवं

नवंग चाप साधकं - धरं त्रिलोक नायकं

रघावंश मंडनं - महेश चाप खंडनं

मीनुं संत रंजनं - सुरारि वृंद भंजनं

मनोज्ञैरि वंदितं - अजादि देव सेवि

बोध विग्रहं - समस्त दूषणा पहं

इंदिरा पतिं - सुरवा करं सतां गं

भवानि क सानुजं - शची पतिं प्रिया नु

द्रि मूलं ये नरा: - भजंति हीन मंत्र

नो भवाणिके - वितर्क बीचि संयु

विवेक वासिन: सदा - भजंति मुक्तये

इंद्रिया दिकं - प्रयांति ते गतिं

CHAPTER THIRTY-TWO

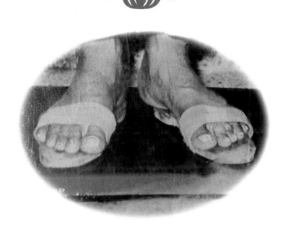

RETURN TO INDIA

When Asha Devi and Deepak landed in Mumbai, their sole concern was Dhyanyogi-ji's recovery. They assumed the Indian disciples would join them in their efforts, and were surprised when many greeted them with suspicion—and some, with anger. For most of the Indian students, these strong feelings arose out of the love they felt for their guru. Dhyanyogi-ji had told them that he would be in America for only three months, yet they had not seen him for four years. They were starving for his darshan. Others felt that Dhyanyogi-ji was too pure a being to remain for long in foreign countries that lacked the spiritual atmosphere, energy and lifestyle he was used to at home. Concerned that their beloved teacher might leave again at any moment, they directed their worry and anger over his condition at Asha Devi, Deepak and American disciples. They believed that in America, Dhyanyogi-ji had given shaktipat without taking adequate precautions, without insisting on sufficient preparation on the part of new disciples.

Despite his abhorrence of noise and crowds, Laxman had flown to India to help care for Dhyanyogi-ji. For almost three months, he shared a room of wall-to-wall mattresses with eight other men, waiting to be called to be with Dhyanyogi-ji. The atmosphere at the flat where Dhyanyogi-ji was staying was so tense, however, that bringing an American into the picture would only create more antagonism. Laxman returned home without even having the chance to see his guru and say goodbye.

Dhyanyogi-ji had an Ayurvedic physician who had great knowledge of the impact of the kundalini energy on the body, so the first order of business was to bring Dhyanyogi-ji to see him. The prescribed treatment included following a special diet and taking herbal medicines. Recovery would take time and require daily home care. Right away, there was a tug of war over who would take charge and provide this. At first, Asha Devi and Deepak both stayed with Dhyanyogi-ji and tended to him, but Asha Devi's parents had missed her terribly and they urged her to come home. As difficult as it was for her to leave Dhyanyogi-ji's side while he was so ill, she went to be with her family in Ghatkopar.

During Dhyanyogi-ji's first year back in India, Deepak brought him from one place to another. For the first month, Dhyanyogi-ji stayed at Shivkumar Daga's home. He spent the next month with the Pandyas, and then moved to the Pathak's. After three months, in January 1981, Dhyanyogi-ji expressed a wish to go back to Bandhwad. He had not yet seen the villagers since his return, and, given the time and expense necessary for travel to Mumbai, it was impossible for them to come to him. The trip to Bandhwad included a flight to Ahmedabad and a four-hour drive from there, but after only two days in the remote village, it was clear that the primitive conditions of the ashram were taking a toll on Dhyanyogi-ji's health. He accepted a request from the Queen of Limbdi to let her tend to him at her palace. The accommodations there weren't luxurious, but they were more comfortable than the ashram, and the palace security would protect him from too many visitors so he could get rest. After an exhausting day traveling to Limbdi, he and Deepak remained there for a month. Next, they traveled several hours farther west to the home of a disciple in Rajkot for a short visit before making the long journey back to Mumbai.

Six months after Dhyanyogi-ji returned to India, when Laxman had moved back to the Yreka area, Kusum Sheth called him and gave him a message from Asha Devi and Deepak: Dhyanyogi-ji wanted to return to America. Could he come back to Mumbai and help? "I went," Laxman recalled. "My suitcase didn't show up, so all I had was warm clothing. I stayed in a floozy hotel over the bus station, and waited for three days to receive word that it was time to get Guruji. But at the last minute, it was decided that he was too sick to go, so I left for America that night."

During this period, Dhyanyogi-ji was very ill. He was barely eating, surviving on several tablespoons of mung broth a day. His body was weak, he was unable to walk, and he hardly spoke. As always, there was a time scheduled each afternoon for darshan, but there were no conversations, no lingering, informal gatherings. Disciples came, bowed to him, and left right away.

Why, when it seems obvious that staying in one place would have been better for his convalescence, did Dhyanyogi-ji shuffle from one house and city to another? Perhaps he simply didn't want to turn down his devotees when they begged him to come and stay with them, just as he insisted on giving shaktipat to anyone who asked, and scolded disciples who spent their precious rupees on bus fare to come see him. Compassion and sacrifice for his students was a way of life for Dhyanyogi-ji, yet it appears there was something more going on. In 1982, Daksha Doctor visited Dhyanyogi-ji and asked him about his condition, but he said they could not discuss it. The significance of his health crisis and the events surrounding him at this time were something that he alone understood.

Although it seemed he was incapacitated, absorbed in an inner state and disconnected from external events, he was, in fact, acutely aware of what was going on around him—the impact of his illness, the animosity disciples were directing towards Asha Devi and Deepak, and the rivalries that had developed while he was away. Furthermore, he took firm actions to deal with these issues. In the rare moments in which he spoke, he communicated to those close to him that he wanted his work to go on, both in India and in the United States, despite the state of his health. He reconfirmed that Asha Devi was his spiritual heir, that she and Deepak would be continuing his mission, and that in their absence, only Swamiji was endorsed to do his work in India.

Above all, Dhyanyogi-ji worried about Asha Devi's well-being. For nearly 10 years, he had personally sheltered her, and now he could no longer do so. He spoke with some of his closer disciples in Mumbai about his desire that she and Deepak marry. He explained that she needed someone with her who could safely and knowledgeably awaken her from deep states of meditation, as well as someone who could help her to continue his work in America. These elders recommended that he give his blessings for the marriage right away. So on June 26, 1981, Dhyanyogi-ji quietly performed a simple ceremony for the couple at the Pathak's home. In the presence of only his long-time disciples Dr. and Mrs. Kedarnath Pathak and Mr. Dahyabhai Pandya, he had Asha Devi and Deepak place a flower garland around the other's neck, and gave them his blessings, with the understanding that they would have a formal, public wedding once they were back in the United States.

Several weeks later, Dhyanyogi-ji returned to Bandhwad and stayed there for three months. Deepak hadn't accompanied him this time, and when Deepak wanted to visit, the attendants at the ashram wouldn't allow him to come because they were afraid that he would take Dhyanyogi-ji back to America, even against his will. This was an inherently absurd concern. No ordinary person could control a yogi like Dhyanyogi-ji, and if he wanted to either stay in India or return to America, nothing and no one could stop him. According to the teachings of Dhyanyogi-ji himself, all that had happened was by divine will, to which he was completely surrendered. Years earlier, someone had asked Dhyanyogi-ji, "What can you *not* do?" and Dhyanyogi-ji had answered, "I cannot do anything wrong." This was not a statement of pride. It was an affirmation that he was an instrument of God's energy.

Dhyanyogi-ji refused to stay at the ashram after Deepak was turned away. His departure from Bandhwad was more significant than anyone realized at the time. After having lived there for over 50 years, he visited the ashram only once more, eight years later.

When Dhyanyogi-ji left Bandhwad in October 1981, he went to Ahmedabad, and Deepak came to see him there. At that point, Asha Devi's and Deepak's visas required that they return to the United States, or their resident status would be jeopardized. Dhyanyogi-ji told Deepak not to worry about him, but to go back to America to continue his work. Earlier, Asha Devi protested that she couldn't bear a separation from him, but Dhyanyogi-ji said, "You are my limb, a part of myself. We can never be separated." With a heavy heart, Deepak left India, consoled only by the knowledge that Dhyanyogi-ji planned to return to the

United States as soon as he was healthy enough to travel. Asha Devi flew back to America a few weeks later.

Once Asha Devi and Deepak had gone, Dhyanyogi-ji went back to Mumbai and stayed at the Pathak's flat for six months. By that time, he had gained a little strength. He was eating and could walk. Given his improvement, in March 1982 he began the 48-hour journey to Bihar for the inauguration of the hospital, and he planned to visit disciples along the way. But when he reached Ahmedabad, his travels came to a halt. His disciples there did not take him on to the hospital in Bihar, nor did they take him

Godhra, 1982

back to Mumbai, for fear he would fly off to America. A member of the family that was hosting him in Ahmedabad died, so for the traditional mourning period of two weeks, Dhyanyogi-ji went to stay at the home of Pravin and Manjula Gajjar. This is where he would spend the remaining years of his life.

The Gajjar's flat was located in Navrangpura, a pleasant residential section of the city, with tree-lined streets filled with birdsong. Dhyanyogi-ji was given a sunny room, with simple furnishings. Pigeons flew in and out of his window, and a pair made their nest on top of the armoire against the wall. He said that the birds and even the insects that shared the space with him were saints doing mantras, just like the creatures in the cave at Bandhwad. Although he rarely left this little room, the flow of the breeze, the quiet peaceful atmosphere, all made it seem like he was still living in nature.

For any person who walks a spiritual path and works with a teacher, there comes a time of extreme chaos, confusion and negativity. Even in the lives of great teachers, there may be at times one or more personalities that cause not just problems, but even pain and suffering, and damage to the spiritual work that helps humankind. Yet in almost all cases, the guru in the middle of all this chaos remains surprisingly quiet and often even removed and detached from it, like the center of a storm. This phase is known as the guru's *leela*, a Sanskrit term that means "divine play."

When Lord Vishnu incarnated as Ram and lived as a man—who fell in love, was betrayed and robbed of his kingdom, fought battles, endured heartbreaks, and suffered losses as if they were real—that was leela. Most of us are lost in the events of our lives, taking them at face value. But God-realized beings are aware of the play of the universe and the reasons for it, even if they don't break out of their roles. There may be subtle, karmic reasons the guru foresees for maintaining detachment, but these are beyond the grasp of the intellect and appear to serve no practical, tangible function. Yet this leela can go on for long, long periods.

When Dhyanyogi-ji fell ill, it looked to some like he was having his leela. Until his illness, he had been a free spirit, his physical mobility unconstrained by anyone else. Now it seemed as if he were allowing others to dictate his movements in a completely uncharacteristic way. Even when he originally agreed to move to Bandhwad—the first time he seemed to acquiesce to the wills of others—it was with the understanding that he was free to leave. Now, it was as if a handful of Ahmedabad devotees were able to keep him confined to the flat in Navrangpura and to monitor other people's access to him, ostensibly because they were protecting him so that he could rest and recover. Public darshan was limited to a few minutes each afternoon, and some devotees recalled receiving their darshan from the hall outside his room, which they were not permitted to enter. For them, the pain of Dhyanyogi-ji's sickness was multiplied by the heartbreak of not being able to spend time with him.

The guru's leela often serves as a testing ground for disciples, many of whom grow frustrated and leave the path during this period. But the guru may simply be challenging them: Do they really want to reach God, or are there still remnant desires, hopes, dreams to be fulfilled before all is left behind and the only desire is God and God alone?

Haresh Chudasama from Pune remembers that once he was in Ahmedabad and wanted to visit Dhyanyogi-ji, but was turned away. After his return home to Pune, a manager from his shop named Venkat came to see him. Venkat told Haresh that he had just had an unusual dream in which he saw an old man with a beard wearing a white dhoti, who said, "Ask Haresh Chandra why he came to my city and didn't visit me?" Venkat had no idea who the old man was. Haresh showed him Dhyanyogi-ji's picture and Venkat exclaimed, "That's him!"

The Gajjars provided a home for Dhyanyogi-ji at considerable sacrifice, caring for him with great devotion. But Dhyanyogi-ji was not encouraged to walk or take exercise, so increasingly, he became bedridden. On the surface, he surrendered to these circumstances. Deepak later commented that he knew that Dhyanyogi-ji was capable of getting up and walking out of the apartment any time he wanted, but for some reason, he didn't.

Once, after a visit to the Hansol ashram, Dhyanyogi-ji was waiting in the car while two of his disciples argued about who would carry him upstairs to the flat. After a few minutes of this, Dhyanyogi-ji got up and walked up the stairs unassisted. But this was rare. For the most part, he maintained a physical appearance of near helplessness.

Dhyanyogi-ji's apparent illness also proved to be a period of tests, trials and tribulations for Asha Devi and Deepak. Except for God and Guru—and a very, very few disciples and members of their families— the world seemed to turn against them for no rhyme or reason. There were all sorts of stories, rumors and accusations against them that took off like a forest fire that could not be controlled. It tested their personal growth and deep bonds with the guru, but also made them consider their own openness and willingness to face the challenges and continue their commitment to hold onto and spread Dhyanyogi-ji's work. In the midst of it all, Dhyanyogi-ji remained cool and quiet, not uttering a word and never saying anything about who or what was right or wrong. He exhibited that absolute state of being just a witness.

One tradition of Tibetan monks is to create beautiful mandalas out of colored sand. For a certain period of time, these sand paintings are on display, and then they are destroyed. The lesson is that noth- ing with form is permanent. It is only the subtlety of the formless that lasts. Dhyanyogi-ji had always taught students to look inward, remind- ing them that their outward attachments were ultimately distractions, impediments to self-realization. His own life had exemplified the neces- sity to give up all attachments. Now, through his actions, it seemed he might be teaching about the subtlety of the guru.

During his years in Ahmedabad, with his physical activity so re- stricted, most of his attention was directed towards activities on the sub- tle level. He spent much of his day sitting up in his bed drawing yantras or writing out mystical calculations. He filled notebooks with writing that no one else was able to decipher or interpret. Other times, he lay in bed silently chanting the *Sundarkand*, the chapter of the *Ramayana* where Hanumanji joins Lord Ram to defeat Lord Ravana.[57]

Occasionally, he showed some interest in external affairs. He expressed concern about Asha Devi and Deepak and their finances now that they were in America without him. He worried about what they were eating and if they had enough help. Every few months, Asha Devi telephoned him. She would shout into the phone, crying with joy at hearing his voice and at the pain of missing him, and he'd always say, "Don't cry." But overseas calls were expensive and the connections to Ahmedabad were scratchy, so their conversations were brief.

When disciples came to him with their problems, he was eager to help. He gave people the yantras he had drawn. Some received *Chamundayai*, a form of the Divine Mother, while others took home nine-planet yantras that addressed astrological difficulties. Jennifer and Craig, a couple who went to see Dhyanyogi-ji in 1988 for his blessing to conceive a child, said that he seemed quite happy that they'd asked and grew very animated when he taught them a mantra. But never again did he outrun his disciples, or rock in his seat with laughter as he teased them. His mood continued to be serious and introverted, and when he did intervene in the lives of his devotees, it was usually on the subtle plane.

In 1986, the headman from Bandhwad was wrongly accused of a murder. Evidence had been planted to make it appear that he was guilty. Dhyanyogi-ji said he would help, and when the case went to court, new evidence was discovered that proved that the headman hadn't been present at the time of the crime.

Not long after this incident, Magan, the headmaster of Samskardham, Dhyanyogi-ji's school in Bandhwad, and his family were on vacation when his son took sick. Magan brought the boy to a doctor, but it was too late, and he died. Magan's wife could not accept that her son was gone. Silently, she had been appealing to Dhyanyogi-ji. "We've been doing your seva," she prayed. "You can't let him die." Magan brought him to another physician in the hopes that he could revive him, and this doctor agreed to work on him. Finally, however, it looked as if there was no hope. But just when the doctor told them he had given up, the boy sat up, to the astonishment of everyone present.

The very next day, the family went to Ahmedabad to thank Dhyanyogi-ji. After they left to return to Bandhwad, Mrs. Gajjar

---

[57]Dhyanyogi-ji's writing shown at the beginning of this chapter is a verse from a prayer to Lord Ram in the *Ramayana*. It translates: "I bow to you. You are affectionate to your devotees. You attract them with your compassion. I worship your lotus feet, the heaven of the desireless."

approached him. She had noticed the day before that he seemed to be in an unusual state at the time when Magan's son had died. She had asked him what was wrong, and he had answered her vaguely, "Nothing, but it's going to be hard," and seemed to go into a deep sleep. Now, she asked if at that moment, he had left his body to go and save the boy. He said yes, and it had been very difficult.

In March 1989, Dhyanyogi-ji finally returned to Bandhwad, after eight long years. The occasion was the dedication ceremony for the new Radha-Krishna temple, which he had ordered built many years earlier, after the old temple collapsed and left the temple murtis without a home. The dedication ceremony was to be a huge, day-long celebration, for the disciples had also built temples for Ganesh, Lord Shiva and Ambaji. The ashram expected to feed 6,000 to 7,000 people, but 10,000 appeared for the feast. Just as the servers had run out of food at the dedication of the Hanuman temple spire in 1966, the pots at the Radha-Krishna celebration were soon empty. At Dhyanyogi-ji's instruction, Asha Devi covered the serving platters and repeated some mantras, and once again there was enough for everyone.

As important as Bandhwad had been to him, this was the last time Dhyanyogi-ji went there. With this one exception, once he moved to Ahmedabad he never traveled farther than Hansol ashram, only half an hour away from the flat. On holy days, he was carried down to a car in a chair and driven to Hansol. Other than that, he remained sequestered in the flat in Navrangpura.

Remaining quiet and secluded enabled Dhyanyogi-ji to move his students beyond their attachment to the physical form of the guru. "His accessibility was very special," Deepak said, "but it may have kept people from relating enough to the subtlety. Usually saints at his level are more physically removed. Ranchodasji, for example, told his disciples to leave him, and he would disappear in caves, keeping silent for years. In a sense, this is what Dhyanyogi-ji was doing now."

During this time, Dhyanyogi-ji sent Moti a tape with a message: "Moti, continue doing your sadhana."

"It seemed to me that his illness forced us, his disciples, to focus on what was most essential," reflected Moti. "The walks, the talks, the wonderful darshans with chai—as well as the trials and rumors surrounding his last months in America—were all clearly becoming

Bandhwad, room housing Radha Krishna before 1979

Bandhwad temple, 1989

Bandhwad Radha Krishna murtis 1989

Bandhwad Shiva lingam, 1989

Bandhwad Ambaji, 1989

Bandhwad Hanuman temple, 1989

Asha Devi's bedroom, Bandhwad 1989

secondary to the real goal, the final goal. If there was any underlying lesson, it seemed to be that the spiritual path is not for the intellect, which cannot comprehend all things, or control all things, but for the heart, which is perhaps able to be enlightened to the degree that the intellect surrenders to God and Guru."

"Guruji had been in the ultimate father role," said Laxman, "even to the point of being ridiculous. We'd ask him what kind of toothpaste to use. Now he'd changed. There was no way to process what was happening, so I took my spirituality internally. What I internalized most strongly was Hanumanji. That was what Guruji portrayed: the ultimate servant. He was a manifestation of that noble state, but now it was no longer physical."

Two years later, the storm that was Dhyanyogi's leela had passed. Asha Devi and Deepak felt that their period of trials was over. They were back on track, resuming his work with a new future and newer challenges. By God's and Guru's grace, they were able to hold on and be used as tools by the Divine. The storm had indeed done a lot of damage, but at least the sun was bright and warm, and the infinite sky as blue as Vishnu.

CHAPTER THIRTY-THREE

"I AM ALWAYS WITH YOU"

June, 1981

Dear Brothers and Sisters,

I was happy to receive letters from you. My health continues to improve slowly. I am still quite weak. I am aware that you are all very anxious about my return to the United States.

Because of present circumstances, it will not be possible for me to return there in the near future. When I am completely well, I need to take care of a lot of things here. My Indian disciples have waited four years, so they also deserve to spend some time with me. But I assure you that I will come back as soon as it is possible. In the meantime, I advise you to continue your sadhana with patience, and when the time is right, I will be physically present there. When Lord Ram left Ayodhya, the people had to wait 14 years for his return. But I am sure you won't have to wait that long.

When the Lord wishes, and when we are destined, we shall meet again. The present time is difficult, and I have to go through some suffering. It may take a while longer, but it will end. I am very happy that the ashrams and disciples are progressing in spite of my physical absence. There is one important lesson you all need to learn. Learn to have faith in the words, "I am always with you."

Asha Devi sends her blessings to all of you. May God bless you.

—Dhyanyogi[58]

Dhyanyogi-ji was keenly aware that his American disciples were feeling lost. It was for this reason that he was anxious that Asha Devi and Deepak return to the United States. When they arrived back in California to pick up the threads of his work in the autumn of 1981, they found disciples still shaken by the sudden and mystifying onset of Dhyanyogi-ji's illness and departure. Although he may have been teaching his students to be strong in their faith and to relate to him on the subtle plane, most were unable to weather the dramatic change in their relationships with him. Caught in their confusion about how someone who was so vital, so interested in them personally, could transform into someone so sick and distant, many had drifted away. The once closely-knit groups of students had scattered, group practices had fallen off, and the ashrams were foundering.

The staff at the ashrams encouraged disciples to focus on their spiritual practices. They wrote a message in the *Dhyanyoga Centers Newsletter* to that effect.

Before Guruji left for India, he told us that this was a difficult time for gurus and disciples. He urged us not to waste time, but to concentrate our attention on spiritual work. In his physical absence, it is good to remember his frequent remark that he is always with us. But it is also our faith and will power that will carry us forward, through all difficulties. Many disciples will remember his statement that apparently difficult times are only Maya, and are like clouds covering the sun. But the sun continues to shine, and the clouds pass over. "I am taking you to the

---

[58]*Dhyanyoga Centers Newsletter,* June 1981

sun," he promised. With hearts full of love, let us continue our
sadhana and joyfully await fulfillment of these glorious words.[59]

But it appeared to be a losing battle. At Swargadham, the ashram in
Yreka, disciples were struggling not only with the loss of Dhyanyogi-ji's
physical presence, but also with the difficulties of rural life. During its
first year, the population of the ashram had grown to about 25 and there
was a mounting sense of excitement. Accommodations were simple, but
basic needs had been met. Several residents worked in Larry and Lisa
Cooper's bakery/café in town. But when Dhyanyogi-ji fell ill, the harmony
in the ashram was disrupted. The challenges of the remote setting began
to eclipse the initial enthusiasm. It was hard to find work, social life was
limited, and now they had lost contact with him. Conflicts arose between
ashram members over their interpretations of Dhyanyogi-ji's instructions.
Some wrote to Dhyanyogi-ji in the summer of 1980 asking for direction,
but he had been too sick to respond. Despite the uplifting moments of
leading a spiritual life, residents felt discouraged and hurt, and some
began to move away. By the time Asha Devi and Deepak returned, the
construction of the ashram had come to a halt. The cabins had been "red-
tagged" because they weren't up to code, the building permits had expired,
and new restrictions had been imposed by the Department of Forestry to
protect the deer that wintered there. Although some disciples remained on
the land and several were still working at the bakery, most had left.

Unlike Swargadham, the Soquel ashram was located in an area
bursting with New Age activities and opportunities, and after Dhyanyogi-
ji returned to India, it continued to operate for two years. New people
moved there, even some who had never met him in person. But over
time, devotees there were also increasingly disheartened by his absence.
Some lost faith and stopped doing spiritual practices, and the group
energy dissipated. For many, when Asha Devi and Deepak came back
without Dhyanyogi-ji, it was the final blow.

Asha Devi had worked side by side with Dhyanyogi-ji, and the summer before he left, he had made it clear that she would be taking over
his work. Now that she was back, she had organized group meditations
and local retreats. But disciples still assumed that things would *really*
start up again when Dhyanyogi-ji returned. To some extent, even Asha
Devi and Deepak were waiting. After all, when he sent them back to

[59]*Dhyanyoga Centers Newsletter,* 1981

America, Dhyanyogi-ji had said, "You go and I will come." Yet they also felt the imperative to keep his work alive.

"These were very hard times for us," Deepak recalled. "Since the time she was 14, Asha Devi had never been without her Guruji. To be separated from him was extremely painful. Although the mighty eagle had been taught by the mightier eagle to fly, to soar high by herself, the shadow of the teacher had always been there. But alas, now the wings that needed to carry the burden were heavy, very heavy. Yet the work had to be done. The name and fame, the glory and the greatness of the Guru, and, most of all, his work—to bring each and every soul to its resting place—had to be continued. She had promised to do his work, and the will and determination were present in her."

"I missed the physical reality of Guruji, of course, " said Asha Devi, "but true to his words, 'I am always with you,' he was always there. I always felt his presence. That subtle plane was becoming a more tangible reality."

"Since the age of 13," Deepak went on, "I was also beneath the Guru's wings. I never felt I could be on my own. There is a story that tells of a man who, at the time of death, has a vision of his life as if he was looking back at his footprints across time. Most of the way, there were two sets of footprints, and he understood that one set was his own, and the other were the prints left by God. But, to his surprise, at the most difficult times of his life, he saw only one set of footprints. Hurt, he asked God why He abandoned him at his most needy moments. God replied that the one set of footprints he was seeing were the prints of God; He had carried the man through those painful times. Like the man in this story, I felt and feel that it is the Guru who is always carrying me in good and bad times. But how could I run to the physical being of the Guru whenever I needed him now that he was 10,000 miles across the ocean? Yet the work needed to continue at any cost of pain and sacrifice. In the midst of all hardships, opposition and difficulties, the seeds that Guruji had laid—now little sprouts—had to be brought to bear fruit, the fruit of meeting God. New seeds had to be laid. As the numbers increased, Mother Earth would become more peaceful, more restful, for Her weary travelers."

One as yet uncompleted piece of Dhyanyogi-ji's instructions to Asha Devi and Deepak was their marriage ceremony. Dhyanyogi-ji wrote them a note, intended for publication in the newsletter:

Dear Asha and Deepak,

It is my heartfelt wish that you two marry. In it my blessings are with you. I pray to God that you two will be happy in your life together, and that He always showers His grace upon you. The purpose of this wedding is so that you two can carry on my work together. Again, I bless you both and pray to Shri Ram and Shri Hanumanji to shower their grace upon both of you, and give you both strength and help in my work for the welfare of humanity.

Dhyanyogi-ji[60]

In the spring of 1982, Asha Devi and Deepak announced that they would be married in Berkeley, California on January 22, 1983, Dhyanyogi-ji's next birthday according to the Indian lunar calendar. After the wedding, Asha Devi and Deepak sent a letter to the disciples.[61]

Dear Brothers and Sisters,

We hope and pray that you are well and doing your sadhana regularly. On the occasion of Guruji's birthday, he sends his blessings to all of you: "May you all be happy. May you all reach your ultimate goal in life and have steady devotion and love for the Lord."

On January 22, we celebrated Guruji's birthday in Berkeley. There, group shaktipat was also performed, and we all felt Guruji's presence strongly. Also, due to various circumstances in the recent past, Guruji has expressed his wish that we should be married, as we have to live together to continue his work here. So, on the evening of the 22nd, we had a simple marriage ceremony. This relationship has been established only as it is

[60] *Dhyanyoga Centers Newsletter*, February 1983
[61] *Dhyanyoga Centers Newsletter*, February 1983

Guruji's wish, and only with the goal of doing Guruji's work and serving humankind to the best of our capabilities. With God's and Guru's grace, and the love and cooperation from all of you, we have no doubt that we will be able to keep the flame of Guruji's work glowing forever.

We thank disciples for their good wishes and gifts, and for their presence at the birthday celebration and wedding.

With love and blessings,
Asha Devi and Deepak

There was to be a reception for the families in Mumbai, so Deepak left for India right away and Asha Devi joined him two months later. Immediately after the reception, they went to see Dhyanyogi-ji in Ahmedabad, and were alarmed to find that he was still very ill and again had stopped eating. They wanted to stay and care for him, but nothing had changed as far as Dhyanyogi-ji was concerned. As always, his only concern was for the continuation of his work.

Since his return, his Indian disciples had been asking him for the Vajra Panjar teachings that he had given out in America. He had told them that when Asha Devi came back to India, she would offer the retreat, so Asha Devi and Deepak gave the first Indian Vajra Panjar retreat in the spring of 1983 in Mumbai. Then, Dhyanyogi-ji sent them back to America with a letter to his students there.

Pranayama at Vajra Panjar retreat, Mumbai

Dear Disciples,

My heartiest blessings to all of you. It has been a very long time since I have communicated with any of you, but all of you have been in my heart especially because Asha Devi and Deepak have been with you.

Asha Devi and Deepak have come to India and removed a lot of worries I had about them. I feel responsible for them and I want to see their welfare and happiness in every way. I have learnt from them that they enjoy your love and support, and this gives me great joy and satisfaction.

My health is still not at its best. But all will be well when the time is right. Don't lose faith but continue your sadhana with love, patience and devotion. I understand you are all longing for my physical presence, but I cannot promise when I shall be able to return. As long as Asha Devi and Deepak are there for all practical purposes I am there also. Remember "I am always with you."

I have granted special powers to both Asha Devi and Deepak and they will continue my work as they are guided. [62]

Asha Devi and Deepak returned to California in the summer of 1983, no longer holding the hope that Dhyanyogi-ji would be joining them soon. Added to this loss, they were faced with the fact that the Soquel ashram was no longer financially viable. When Robert Pugh had originally offered the property, he had given Dhyanyogi-ji the option to buy, but Dhyanyogi-ji felt it made more sense to rent it and see how things worked out. Now the lease on the property had expired, Asha Devi and Deepak had no funds with which they could purchase it, and with so few people actively involved with the ashram, it made no sense to try to keep it. Asha Devi and Deepak were prepared for something like this to happen, but letting go of the Soquel ashram also meant that they would lose their home. Things looked grim. "At that timely moment," said Deepak, "God, who continuously helped Dhyanyogi-ji, manifested His grace again, and Dr. Alan and Nancy Lee offered us their house in Clayton, California. Dhyanyogi-ji had once referred to their home saying, 'This is my temple,'

---

[62]*Dhyanyoga Centers Newsletter,* August 1983

so we gratefully accepted their hospitality."

In November 1983, Asha Devi and Deepak, along with two other couples who were close disciples—Moti and Govindaram Newman, and Mike and Lalita Heckathorn—moved to the Lee's house. For a few months, they led a simple and disciplined life, waking daily at 4:00 a.m. to meditate, and, like Dhyanyogi-ji, following a fixed schedule for meals and walks. Time was dedicated for personal anusthans, and they invited other disciples to come join them. They held meditation programs and celebrated special holy days. Although she wasn't traveling much, Asha Devi stayed in touch with devotees in other parts of the country and worked to maintain their sense of being part of Dhyanyogi-ji's family of disciples. In February 1984, she asked disciples all over the world to simultaneously meditate for five minutes "to further improve Guruji's health and strengthen the spiritual bonds among disciples with the guru."

Early in 1984, Asha Devi began receiving requests from disciples on the east coast to come to their areas and offer public programs and shaktipat. Tom Thompson and Janaki Pierson invited her to Connecticut, Pravin and Daksha Doctor to New Jersey, Jyotindra Desai to Colorado, and Dr. Bindra to Cleveland, Ohio. The quiet period in Clayton was over after only a few months. They began to travel as they had with Dhyanyogi-ji, giving programs five or six days each week. In each place they went, old groups became reinvigorated and expanded and new ones formed. In response to disciples' requests, Asha Devi began to offer the Vajra Panjar series of retreats on both coasts, so many more people joined in with these more advanced practices. During their personal meditations, Asha Devi and Deepak received instructions from Dhyanyogi-ji guiding them about what and how to teach. They began to offer a new retreat that they called the "Applied Vajra Panjar" to realize Dhyanyogi-ji's vision of advanced students practicing the Vajra Panjar techniques in a group to work for world peace.

"It was difficult to start the work in America again," recalled Deepak, "but at the subtle level, all problems were resolved by Guruji's energy and grace."

Dhyanyogi-ji was 10,000 miles away, yet it was not unusual for people in America to report experiences of him. Some described receiving shaktipat from him in dreams or during meditation. Each year, 20 to 30 people came to meet Asha Devi saying that they'd had a vision of

Dhyanyogi-ji, and that this was what had led them to her. For example, a woman from Connecticut described having a "clear inner vision of a man standing on my right side, guiding me." She went to the yoga center in Woodbury run by Tom Thompson and Janaki Pierson, saw a picture of Dhyanyogi-ji, recognized him as the man she'd been seeing, and ultimately received shaktipat from Asha Devi.

Whenever Asha Devi gave shaktipat initiation to a group of people, one or two would report having seen Dhyanyogi-ji come and touch their heads with a rose. Once, after receiving the initiation, a 6-year-old child in Boston, Massachusetts whispered to her mother, "Did you see Guruji?" She told her mother that Dhyanyogi-ji had come, stood in front of her, and blessed her.

Daya, a devotee from Maine, said that Dhyanyogi-ji appeared to her during her shaktipat initiation and that he kept saying things that struck her as very funny. She worried that it might be disrespectful to laugh out loud, given the significance of the ceremony. "But he said, 'The best place to laugh is in church!' and that made me laugh even harder," recalled Daya. "Each time I laughed, my body tingled and emptied out everything. The harder I laughed, the more clean I felt. Guruji was making movements like zipping everything open and kicking up water at the shore of an ocean. I felt like a happy child or like how animals sometimes seem happy. My body was perfectly straight, my feet were together, and I had no other body movements except for the shaking of my laughter. Later, Asha Devi gave me the spiritual name Daya, which means one who is always compassionate. I didn't really think it fit me, but Guruji told me, 'Perhaps there are things about yourself that you do not know,' and then I felt happy with the name. For me, Guruji is always there, is so easy to be around, so full of joy and life. I wish I could visit him in India, but I feel I do get to see him. In a sense, that is like visiting him too."

John, a student from Boston, wrote about an experience he had at his first Vajra Panjar retreat. "Guruji taught me a lesson about his undying love for his disciples. I had a vision in which he and I were standing on a tower used for observing the stars. It felt as though I was reliving a scene from a past life in which he was both my astrology teacher and my spiritual teacher. I felt that he and I had spent many a night on that tower studying and marveling at the stars. This one night, I asked if I would need to reincarnate into the physical world again before I would be free. Guruji replied that yes, I would have to take birth again. I started to cry, and I asked him, 'But what if I don't remember you? What if I don't find you again?' He hugged me and replied, 'Don't worry. I will remember you and I will find you.'"

"During the first few weeks after the shaktipat ceremony," a new disciple from Connecticut reported, "I saw and felt Guruji and Asha Devi meditating with me. Guruji nodded to me, or used hand signals to approve or to have me change what I was doing. Twice he came and placed his hands on my head. I had a clear image of being in a room with them and others. When I described the room to two disciples who have been to India, they recognized the room as the one in which they had meditated with Guruji when they visited him."

Another wrote, "I didn't know exactly what to expect when I went to take shaktipat. I had been feeling a build-up of energy in the area of my heart. When Asha Devi touched me with a rose, I felt all the pressure dissolve. I saw Asha Devi enter within me, then Guruji, then the whole line of masters. The next thing I knew, I was in India. It was very vivid, not like a dream. I could see the sights and smells of a city. Then I was in a jungle and a Bengal tiger was nearby and I felt unprotected. Once again, the whole lineage of masters appeared and as I began to feel completely protected, the tiger sat down. I realized I was totally protected by the love flowing from the line of masters in this path."

Although many experienced Dhyanyogi-ji's presence, a marked shift was taking place. For people who took shaktipat from this point on, Asha Devi was the Guru. Those who had known her when she was first with Dhyanyogi-ji, who were used to thinking of her as a young girl standing silently beside him, began to experience her in a very different way. Asha Devi was stepping into the position for which Dhyanyogi-ji had prepared her.

"When I think of those times," said Bhailal Suthar, "the most incredible thing was the transformation I saw in Asha Devi. When she and Guruji first came to stay with us in New Jersey, Ma[63] was very young. She watched TV to learn English and was curious about my daughter's dolls. Guruji told us to bow down to her because she was a divine being but we laughed. 'How could she be divine? She is like a child!' We didn't understand. Then I saw her a couple of years later

---

[63]Ma was a name by which Asha Devi was called, because in India, women are seen as manifestations of the Divine Mother, and this was especially true of a woman saint.

after she came back from India, without Guruji and she was completely changed. She was serious and divine, just like Guruji had been. I realized how wrong I had been."

"When I first met Asha Devi," Tom Thompson recalled, "Guruji was still training her to stay in the body and control her energy, and he was teaching Deepak to take care of her when she went into deep meditative states. In those days, it seemed like she'd rather go on some mountaintop with Guruji rather than deal with all the disciples, but he trained her and she became the Guru. At first she and Deepak were just there as disciples, but Guruji began making more demands on them to function on another level. Ma was going to be the Guru and he wanted her to do it well. She was very shy then and would rather just be in samadhi and not deal with all the nonsense of the material world. But the transition happened over a period of time. Especially after Guruji left America.

"I remember a very profound experience I had with her when I really began to understand who she was. I came home from work late and everyone else was in bed. She was waiting to call India, to call Guruji. She was sitting on the floor and I sat down with her. It was a very informal situation. I asked her, 'Do you experience God all the time?' and she laughed and said yes and looked at me, and I had a direct experience of God for just a few seconds. Everything opened up in that moment."

Deepak later speculated that although Dhyanyogi-ji said he was coming back to America, he had probably made the decision not to do so. Perhaps withdrawing into his internal state and sending Asha Devi back without him was his way of dimming his glow so that hers could be seen more clearly, so she could assume her position as head of the lineage. Without Dhyanyogi-ji's physical presence, disciples deepened their connections to Asha Devi. "Guruji's personality was gone," Janak said. "Now, she was the one who had the relationships with disciples. Guruji was like Johnny Appleseed, tossing off the seeds, opening the way, but Asha Devi was here to make sure the seeds grow, to pull out the weeds and keep the gardens growing."

While Asha Devi's activities increased, Dhyanyogi-ji's life became more and more secluded. Contact between them was limited to their occasional phone calls. Then the intuition came to Asha Devi to bring a group of disciples to India on a pilgrimage to see Dhyanyogi-ji and visit

other powerful spiritual spots. In the fall of 1985, after visiting the places that had been especially meaningful to Dhyanyogi-ji—Mount Abu, Ambaji, and, of course, Bandhwad—and performing the anusthan of collecting water from the Himalayas and carrying it to Rameshwaram, the group of 50 students piled into the small sitting room of the Gajjar's flat in Ahmedabad to receive Dhyanyogi-ji's darshan. After five years, American disciples were finally able to see him. When the tour was over, Asha Devi and Deepak stayed on in India to visit with Dhyanyogi-ji and he told them where they should take the group "next time." With this remark, pilgrimages to India became a regular feature in Dhyanyoga Centers' events.

Upon their return to America in the winter of 1986, Deepak and Asha Devi, who was now known as Asha Ma, Mother of Hope,[64] were greeted with news that they'd lost their home, just as they had the previous time they'd come back from India two years before. The Lees were selling their house in Clayton and Asha Ma and the others living with her would have to move right away. Resources were scant and once again, Asha Ma and Deepak found themselves without a roof over their heads. A solution presented itself immediately, however. Frank and Jill Thomas had moved from Nevada to San Francisco, and they invited Asha Ma and Deepak to live with them. "They were God in disguise," Deepak said. "They not only opened their home and hearts for us, they brought groceries, went around town putting up posters announcing meditation programs, and helped with Guruji's work in ways that far exceeded our expectations. They were our saviors in many ways, and Guruji's work was able to reestablish strong, firm and deep roots through their love and support. It is from here that we were able to build a foundation to further reach the seeking souls. Although we had agreed that we would stay with them for two years, we ended up living with them for four."

When Dhyanyogi-ji heard about their move, however, he was concerned about Asha Ma and Deepak not having a permanent place to stay. For years, since the time when Dhyanyogi-ji was in America, they had

---

[64]The change grew from the discomfort some Westerners felt with the word "Devi," which means Goddess.

Jill Thomas doing puja to Asha Ma

been looking for a property that could serve as both a meditation center and a residence. Now Dhyanyogi-ji advised them to separate the two, because zoning laws made it so difficult to do public activities in a residence. He said that first they should find a place to live, and then purchase a meditation center.

It wasn't until 1989 that Asha Ma bought her own house, and years after that before Dhyanyoga Centers purchased property for a center, but Dhyanyogi-ji's instructions signified the first step toward reestablishing physical roots for his work in America, this time under Asha Ma's guidance.

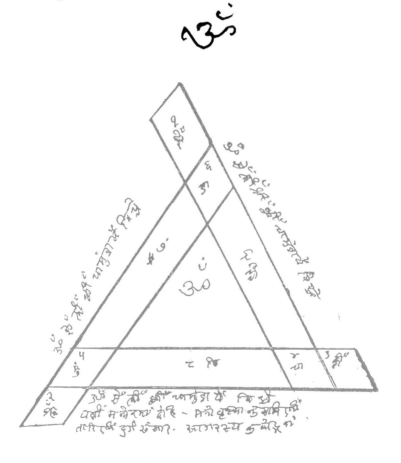

Yantra of the Divine Mother drawn by Dhyanyogi-ji

CHAPTER THIRTY-FOUR

PILGRIMAGES TO DHYANYOGI-JI

When Asha Ma and Deepak brought groups to India, the American disciples who were with Dhyanyogi-ji for the first time since he had returned to India saw a very different man than they remembered. Since his illness, he seemed more serious and spoke little. Indian disciples were accustomed to being with Dhyanyogi-ji in silence. This was not so different from how he had been before, and they'd had time to adjust to the physical changes caused by his years of illness. But Americans had known him to be—or had heard stories about his being—outgoing, curious and playful. Now it appeared that he had withdrawn his interest in the external world, and his frail physical façade led them to believe that his spiritual power had weakened. Furthermore, there were reports from other visitors that when they went to him for spiritual guidance; he turned them away, directing them to Asha Ma. "I have given all of my energy to her," he would tell them.

In fact, Dhyanyogi-ji had lost neither his interest in world affairs nor his energy. He followed the news closely, especially regarding politics. He was concerned, more than ever, with working for world peace. As for his spiritual work, he continued to be available for brief darshan in the afternoons, and he gave shaktipat initiation to crowds of 75 to 100 people at the Hansol ashram on his birthday and Guru Purnima. In January 1992, a devotee named Doug received the initiation from the now 114-year-old Dhyanyogi-ji. "One by one, 75 of us were brought in front of him," Doug remembered. "It took over two hours for him to initiate everybody. I never expected him to have such stamina. And when he pushed his thumb into my third eye, there was not a hint of frailty. He had as much physical strength in his hand as I had ever felt, let alone the force of his energy. It felt like he would push his thumb right through my head."

Dhyanyogi-ji performing shaktipat at Hansol ashram, 1992

"When I first saw him," remarked Stan, a devotee from Chicago who'd known Dhyanyogi-ji in America, "I have to admit that I thought I should pray *for* him instead of *to* him. He looked very old and weak. When I had last seen him, he was 101 years old and doing headstands and walking so fast I couldn't keep up with him. Now he looked completely changed. Then, one day, Asha Ma told me to sit right in front of him. I did, and I got one of those very powerful glances from him that I remembered all too well. When those X-ray like eyes penetrated my very soul, I knew Guruji was still Guruji."

"I remember the first time I ever met Guruji," said another devotee. "It was on the 1988 trip to India. I bowed and touched his feet and as soon as I stood up, I felt as if I had been thrown across the room. I landed against the wall. Tears welled up in my eyes and I felt a deep sense of desolation. I felt as if I were being released from my bondage to all my old pain, as if he had just awakened me from a horrible dream. I could remember the dream, but I knew it wasn't real. This happened within seconds of touching his feet. That was the impact of his energy."

Dhyanyogi-ji's spiritual power was so strong that his image as an invalid seemed absurd. Yet he kept it up. This behavior discouraged any attachment to his outer personality. When Janak saw Dhyanyogi-ji in

1991, after not having seen him for 11 years, "I felt like an idiot," he confessed. "I walked into the room and said 'hi' as I would have done when I used to visit him in California, and then I realized that it was a whole different thing happening now. He was in another realm. He was channeling the energy, but his personality was gone. He was like a living Shiva Lingam. Now it was like going to see the Oracle—you ask your question and get your answer—no small talk, just the answer."

On one particular evening in 1991, several American disciples were visiting Dhyanyogi-ji in his Ahmedabad room. No one was there to translate for them. One woman asked a question that had been deeply troubling her. "Why do such terrible things as child abuse and rape happen in the world?" Dhyanyogi-ji made a brief verbal response. "Don't worry," he said, "it's all part of it." Then he began tapping his fingers on the side of his bed frame. He tapped several rhythms for about a half an hour. According to Doug McLeod, who was present and able to keep his eyes open while the rest of the disciples were in deep meditation, Dhyanyogi-ji would occasionally turn and make mudras or some sort of greeting to a picture of Lord Ram next to his bed. Then he resumed tapping.

"It was as if time itself had stopped," Ellen recalled. "I felt like Guruji had molecularly restructured my body, altered me on a cellular level. He gave me a brief experience of awareness beyond duality, and I felt as if he had imparted the knowledge of creation directly into my blood stream, so that I understood it physically, not intellectually. At one point, I noticed an ant on the floor and felt the absolute bliss of this ant

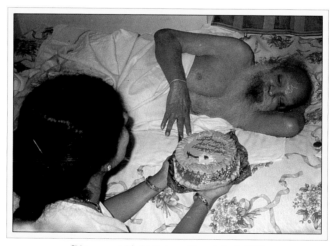

Dhyanyogi-ji's birthday, Ahmedabad, 1992

that lived on the floor of this divine being's room. When Guruji stopped tapping, our darshan was over, and the five of us went outside. I asked the others, 'Did that really happen?' Each of us had had an equally profound meditation. Dorothy said that a longstanding question had been resolved, Joanne that her desire to experience unconditional love had been fulfilled. We were all disoriented and overcome with gratitude. Bewildered as we were, none of us doubted that Guruji had just worked on us, blessed us, changed us deeply in some inexplicable way. Many years later I learned that he had been tapping the *Sundarkand*, the chapter in the *Ramayana* that tells how Hanumanji saved Sita by leaping across the ocean to Lanka."

For the 1991 group tour, Dhyanyogi-ji had told Asha Ma to make the pilgrimage so dear to him that he had attempted several times but completed only once—to collect Ganges water from the glacier at Gaumukh, the actual source of the Ganges, and carry it down to the Shiva temple in Rameshwaram. His American disciples hoped to do the anusthan for their own evolution, but also in his name. The climb from Gangotri, the tiny village closest to Gaumukh, to the glacier itself was treacherous, and the altitude caused problems for many. A disciple named Jan Handel wrote about the challenges she faced on this hike.

"I walked the many miles up to Gaumukh, the very source of the holy Ganges, and most of the way back at a surprisingly brisk and steady pace, with my trusty Himalayan mountain stick steadying me every step of the way. My stamina was far greater than I ever would have expected, given the harsh realities of a mountain trek and my notoriously lazy life. But everything was different here. This was India! From the moment I stepped off the airplane, I was charged with energy. Not only was it the incredible excitement I felt knowing that Asha Ma would soon be leading us to Guruji, but I seemed to be vibrating with the energy of India itself. I hadn't slept hardly at all during the days leading up to the trek, yet I seemed none the worse for it.

"But on a particular hill, on this winding mountain path somewhere between Gaumukh and Gangotri, the energy vanished and I suffered a sudden, overwhelming fatigue. As I struggled to reach the top of the hill, I was forced, by sheer exhaustion, to stop half the way up. Completely out of breath, my layers of clothes drenched with perspiration, it was all I could do to prop myself up against a rock ledge. I couldn't imagine how I would get myself down to the camp but the possibility of not being able to finish this journey on my own two feet was too upsetting even to contemplate. In my desperation, I prayed to Guruji and suggested that if I were truly supposed to complete this spiritual mission, a little divine intervention would be necessary, in my humble opinion! A few minutes later, I leaned forward on my walking stick and then took a couple of tentative steps. As the tip of the stick moved behind me, I felt a subtle but unmistakable force move me forward. I took another step and again, I felt the same push from behind. Whoa! It was like having a strong wind blowing at my back, but without the air! I continued walking until I was over that hill and the next and the one after that. A few more times along the way, I was again forced by fatigue to stop but each time I asked Guruji for help and each time, my magic walking stick came alive with energy and moved me forward, until I finally arrived in Gangotri, my destination. Though I quickly recovered from my mountain trek, it took a bit longer to process the experience with the walking stick!

"Some days later, as I sat at Guruji's feet with Asha Ma and Deepak and the rest of our group, I explained to Guruji what had happened on that mountain. I told him that I had felt like he was right there with me whenever I needed him, and then I asked, 'Guruji, I was wondering if you are always that close?'

"When I started to ask the question, I was in my head (the land of all questions!) but by the time I got to the end, I had fallen into my heart and I suddenly burst into tears. I did not hear Guruji's voice over my noisy sobs but I was able to regain control in time to hear Deepak translate his response. 'Guruji had been paying extra close attention to our group,' Deepak explained, 'because of the dangers on the mountain, but he is *always* with us, helping us.' As Deepak translated, his voice cracked and he, too, suddenly began to cry. At that point, I lost it again and in between my own wrenching sobs, I could hear people crying all around me.

"That was a truly indescribable moment—one, in which, I believe, there was a collective experience of clarity. It was a moment when those of us so blessed to be sitting in that little room in Ahmedabad fell into our hearts and suddenly glimpsed the true nature of our guru—our supremely loving, omnipresent, guide and protector. Our tears were the spontaneous expression of our deepest love and gratitude.

Hansol, 1991, Asha Ma and Deepak visiting Swamiji

"I hold the memories of these magical times along the path and, in my low periods, I reach for them. Then my memories, like my walking stick, propel me up the hill."

The trips to India created an opportunity for American and Indian disciples to finally meet each other face-to-face. This helped to reduce the remnants of suspicion and jealousy that had troubled many devotees from both places. A sense of connection grew between the disciples from East and West that culminated in 1992, when they worked together at an eye camp in Bandhwad that Dhyanyogi-ji had asked Asha Ma to arrange.

Eye camps are free temporary clinics where people without access to medical care can receive cataract surgery at no cost. In India, many people living in isolated, rural places go blind from cataracts because of their utter lack of resources. The eye camp, held at Dhyanyogi-ji's school, was a collaborative effort. Funds had been collected in America to cover the costs. The children who lived at Samskardham went back to their villages to find out who needed the surgery. Physicians from nearby Radhanpur volunteered to go and evaluate the patients. Villagers and other disciples set up the eye camp on the grounds of the school, and for five days, they cooked and served three meals a day for the nearly 300 patients and the family members who were tending to them while they

Eye Camp, Bandhwad, 1993

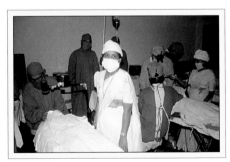

Eye surgery at the eye camp

Medical Camp, Nikora, 2000

received the surgery and aftercare. Twenty-five American disciples came to Bandhwad to join the Indian disciples doing seva.

At the same time that Dhyanyogi-ji's work was expanding in these ways, he himself seemed to continue to fade from the world of forms. In 1991, he had fallen out of his bed in Ahmedabad. As he explained it, one of the cows at the Bandhwad ashram had come to him at the subtle level and kicked him to let him know that she and the other cows were being neglected. Dhyanyogi-ji contacted the ashram to resolve the problem and sustained no lasting injuries. But soon after the 1991 group tour, too weak to keep his balance, Dhyanyogi-ji had fallen again while attempting to stand up, and this time, he didn't recover. Unable to sit up, his mobility had been even further reduced. He stopped his infrequent visits to the Hansol ashram. He stopped performing shaktipat. He encouraged Asha Ma to establish a new ashram near Mumbai. He said they should go and look at land, take photographs of the properties, and then he'd tell them what to purchase once he'd seen the photographs. Lest there be any more challenges to Asha Ma's and Deepak's right to work on his behalf, Dhyanyogi-ji wrote an official letter:

This is to inform each and every disciple, and all others concerned, that on the day of 26 January 1992, I, the undersigned, granted complete permission with full confidence, to my disciples, Ashama Deepak Pathak and Deepak Kedarnath Pathak, to carry on all my works in India, U.S.A., or in any other country. This is done without any kind of pressure from anyone, and I grant this permission of my own free will.

I would also like to inform all concerned that I also appoint Ashama Deepak Pathak and Deepak Kedarnath Pathak as my spiritual heirs and foremost authorities after me. I would like to add that I have given to Ashama Deepak Pathak all my collective spiritual energies.

For these reasons, on my behalf, henceforth they have my blessings and command to perform all activities of meditation, shaktipat initiation, meditation retreats or any other related activities both spiritual and material.

Besides Ashama Deepak Pathak and Deepak Kedarnath Pathak, I have not given such authority to anyone. Therefore if, besides the two above-mentioned disciples, if anyone else performs shaktipat initiation, then it will be considered unauthorized and whatever negative results come about will be the responsibility of the person concerned.

If any person was granted any such authority earlier, it is revoked with this letter, with one exception. In the physical absence of Ashama Deepak Pathak and Deepak Kedarnath Pathak in India, Swami Shri Vijay Krishna Bhartiji can conduct shaktipat initiation, meditations, and retreats. Of this, all disciples should take note.

Signed this 26 day of January, 1992 in Ahmedabad, India
Dhyanyogi Madhusudandas

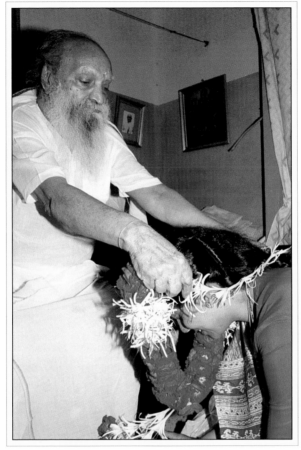

Dhyanyogi-ji blessing Asha Ma

In December 1992, while Asha Ma and Deepak were visiting Dhyanyogi-ji in Ahmedabad with a group of students before the eye camp, Dhyanyogi-ji made a formal statement in which he reiterated that he had passed all of the energy of the lineage to Asha Ma. Following his announcement, he gave Asha Ma and Deepak the spiritual names of Anandi Ma[65]—one who puts others in bliss and remains in bliss—and Dileepji—winner of hearts. His act of giving them spiritual names signified breaking their ties from their previous life. He had now placed them in full charge of his work.

ॐ

---

[65]Dhyanyogi-ji also stated that Anandi Ma was a manifestation of the Divine Mother in the form of Ambaji.

CHAPTER THIRTY-FIVE

MAHASAMADHI

Although Dhyanyogi-ji was still interested in how his work was progressing, he had retired. He lay on his bed, under a soft, woolen shawl, rarely moving at all. His skin glowed, his body appeared to have an unexpected firmness, given his age and immobility, and his gaze was still penetrating. But most of all, it was the power of sitting in his presence that stunned his visitors. People who met him during this time described him as being less a person than sheer energy. "Guruji was more than a man," said one devotee. "He was a force. A realized yogic master has aligned himself with nature, understood what the Buddhists call 'emptiness,' evolved to point where he can control his own prana, and determine the moment of his own death. When you know such a man, you feel you are in contact with the source of everything."

In December 1992, when the group of disciples who came to work on the eye camp visited with Dhyanyogi-ji, many felt suffused with an overwhelming love. "Think of how you feel when you're so in love that you feel it towards everyone—not just your beloved—and increase that love by a thousand fold," Ellen said. "Someone asked Guruji why we were feeling this and he answered, 'This is what it's like at the source.' When I gazed at him, I felt as if I was looking into the opening of a deep chasm, inside of which the fire that generated the sparks of life was burning. This is how I experienced his oneness with God. He *was* that source."

"The love in the air was tangible," said Radhika, another devotee who was in that group. "The feeling of love was so thick, you could push through it, whip it up. I remember that before I met Guruji, I was afraid that I wouldn't like him or believe in him. But when our eyes met, I fell into his eyes like you'd fall into outer space, just spiraling inside him in total bliss. Poetic words sprang into my mind—words like lotus-eyed and precious one—and I was never one for poetry. Everyone in the room was lost and I couldn't see Guruji. I was inside of him. Then I came down for a landing into my body. Never before or since have I felt like that. I came away feeling like I'd finally met God. He was God."

Yet Dhyanyogi-ji's transformation from dynamic, agile, vigorous yogi into this more unearthly presence had happened in stages, and since he'd always seemed to be a mythical figure, it was business as usual for his disciples. In 1994, Anandi Ma and Dileepji planned the next trip to India. This time, at Dhyanyogi-ji's suggestion, they would begin the tour in the Himalayas, visiting the Valley of Flowers—an area at an altitude of 12,000 feet, which, after the rainy season, was covered with pink orchids. They would also hike to nearby Hemkund, a place sacred to the Sikhs, where at an altitude of 15,000 feet stood the only Laxman temple in India. Following these rigorous treks, the group would go to Calcutta to visit the Kali temple and Ramakrishna's ashram, and then travel to Ahmedabad to see Dhyanyogi-ji.

Between the steep climbs, high altitudes, and the cold and rainy weather, the weeks in the mountains were challenging, and the close group living intensified tour members' reactions to the conditions. Everyone was at the edge of what they could physically and mentally tolerate. By the time the group arrived in Calcutta on the verge of collapse, they were grateful just to have beds and warm temperatures. As it turned out, however, the emotionally charged period had only just begun. Early the next morning, Anandi Ma received a phone call from Ahmedabad with the news that Dhyanyogi-ji had been having chest pains. Frightened by his condition, the Gajjars had brought him to the hospital, where he was admitted for observation overnight. Alone in his room, he sat up on his bed, went into meditation, and took mahasamadhi.

"News of Guruji's mahasamadhi instantly put everything into perspective for me," said a devotee named Sally. "The physical hardships of the mountains and monsoonal India at once seemed totally inconsequential and profoundly meaningful. We had all been pushed to our physical and emotional limits—cleaned out, burned up—to be ready for this ultimate experience."

Dileepji later wrote, "Just a couple of days before the disciples were to have their golden moment to be with Guruji, we were shattered by a phone call giving us the shocking news that Guruji had freed himself from the physical cage. The call came at 3:00 a.m. on August 29, Lord Krishna's Birthday. It was Lord Krishna who had appeared to Guruji's mother in a dream to tell her about the coming of this great child, and it was He who called him away. The sun that shone so brightly bringing light, nay life itself to thousands, had finally set. Humanity had lost yet another of its priceless gems. Such a being would perhaps never be born again. At that moment, our lives seemed empty."

Many wondered why Dhyanyogi-ji chose that night to take mahasamadhi. Anandi Ma and the group of disciples were only three days away. Perhaps he chose that day because it was Lord Krishna's birthday, but some speculated that if Anandi Ma had been by his side, their deep bond might have made it more difficult for him to leave, keeping him tied to his body.

Anandi Ma and Dileepji were in a state of grief bordering on shock. Accompanied by Bipin and Kirti Pancholi, they left Calcutta immediately, and the rest of the group followed that evening. Anandi Ma later wrote an account of what the first 24 hours were like. "When Dileepji's brother called to give us the heart-wrenching news of Guruji leaving us all, the initial interaction was that my prana was pulled out of my body, my heart was torn by some unknown hands, my senses began to withdraw. I had lost everything. The world was empty. There was nothing but a state of void. At the same time the mind, however, began to remind me of Guruji's desire and my promise to continue his work. This pulled me back together, yet I was hurt. How could I still be living?

Why was I not blessed like Lord Ram's father who passed on once he lost his son?[67] How could I continue to exist when my Guru was gone? Guruji's voice rang like loud bells within me. I had to think of the disciples first and not myself. Many were for the very first time just waiting for the moment to quench the thirst of their eyes with his darshan. They needed to be cradled and comforted. I thus collected myself and began to prepare mentally to give that support and love which Guruji had given and taught me to give to one and all."

While local Ahmedabad disciples collected what was required for the cremation ceremony, Anandi Ma prepared Dhyanyogi-ji's body so that disciples could have the chance to see him and touch his feet. They dressed him, propped him up on huge blocks of ice, and put his hands back into the mudras they had formed at the moment of his mahasamadhi.

Dhyanyogi-ji's body kept at Hansol ashram after his mahasamadhi

"Once I arrived in Ahmedabad and entered the hall in which Guruji was seated, I had a very strange, paradoxical feeling," Anandi Ma recalled. "The outer news which the senses perceived was 'Guruji is gone,' but my inner feeling was that he was very much there. I laughed at myself. I will never lose my guru. He has held my hand tight and firm. That grip will never be lost. He had once said, 'Even Brahma cannot separate us.'"

Word of his mahasamadhi spread among devotees in India and America. Those who could get there came to Hansol. Those who couldn't gathered in their local groups to chant. In India, it is customary to chant through the night on Lord Krishna's birthday, so many devotees were already chanting together when they learned of Dhyanyogi-ji's mahasamadhi. Those on the group tour sang through the night in the Mumbai airport, while waiting for their morning flight to Ahmedabad.

"It was a small miracle that they were all able to get a flight so quickly," remembered Anandi Ma. "With their arrival, the hall was filled with an emotional charge of love and sadness, of faith and despair. It felt like the very walls of the hall would melt. The love of the

---

[67]This refers to the grief of King Dasharath in the *Ramayana*.

disciples for their Guru would melt the hardest stone on earth today. Beyond all this was Guruji—overriding all that intense emotion, his love and grace poured, poured like the wildest torrential rainstorm ever. Drenching every pore of his dear ones. It felt like he was saying, 'Arise, awake, go forward. I am with you always, as I have said over and over again. I have gone nowhere. I am everywhere. See me. Look at me with your inner eye. I am in your heart, your mind, your very being. You and I are one.'"

"I walked into the hall with the expectation of smelling death, hearing death, tasting death, feeling and seeing death," recalled Suzanne, a devotee who had come to India to meet Dhyanyogi-ji for the first time. "I braced myself against the conflict I thought I would feel because I was still living and Guruji was not. But this conflict was challenged the minute I stepped into the hall. Guruji had not gone anywhere. He was still with us. He was sitting up, not in a casket, and his energy, his spirit and his being filled the hall with a still aliveness that contained every impulse in creation. He was the hub of the wheel of life, and all the activity around him was on his behalf, for his glory and animated by him.

"We had been expecting to see Guruji for the last month, building up to it with great momentum. Now that he had left the body, it felt like having to stop a freight train. How could we believe that there was no more Guruji? We had to go to another level of understanding. We had to veer the train to another track, the track of going beyond what was presented to us with our five senses and rather go to where Guruji was still living—in the more subtle realms of our being, deep within our hearts."

The American and Indian disciples sang together as each took turns going up to bow to Dhyanyogi-ji's body for the very last time.

"After each devotee received their final darshan," recalled Anandi Ma, "we prepared for the ceremonial bath. Sacred mantras were recited and as the chanting began, I felt a radiance from Guruji's body spread to every person there. As Dileepji sprinkled Ganges water, a beautiful fragrance of rose emerged from Guruji's body.

"In Indian traditions, a woman is not permitted to participate in certain rites, so I was given a chair to sit on as the bathing began. I felt pain within me, so I prayed, 'Oh! Guruji, if my faith and devotion to your feet is true in thought, word and deed, then please give me this opportunity to join in the final rites.' Then I heard Guruji's voice saying, 'Get up. Why are you still sitting?' That gave me the strength and courage I needed. I began to give the ingredients, like sandalwood paste, clothing and Ganges water. I placed the leaves of tulsi and a small piece of gold and silver in his mouth, and I applied sandalwood paste on his forehead. I covered his body with a shawl, offered a flower garland, and sang the arati. Once again, the impossible had been made possible by Guruji's grace."

After this ritual bath, the procession across the Hansol ashram grounds to the cremation site began. Several men carried Dhyanyogi-ji on their shoulders, and a throng of disciples surrounded them throwing white and red powders, flowers and coins. There was deafening noise from bells and drums and voices shouting, "*Sadaguru deva ki Jaya! Dhyani Maharaj Shri Madhusudandasji ki Jaya*!" Glory to the Guru! Victory to Dhyanyogi-ji! By the end of the 100-yard procession, the crowd was covered from head to toe with the red and white powders, their appearance suggestive of flames.

The body was placed on a platform and covered with sandalwood. Several Brahmins circled the pyramid of logs, their backs covered in red kumkum, as Anandi Ma joined them in lighting the sacred fire. After a breath, she stepped down from the platform and, along with the other disciples, performed what is called the *pradakshina*, which literally means walking around the center of the universe. As the smoke and flames rose, the mourners walked around Dhyanyogi-ji's body three times, before sitting down on the ground facing the funeral pyre, and meditating.

Lighting the sacred fire

"As I watched the fire burning," one devotee wrote, "I kept remembering how Anandi Ma had told us that Guruji said, 'My house is on fire. Loot as much as you can!' Here was the ultimate expression of this—he was on fire and his energy whirled around us. It was ours for the taking."

"The cremation was both solemn and joyous," said another. "It was agonizing to say goodbye, yet there was something glorious about the realization that Guruji was finally totally free from the limitations imposed by the physical body. When a river merges with the ocean it becomes larger. It is no longer confined by its banks. Guruji's complete merging with God expanded him." Cheryl, a devotee from New York, wrote, "The embers rose to heaven and there was a tremendous mingling of being, as if Guruji was embracing the universe, and there was not sorrow."

"Before we began to meditate," recalled Anandi Ma, "I looked up in the sky and saw Guruji along with some forms of deities. At the same time, I saw a much larger crowd of disciples present than were actually there. The sky was extremely bright white with golden rays. Guruji appeared in a beautiful body with a profound smile and such a state as was never seen when he was in the body itself. His body shone like gold, his eyes shone such light that even the deities present there were honoring Guruji. Then a chariot came in which Guruji sat and he, along with the deities, began to pour a silver-like fluid on the people below, but all this fell only on my head and not anywhere else. I was immersed in it. I felt a very pleasing and cooling effect; at the same time I felt as if I had eaten something extremely sweet. I was immersed in a state of bliss that was unique. I felt Guruji had now spread his body through me and through his disciples. He now lived in every heart. Every moment he continued to guide me."

Vedic tradition dictates each step to be taken when a saint passes on. After the cremation, there were rituals to complete. Dhyanyogi-ji had told Anandi Ma that after he left his body, his remains should be placed in the holy Narmada River. The 800 mile-long river is lined with ashrams. It is said that pilgrims who walk from one side of the mouth of the river at the Arabian Sea, along the river and back to the other side of the mouth will attain enlightenment. Since they cannot carry money with

The site on which Dhyanyogi-ji was cremated

them, the ashrams along the banks of the Narmada take in these pilgrims and provide them with meals and a bed. Dileepji said that Dhyanyogi-ji chose the Narmada "because it was the closest spot with the highest spiritual energy. Characteristically, he picked it for *our* convenience."

As the time approached for the rituals at the Narmada, it began to rain steadily and heavily. Floods were reported, and the banks of the river turned into thick, deep, mud. It seemed likely that Anandi Ma would have to change the location for Dhyanyogi-ji's final rites. Despite the weather, Anandi Ma, Dileepji, a group of devotees and a priest from a Shiva temple near the Gajjar's flat kept to their schedule and trudged through two feet of mud to complete the three days of ceremonies at the Narmada. Afterwards, the group continued on to Bodhgaya, the place mentioned in the scriptures as the most powerful for rites for the on-going journey of the soul.

Final rites of offering ashes at the Narmada River

"Sixteen days after his mahasamadhi, we made the final offerings at Gaya," recalled Anandi Ma, "As we were meditating in Bodhgaya, I had a vision in which Guruji's form appeared spreading from the earth to the sky. He split my head into two, and his form emerged from my head. 'I have not gone anywhere. I am within you. You are a part of my being.'"

After the final rites were concluded, Anandi Ma honored Dhyanyogi-ji by arranging to feed 500 sadhus and donating a cow and her calf in his name at a Krishna temple in Ahmedabad. She organized a feast to feed people in Bandhwad, and later hosted others in California, Massachusetts and Connecticut. Disciples all over America donated to soup kitchens and served meals at shelters in his name. The only step remaining was to build a shrine in which to keep the small portion of the remains from the cremation that had been set aside.

Over the next year, reactions to the Dhyanyogi-ji's mahasamadhi varied. Some devotees described falling into depressions, feeling hopeless and despondent. Others experienced his energy as even stronger now, as if it had expanded with his liberation from the body. "Guruji is the promise of love fulfilled, and he is still with us," Mala said. "After

Guruji's mahasamadhi, Anandi Ma and Dileepji told us to remember that he is now in every atom of our bodies. I try to practice this every day. In every blossom, I see Guruji smiling at me. His touch is the caress of a soft, sudden breeze. And when I wake up to the sound of birds singing, it's his voice I hear."

Some expressed relief that he was freed from the trap that his body had become during the final years of his illness. "Maybe," Janak wondered, "just as Lord Ram stayed in the forest for 14 years of exile for the sake of his people, Guruji stayed in his body for 14 years, from the onset of his illness in 1980 until his mahasamadhi in 1994, to work out the karma of his people."

Several of the oldest and closest disciples—Swamiji, Kaka Patel, and Mrs. Manjula Gajjar—passed on in the year following Dhyanyogi-ji's death. Dr. Kedarnath Pathak had died the year before. In the *Ramayana*, when Lord Ram leaves his body by walking into the river, the people of Ayodhya followed him, not wanting to remain behind. It was as if these devotees, for whom Dhyanyogi-ji was the center of their existence, accompanied him.

"In life's journey, we all experience low and high tides of happiness and joy on one end, and pain and sorrow on the other," Anandi Ma wrote. "On the peaks of happiness one feels at the top of the world, and in the lowest ravines of pain and sorrow one feels like one is passing through an infinite black hole from which there is no escape.

"The day I met Guruji and the years that followed were the Himalayan peaks of infinite bliss, peace, joy, happiness, beauty, glory, love, compassion, light, a heart-opening, a mind-boggling era. Being with Guruji, what else could one ask for, what could be lacking in life?

"In 1980, after we took him to India and I had to separate from him for the first time in several years, I began to be taken downwards in a human emotional way, away from those peaks. Yet I knew that in spite of this physical separation and my attachments it was all for the greatest principle of his life—the welfare of all humankind. I had to sacrifice and spread his words and love as he wished me to do.

"On that darkest night ever of Lord Krishna's birthday, the news of Guruji's mahasamadhi took me to that infinite black hole. Yet even in that darkness, there was a small but bright ray of light, love, hope and peace. My Guru had left me but he was still with me, leading me on.

"I feel it is Guruji who works every moment of my life. As written in the *Ramayana*, I feel I am a puppet in my master's hands. His presence is felt continuously. Occasionally, I do miss him and pray, 'Oh Guruji, call me towards you. I am left here without any support. There is nothing left here for me.' But right away his commands, his sankalpa, spring up and I say, 'This body, this life, is yours. Use it as your tool to complete your goal—*the Welfare of All Humankind*.' "

Soon after the cremation, Dhyanyogi-ji appeared to Dileepji in a dream. He sat up from the funeral pyre, threw out a burning pillow and said, "The world may say I have taken mahasamadhi, but that is not true." Dileepji took the dream to be a reassurance from Dhyanyogi-ji that although Dileepji missed him painfully, in reality he was still here.

One thing is certain. Just as devotees reported experiences of Dhyanyogi-ji when he was alive but not physically with them, people continue to have visions of him or a sense of his presence after his mahasamadhi.

In 1996, Anandi Ma was invited to teach at an International Kundalini Conference in Todtmoos, Germany. It was here that Claudia, a Catholic theologian, met her. "My first contact with Anandi Ma in Todtmoos was very brief but made a deep impression on me," Claudia wrote. Unprepared to take shaktipat on the spot, she took home information on how to receive the initiation at a distance. "But once I got back home," Claudia continued, "my experiences with Anandi Ma seemed very strange to me, and I put them aside. Then I had a vision while I was meditating. I saw Guruji and Anandi Ma sitting at my side and offering me help on my spiritual path. The experience was so powerful that I felt that either I had to stop meditating completely, or I had to take this seriously, and write and ask for shaktipat.

"During the next four months I was going through about the hardest time in my life. I was in psychotherapy, dealing with my family background. During the Nazi period, my family had been torn apart. One side of my family was Jewish, but there were several Nazis on the other. While I worked in therapy to try to face this painful history, all my religious concepts broke down. I was confronting the darkest side of humankind, not just what happened to my family, and I was plagued with fears and terrible images. Listening to Anandi Ma's chanting tapes was one of the few things I could hold onto. But in my prayers, it was easier for me to relate to Guruji. As a Catholic, I was familiar with the idea that saints, even after their death, help and support people. It was in accordance with my tradition to have an inner dialogue with Guruji, and this relationship became essential to me. I felt that I had gotten in contact with questions that were far beyond my ability to handle, and that this Indian guru came to carry me through this time. This was even before I received shaktipat.

"However, the conflict between my theological concepts and my experience of Ma's and Guruji's presence in my life caused me tension. I felt stuck. One time, I brought all my confusion, gratitude and doubt—all this together—to the feet of Guruji. I was lying on the ground and I saw him standing before me. First, severe kriyas went through my body, then an intense energy flow followed. I felt completely accepted by him with all my chaos. It was like receiving shaktipat in that moment.

"Several months later the tension of being a Roman Catholic theologian and having a Hindu guru was resolved by an experience I had during the celebration of the Eucharist. I was following the service, but Sanskrit mantras were constantly coming into my mind. Both ways of worship pulled for my attention. But then, at the climax of the celebration, when the priest repeats Christ's words over the bread: 'This is my body for you,' I saw Guruji looking at me saying the same: 'This is my life for you.' Christ's love and Guruji's love—it was just the one divine love, far beyond my understanding."

In 2003, a woman who ran a yoga center in Mexico called a Dhyanyoga Centers' contact person. She said that in her meditations, a man had been teaching her how to teach yoga. The man identified himself as Madhusudandas. She told him she didn't understand the name, and then he said his name was Dhyana. At first, the caller thought he meant "Diana," and was confused by his having a feminine name. Then someone gave her a *Yoga Journal* magazine and she read an ad for the book *Shakti*. She decided to buy the book, and when she opened it, and saw the photograph of Dhyanyogi-ji, she recognized him as the man who was her teacher.

"After Dhyanyogi-ji's mahasamadhi, I realized that the energetic, devoted practices of one man can move the world," wrote a student named Eric, "and I resolved to practice more deeply to try to reach the final goal in this life...I am slowly increasing the intensity of my practices. Guruji's example is a sufficient prod. And of course the energy he and Anandi Ma send makes this possible. I will always be grateful that Guruji chose to come to this world and rescue those of us crying out in the darkness, and I will always be grateful that Guruji brought Anandi Ma and Dileepji to America."

Dhyanyogi-ji once wrote, "The relationship between guru and disciple is the supreme relationship in human existence, even superior to that between mother and child. The mother only gives physical birth but the guru leads you onto the path to liberation. If the guru is perfected, he or she need not be physically present. He or she can give you guidance from anywhere. It is the perfection of the guru and the relationship of guru and disciple that matters. Then physical limits are transcended."[68]

All my blessings with love
आयुष्मान् धनवान् सदा सुखी भव.

may god bless you
Dhyan yogi

Long life, prosperity, be happy always.

Afterword

Shri Anandi Ma and Dileepji continue Dhyanyogi-ji's work in America, India and Europe. After his mahasamadhi, in accordance with his wishes, they purchased land in Nikora, a small village near Bharuch, Gujarat, on the banks of the holy river Narmada, near where Dhyanyogi-ji's final rites were performed. They have built an ashram there, called Dhyani Dham, and are in the process of constructing a temple that will house his mahasamadhi shrine.

To fulfill Dhyanyogi-ji's desire to offer medical services to those who cannot afford them, there is a free medical clinic at Dhyani Dham each Sunday that serves the local people. Every year, the ashram hosts a weekend medical camp to provide services for a thousand patients coming from greater distances. Free cataract surgeries are arranged through this service.

In 1999, Dhyanyoga Centers bought seven acres of land in Antioch, California where they are building a meditation center, so there will also be a physical place in America to hold Dhyanyogi-ji's energy and the energy of his disciples now and for future generations.

Dhyanyogi-ji's four years in America will be the subject of Volume 2 of *This House is on Fire*.

Note: Dhyanyogi-ji started Dhyanyoga Centers in America and gave ultimate authority to Anandi Ma and Dileepji to continue his work there. Later, he expanded this and asked them to do his work all over the world. Dhyanyoga Centers, Anandi Ma, and Dileepji are not in any way affiliated with any other person or organization that uses the name of Shri Dhyanyogi Madhusudandasji.

Proposed temple at Dhyani Dham in Nikora; Construction began in 2003.

Washroom Facilities

Smruti Mandir

Guruji's Memories
& Spiritual Library

Architectural model, 2003

Meditation Center   Changing Room   Holy Bath Place

Mā's Residence   Anusthan Cave

Acknowledgments

This book represents an international, multicultural, multilingual group effort. We began with *A Pathway to the Self*, the biography of Dhyanyogi-ji written in Gujarati by Pranav Parekh, published in India in 1972. It was Pranav who interviewed Dhyanyogi-ji extensively about his childhood, and recorded early experiences of Indian disciples with Dhyanyogi-ji. Chaturbhai Patel translated *A Pathway to the Self* into English, and then a series of devotees including Lalita and Mahendra Heckathorn, Doug McLeod, Marsha Newman, Margaret Herrell, Cheryl Amand, and Jan Handel typed and edited sections of the book. Jyoti identified scores of places in the text that required more explanation. Eric and Sally Biggar organized the manuscript chronologically, filled in missing historical and geographical information, rewrote and expanded the entire text. Without Eric and Sally, this book would never have been possible.

We want to thank all of the disciples who shared their recollections and sometimes very personal experiences with Dhyanyogi-ji, in particular Carl Kuntz, Will Laxman Hartzel, Shanta Gabriel, Janak Koch, Tulsi Gottfredson, Marsha Moti Newman, Kanta Lipsky, Sushila and Pranav Parekh, Rajan and Satish Menon, Kusum Sheth, and Daksha and Pravin Doctor. We can't name every person who made an important contribution, whether large or small, but we are indebted to each one.

Our work was greatly enriched by two of Dhyanyogi-ji's closest disciples, Swami Vijay Krishnabharati and Dr. Kedarnath Pathak, who wrote down their experiences with Dhyanyogi-ji and left these with Dileepji so that they would be available for future use. Pravinji Jani was very generous with his time, counsel, and memories, helping us to understand the context of Dhyanyogi-ji's work. Without him, we would not have been able to so deeply convey the quality of Dhyanyogi-ji's relationship with Anandi Ma.

We thank Lydia Leovic Towery and Jan Handel for letting us use their beautiful photographs, and our proofreader, Virginia Villalon, for making herself available at just the perfect moment.

Kajal Dhabalia, Trupti Mannina, Janani English and Doug McLeod read chapters, made suggestions, and held our hands. Without them, we would have lost our way. Our thanks to Moti Newman, Michael Taft and Linda Johnsen, who read our drafts, gave us encouragement, and assured us that Dhyanyogi-ji was here. Michael also offered invaluable editing suggestions.

We appreciate the designers at Insight Design and the team at Palace Press who envisioned this finished project before any of the rest of us dared to, and who threw themselves into creating this beautiful book.

We are deeply grateful to Shri Anandi Ma and Dileepji for the priceless opportunity to do this seva. They spent hours talking to us, writing down their memories, guiding and inspiring us. They personally selected all the photographs and explained the history behind them. Dileepji wrote pages of stories, scriptural references, and corrected the manuscript repeatedly. His patience and his ability to consistently deepen our understanding of the events of Dhyanyogi-ji's life were unceasing. Words cannot express how we felt as we listened to them tell stories of Dhyanyogi-ji, their eyes filling with tears of love or dancing with joy as they remembered their days with him. Throughout all of our conversations, it was their constant wish that his love, compassion, gentleness and simple nature be conveyed to the world, for the purpose of helping others to grow spiritually. They helped us remember that the goal of his work and his life was to take us all inside, to our own true selves. They impressed upon us that his energy is no less available to us now than when he announced to some disciples massaging him, "Energy, free of charge!"

Finally, we bow to the lotus feet of Shri Dhyanyogi-ji. Without his blessing, we could never have written a word.

Glossary

Ajna The chakra at the third eye. It is only with the opening of the ajna chakra that we can attain realization.

Anusthan A focused spiritual practice, concentrated with respect to number of days and hours per day, during which the sadhak follows a disciplined diet and keeps celibacy.

Arati An offering. Normally five wicks are lit on a lamp and waved in front of a statue or guru.

Asan Ideally, a silk or woolen cloth used to sit on during spiritual practices, which acts as an insulator of the energy.

Aum The bija mantra from which all sound, and all creation, derives.

Asana Hatha yoga posture.

Ayurveda One of the Vedas—the Veda of life—in which the traditional medicine of India is revealed.

Baba A term often used to address a saint or a spiritual teacher. In some communities it may be used to address one's father.

Bhagavad Gita The essence of the Vedas, in which Lord Krishna teaches his disciple Arjuna.

Bhajan A devotional song.

Bhakti Devotion.

Bhandara Feast to honor a great being or saint.

Bhastrika "The bellows;" a type of pranayama (breathing technique) which is forceful and rapid.

Bhav samadhi State of meditation in which the soul of the person identifies and merges with a particular form of the Divine with qualities, and is manifested physically.

Bhuta Shuddhi mantra A mantra specific for purification of the three bodies: the physical body; the subtle or astral body, which includes the chakras and nadis; and the causal body, which is the storehouse of the person's karma.

Bija mantra The essential energy of a mantra concentrated in a single letter. Just as a tree is embedded in its seed, the mantra is contained in its seed letter.

Brahma Aspect of God as the creator.

Brahman The priest-scholar caste, i.e., one who comes from Brahma.

Chakra A circle, normally referring to the energy centers in the subtle body along the spinal column.

Darshan Vision; to let the eyes fall upon God or Guru.

Dham Site, place.

Dharma Right conduct and behavior.

Dhoti A three to four yard cloth that is used for clothing by males.

Dhyan Meditation.

Garba A traditional folk dance of Gujarat to sing praises of the Divine Mother.

Ghat Mountain peaks, or stone or concrete banks constructed on rivers to provide bathing access.

Guru Spiritual guide.

Guru Purnima The full moon day in July which is dedicated to worshipping the Lord through the spiritual teacher.

Guru seva Service to the guru.

Guru Tatwa The divine principle through which God's energy works in the universe through the spiritual teachers and saints.

Ida The flow of energy on the left side of the spinal column (moon).

Ishta-devata The principal form of worship chosen by an individual.

Japa Repetition of a mantra or divine name.

Jnana Inner knowledge.

Jyotir-lingam An aspect of Shiva's appearance that is spontaneous and not man-made.

Karma Action.

Kirtan Chanting of divine names.

Kriya Spontaneous movement brought about by awakened kundalini; a technique.

Kundalini The three-coiled serpentine divine energy present in every individual.

Lakh 100,000.

Laxman The brother of Lord Ram known for his devotion and service.

Leela God's play of consciousness; usually refers to phenomena that cannot be explained logically.

Lingam An elliptical shaped stone representative of Lord Shiva—it has no center, no beginning or end.

Mahant The chief spiritual person of a temple or ashram.

Mahasamadhi The state of union achieved by a realized person, i.e., leaving the body consciously by will.

Mahatma A great soul.

Mala Rosary; 108 beads strung together to use for repeating a mantra or divine name.

Mantrochar A set of mantras chanted together.

Maun Observing silence.

Maya God's energy as illusion.

Moksha Liberation.

Muladhara The first chakra at the base of the spine.

Murti A statue.

Nadi A channel of the flow of energy in the subtle body.

Navaratri The nine nights of war between good and evil, i.e. Ram vs. Ravana; ideal time for spiritual practices.

Nirvikalpa samadhi The state of consciousness that transcends will and doubt.

Padmasana The lotus pose, ideal for meditation.

Pingala The channel of energy on the right side in the spinal column (sun).

Pradakshina The act of walking around a divine statue or being, usually four times.

Pran Pratistha An invocation ceremony to enliven a new statue, to bring in the vital divine force.

Prana The vital force.

Pranayama The fourth limb of yoga.; breathing techniques to control the breath and thus, the mind.

Prasad Gift from God, usually fruit or food.

Puja The 16-step (or more) act of worship.

Raja yoga "Royal path of yoga;" path to realization, ascribed to Patanjali, through concentration, meditation and samadhi.

Ram The incarnation of Vishnu who killed Ravana.

Ramayana The scripture that tells the story of the life of Lord Ram.

Rishi Seer of the scriptures.

Sadguru The true/final spiritual guide.

Sadaguru deva ki jai Glory to God as Guru.

Sadhu A renunciate.

Sadhak A student.

Sadhana Spiritual practice and discipline.

Sahasrar The 1000-petaled chakra at the crown of the head.

Samadhi The state of union between soul and God.

Samskara The impression of the mind brought over from past lives or learned in childhood.

Sankalpa Resolution; firm action; request for divine help and guidance.

Sanyas Renunciation.

Sanyasi One who has taken the vows of sanyas, renunciation.

Satsang To be in the company of truth, i.e., a spiritual being.

Sattva Pure, noble quality.

Satyam Truth.

Seva Service.

Shakti Divine Mother; God's energy.

Shaktipat The process of transmitting energy from teacher to student.

Shivam Of Shiva; the state of unity of soul with its creator-self.

Shraddha ceremony The rites performed after the death of a person by the eldest son, to help the soul on its onward journey.

Siddhi A perfected state.

Sita Of the earth, i.e. Sita, the wife of Lord Ram.

Sundaram The one who is beautiful.

Sushumna The energy pathway in the middle of the spinal column within which the kundalini operates.

Swami Usually refers to a renunciate.

Tamas Dark quality of inertia.

Tapas Austerity.

Tilak A mark of sandalwood paste or kumkum (red powder) applied at the third eye center.

Upanishads Scriptures stating the true knowledge of the Supreme Spirit.

Vedas Scriptures directly revealed by the Supreme Being Brahma.

Yagna A ceremony in which offerings are made through fire, the fire being experienced as the very mouth of the Lord.

References

Dass, Ram *Grist for the Mill.* Berkeley, CA: Celestial Arts, 1987.

Isherwood, Christopher. *The Song of God: Bhagavad-Gita.* New York: New American Library, 1972

Jnaneshwar, Shri. *Jnaneshwari.* Trans. M. R. Yardi. Pune, India: Jairaj Ad-Print, 2002*

Johnsen, Linda. *Daughters of the Goddess.* St. Paul, MN: Yes International Publishers, 1994

Madhusudandas, Shri Dhyanyogi. *Brahmanada: Sound, Mantra, and Power.* Santa Cruz, CA: Dhyanyoga Centers, 1979

> *Death, Dying and Beyond.* Santa Cruz, CA: Dhyanyoga Centers, 1979
>
> *Light on Meditation.* Santa Cruz, CA: Dhyanyoga Centers, 1978
>
> *Message to Disciples.* Mumbai, India: Shri Dhyanyogi Mandal, 1968
>
> *Shakti: An Introduction to Kundalini Maha Yoga* Antioch, CA: Dhyanyoga Centers, 2000
>
> *Yoga Dipika.* Pasadena, CA: Dhyanyoga Centers, 1979

Sannella, Lee. *The Kundalini Experience: Psychosis or Transcendence?* Lower Lake, CA: Integral Publishing, 1992.

Saraswati, Swami Satyananda, trans. *Chandi Path.* Napa, CA: Devi Mandir Publications, 1997.

Tirtha, Swami Vishnu. *Devatma Shakti.* Delhi, India: Rishikesh, India: Vigyan Press, 1993*

Tulsidas, Shri. *Shri Ramacharitamanasa.* Trans. R.C. Prasad. Delhi, India: Motilal Banarsidass Publishers, 1994.*

Vivekananda, Swami. *Raja Yoga.* New York: Ramakrishna-Vivekananda Center, 1982*

*These books were recommended reading by Dhyanyogi-ji.